P9-DWY-505

NO REFUND IF REMOVED

B 63.00

7559 USED BOOK

JUL 2 3 2003

Santa Rosa JC Book Store

Informal Logic

USED BOOK

DEC 1 5 2019

Santa Rosa JC Book Store

Informal Logic
THIRD EDITION

Irving M. Copi
The University of Hawaii at Manoa

Keith Burgess-Jackson
The University of Texas at Arlington

Prentice Hall, Upper Saddle River, New Jersey 07458

LIBRARY OF CONGRESS CATALOGING-IN-PUBLICATION DATA

Copi, Irving M.
    Informal logic / Irving M. Copi, Keith Burgess-Jackson.—3rd ed.
      p.   cm.
    Includes index.
    ISBN 0-13-229048-0
    1. Logic. I. Burgess-Jackson, Keith. II. Title.
    BC71.C68   1995
    160—dc20   95-33207

Acquisitions editor: Ted Bolen
Manufacturing buyer: Lynn Pearlman
Cover photograph: Ireland stones, Fulvio Roiter/The Image Bank
Editorial assistant: Meg McGuane

 © 1996, 1992, 1982 by Prentice-Hall, Inc.
Simon & Schuster/A Viacom Company
Upper Saddle River, New Jersey 07458

Printed in the United States of America

10 9 8 7 6 5 4

ISBN 0-13-229048-0

Prentice-Hall International (UK) Limited, *London*
Prentice-Hall of Austria Pty. Limited, *Sydney*
Prentice-Hall Canada, Inc., *Toronto*
Prentice-Hall Hispanoamericana, S.A., *Mexico*
Prentice-Hall of India Private Limited, *New Delhi*
Prentice-Hall of Japan, Inc., *Tokyo*
Simon & Schuster Asia Pte. Ltd., *Singapore*
Editora Prentice-Hall do Brasil Ltda., *Rio de Janeiro*

To Sophie and Ginger,
the loves of my life.

—K.B.-J.

*In a republican nation, whose citizens are to be led
by reason and persuasion and not by force,
the art of reasoning becomes of first importance.*

—Thomas Jefferson

Contents

Preface

The aim of this third edition, as of those preceding it, is to help students think more clearly, critically, and competently—to sharpen their native reasoning abilities. It is addressed primarily to students in Informal Logic or Critical Thinking courses at the university level, although there is no reason it cannot be used in advanced high school courses or by university professors in other fields (English, communication, speech, journalism, linguistics, even science). Unlike traditional logic texts, which are heavily (and necessarily) laden with symbols and jargon, this book is written in plain English to the extent possible. It focuses on arguments and explanations as they occur in natural language.

Informal logic is now widely (if not universally) recognized as a discipline in its own right. At one time it was viewed as "baby logic," which suggests immaturity, lack of rigor, and perhaps lack of seriousness and importance. This—in our view, fortunately—is changing. There are now journals, monographs, and academic conferences devoted to the subject. Attention is being drawn, or rather redrawn, to such topics as argumentation, discourse analysis, fallacies, definition, and analogy. Interdisciplinary work is being done by philosophers and linguists, philosophers and psychologists, and philosophers and rhetoricians (among others). Moreover, as science and technology loom progressively larger in our lives, the need for a basic understanding of scientific concepts, methods, and reasoning increases. This book provides that understanding.

New to the third edition

The general structure of the first two editions has been preserved. Two chapters (chapters 3 and 6) have been substantially rewritten for the third edition, one of them (chapter 3) completely. Chapter 3 now contains a discussion of twenty informal fallacies divided into four sections, each with a set of exercises. The section on formal fallacies has been deleted as being inappropriate to a work in informal logic. The fallacies selected for discussion are among those most commonly committed (and therefore, practically speaking, most in need of study). Since informal fallacies, by definition, can be detected only by examining the content of the argument or the context in which the argument is

ix

made, every effort is made to distinguish those arguments of a particular form that are fallacious from those that are not. The inculcation of this *skill*, this "knowledge-how" as opposed to "knowledge-that," is, or should be, the instructor's aim.

Chapter 6 retains the material on the nature of causation but contains a new discussion of Mill's methods of experimental inquiry as well as more accessible charts and all new, up-to-date exercises. The aim of the revision is to show that Mill's methods are still used by both laypeople and practicing scientists, even if reference is seldom made to Mill. The section of chapter 4 dealing with verbal disputes and definitions is omitted in this edition on grounds that it duplicates material discussed in section 2.5. Numerous changes of a lesser sort have been made throughout the book. As before, every fifth exercise (indicated by a square) is solved in an appendix at the back of the book. We hope that the solutions manual is of use to instructors.

Uses of the text

A course in informal logic can serve as a terminal course or as preparation for more advanced or specialized courses in logic; but it should not be viewed as inferior to or parasitic on the traditional logic course. Informal logic has objectives, techniques, methods, and theories—not to mention problems!—of its own. The book is designed for and can be covered in a single semester-length course, although one or more sections may have to be omitted to accomplish this. The chapters, while cross-referenced, are substantially independent of one another, so an instructor can discuss them in any order he or she pleases.

An ambitious instructor with good students may wish to supplement this text with another—say, on scientific reasoning or on the effect of television, show business, and other forms of entertainment on critical-thinking abilities. The authors have used and recommend the following as supplements: Thomas Gilovich, *How We Know What Isn't So: The Fallibility of Human Reason in Everyday Life* (1991); Neil Postman, *Amusing Ourselves to Death: Public Discourse in the Age of Show Business* (1985); and Neil Postman and Steve Powers, *How to Watch TV News* (1992). Obviously there are many other good candidates. The instructor may wish to experiment.

ACKNOWLEDGMENTS

The authors would like to express their continuing gratitude to those who made constructive criticism during the preparation of the first and second editions: Richard W. Behling of the University of Wisconsin at Eau Claire; Thompson M. Faller of the University of Portland; David Nakamura of the University of Hawaii at Manoa; Perry Weddle of California State University at Sacramento; R.G. Wengert of the University of Illinois; and J.-C. Smith of Youngstown State University. We thank four anonymous reviewers for their input into the third edition. As always, we are grateful to our students for lively classroom discussions; to our colleagues at the University of Hawaii at Manoa and the University of Texas at Arlington, respectively; and to our editors Maggie Barbieri and Ted Bolen. Readers who wish to comment on the present edition may contact the authors by e-mail at d284kbj@uta.edu. We thank you in advance.

I.M.C.
K.B.-J.

Introduction

1.1 THE NATURE AND UTILITY OF LOGIC

Logic, as a discipline is concerned with reasoning. Its concern is to distinguish good reasoning from bad, or better from worse. Logic is both an art and a science. As a science logic investigates, develops, and systematizes principles and methods that can be used to distinguish correct and incorrect reasoning. The science of logic has its own professional jargon and technical notation, like other advanced sciences such as mathematics, physics, and chemistry. But as an art or craft, logic can be equated with "logical ability" and includes a family of related skills that have many applications. Among these applications are problem solving, weighing evidence, marshaling evidence and constructing arguments for or against a disputed proposition, analyzing a problem into components that may usefully be dealt with separately, detecting and exposing mistakes in reasoning (including one's own), and clarifying issues, often through defining or redefining the key terms on which disputes frequently turn. In doing or studying informal logic, the aim is to develop and strengthen these skills.

Logical skills are valuable and important. Each of us is a constant target for those who want to influence our beliefs, actions, and feelings. In our free society, others cannot simply demand that we think, act, and feel as they tell us to. They must persuade us. Often they have their own benefit or advantage in mind rather than ours. So we should not let ourselves be persuaded too easily. We should believe only on the basis of evidence, act only for good reasons, and require that our feelings or attitudes be in harmony with our most deeply held commitments and sense of self. In general, we ought to let our beliefs be guided by the careful weighing of argument and evidence. Where a proposed action could have serious consequences, we should have good reason for doing it. Here is where logical skills can protect us from being unduly influenced by media commercials, slanted "news" stories, and politicians' promises.

Another benefit of developing logical skill comes when we try to understand complex situations and think things through. As the great American philosopher Charles

Sanders Peirce (1839–1914) remarked long ago, "The object of reasoning is to find out, from the consideration of what we already know, something else which we do not know."[1] To achieve this object, to extend our knowledge by reasoning, we must reason well rather than poorly. In order to infer correct and useful conclusions from what we already know, we must possess and apply the logical skills that constitute the art of logic. As Peirce went on to remark, "We come to the full possession of our power of drawing inferences, the last of all our faculties; for it is not so much a natural gift as a long and difficult art."[2] Indeed, sometimes in the process of reasoning we find that we are working with less than maximum effectiveness; depending on slogans rather than using our intelligence, avoiding the work of thinking by appealing only to habit, stereotypes, stale maxims, and vague generalities.

Finally, logical skills are valuable because they contribute to both fruitful cooperation and effective leadership. We live in communities with others, and some of our needs and wants can be satisfied only by the efforts of many people working together toward common goals. That presupposes agreement on goals and on ways to achieve them. In reaching such agreement, one must try to avoid being persuaded by others on insufficient grounds. Here the recognition of bad reasoning is important. But it is also important to be able to persuade others to agree on what is the best route to the best goal. Careful, constructive, *logical* thinking is not only a basis for productive collaboration, but the hallmark of effective and dependable leadership.

As in developing any other skill, from macramé to swimming, practice is essential. One learns by doing. The problems contained in this book are probably the most important part of it. You will surely strengthen your logical skill by taking the time and making the effort to do the exercises.

1.2   PREMISES AND CONCLUSIONS

To clarify the explanation of logic offered in the preceding section, it will help to set forth and discuss some of the special terms logicians use in their work. *Inference* is commonly defined as a process in which one proposition is arrived at and affirmed on the basis of one or more other propositions accepted as the starting point of the process. To determine whether an inference is correct, the logician examines those propositions that are the initial and end points of that process and the relationships between them.

Propositions are either true or false, and in this they differ from questions, commands, and exclamations. Only propositions can be either asserted or denied. Questions may be asked and commands given and exclamations uttered, but none of them can be affirmed or denied, or judged to be either true or false.

It is customary to distinguish between sentences and the propositions they may be uttered to assert. Two sentences, which are clearly two because they consist of different words differently arranged, may in the same context have the same meaning and be uttered to assert the same proposition. For example,

---

[1]   Charles Sanders Peirce, "The Fixation of Belief," *Readings on Logic,* 2d ed., ed. Irving M. Copi and James A. Gould (1972), p. 60.
[2]   Ibid., p.- 59.

John loves Mary.
Mary is loved by John.

are two different sentences, for the first contains three words, whereas the second contains five; the first begins with the word "John," whereas the second begins with the word "Mary," and so on. Yet the two sentences have exactly the same meaning. We use the term "proposition" to refer to what such sentences as these are typically uttered to assert.

The difference between sentences and propositions is brought out by remarking that a sentence is always a sentence of a particular language, the language in which it is uttered, whereas propositions are not peculiar to any language. The four sentences

It is raining.
Está lloviendo.
Il pleut.
Es regnet.

are certainly different, for they are in different languages: English, Spanish, French, and German, respectively. Yet they have a single meaning, and in appropriate contexts may be uttered to assert the proposition of which each of them is a different formulation. In different contexts exactly the same sentence can be uttered to make very different *statements*. For example, the sentence

The present president of the United States is a former senator.

could have been uttered in 1973 to make a (true) statement about Richard Nixon, but might have been uttered in 1991 to make a (false) statement about George Bush. In those different temporal contexts, the sentence in question would be uttered to assert different propositions or to make different statements. The terms "proposition" and "statement" are not exact synonyms, but in the context of logical investigation they are used in much the same sense. Some writers on logic prefer "statement" to "proposition," although the latter has been more common in the history of logic. In this book the terms will be used interchangeably.

Corresponding to every possible inference is an *argument*, and it is with these arguments that logic is chiefly concerned. An argument, in the logician's sense, is any group of propositions of which one is claimed to follow from the others, which are regarded as providing support or grounds for the truth of that one. Of course the word "argument" is often used in other senses, such as "disagreement" or "quarrel," but in logic it has the special sense explained. An argument is not a mere collection of propositions, but has a structure. In describing this structure, the terms "premiss" and "conclusion" are usually employed. The *conclusion* of an argument is the proposition that is affirmed on the basis of the other propositions of the argument, and these other propositions, which are affirmed (or assumed) as providing support or reasons for accepting the conclusion, are the *premisses* of that argument.

The simplest kind of argument consists of just one premiss and a conclusion that is claimed to follow from it or to be implied by it. An example in which each is stated in a separate sentence is the following:

> The investigation of supernatural phenomena lies outside the realm of science. Therefore, science can neither prove nor disprove the existence of God.[3]

Here the premiss is stated first and the conclusion second. But the order in which they are stated is not significant from the point of view of logic. (It may, however, have rhetorical significance.) An argument in which the conclusion is stated in the first sentence and the premiss in the second is:

> Moreover, cutting Social Security will not improve the deficit problem. As Martin Feldstein, chairman of the Council of Economic Advisers, has noted, Social Security is funded by separate payroll taxes and contributes not a cent to the deficit.[4]

In some arguments the premiss and conclusion are stated in the same sentence. Following is a one-sentence argument whose premiss precedes its conclusion:

> The solar system is much younger than the universe (only 4.5 billion years compared with 10 to 15 billion years), and so it must have formed from older matter that had a previous history.[5]

Sometimes the conclusion precedes the premiss in a one-sentence argument, as in the following example:

> The budget deficit will not be brought under control because to do so would require our elected leaders in Washington to do the unthinkable—act courageously and responsibly.[6]

When reasons are offered in an effort to persuade us to perform a specified action, we are presented with what is in effect an argument even though the "conclusion" may be expressed as an imperative or command. Consider, for example, the following two passages:

> Wisdom is the principal thing; therefore get wisdom. . . .[7]

and

---

[3] James A. Hopson, letter to the editor, *The New Republic,* 12 September 1983, p. 4.
[4] Daniel Patrick Moynihan, "Reagan's Bankrupt Budget," *The New Republic,* 31 December 1983, p. 20.
[5] Roy S. Lewis and Edward Anders, "Interstellar Matter in Meteorites," *Scientific American* 249 (August 1983), p. 66.
[6] Bruce Crutcher, letter to the editor, *U.S. News & World Report,* 19 December 1983, p. 4
[7] Proverbs 4:7.

> Neither a borrower nor a lender be;
> For loan oft loses both itself and friend.[8]

Here too the command may either precede or follow the reason (or reasons) offered to persuade the hearer (or reader) to do what is commanded. For the sake of uniformity and simplicity, it is useful to regard commands, in these contexts, as no different from propositions in which hearers (or readers) are told that they should, must, or ought to act in the manner specified in the command. Exactly what difference, if any, there is between a command to do something and a statement that it should, must, or ought to be done is a difficult problem that need not be explored here. By ignoring that difference (if there really is one), we are able to regard both kinds of arguments as structured groups of propositions.

Some arguments offer several premises in support of their conclusions. On occasion the premises are enumerated as first, second, third—or as (a), (b), (c) in the following argument, in which the statement of the conclusion precedes the statements of the premises:

> To say that statements about consciousness are statements about brain processes is manifestly false. This is shown (a) by the fact that you can describe your sensations and mental imagery without knowing anything about your brain processes or even that such things exist, (b) by the fact that statements about one's consciousness and statements about one's brain processes are verified in entirely different ways, and (c) by the fact that there is nothing self-contradictory about the statement "X has a pain but there is nothing going on in his brain."[9]

In the following argument the conclusion is stated last, preceded by three premises:

> Since happiness consists in peace of mind, and since durable peace of mind depends on the confidence we have in the future, and since that confidence is based on the science we should have of the nature of God and the soul, it follows that science is necessary for true happiness.[10]

Counting the premises of an argument is not terribly important at this stage of our study, but it will gain importance as we proceed to analyze and diagram more complicated arguments. To list the premises of the preceding arguments, we cannot appeal simply to the number of *sentences* in which they are written. That they are all in a single sentence should not be allowed to disguise their multiplicity.

It should be noted that "premiss" and "conclusion" are relative terms: one and the same proposition can be a premiss in one argument and a conclusion in another. Consider, for example, the argument:

> Now human law is framed for the multitude of human beings. The majority of human beings are not perfect in virtue. Therefore human laws do not forbid all vices. . . .[11]

---

8   William Shakespeare, *Hamlet,* I, iii.
9   U. T. Place, "Is Consciousness a Brain Process?" *The British Journal of Psychology* (February 1956).
10 Gottfried Leibniz, *Preface to the General Science.*
11 Thomas Aquinas, *Summa Theologica,* I-II, Question 96, Article 2.

Here the proposition *human laws do not forbid all vices* is the conclusion, and the two propositions preceding it are premisses. But the given argument's conclusion is a premiss in the following (different) argument:

> . . . vicious acts are contrary to acts of virtue. But human law does not prohibit all vices, as was stated. Therefore neither does it prescribe all acts of virtue.[12]

No proposition by itself, in isolation, is either a premiss or a conclusion. It is a premiss only where it occurs as an assumption in an argument. It is a conclusion only where it occurs in an argument in which it is claimed to follow from propositions assumed in that argument. Thus "premiss" and "conclusion" are relative terms, like "employer" and "employee." A person alone is neither employer nor employee, but may be either in different contexts: employer to one's gardener, employee of the firm for which one works.

The preceding arguments either have their premisses stated first and their conclusions last, or their conclusions stated first, followed by their premisses. But the conclusion of an argument need not be stated either at its end or at its beginning. It can be, and often is, sandwiched between different premisses offered in its support. This arrangement is illustrated in the following:

> Iran's chargé d'affaires in Beirut, Mehdi Amer Rajai, said, "If America enters the war, all hostages in Iran will be killed. Therefore, America will not do any such thing, especially now that the American elections are close and the death of the hostages will not be to [President] Carter's advantage. . . ."[13]

Here the conclusion that *America will not enter the war* is asserted on the basis of the propositions that precede and follow it.

To carry out the logician's task of distinguishing good from bad arguments, one must be able to recognize arguments when they occur and to identify their premisses and conclusions. Given that a passage contains an argument, how can we tell what its conclusion is and what its premisses are? We have already seen that an argument can be stated with its conclusion first, last, or between its several premisses. Hence the conclusion of an argument cannot be identified in terms of its position in the formulation of the argument. How, then, can it be recognized? Sometimes recognition is facilitated by the presence of special words that attach to the different parts of an argument. Some words or phrases typically serve to introduce the conclusion of an argument.

We call such expressions *conclusion-indicators*. The presence of any of them often, though not always, signals that what follows is the conclusion of an argument. Here is a partial list of conclusion indicators:

therefore	we may infer
hence	I conclude that
thus	which shows that

---

12 Ibid., Article 3.
13 Alvin B. Webb, *Honolulu Advertiser,* 2 October 1980, p. 4.

so	which means that
ergo	which entails that
accordingly	which implies that
in consequence	which allows us to infer
consequently	points to the conclusion that
proves that	establishes
as a result	justifies
it follows that	supports

Other words or phrases typically serve to mark the premisses of an argument. Such expressions are called *premiss-indicators.* The presence of any one of them often, though not always, signals that what follows is a premiss of an argument. Here is a partial list of premiss-indicators:

since	the reason is that
because	for the reason that
for	may be inferred from
as	may be derived from
follows from	may be deduced from
as shown by	in view of the fact that
inasmuch as	given that
as indicated by	granted that

Once an argument has been recognized, these words and phrases help us to identify its premisses and conclusion.

But not every passage containing an argument contains these special logical terms. Consider, for example:

> A little neglect may breed great mischief . . . for want of a nail the shoe was lost; for want of a shoe the horse was lost; and for want of a horse the rider was lost.[14]

Although it might be regarded as *stating* a well-known truth, and then *illustrating* it by reference to the missing horseshoe nail and the consequent loss of the rider, it can at least equally well be understood as an argument whose conclusion is stated first and followed by three premisses that are claimed to support it. A somewhat more complicated example of an argument in whose formulation neither conclusion-indicators nor premiss-indicators appear is the following:

> It takes obtuse reasoning to inject any issue of the "free exercise" of religion into the present case. No one is forced to go to the religious classroom and no religious exercise or instruction is brought to the classrooms of the public schools. A student need not take religious instruction. He is left to his own desires as to the manner or time of his religious devotions, if any.[15]

---

14   Benjamin Franklin, *Poor Richard's Almanac* (1758).
15   Justice William O. Douglas, for the U.S. Supreme Court, *Zorach v. Clauson,* 343 U.S. 306 (1952).

Here the conclusion, which can be paraphrased as "the present case has nothing to do with the 'free exercise' of religion," is stated in the first sentence. The last three sentences offer grounds or reasons in support of that conclusion. How can we know that the first sentence states the conclusion and that the other three express premisses? Context is enormously helpful here, as indeed it usually is. Also helpful are some of the phrasings used in expressing the various propositions involved. The phrase "it takes obtuse reasoning to inject . . ." suggests that the question of whether "free exercise" of religion is involved in the case is precisely the point of disagreement. It suggests that someone has claimed that there is an issue of religious freedom in the case and that the court rejects that claim and must therefore argue against it. The other propositions are formulated in matter-of-fact terms, suggesting that there is no dispute about them, and thus no question of their being acceptable as premisses.

These examples show that not every passage containing an argument contains an indicator word. The converse of this is also true: Not every occurrence of an indicator word serves to indicate either a premiss or a conclusion. Here is an example of the use of the word "since" (a premiss-indicator) to indicate something other than a premiss:

> Since [Mikhail] Gorbachev became President [of the Soviet Union] in March, he has tried to wield the extra powers of the office to steer the country away from a centralized system, where everyone took orders from above, toward a society where decisions would come from below and be coordinated with a vastly reduced administrative center.[16]

The proposition *Mikhail Gorbachev became President of the Soviet Union in March* is not a premiss, for the author is not claiming that it supports any other proposition. Instead, it marks a point in time after which certain other events are alleged to have happened. The word "since" in this passage has temporal rather than logical significance.

Here is an example of the use of the word "thus" (a conclusion-indicator) to indicate something other than a conclusion:

> From the beginning, federal judges have been tempted to do more than to resolve concrete cases and controversies; the impulse to shape public policy more broadly is a strong one. Thus the Marshall Court sought to flesh out the meaning of the commerce and contracts clauses; the Taney Court hoped once and for all to silence the political storm over slavery; the so-called laissez-faire Court brandished its doctrinal contrivance of "liberty of contract"; the New Deal court moved to support ever greater centralization of governmental power; the Warren Court hammered out policies to desegregate society; and the Burger Court attempted to fashion a national policy on abortion.[17]

The author of this passage begins by making a general point about the Supreme Court. He then illustrates that point by citing a number of examples. The word "thus" indicates that what follows is an illustration.

---

[16]   John Kohan, "Gorbachev's Home Remedy," *Time* 136, 17 September 1990, p. 28.
[17]   Gary L. McDowell, "Congress and the Courts," *The Public Interest* (Summer 1990): 90–91.

Not everything said in the course of an argument is either a premiss or the conclusion of that argument. A passage that contains an argument may also contain other material, which may sometimes be irrelevant, but which often supplies important background information that enables the reader or hearer to understand what the argument is about. For example, consider the argument contained in the following passage:

> Untreated chronic glaucoma is a leading cause of painless, progressive blindness. Methods for early detection and effective treatment are available. For this reason, blindness from glaucoma is especially tragic.[18]

The third proposition contained in this passage is the conclusion. The second proposition is the premiss. The first proposition is not part of the argument at all, strictly speaking. But its presence permits us to understand that the *available methods* referred to in the premiss are methods for early detection and effective treatment of *chronic glaucoma.*

If we wished to give a *complete* analysis of the preceding argument we might want to rephrase its constituent propositions as follows:

> *Premiss:* Methods for early detection and effective treatment of chronic glaucoma are available.
> *Conclusion:* Blindness from chronic glaucoma is especially tragic.

Another illustration of this point is found in one of Arthur Schopenhauer's (1788–1860) essays:

> If the criminal law forbids suicide, that is not an argument valid in the Church; and besides, the prohibition is ridiculous; for what penalty can frighten a person who is not afraid of death itself?[19]

Here the material before the first semicolon is neither premiss nor conclusion. But without some such information we should not know what "prohibition" the conclusion refers to. Here the conclusion is *the criminal law's prohibition of suicide is ridiculous.* The premiss offered in its support is *no penalty can frighten a person who is not afraid of death itself.* This example also shows that propositions can be asserted in the form of "rhetorical questions," which are used to make statements rather than to ask questions, even though they are interrogative in form.

In analyzing this argument, and the earlier one from the Supreme Court decision, it was helpful to rephrase some of their constituent propositions. The purpose in each case was to minimize our dependence on their contexts for an understanding of the arguments and of the roles played in them by their constituent propositions. This will be a pervasive concern in much of the rest of this book. We

---

[18] *The Harvard Medical School Health Letter* (April 1979), p. 2.
[19] Arthur Schopenhauer, "On Suicide," *Complete Essays of Schopenhauer,* Book V, *Studies in Pessimism,* trans. T. Bailey Saunders (1942), p. 26.

often want to focus on a proposition itself: we might want to know whether it is true or false, what it implies, whether it is implied by some other proposition, or whether it is a premiss or the conclusion of a given argument. In such cases it will be useful to have a statement of the proposition that can be understood as independently of context as may be possible.

Sometimes the propositional nature of a constituent of an argument is disguised by its expression as a noun phrase rather than a declarative sentence. This occurs in the following:

> The usual argument about the depressing effects of a large deficit runs like this: Big deficits cause high interest rates. High interest rates depress expenditures for business investment, housing, and automobiles. The economy cannot recover unless business investment, housing, and automobiles recover.[20]

Here the words preceding the colon seem simply to characterize what follows the colon as "the usual argument." But what follows the colon is not a whole argument but the premisses of an argument. That argument's conclusion is the proposition that a *large deficit has a depressing effect,* which is expressed (in the words preceding the colon) by the noun phrase "the depressing effects of a large deficit."

Although every argument, by definition, has a conclusion, the formulations of some arguments do not contain explicit statements of their conclusions. How can such an argument be understood and analyzed? The unstated conclusion of such an argument often is indicated by the context in which the argument occurs. Sometimes the stated premisses inescapably suggest what the unstated conclusion must be, as in

> If he's smart, he isn't going to go around shooting one of them, and he's smart.[21]

Here the context is required for us to know what "one of them" might be. But the context is not strictly needed for us to know that the conclusion is

> He isn't going to go around shooting one of them.

Another example of an argument with an unstated conclusion is:

> It could hardly be denied that a tax laid specifically on the exercise of these freedoms would be unconstitutional. Yet the license tax imposed by this ordinance is in substance just that.[22]

Here the two stated premisses of this argument can be rephrased as

---

[20] Herbert Stein, "Deficits Are Not Depressing," *The Wall Street Journal,* 12 January 1983, p. 28.
[21] George V. Higgins, *The Friends of Eddie Coyle,* p. 121.
[22] Justice William O. Douglas, for the U.S. Supreme Court, *Murdock v. Commonwealth of Pennsylvania,* 319 U.S. 105 (1943).

1. A tax laid specifically on the exercise of these freedoms is unconstitutional.
2. The license tax imposed by this ordinance is a tax laid specifically on the exercise of these freedoms.

And from these premisses—especially as rephrased—the unstated conclusion of Justice Douglas's argument is inescapable:

The license tax imposed by this ordinance is unconstitutional.

Some of you might be put off at being told that in analyzing an argument with an unstated conclusion you must already know what follows logically, or what might seem to the arguer to follow logically, from the stated premisses. After all, it is logic that you are supposed to be learning from this book! How can the book presuppose that you already know logic? If you did, why would you be studying the subject? This objection is not difficult to answer. Some logical ability is presupposed in the study of any subject, including logic itself. The study of logic can be expected to *sharpen* your logical sense, *improve* your ability to analyze arguments, and *develop* your capacity for appraising arguments as good or bad, or as better or worse. But some logical sense must be there to be sharpened, and some analytical ability must already exist to be improved. As C. I. Lewis (1883–1964), an important contemporary logician, wrote:

The study of logic appeals to no criterion not already present in the learner's mind. . . . for the very business of learning through reflection or discussion presumes our logical sense as a trustworthy guide [23]

In summary, an argument is a group of propositions of which one, the conclusion, is claimed to follow from the others, which are premisses. Propositions typically are expressed in declarative sentences, but they sometimes appear as commands, rhetorical questions, or noun phrases. An entire argument can be stated in a single sentence, but often several sentences are employed in its formulation. In the presentation of an argument, its conclusion may either precede or follow all the premisses, or it may come between two of them. Or the conclusion may not be stated explicitly, but be made clear by the context or implied by the very statement of the premisses. The presence of special terms functioning as premiss-indicators or conclusion-indicators often helps us to identify and distinguish the premisses and conclusion of an argument. A passage containing an argument also may contain propositions that are neither premisses nor conclusion of that argument, but present information that helps the reader or hearer understand what the premisses and conclusion are about. In analyzing an argument, often it is useful to distinguish separate premisses that may be conjoined in a single sentence. And in reporting the result of our analysis of an argument into its premiss or premisses and conclusion, it is customary and helpful to formulate each single premiss, and the conclusion, in a separate declarative sentence that can be understood independently of the context.

---

[23]   C. I. Lewis, *Mind and the World-Order* (1929), p. 3.

EXERCISES

Identify the premisses and conclusions in the following passages, each of which expresses just one argument.[24]

■ *1.* Climate models suggest that during the next century the average values of temperature and precipitation are likely to change over large areas of the globe. As a result, widespread adjustments are likely to occur in the distribution of terrestrial vegetation.

> —WILLIAM H. SCHLESINGER ET AL., "Biological Feedbacks in Global Desertification," *Science* 247 (2 March 1990), p. 1043

2. Are politicians (and the people who elect them) selfish? Of course they are: they are human.

> —"Beating the System," *The New Republic,* 5 November 1990, p. 7

3. We discern neither a historical nor a modern societal consensus forbidding the imposition of capital punishment on any person who murders at 16 or 17 years of age. Accordingly, we conclude that such punishment does not offend the Eighth Amendment's prohibition against cruel and unusual punishment.

> —JUSTICE ANTONIN SCALIA, for the U.S. Supreme Court, *Stanford v. Kentucky,* 492 U.S. 361 (1989)

4. Everyone dies; I am someone, so I will die.

> —THOMAS NAGEL, *The View From Nowhere* (1986), p. 225

■ *5.* The evidence of sexologists strongly indicates that women whose partners are aggressively uncommunicative have little chance of experiencing sexual pleasure. But it is not reasonable for women to consent to what they have little chance of enjoying. Hence it is not reasonable for women to consent to aggressive noncommunicative sex.

> —LOIS PINEAU, "Date Rape: A Feminist Analysis," *Law and Philosophy* 8 (August 1989), p. 239

6. Forty percent of the world's people live in India and China. Therefore, government policies bearing on population growth in the two countries have a significant relevance to the size and well-being of the human population as a whole.

> —"Science and the Citizen," *Scientific American* 249, (July 1983), p. 60

7. Forbear to judge, for we are sinners all.

> —WILLIAM SHAKESPEARE, *Henry IV,* Part II, Act III, Scene III

8. Since there are no mental diseases, there can be no treatments for them.

> —THOMAS S. SZASZ, quoted in *Taking Sides: Clashing Views on Controversial Bio-Ethical Issues,* ed. Carol Levine (1984), p. 179

9. He that loveth not knoweth not God, for God is love.

> —I John 4:8

■ *10.* The pastoral letter fully deserves the wide audience it seeks. It is a thoughtful and comprehensive effort to bring religious and moral principles to bear on nuclear weapons.

> —MCGEORGE BUNDY, "The Bishops and the Bomb," *The New York Review of Books* 30, 16 June 1983, p. 3

---

[24] Solutions to exercises preceded by a black square will be found at the back of the book on pages 284–310.

11. [The characteristic feature of the environment is that, for most practical purposes, nobody owns it.] Hence, [it is used and misused by individuals, firms, and, for that matter, public bodies as well, without any automatic restraint in the form of some obligation to compensate the owner for its use or to pay some other form of charge for its use.]

—WILFRED BECKERMAN, *Two Cheers for the Affluent Society* (1974), pp. 20–21

12. [H]e [James Q. Wilson] strenuously argues that [it is possible to influence events without knowing their causes.] This is a point that should be obvious: [one can extinguish a fire without knowing what caused it.]

—ERNEST VAN DEN HAAG, "Thinking About Crime Again," *Commentary* 76, December 1983, p. 73

13. [Put off thy shoes from off thy feet,] for [the place whereon thou standest is holy ground.]

—Exodus 3:5

14. Moreover, [the similarity in shape between the edges of two continents that today are separated by thousands of kilometers] (for example the eastern edge of South America and the western edge of Africa) shows that [they rifted apart.]

—VINCENT COURTILLOT and GREGORY E. VINK, "How Continents Break Up," *Scientific American* 249, July 1983, p. 43

■ **15.** I begin, then, with these preliminary considerations: [that a free society is a pluralistic society,] that [a pluralistic society is one with countless propaganda from many sources] and that [coping with propaganda requires a wide-spread critical intelligence which is largely the product of education.] *all P, no C*

—RICHARD M. WEAVER, "A Responsible Rhetoric," *The Intercollegiate Review* 12, Winter 1976–77, p. 82

16. Q. Doesn't the death penalty verge on the kind of "cruel and unusual punishment" that the Constitution prohibits?

A. [The men who wrote the Constitution didn't see it that way.] The proof is contained in the language of the Constitution itself. [The due-process clauses of the Fifth and Fourteenth Amendments both speak of the necessity to provide due process when depriving a person of life.]

—WALTER BERNS, interview in *U.S. News & World Report,* 20 April 1981, p. 49

17. [Power is not equally distributed in the marketplace,] nor are [information and knowledge (which are a form of power);] hence [the need for ethical standards and rules.]

—LEONARD SILK, *Economics in Plain English* (1978), p. 42

18. [Being married, rather than restricting him, provides a man even greater freedom than being single] because [he need not worry about day to day chores, cleaning the house, making dinner, spending long hours with the children, or anything else to do with the home.]

—JONATHAN L. FREEDMAN, "Love + Marriage = Happiness (Still)," *Public Opinion,* November–December 1978

19. Courtly love was understood by its contemporaries to be love for its own sake, romantic love, true love, physical love, unassociated with property or family, and consequently focused on another man's wife, since only such an illict liaison could have no other aim but love alone.

—BARBARA TUCHMAN, *A Distant Mirror, The Calamitous 14th Century*

■ *20.* Citizens who so value their "independence" that they will not enroll in a political party are really forfeiting independence, because they abandon a share in the decision-making at the primary level: the choice of the candidate.

—BRUCE L. FELKNOR, *Dirty Politics*

21. We cannot for a moment believe that knowledge has reached its final goal, or that the present condition of society is perfect. We must therefore welcome from our teachers such discussions as shall suggest the means and prepare the way by which knowledge may be extended, present evils be removed and others prevented.

—THE UNIVERSITY OF WISCONSIN BOARD OF REGENTS, 1894, quoted in Richard Hofstadter and Walter P. Metzger, *The Development of Academic Freedom in the United States*

22. The patterns of industrial production in this country, and the manipulation of consumer demands by the corporate sector, have led to such a profligate use of energy that American consumption is now many times higher than the world average. The quickest way, therefore, to deal with over-consumption and "scarcity" is by conservation.

—ALAN S. MILLER, "Energy Ethics for America: 1980," *Journal of Current Social Issues*, Winter 1980

23. [Members of a twelve-member faculty committee at the Colorado School of Mines] . . . say that future engineers will be called on increasingly to work on interdisciplinary teams and be faced with greater public scrutiny and government regulation. Accordingly, says the faculty report, the school should help students develop a "broader view of the social and political implications of [their] actions, better communicative skills, more intellectual mobility, better management capabilities, and a higher commitment to the preservation of the environment."

—ROBERT L. JACOBSON in *The Chronicle of Higher Education*, 9 July 1979

24. Since, the argument runs, *McDonald v. Santa Fe Trans. Co., supra,* settled that Title VII forbids discrimination against whites as well as blacks, and since the Kaiser-U.S.W.A. affirmative action plan operates to discriminate against white employees solely because they are white, it follows that the Kaiser-U.S.W.A. plan violates Title VII.

—JUSTICE WILLIAM BRENNAN, JR., for the U.S. Supreme Court, *United Steelworkers v. Brian E. Weber et al.,* 78 USLW 432 (1979)

■ *25.* As Adam Smith long ago noted, monopoly is the enemy of good management, since it destroys incentive to control corporate expenses and maintain maximum production.

—JIM HIGHTOWER, "Food Monopoly," *The Texas Observer,* 17 November 1978

26. By a rough rule of thumb, economists reckon that to secure one unit of income you have to invest three times as much capital. So, even to keep pace with a three-percent increase in population, a nation has, roughly speaking, to invest nine percent of its national income each year.

—BARBARA WARD, *The Rich Nations and the Poor Nations*

27. . . . since the elderly have always had a higher cancer rate, and since we now have more older citizens, the absolute increase in the number of cancer deaths is not an indication of any kind of "environmental breakdown."

—TED DIENSTFREY, in *The Public Interest,* Summer 1979

28. Good sense is of all things in the world the most equally distributed, for everybody thinks himself so abundantly provided with it, that even those most difficult to please in all other matters do not commonly desire more of it than they already possess.

—RENÉ DESCARTES, *A Discourse on Method*

29. A gray surface looks red if we have been looking at a blue-green one; plain paper feels smooth if we have been feeling sandpaper or rough if we have been feeling plate glass; and tap water tastes sweet if we have been eating artichokes. Some part of what we call red or smooth or sweet must therefore be in the eyes or fingertips or tongue of the beholder, feeler, or taster.

—B. F. SKINNER, *Beyond Freedom and Dignity*

■ **30.** Thinking is a function of man's immortal soul. God has given an immortal soul to every man and woman, but not to any other animal or to machines. Hence no animal or machine can think

—A. M. TURING, "Computing Machinery and Intelligence," *Mind* 59, 1950

31. If there were to be any difference between a girl's education and a boy's, I should say that of the two the girl should be earlier led, as her intellect ripens faster, into deep and serious subjects. . . .

—JOHN RUSKIN, *Sesame and Lilies*

32. Roman Catholic faith gives a God-given role to the hierarchical magisterium of pope and bishops as the official and at times even infallible teachers on questions of faith and morals. The Roman Catholic theologian precisely as such must recognize the role of the hierarchical magisterium and therefore is not and cannot be free to come to a conclusion in opposition to Catholic faith or to the divinely constituted hierarchical teaching office in the Church.

—CHARLES E. CURRAN, "Academic Freedom: The Catholic University and Catholic Theology," *Academe,* April 1980

33. Last year we had a serious infestation [of Medfly] that threatened the agricultural economy of California. Then aerial application of malathion began. This year we have none. How anyone can write that malathion may have had no effect is mind-boggling, entomologically and logically.

—CLARK BIGGS, letter to the editor, *Newsweek,* 29 November 1982, p. 6

34. Those who in ancient times gave good government were sages, and those who in later times have given good government are likewise sages. The virtue of the sages then and now does not differ, and therefore their government, anciently and today, is likewise not different.

—WANG CH'UNG, *Critical Essays,* quoted in *A History of Chinese Philosophy* by Fung Yu-lan, Vol. 2, p. 158

■ *35.*   Does the United States have vital interests in Central America? The truth is it does not. U.S. trade with the area is minuscule. Our investment in the area is insignificant. Overblown Pan-American rhetoric aside, we share few values with the countries of Central America. Except for Costa Rica, the region has not known democracy and the governments have traditionally allowed a few corrupt families to run whole countries like giant plantations for private profit.

—CHARLES WILLIAM MAYNES, "Central America Testing U.S.," *Los Angeles Times Service,* 13 June 1983

1.3   DIAGRAMS FOR SINGLE ARGUMENTS

Many argumentative passages contain more than a single argument, and it often happens that the conclusion of one argument serves as a premiss for another. Sometimes there are more than two arguments, and they are so articulated that an extended line of reasoning cascades through several arguments to reach a final conclusion. In such argumentative passages there is a flow, a general direction, along which the speaker or writer intends the hearer or reader to follow.

To understand such complex support for a final conclusion, certainly to appraise such an extended argument as good or bad, cogent or faulty, one must be aware of the entire structure. One must try to see how the single arguments in the passage are so arranged as to lead one rationally to accept that final conclusion.

That is more difficult to accomplish in an oral presentation than in a written passage. But acquiring facility at analyzing a written argumentative passage will help one to develop the habits and insights required to cope with spoken arguments.

To deal with the problem of analyzing complex argumentative passages, it is useful first to establish a standard method of analyzing and diagramming single arguments. That will enable us to fit them clearly into the complex argumentative structure in which they may play a leading or bridging role. A complex argumentative passage can best be understood by one who can analyze its component argumentative parts and can recognize and articulate those parts in the larger whole.

Practicing these skills will help the student to read more carefully and thus with greater comprehension. These skills enable their possessor to see with maximum clarity what conclusion is being urged, on the basis of what evidence, and exactly how the speaker or writer claims that the premisses relate to the conclusion. These logical skills also help students organize their own arguments more effectively. Such organization involves marshaling the evidence for our conclusions in the clearest possible fashion and formulating the premisses offered in support of our conclusions with maximum force and directness.

A useful method of analyzing and diagramming argumentative passages was devised some years ago by Professor Monroe Beardsley.[25] With only minor modifications, we follow his lead in this matter. A diagram of something is a spatial representation of it, like a blueprint of a building or a machine, a graph showing population or income distribution, or a wiring diagram for electrical equipment. We will adopt the convention of placing the argument's conclusion below its premiss or premisses and will use an arrow as our diagrammatic conclusion-indicator. As a first approximation to our diagrams, we set forth the argument

> Since light has a finite velocity the astronomer can never hope to see the universe as it actually exists today.[26]

as

> Light has a finite velocity.
> ↓
> The astronomer can never hope to see the universe as it actually exists today.

and the argument

> . . . lawyers are increasingly the most important service group in society because by and large people do not do much of significant secular importance without first consulting a lawyer.[27]

whose conclusion is stated first and its premiss second, as

> By and large people do not do much of significant secular importance without first consulting a lawyer.
> ↓
> Lawyers are increasingly the most important service group in society.

When we encounter arguments with two or more premisses, rearranging them becomes more tedious, and our diagrams become too cluttered. It is convenient to number the constituent propositions in the order of their occurrence in the passage and to let the numerals assigned to them, enclosed in circles, appear in our diagrams instead of the full sentences in which they are stated. When constructed in this way, a diagram displays the structure of the argument with maximum clarity. In numbering the premisses and conclusions of arguments, it is helpful to put brackets around each one, with its circled numeral either above it or directly in front of it, as in the following letter:

> As a Ph.D. student in operations research at Cornell University, I can state from experience that ① [professors moonlighting as consultants . . . are not

[25]   Monroe C. Beardsley, *Practical Logic* (1950).
[26]   Maarten Schmidt and Francis Bello, "The Evolution of Quasars," *Scientific American*, May 1971.
[27]   William A. Stanmeyer, "Legal Education and Lawyers," *The Intercollegiate Review*, Fall 1979, p. 20.

shortchanging their students.] ② [Money from consulting contracts has helped to finance many a graduate student's education.] More important, ③ [students often serve as research assistants under such contracts and can gain valuable experience while still in school.]²⁸

Now we can use the circled numerals to represent the propositions they label, and diagram the argument in this way:

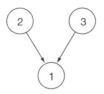

In this argument each of the two premisses supports the conclusion *independently*. Each supplies some warrant for accepting the conclusion and would do so even in the absence of the other premiss.

A decision must be made at this point about the "arithmetic" of such arguments. Should we count this as a single argument with two premisses and one conclusion, or should we say that here we have two arguments with the same conclusion? Emerging practice is to say that it is *one* argument with two independent premisses. The principle seems to be that the number of conclusions determines the number of arguments. So by a "single argument" we mean an argument to a single conclusion, regardless of how many premisses are adduced in its support.

Not every premiss in an argument provides the kind of independent support for the conclusion that those in the preceding argument do. Some premisses must work together to support their conclusion. When this happens, the cooperation they display can be exhibited in the argument's diagram. This situation is illustrated by the following argument. Incidentally, it may be useful to circle any premiss-indicators or conclusion-indicators that are in the argument being analyzed.

Helms's lawyer was Edward Bennett Williams, who is regarded as perhaps the best criminal lawyer in the country. (Since) ① [Helms had clearly lied under oath to a congressional committee,] and (since) ② [it is a crime to. lie under oath to a congressional committee,] ③ [Williams didn't have a lot going for his client in the way of a legal defense.]²⁹

Here neither of the two premisses supports the conclusion independently. If Helms had *not* lied under oath, the fact that lying under oath to a congressional committee is a crime would have no bearing on the argument's conclusion. And if such lying were *not* a crime, Helms's lying would not have impaired his legal defense. Each premiss supports the conclusion through the *mediation* of the other premiss. *Both* are needed,

---

²⁸   Howard M. Singer, *Newsweek*, 24 July 1978, p. 7.
²⁹   Richard Harris, "Reflections (Richard Helms)," *The New Yorker*, 10 April 1978, p. 54.

in contrast to the independent or *immediate* support for its conclusion that each premiss provided in the argument about professors working as consultants. That the two premisses work cooperatively in this argument, rather than independently, is represented in the diagram by connecting their circled numerals with a horizontal brace, as shown, with a single arrow leading from the pair of them to the conclusion.

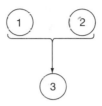

In an argument containing three or more premisses, one (or more) might provide independent support for the conclusion, while two (or more) of the other premisses provide support only in combination. This situation is illustrated by the following argument:

①[Desert mountaintops make good sites for astronomy.]
②[Being high, they sit above a portion of the atmosphere, enabling a star's light to reach a telescope without having to swim through the entire depth of the atmosphere.] ③[Being dry, the desert is also relatively cloud-free.] ④[The merest veil of haze or cloud can render a sky useless for many astronomical measures.][30]

Here propositions ② ③ and ④provide support for proposition ① which is the conclusion. But they offer their support in different ways. The single statement ②by itself supports the claim that mountaintop locations are good sites for telescopes. But the two statements ③and ④must work together to support the claim that desert locations are good sites for telescopes. The diagram showing this difference is:

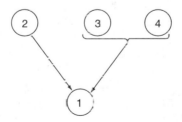

The following is an argument in whose formulation the conclusion is sandwiched between two premisses:

[30]Blanchard Hiatt, *University of Michigan Research News* 30, August-September 1979, p. 5.

Since ①[morals . . . have an influence on the actions and affections] it follows that ②[they cannot be deriv'd from reason;] . . . because ③[reason alone as we have already prov'd, can never have any such influence.] [31]

The diagram for David Hume's (1711–76) argument is

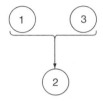

This arrangement of premisses and conclusion might suggest that the author, after stating a premiss and inferring a conclusion, belatedly realized that another premiss was needed and added it as an afterthought. That probably does not account for the arrangement of propositions in Hume's argument, however. It is more likely that he realized that his reader might not *remember* the second premiss, which Hume had established as the conclusion of another argument some forty-three pages earlier in his book.

For various reasons, including attempting to maximize rhetorical effectiveness, people do not always make the conclusions of their arguments explicit. When this occurs, the conclusion can be represented in the argument's diagram by enclosing its numeral in a broken circle. Consider the following example:

What was striking was that ①[every politician or journalist I talked to, including the young intellectuals who back the PLO, claimed that Egyptian young people would not want to fight again.] . . . ②[Moreover, the widening of the Suez Canal is now going forward and the cities on its banks are being rebuilt.] ③[A nation planning to make war would not be likely to block its route of attack in this way.] [32]

The first thing to notice is that this argument has an unstated conclusion, which we number in the way indicated:

④[Egypt will not attack [Israel] across the Suez Canal again.] Having all its propositions indicated and labeled, we can represent the argument by the following diagram:

---

[31] David Hume, *A Treatise of Human Nature,* p. 457.
[32] Arthur Hertzberg, "The View from Cairo," *The New York Review of Books,* 26 June 1980, p. 45.

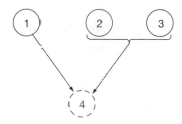

EXERCISES

Diagram the arguments in the following passages, each of which expresses a single argument.

■ *1.* Incidentally, I never miss [Roseanne Barr's TV] show. I never see it, so I never miss it.
—BLACKIE SHERROD, *The Dallas Morning News,* 29 July 1990, p. 4B

2. Potatoes are exceptionally nutritious: they are rich in potassium, iron, magnesium, vitamins B and C, and complex carbohydrates, have a better quality protein than soybeans and are 99.9% fat-free.
—"Science and Technology," *The Economist,* 13 October 1990, p. 90

3. [W]hile it is possible to make objective measurements of physical properties such as weight and speed, it is not possible to make such measurements of artistic value, because people having different values and preferences do not agree and cannot be brought to agree on how to determine the presence of that attribute or even how to define it.
—RICHARD A. POSNER, "Art for Law's Sake," *The American Scholar* 58, Autumn 1989, p. 514

4. Penn [the University of Pennsylvania] argues that since the new use of the drug [Retin-A] was developed at least in part in its own laboratories and tested on patients in university facilities, the university has a claim to ownership.
—ELIOT MARSHALL, "Penn Charges Retin-A Inventor with Conflict," *Science* 247, 2 March 1990, p. 1028

■ *5.* If we have known freedom, then we love it; if we love freedom, then we fear, at some level (individually or collectively), its loss.
—A. BARTLETT GIAMATTI, *Take Time for Paradise: Americans and Their Games* (1989), pp. 104–105

6. Since we never are going to have the unlimited resources of the Republicans, we have to put the resources we do have to the best possible use.
—SENATOR EDWARD M. KENNEDY, "The Democratic Report," *Fund for a Democratic Majority,* Summer 1983, Washington, D.C., p. 3

7. . . . we often learn about causes from cures: if ingesting a chemical cures a disease, we may learn that the disease was caused by a lack of that chemical.
—ERNEST VAN DEN HAAG, "Thinking About Crime Again," *Commentary* 76, December 1983, p. 73

8. Deficits are bad because they enable our representatives to vote for spending without having to vote for taxes to pay for the spending.

—MILTON FRIEDMAN, "Why Deficits Are Bad," *Newsweek*, 2 January 1984, p. 56

9. The rule in the diamond district is that no stranger is ever admitted to these private offices. Since dealers commonly carry on their persons millions of dollars worth of diamonds, such stringent precautions are indispensable.

—EDWARD EPSTEIN, "The Carat Tzimmes," *Moment*, 7 June 1982, p. 55

■ **10.** Modern technology can tell us very well, down to the millimeter; what the brain matter of a baby's cortex is, and thus we know very accurately through brain scans and other tests what sort of life is in store for deplorably handicapped infants.

—DR. HARRY JENNISON, "Should Uncle Sam Protect Handicapped Babies?" *U.S. News & World Report*, 16 January 1984, p. 64

11. Hunting, particularly . . . the hunting of large animals, is so complicated, difficult and hazardous that the cooperation of numerous individuals is needed. It can be inferred, therefore, that Peking man was more likely to have been living in a group than in solitude when he began to hunt deer.

—WU RUKANG and LIN SHENGLONG, "Peking Man," *Scientific American* 248, June 1983, p. 94

12. . . . since reduction of sodium may prevent the development of hypertension in some people and since a high-salt diet is almost certainly not beneficial, reduced salting of food and reduced consumption of salty snack foods is probably a good idea.

—"Science and the Citizen," *Scientific American* 249, August 1983, p. 60

13. "In order to sell, you have to develop a positive attitude, and in order to develop a positive attitude, you have to exercise," says a chic young woman attempting to motivate a team of middle-aged salesladies before opening time.

—MARY-LOU WEISMAN, "Neiman-Marcus, The Movie," *The New Republic*, 31 December 1983, p. 26

14. Dr. Oliver Wendell Holmes once laid out the dictum that the key to longevity was to have a chronic incurable disease and take good care of it. Even now, 150 years later; this works. If you have chronic arthritis you are likely to take a certain amount of aspirin most days of your life, and this may reduce your chances of dropping dead from coronary thrombosis. When you are chronically ill, you are also, I suppose, less likely to drive an automobile, or climb ladders, or fall down the cellar stairs carrying books needing storage, or smoke too much, or drink a lot.

—LEWIS THOMAS, *The Youngest Science* (1983), p. 149

■ **15.** A just society cannot possibly pay everyone the same income, since the aptitudes and efforts of individuals diverge dramatically, and since the common good is far better served, accordingly, by systematic inequalities of reward.

—MICHAEL NOVAK, *Commentary* 76, December 1983, p. 30

16. To say I believe in spanking children implies that spankings are in some way essential to their proper upbringing. I do not hold that opinion; therefore, I do not believe in spankings.

—JOHN ROSEMOND, "Parent Power," syndicated column, 30 August 1983

17. No human subject may be used in a medical experiment without his informed and freely given consent. But prisoners, by virtue of their total custody, cannot give free and uncoerced consent. Hence prisoners—no matter how valuable experimentation with their cooperation may prove—must be excluded from all populations of subjects in medical experimentation.

> —CARL COHEN, "Medical Experimentation on Prisoners," in *Taking Sides: Clashing Views on Controversial Bio-Ethical Issues,* ed. Carol Levine (1984), p. 213 (It should be remarked that Professor Cohen regards this argument as unsound.)

18. This letter is concerning vandalism in the parks. The reason I am against this is, first of all, the innocent people have to pay more taxes to pay for the damage caused by the vandals. The second reason is because it defaces the parks for the people that like to visit the parks.

> —ERIK DERYEE, "Park Vandalism," letter to the editor, *The Honolulu Advertiser,* 8 May 1982, p. A-13

19. Dost thou love Life? Then do not squander Time; for that's the stuff Life is made of.

> —BENJAMIN FRANKLIN, *Poor Richard's Almanac,* 1746

■ *20.* Q. Dr. Koop, why does the government need to intervene in the treatment of handicapped infants?

A. The Rehabilitation Act of 1973 states that it is illegal in any institution that receives federal aid to discriminate against anyone on the basis of race, creed, color, religion, ethnic origin or handicap. We have good evidence that many children are deprived of their civil rights by being treated in a different way than they would be treated if they were not handicapped.

> —Interview with Dr C. Everett Koop, *U.S. News & World Report,* 16 January 1984, p. 63

21. Given the diagnostic deficiencies of psychiatry, given its philosophical weaknesses, given its poor therapeutic record, given the manner in which it has been abused at times for political purposes, given the way psychiatry has been employed at times to pervert justice, or even for the purpose of sexually exploiting patients, we should rethink accustomed notions concerning the nature and treatment of mental disease.

> —LEWIS H. GANN, "Psychiatry: Helpful Servant or Cruel Master?" *The Intercollegiate Review,* Spring/Summer 1982, pp. 111–12

22. Since all judges first were lawyers, since lawyers are notorious for their low tolerance of criticism, and since lawyers-become-judges were first law students on a steady diet of the adversary system, it is a rare judge who will admit that this process is often inappropriate for solving social and political problems.

> —WILLIAM A. STANMEYER, "Legal Education and Lawyers," *The Intercollegiate Review,* Fall 1979

23. Prisons are . . . necessary. The existence of prisons and the prospect of incarceration make up a backdrop of deterrence that keeps the crime rate from overflowing. Prisons also serve the melancholy social task of consuming the youth of violent offenders and returning them to the community drained of the vitality necessary for aggression. Finally, prison sentences serve the morally unifying and emotionally releasing purpose of expressing communal reprobation through ceremonies of degradation that bind people together in separating them from the criminal.

—GRAHAM HUGHES, "American Terror," *The New York Review of Books,* 25 January 1979

24. For years the GOP was impervious to untested new ideas. It also was impervious to tested old ideas, but about 97 percent of all ideas are false, so there is something to be said for a party that has nothing to do with any of them.

—GEORGE F. WILL, "Waltz of the Lame Ducks," *Newsweek* 6, December 1982, p. 158

■ *25.* Over the last quarter-century, as this is written, the average work week in industry has increased moderately. The standard work week has declined, but this has been more than offset by increased demand for overtime work and the companion willingness to supply it. During this period average weekly earnings, adjusted for price increases, have nearly doubled. On the evidence, one must conclude that, as their incomes rise, people will work longer hours and seek less leisure.

—JOHN KENNETH GALBRAITH, *The New Industrial State*

26. . . . the simplest form of the theological argument from design, once well known under the name of "Paley's watch." Paley's form of it was just this: "If we found by chance a watch or other piece of intricate mechanism we should infer that it had been made by someone. But all around us we do find intricate pieces of natural mechanism, and the processes of the universe are seen to move together in complex relations; we should therefore infer that these too have a Maker."

—B. A. O. WILLIAMS, "Metaphysical Arguments," *The Nature of Metaphysics,* ed. D. F. Pears

27. Zen liberates all the energies properly and naturally stored in each of us, which are in ordinary circumstances cramped and distorted so that they find no adequate channel for activity. This body of ours is something like an electric battery in which a mysterious power latently lies. When this power is not properly brought into operation, it either grows mouldy and withers away or is warped and expresses itself abnormally. It is the object of Zen, therefore, to save us from going crazy or being crippled.

—DAISETZ TEITARO SUZUKI, *Essays in Zen Buddhism*

28. . . . the really important role that women serve as housewives is to buy *more things for the house.* In all the talk of femininity and woman's role, one forgets that the real business of America is business. But the perpetuation of housewifery, the growth of the feminine mystique, makes sense (and dollars) when one realizes that women are the chief customers of American business. Somehow, somewhere, someone must have figured out that women will buy more things if they are kept in the under-used, nameless-yearning, energy-to-get-rid-of state of being housewives.

—BETTY FRIEDAN, *The Feminine Mystique*

29. Every time an obscenity case is to be argued here, my office is flooded with letters and postal cards urging me to protect the community or the Nation by striking down the publication. The messages are often identical even down to commas and semicolons. The inference is irresistible that they were all copied from a school or church blackboard. Dozens of postal cards often are mailed from the same precinct.

—JUSTICE DOUGLAS, concurring opinion, 383 U.S. 413

■   ***30.***   There is no such thing as free will. The mind is induced to wish this or that by some cause, and that cause is determined by another cause, and so on back to infinity.

—BARUCH SPINOZA, *Ethics*

31.   First, the *personality and character*—which are really synonymous—*take their form during the first six or eight years of life.* During this period of infancy and childhood, we select and develop the techniques which gain us satisfaction, defend us against threats, and become the tools in coping with the endless variety of problem situations that will be encountered later in life. It is during this time that we develop our methods of relating ourselves to other people and undergo the experiences which determine the strength and weaknesses within our personality. As adults we are not able to remember the details of these formative years. Therefore, we cannot understand our own behavior fully.

—WILLIAM C. MENNINGER, "Psychiatry for Everyday Needs," *Perspectives in Medicine—The March of Medicine,* 1948

32.   In 1972 Justice Thurgood Marshall wrote that "punishment for the sake of retribution is not permissible under the Eighth Amendment." That is absurd. The element of retribution—vengeance, if you will—does not make punishment cruel and unusual, it makes punishment intelligible. It distinguishes punishment from therapy. Rehabilitation may be an ancillary result of punishment, but we punish to serve justice, by giving people what they deserve.

—GEORGE F. WILL, "The Value of Punishment," *Newsweek,* 24 May 1982, p. 92

33.   However proper or safe it may be in governments where the executive magistrate is an hereditary monarch, to commit to him the entire power of making treaties, it would be utterly unsafe and improper to intrust that power to an elective magistrate of four years' duration. It has been remarked, upon another occasion, and the remark is unquestionably just, that an hereditary monarch, though often the oppressor of his people, has personally too much at stake in the government to be in any material danger of being corrupted by foreign powers. But a man raised from [the] station of a private citizen to the rank of Chief Magistrate, possessed of but a moderate or slender fortune, and looking forward to a period not very remote when he may probably be obliged to return to the station from which he was taken, might sometimes be under temptations to sacrifice his duty to his interest, which it would require superlative virtue to withstand. An avaricious man might be tempted to betray the interests of the state to the acquisition of wealth. An ambitious man might make his own aggrandizement, by the aid of a foreign power, the price of his treachery to his constituents. The history of human conduct does not warrant that exalted opinion of human virtue which would make it wise in a nation to commit interests of so delicate and momentous a kind, as those which concern its intercourse with the rest of the world, to the sole disposal of the magistrate created and circumstanced as would be a President of the United States.

—ALEXANDER HAMILTON, *The Federalist Papers,* Number 75

34.   An amusing observation relevant to the effects of rapid change was made among Hopi Indians. A young Hopi, American schooled, may be contrasted with his father. His father believed that when he trod on the tracks of a snake, he would get sore ankles unless he took himself to the medicine man who could prevent this by incantation. This he believed without question, and visiting the medicine man prevented his ankles from becoming sore. But his American-schooled son, who no longer believes in the powers of the medicine man, considering him a humbug, refuses to consult him, and does get sore ankles after walking in the track of a snake. The implication is that in a rapidly changing society, anxiety-inducing factors outlive anxiety-resolving factors.

—HAROLD G. WOLFF, "The Mind-Body Relationship"

■ *35.* The United States economy is still the most powerful in the world; and if the country's position as a manufacturer is now less secure, its position as supplier of food to the world was never more important. Unlike France, Italy, or England, it has no opposition party whose policies would force large-scale adaptations of the system or an attempt at conversion to socialism. The American recession, costly though it has been, has not produced serious political or social unrest. We have been mercifully spared Europe's terrorism. America's inflation is still below that of most of the rest of the industrial world, and the prices of shares on its stock exchanges are, by comparative standards, cheap. Thus, by all the criteria of history or common sense, the dollar would seem to be one of the soundest, not one of the frailest, currencies.

—ROBERT L. HEILBRONER, "Reflections: Boom and Crash," *The New Yorker,* 28 August 1978

1.4   RECOGNIZING ARGUMENTS

Thus far the reader's attention has been directed to passages already identified and labeled as expressing arguments. There the problems were, first, to distinguish their premises and conclusions; and second, to diagram the arguments to exhibit their structures more clearly. In this section we consider the prior problem of deciding whether an argument is present in a given passage.

The presence or absence of premiss-indicators or conclusion-indicators is helpful, though not always decisive, as was noted in section 1.2. Extremely important is the context in which the passage (spoken or written) occurs. In a formal debate in a law court or in a legislative chamber, one naturally *expects* to encounter arguments. And the announced or scheduled agenda in such contexts helps us to understand what is being asserted in alleged support of *what* conclusion. Other argumentative contexts include the editorial pages of newspapers, articles in scholarly journals, and commercial advertisements.

A proposition by itself is not an argument. A proposition is said to be "true" or "false," whereas we use different terms to describe analogous characteristics of arguments, such as "correct" or "incorrect," "valid" or "invalid," "sound" or "unsound," "demonstrative," "probable," "plausible," or "fallacious."

An argument is a group of propositions of which one, the conclusion, is claimed to be true on the basis of other propositions, the premises, that are asserted as providing grounds or reasons for accepting the conclusion. The several propositions contained in an argument, that is, the argument's conclusion and its premises, are said to be *constituents* (or *constituent propositions*) of the argument. But not every passage containing several propositions is an argument. Consider the following (full) paragraph from a history book:

> Petersburg, too, was occupied by Federal troops, but destruction there was largely averted. At a private home President Lincoln and Gen. Grant conferred. Mr. Lincoln reviewed the troops passing through the city, which had undergone more than nine months of siege.[33]

Here every proposition contained in the paragraph is asserted, but no claim is made, either explicitly or implicitly, that any of them provides grounds or evidence for any other. So no argument is present.

It is useful to remark at this point that not only arguments, but also some compound propositions, contain two (or more) other propositions of which both (or all) are asserted. The several propositions contained in a *compound* proposition are said to be *components* (or *component propositions*) of the compound proposition. For example, the first sentence of the paragraph just quoted is a conjunction of the two propositions *Petersburg was occupied by Federal troops* and *destruction there* [in Petersburg] *was largely averted,* which are conjoined by the word "but." Other conjunctions are simpler, for example, "Roses are red and violets are blue" or "Jack and Jill went up the hill." Still others are more complex, as when they have more than two components, or when their components are themselves compound. It is obvious that asserting the conjunction of two propositions is strictly equivalent to asserting each of the component propositions itself.

But that is not true of other kinds of compound propositions. In alternative or disjunctive propositions, such as

> Circuit Courts are useful, or they are not useful.[34]

and

> Either wealth is an evil or wealth is a good.[35]

neither of their components is asserted; only the compound either-or-alternative propositions are asserted. And in hypothetical (sometimes known as conditional) propositions such as

> If Pluto, according to Halliday's calculations, had a diameter of more than 4,200 miles, then an occultation would have occurred at McDonald [observatory at Fort Davis, Texas].[36]

and

> If the President defied the order, he would be impeached.[37]

---

[33]   E. B. Long, with Barbara Long, *The Civil War Day by Day, an Almanac 1861–1865,* p. 665.

[34]   Abraham Lincoln, annual message to Congress, 3 December 1861.

[35]   Sextus Empiricus, *Against the Logicians.*

[36]   Thomas D. Nicholson, "The Enigma of Pluto," *Natural History* 76, March 1967.

[37]   Victoria Schuck, "Watergate," *The Key Reporter* 41, Winter 1975–76.

neither of their component propositions is asserted; only the compound "if-then" hypothetical propositions are asserted. So in diagramming an argument one must diagram each alternative proposition and each hypothetical proposition as a single (compound) proposition, because each constituent proposition of an argument is asserted in that argument, either as one of the premises or as the conclusion.

Because neither alternative propositions nor hypothetical propositions involve the assertion of their component propositions, they are not—by themselves—arguments. In this respect a hypothetical proposition is different from an argument that might resemble it very closely.

Consider the hypothetical proposition

If objects of art are expressive, they are a language.

Neither its first component proposition, *objects of art are expressive,* or its other component proposition, *they* [objects of art] *are a language,* is asserted. What is asserted is only that the former implies the latter, but both could be false for all the statement in question says. No premiss is asserted, no inference is made, no conclusion is claimed to be true: There is no argument here. But consider the following:

Because objects of art are expressive, they are a language.[38]

Here we do have an argument, as is suggested by the presence of the premiss-indicator "because." The proposition *objects of art are expressive* is asserted as a premiss, and the proposition *they* [objects of art] *are a language* is claimed to follow from that premiss and is asserted to be true. A hypothetical proposition may look like an argument, and, as we saw earlier; it may be a constituent of an argument, but it is not—by itself—an argument; and the two should not be confused.

Context, however, is extremely important here. Included in context is what can be called "common knowledge." For example, it is common knowledge that society has not yet finally settled matters of justice and retribution. In the light of this common knowledge, an argument is expressed in the following hypothetical proposition:

If matters of justice and retribution were simple, society would have settled them as easily as it has settled on the advantages of paved roads.[39]

In the given hypothetical proposition the component that is implied, *society would have settled them as easily as it has settled on the advantages of paved roads,* is false. And in the light of this contextual information we immediately infer that the "if" component of that hypothetical proposition must be false also—and that is the unstated conclusion of the argument expressed by the hypothetical proposition in question:

Matters of justice and retribution are *not* simple.

---

[38]   John Dewey, *Art as Experience* (1934), p. 106.
[39]   Diane Johnson, review of Susan Jacoby, *Wild Justice: The Evolution of Revenge, The New York Review of Books* 31, 16 February 1984, p. 40.

To diagram the argument expressed in that hypothetical proposition, we could represent that proposition itself as ① the common knowledge denial of its component that is implied in it as ② and the unstated conclusion that is the denial of its "if" component as ③ So the diagram for the preceding argument is:

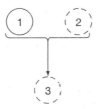

Another example of the same use of a hypothetical proposition to express an argument, this time in a passage containing background information, is the following:

> To date, diplomacy isn't doing the job. The Iraqis won't evacuate Kuwait because the United Nations' secretary-general—or even the garrulous Jesse Jackson—lays on the unction of sweet reason. ①[If Saddam Hussein were reasonable, he wouldn't have invaded Kuwait in the first place.][40]

Here the unstated or missing premiss is supplied by the relevant common knowledge that ②[Saddam Hussein invaded Kuwait.] And the unstated conclusion is that ③ [Saddam Hussein is not reasonable.] This argument is likewise diagrammed as

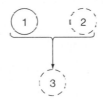

Sometimes, in arguments such as this, the hypothetical proposition has a humorous—and obviously false—component, as in

> If you believe Congress will lower its own pay, then you believe in Santa Claus.

and

> If the Atlanta Braves are the best team in baseball, then I'm a monkey's uncle.

In most cases, the person to whom such an argument is addressed has no trouble filling in the missing propositions. Indeed, people seem to delight in this reconstructive

---

[40] William Murchison, "Prepare for War with Iraq," *The Dallas Morning News*, 5 September 1990, p. 17A.

process. They no more want arguments laid out in excruciating detail than they want jokes explained to them.

We have already remarked that although every argument contains several propositions, not every passage in which several propositions are asserted contains an argument. For an argument to be present, one of those asserted propositions must be claimed to follow from other propositions asserted to be true, which are *presented* as grounds for, or reasons for believing, the conclusion. This claim may be either explicit or implicit. It may be made explicit by the use of premiss-indicators or conclusion-indicators or by the occurrence of such words as "must," "should," "ought," or "necessarily" in the conclusion. But as we saw in section 1.2, the presence of these argument-indicators is not always decisive. Quite a few argument-indicators have other functions as well. For example, if we compare

Since Kleo graduated from medical school, her income is probably very high.

with

Since Kleo graduated from medical school, there have been many changes in medical techniques.

we see that although the first is an argument in which the word "since" indicates the premiss, the second is not an argument at all. In the second the word "since" has temporal rather than logical significance: What is asserted is that many changes in medical techniques developed after Kleo graduated from medical school, without the slightest suggestion that there is any logical or causal connection between her graduation and those changes. These two different meanings of the term combine to give deeper texture to a line from the popular song "Stormy Weather":

Since my man and I ain't together, keeps rainin' all the time.

Such words as "because" and "for" also have other than strictly logical uses. Compare the following two passages:

In inflationary times it is obviously advantageous to borrow money at normal interest rates because dollars will be cheaper and more plentiful when it comes time to repay the loan.[41]

and

I chose the title "Weapons and Hope" for this essay because I want to discuss the gravest problem now facing mankind, the problem of nuclear weapons, from a human rather than a technical point of view.[42]

In the first we have an argument in which the term "because" indicates the premiss, asserting that *in inflationary times dollars become cheaper and more plentiful as time passes*

---

[41]   Robert Heilbroner and Lester Thurow, *Five Economic Challenges* (1981), p. 28.
[42]   Freeman Dyson, "Reflections: Weapons and Hope," *The New Yorker* 6 February 1984, p. 52.

(and loan repayments come due). From that it is inferred that *in inflationary times it is obviously advantageous to borrow money at normal interest rates.* But in the second passage there is no argument. It is not inferred that *Dyson chose the title "Weapons and Hope"* for his essay. That shows itself on the first page of the essay and does not need proving; it is obvious. What follows the word "because" is not offered as evidence, grounds, or reason for believing the preceding proposition, which is more obviously true than any account of what the author aimed to accomplish. What we have here is Dyson's *explanation* for his choice of the essay's title. In both illustrations two propositions are asserted, with the word "because" linking them. But there the resemblance ends.

The difference between these arguments and nonarguments is primarily one of purpose or interest. Either can be formulated in the pattern

Q because *P.*

If we are interested in establishing the truth of *Q,* and *P* is offered as evidence for it, then "*Q* because *P*" formulates an argument, with *Q* its conclusion and *P* its sole premiss. However, if we regard the truth of *Q* as being unproblematic, as being at least as well established as the truth of *P,* but are interested in explaining why *Q* is the case, then "*Q* because *P*" is not an argument but an explanation, with *Q* the fact to be explained and *P* the fact (or set of facts) that does the explaining. In both cases the word "because" functions as a reason-indicator.

Not all examples are so easily classified. One useful technique is to compare the obviousness of the claims contained in the passage. People do not ordinarily try to justify or establish the obvious, such as the fact that dogs bark, though they often try to explain such happenings.[43] Consequently if the reasons provided are less obvious than the claim for which they are given, the passage is probably an explanation. By the same token, people do not ordinarily try to explain nonobvious happenings, such as the expansion of the universe, although they often try to justify such claims. Hence, if the reasons provided are more obvious than the claim for which they are given, the passage is probably an argument. Explanations will be discussed in greater detail in chapter 7.

Recognition and analysis of arguments go hand in hand. Unless it is at least suspected that an argument is present, there is no motivation to apply the method of analysis and to construct a diagram. And often recognition is effected by trying the method of argument analysis and finding that it does apply to the passage in question.

EXERCISES

Some of the following passages express arguments, some express explanations, and some express neither. For those expressing arguments, diagram the arguments. For those expressing explanations, indicate what is being explained and what the expla-

---

[43]   See, e.g., Raymond Coppinger and Mark Feinstein, "'Hark! Hark! The Dogs Do Bark . . .' and Bark and Bark," *Smithsonian,* 21 January 1991, pp. 119–29.

nation is. For those expressing neither, characterize the passage as a compound proposition, a description, a report, or something else.

■ *1.* In my opinion the preamble to the Missouri statute is unconstitutional for two reasons. To the extent that it has substantive impact on the freedom to use contraceptive procedures, it is inconsistent with the central holding in *Griswold.* To the extent that it merely makes "legislative findings without operative effect," as the State argues, . . . it violates the Establishment Clause of the First Amendment.

—JUSTICE JOHN PAUL STEVENS, *Webster v. Reproductive Health Services,* 492 U.S. 490 (1989)

2. From President George Bush down . . . the administration is convinced that China is on the way to becoming a genuine world power. It wants it on America's side. Hence its efforts, since the massacre in Tiananmen Square last year, to keep lines open to the Chinese government.

—"American Survey," *The Economist* 28 July 1990, p. 22

3. If Ellis Island was a paradox, a place where dreams bumped up against bureaucracy, it was no less a place where one of the most powerful currents of American life flowed by.

—RICHARD LACAYO, "Reopening the Gate of America," *Time* 136, 17 September 1990, p. 68

4. Evidence is abundant that human beings are incurably religious. Prehistoric and primitive tribes manifested their religious impulses in animistic and totemistic practices. From the dawn of civilization, a multitude of religions have developed, each very complex.

—MICHAEL PETERSON ET AL., *Reason and Religious Belief: An Introduction to the Philosophy of Religion* (1991), p. 3

■ *5.* A combination of circumstances, present and prehistoric, contributes to the preservation of so many fossils through a region hundreds of miles south and west of Ulan Bator; capital of the Mongolian People's Republic. In the time of the dinosaurs and the rise of mammals, the area was marked by large basins where bones deposited in sand were more certain to become fossilized. In the 40 million years since, the area has been little disturbed by geological turmoil or people. But erosion by wind and weather has exposed the relics of many dinosaurs and early mammals.

—JOHN NOBLE WILFORD, "After 60 Years, Scientists Return to Fossil 'Paradise' of the Gobi," *The New York Times,* 31 July 1990, p. B5

6. Because it takes time for light to travel, looking out into space means looking back in time.

—"Science and Technology," *The Economist* 11 August 1990, p. 86

7. The motives behind General [Benedict] Arnold's decision to betray the Revolution turn out to be money, military status and vanity.

—HERBERT MITGANG, "Benedict Arnold, the Great American Traitor," *The New York Times,* 12 September 1990, p. B2

8. Greg LeMond picked up two prestigious sports awards at ceremonies conducted in New York City. The three-time Tour de France winner was named ABC's Wide World of Sports "Athlete of the Year" for the second consecutive time, and he also received the "Jesse Owens Award."

—"LeMond Receives Sports Honors," *Winning: Bicycling Illustrated,* April 1991, p. 18

9. Custer never thought like an Indian. With most of his peers, therefore, he was doomed to fight Indians with the techniques of conventional warfare.

—ROBERT M. UTLEY, *Cavalier in Buckskin: George Armstrong Custer and the Western Military Frontier* (1988), p. 206

■ **10.** American Express has begun to woo merchants aggressively, in part because it has come under increasing attack from Visa, which has recently been trying to convince merchants that Visa offers a better deal.

—KIM FOLTZ, "Advertising," *The New York Times,* 10 September 1990, p. C8

11. Thomas Moore, the director of domestic studies at the Hoover Institution at Stanford University, argues that poverty statistics overstate the number of poor people because researchers don't add in such noncash benefits as food stamps or Medicaid when calculating family incomes.

—VICTOR F. ZONANA, "Population Puzzle," *The Wall Street Journal,* 20 June 1984

12. . . . a 30-year-old unemployed riveter . . . doesn't want his name used because he is embarrassed by his plight.

—VICTOR F. ZONANA, "Population Puzzle," *The Wall Street Journal,* 20 June 1984

13. If the pollsters and sociologists have properly read the minds and hearts of those they have examined, no institution of this nation, whether government or church or press or academia or any of the so-called professions has the confidence of a majority of the American population.

—PHILIP B. KURLAND, "Is the Constitution Dead, Too?" *The University of Chicago Magazine,* Winter 1984, p. 28

14. I would argue that the country is better off because of the Kemp–Roth tax cut, if only because the budget deficit has imposed a much needed brake on federal social spending.

—MELVYN KRAUSS, "A Tax Cutter's Sad Tale," *Fortune,* 14 May 1984, p. 224

■ **15.** One of the reasons Honolulu businessman Robert W. Hall shot three men at the Waikiki Yacht Club in May 1980 was that he was suffering an allergic reaction to a specific ingredient in wine he drank earlier in the evening, his attorney said in court yesterday.

—*The Honolulu Advertiser,* 22 May 1984, p. A-12

16. Few regimes under guerrilla attack care about their own dispossessed. This is precisely why they are under attack.

—ARTHUR SCHLESINGER, "The Central American Dilemma," *The Wall Street Journal,* 20 July 1983, p. 26

17. If Joan [of Arc] had been malicious, selfish, cowardly or stupid, she would have been one of the most odious persons known to history instead of one of the most attractive.

—GEORGE BERNARD SHAW, Preface to *Saint Joan, Complete Plays with Prefaces,* vol. 2, 1962, p. 266

18. Capriciousness and irrelevant discrimination in the distribution of the death penalty to convicted murderers—and even in the distribution of fines to people who double park—should be corrected, for they outrage our desire for equality, and, above all, allow guilty persons to escape deserved punishment.

—ERNEST VAN DEN HAAG, letter to the editor, *The New Republic,* 23 January 1984, p. 2

19. The main reason the SAT's [Scholastic Aptitude Test's] label remains unchanged, despite all the changes in psychometric opinion about "aptitude" over the past generation, is probably institutional inertia.

> —CHRISTOPHER JENCKS and JAMES CROUSE, "Aptitude vs. Achievement: Should We Replace the
> SAT?" *The Public Interest,* Spring 1982, p. 26

■ **20.** But the peculiar evil of silencing the expression of an opinion is, that it is robbing the human race; posterity as well as the existing generation; those who dissent from the opinion, still more than those who hold it. If the opinion is right, they are deprived of the opportunity of exchanging error for truth: if wrong, they lose, what is almost as great a benefit, the clearer perception and livelier impression of truth, produced by its collision with error.

> —JOHN STUART MILL, "On Liberty," *Essential Works of John Stuart Mill,* ed. Max Lerner (1961),
> p. 269

21. The Iranians made more money delivering 3 million barrels a day than they did at 6 million, because the very action of cutting back doubled the price.

> —ADAM SMITH, *Paper Money* (1981), p. 237

22. If you are one of the 65 percent of Americans who have no fear of flying, there are good reasons for your confidence. Flying on scheduled U.S. carriers is *30 times* safer than traveling the highways by car, and the record is improving. U.S.-certified airlines carried 310 million passengers more than 3 billion miles with only 25 fatalities in 1983—fewer than the number of Americans who died from bee stings.

> —"Can We Keep The Skies Safe?" *Newsweek,* 30 January 1984, p. 24

23. For Birchers [members of the John Birch Society], laetrile is the drug of choice of treating cancer, mainly because they hate the idea that the government can tell them what they can and cannot put into their bodies.

> —JOSEPH NOCERA, "McDonald's War," *The New Republic,* 3 October 1983, p. 13

24. President Reagan has acted much as his predecessors have done in foreign affairs, and for the elemental reason that he is faced with much the same situations.

> —DANIEL PATRICK MOYNIHAN, "Reagan's Bankrupt Budget," *The New Republic,* 31 December
> 1983, p. 19

■ **25.** Businessmen praise competition and love monopoly. The reason is not, as some economists have contended, that monopoly ensures a "quiet life"—it rarely does—but that it promises bigger profits.

> —LEONARD SILK, *Economics in Plain English* (1978), p. 142

26. According to the advertising, all [computer] software is not only fast and powerful but also easy—or, in the jargon, user-friendly. Anyone who believes that, of course, also believes that the check is in the mail and that he may have already won $1 million in the magazine sweepstakes.

> —RICHARD A. SHAFFER, "Software Firms Push to Write Programs for Low-Tech Users," *The Wall
> Street Journal,* 20 April 1984, p. 19

27. Q. Representative Wirth, why do you feel the TV networks should curtail projections of winners until polls close?

A. A democratic society is successful only if people participate in it, and we have very clear evidence that early projection of election returns tends to discourage some people from voting.
> —Interview with Representative Timothy Wirth, Democrat of Colorado, *U.S. News & World Report*, 19 March 1984, p. 27

28. If the Founding Fathers had intended that our most serious political differences should be the province of eminent appointees instead of elected politicians, they would have given us a mandarin oligarchy instead of Congress.
> —EDITORIAL, "The Latin America Commission," *The Wall Street Journal*, 20 July 1983, p. 26

29. If our weapons are vulnerable to attack or if they have very high value relative to the forces needed to knock them out, that would be very dangerous.

Therefore, both sides should try to move away from reliance on stationary, multiwarhead ICBM's. If they are stationary, their location is known and they can be struck; if they have multiple warheads, they became lucrative targets in the sense that a single Soviet warhead could knock out several of our warheads.
> —Interview with Lt. Gen. Brent Scowcroft, Chair, President's Commission on Strategic Forces, *U.S. News & World Report*, 5 December 1983, p. 31

■ **30.** The Russians have become more cautious in the third world because of a combination of their own economic weakness, the unpredictability of many of their assumed new friends, the Reagan administration's reassertiveness, South Africa's recent pugnacity.
> —"Russia's Road South," *The Economist*, 17 March 1984, p. 16

31. Manufacturers (or their shareholders) who can pollute free of charge make bigger profits than if they were obliged to cover the full social costs of their production, including the external costs generated by their pollution. And the purchasers of the goods and services concerned buy them at lower prices than if the prices covered the full social costs. Hence, the manufacturers and consumers of the particular products concerned gain at the expense of the victims of the pollution.
> —WILFRED BECKERMAN, *Two Cheers for the Affluent Society* (1974), pp. 134–35

32. "The reason the aircraft was shot down," said Tommy Toles, aide to Representative Larry McDonald, the day after Korean Airlines Flight 007 was downed by a Soviet fighter jet, "was because Congressman McDonald was a passenger."
> —JOSEPH NOCERA, "McDonald's War," *The New Republic*, 3 October 1983, p. 12

33. The sole reason we can now feel concerned about the quality of life instead of worrying where the next meal is coming from is that through our great industries we have, as a society, built up immense material wealth.
> —PHILIP SADLER, quoted in Wilfred Beckerman, *Two Cheers for the Affluent Society* (1974), p. 66

34. Trying to kill inflation and instill such virtues as discipline and farsightedness is a gamble because pain is immediate and social benefits are delayed, and in the interval the public may turn out the government.
> —GEORGE F. WILL, "Britain's Purging Fire," *Newsweek*, 20 June 1983, p. 88

■ **35.** Important voices, both internal and external to the university community, are suggesting that academic tenure may be inconsistent with the vitality of higher education in the coming decades. Tenure, some would argue, not only works to shield incompetency, create a kind of "academic aristocracy," and block the access of women and minorities to university positions, but also deprives a university community of the necessary flexibility and adaptability to meet the particular demands of the 1980s and 1990s.

—HAROLD T. SHAPIRO, "The Privilege and the Responsibility: Some Reflections on the Nature, Function, and Future of Academic Tenure," *Academe,* November–December 1983, p. 3a

36. . . . rapid responses to calls for [police] service do not dramatically increase the apprehension of criminals. The reason is that citizens do not call the police until long after a crime has been completed, and the attacker has fled the scene. Given these delays, even instantaneous police responses would do little good.

—MARK H. MOORE and GEORGE L. KELLING, "To Serve and Protect': Learning from Police History," *The Public Interest,* Winter 1983, p. 56

37. The distinguishing mark of our century is not so much Communism's determination to erase democracy from our planet, or its frequent success in pursuing that end, as it is the humility with which democracy not only consents to its own obliteration, but contrives to legitimize the victory of its deadliest enemy.

—JEAN-FRANÇOIS REVEL, "Can the Democracies Survive?" *Commentary,* June 1984, p. 20

38. As campaign consultant Matt Reese once observed, "Teachers are the ideal political organization. They're in every precinct." Moreover, they are generally well-educated, likely to vote, mindful of public affairs, articulate, and possessed of ample spare time.

—CHESTER E. FINN, JR., "Teacher Politics," *Commentary,* February 1983, p. 29

39. . . . changes of the last 25 years have led to what may be called "the de Jouvenel paradox" in modern "fiscal sociology": the frustration of the individual who finds that although his income has doubled, he does not live twice as well as he did before. The reason, of course, is that when income doubles, there is more competition for inherently scarce goods and space. As more people acquire more cars, there is more congestion on the highways. As people travel more, there is more crowding in national parks and beaches. As more enlarge their cultural horizons, they get shuffled along tour lines in the Vatican, or around the Parthenon, or in the Uffizi. And even though expectations increase, only a few persons can own that desirable location on the mountain or by the sea.

—DANIEL BELL, "The Future That Never Was," *The Public Interest,* Spring 1978, p. 43

■ **40.** The Russian warriors are now armed with nuclear weapons on a vast scale. The strategic rocket forces of the Soviet Union are comparable in size and quality with those of the United States. The Soviet rocket commanders could, if they were ordered to do so, obliterate the cities of the United States within thirty minutes. It has therefore become a matter of some importance for us in the United States to understand what may be in the Soviet commanders' minds.

—FREEMAN DYSON, "Reflections: Weapons and Hope," *The New Yorker,* 20 February 1984, p. 86

1.5   PASSAGES EXPRESSING SEVERAL ARGUMENTS

It was remarked in section 1.3 that the number of conclusions in a passage determines the number of arguments it contains. So a passage in which the two distinct conclusions are inferred from the same premiss or group of premises will count as containing two arguments. A remarkably clear example is the following passage:

> You can read about a country's history and culture, you can pore over travel brochures . . . but you can't get a true feeling for the people and the culture without witnessing both first hand. That's why there is no substitute for sending your children abroad to study, and why hosting a foreign student yourself can be a valuable experience for your family.[44]

Here the premiss is ①[you can't get a true feeling for the people and the culture without witnessing both first hand], the first conclusion is ②[there is no substitute for sending your children abroad to study], and the second conclusion is ③[hosting a foreign student yourself can be a valuable experience for your family]. This passage contains two arguments, as is displayed by the diagram

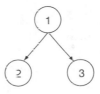

An example of a two-argument passage in which each conclusion is inferred from the same pair of premises is

> . . . to hasten the social revolution in England is the most important object of the International Workingmen's Association. The sole means of hastening it is to make Ireland independent.
> Hence the task of the "International" is everywhere to put the conflict between England and Ireland in the foreground, and everywhere to side openly with Ireland.[45]

The premises here are ① [to hasten the social revolution in England is the most important object of the International Workingmen's Association] and ② [The sole means of hastening it is to make Ireland independent], and the conclusions are ③ [the task of the "International" is everywhere to put the conflict between England and Ireland in the foreground] and ④[everywhere [the task of the "International" is] to side openly with Ireland]. The diagram for this argumentative passage is

[44]   Carol Steinberg, "Family," *Venture*, April 1983, p. 68.
[45]   Karl Marx, letter 141, 9 April 1870, *Karl Marx and Friedrich Engels Correspondence 1846–1895* (1936), p. 290.

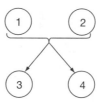

Some passages contain two or more arguments that do not overlap either in their premises or conclusions but have been placed next to each other because of their common subject matter. They may come in simple succession, as in

> She is a woman, therefore may be won;
> She is Lavinia, therefore must be lov'd.[46]

Here the component propositions are ① [she is a woman], ② [she may be won], ③ [she is Lavinia], and ④ [she must be lov'd]. The diagram for this argumentative passage is

Two arguments in a single passage may have their premises and conclusions intertwined, although still independent of each other. In the following passage from John Locke's (1632–1704) influential *Second Treatise of Government,* the two conclusions are stated first, followed by the premises offered in their support:

> It is not necessary—no, nor so much as convenient—that the legislative should be always in being; but absolutely necessary that the executive power should, because there is not always need of new laws to be made, but always need of execution of the laws that are made.

Here the component propositions are ① [it is not necessary or convenient that the legislative [branch of government] should be always in being]; ② [it is absolutely necessary that the executive power should be always in being]; ③ [there is not always need of new laws to be made]; and ④ [there is always need of execution of the laws that are made]. The diagram for this argumentative passage is

---

46   William Shakespeare, *Titus Andronicus,* Act II, Scene I.

which shows that the second argument's conclusion comes between the premiss and conclusion of the first argument and that the first argument's premiss comes between the premiss and conclusion of the second argument, as well as showing that both conclusions are stated before their premisses.

A more interesting arrangement of two or more arguments in the same passage occurs when the conclusion of one argument is also a premiss of another. A simple example is the following:

① [The majority of our college students enroll in higher learning for vocational reasons.] ② [Such students, (therefore,) view their stay at college as a series of hurdles culminating in a credential and a postgraduate job.] (Consequently,) ③ [the values harbored by the majority of students coincide rather precisely with the values of the business establishment in general and the college administrators.][47]

The diagram for this passage is

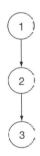

which shows there is an intermediate conclusion, or subconclusion ② which is inferred from the given premiss ① and is itself a premiss from which the final conclusion ③ is inferred.

Another passage of the same complexity but with its constituents differently arranged is

① [The death penalty is further warranted] (because) ② [it is the only practical way to make certain that a murderer will not repeat his crime.] ③ [Under today's permissive, revolving-door justice, it is almost an everyday occurrence

---

[47]   David Slive, letter to the editor, *Academe*, February 1980, p. 59.

to read where a convicted murderer, after serving a relatively short sentence, has killed again.][48]

Its diagram is

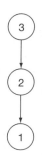

A passage containing a slightly longer "chain" argument is

At first sight it seems plausible to say that (since) ① [reasons can be given for pieces of behaviour we usually call "irrational,"] ② [even this behaviour is, after all, rational, but at the unconscious level.] (It is a short step to the conclusion) that ③ [Freud has shown irrational behaviour to be "really" rational] and that ④ [we are, (therefore), more rational than we usually suppose.][49]

Its diagram is

In some argumentative passages the final conclusion is not inferred from the sub-conclusion alone, but from it together with one or more premises that are adduced

---

[48]   Frank G. Carrington, *Neither Cruel Nor Unusual.*

[49]   Peter Alexander, "Rational Behaviour and Psychoanalytic Explanation," in *Freud: A Collection of Critical Essays,* ed. Richard Wollheim (1974), pp. 306–7.

in additional support for the final conclusion. We have this situation in the following:

> ... ①[wealth is not sought except for the sake of something else,] (because) ② [of itself it brings us no good, but only when we use it, whether for the support of the body or for some similar purpose.] ③[Now the highest good is sought for its own, and not for another's sake.] (Therefore) ④[wealth is not man's highest good.][50]

as the following diagram shows:

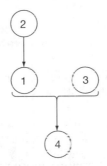

In somewhat more complicated argumentative passages, the final conclusion is inferred from two or more premises that were themselves the conclusions of earlier arguments in the passage. That is the case in the following argument:

> ①[Unlike land-based intercontinental ballistic missiles (ICBM's) such as the Minuteman and its proposed replacement, the MX, SLBM's [sea-launched ballistic missiles] on submerged submarines are difficult to locate accurately;] (hence) ②[they are essentially invulnerable to a preemptive "counterforce" attack and seem certain to remain so for the foreseeable future.] Moreover, ③[U.S. ballistic-missile submarines, by virtue of their range and mobility, are capable of launching a prompt retaliatory strike on the U.S.S.R. from many directions,] (thereby) ④[complicating any attempt to thwart a counterattack by means of an anti-ballistic-missile (ABM) system.] (In short,) ⑤[SLBM's come close to being an ideal deterrent force against a nuclear attack.][51]

whose diagram

---

[50] Thomas Aquinas, *Summa Contra Gentiles, Basic Writings of St. Thomas Aquinas,* ed. Anton C. Pegis.
[51] "Science and the Citizen," *Scientific American* 248, May 1983, p. 88.

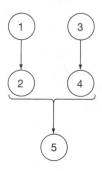

shows that ⑤is inferred from ②and ④, each of which was itself inferred earlier in the passage.

Diagramming another complex argumentative passage reminds us how to treat noun phrases that—in the context—have propositional roles in the argument.

①[Looking ahead, the Labor Department sees manufacturing's share of non-farm jobs, which stood at close to 24 percent in 1969, dropping to about 19 percent by 1990.]

The reasons for the fall are threefold: Because of ②[high interest rates] and ③[low birth rates,] ④[the American appetite for autos, refrigerators and other big-ticket items is waning.] ⑤[More of what is bought here is being produced abroad.] And ⑥[American industry is becoming increasingly automated.][52]

The diagram is

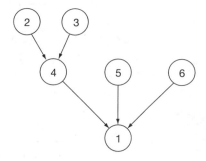

Here bracketing and numbering the noun phrases ②and ③indicates that they are understood to express propositions that (after deleting the word "of") might be rephrased as "interest rates are high" and "birth rates are low."

Sometimes we *assume* a proposition in order to explore its consequences, to see what else would be the case if the proposition in question were true. That amounts to "asserting the proposition for the sake of the argument," and occurs in the following

---

[52]   "Jobs—A Million that Will Never Come Back," *U.S. News & World Report,* 13 September 1982, p. 53.

argumentative passage. For stylistic reasons, to avoid the monotony of saying the same thing in the same way, authors may say the same thing in different ways, that is, they may formulate a single proposition in various different sentences. This also happens in the following passage—as is shown by our assigning the same number to different formulations of the same proposition.

> When ① [the state levies a sales tax,] ② [the cost of the taxed commodity rises.] (Because) ② [the cost of the commodity is higher,] ③ [less of it is sold—gasoline or liquor or cigarette sales, for example, always suffer when taxes are placed on them.]
> (It follows that) ④ [the sales tax must affect individuals other than just the buyers.] ⑤ [The seller of the commodity must bear some of the tax] (because) ③ [his sales have declined] and presumably ⑥ [so has his income.] ⑦ [The workers or other suppliers of services who produce the commodity will also be penalized,] (because) ③ [less of the taxed commodity will be bought] (and therefore) ⑧ [fewer people will be employed making it.] In other words, ⑨ [the incidence, or burden, of a tax is often much more complex than appears on the surface.][53]

The following diagram presents the logic, if not the rhetoric, of the passage in question.

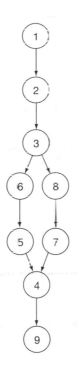

---

[53] Robert Heilbroner and Lester Thurow, *Five Economic Challenges* (1981), pp. 60–61.

EXERCISES

Analyze and diagram the arguments in the following passages, each of which expresses more than one argument.

■   *1.* Opponents of the death penalty sometimes argue for its abolition on the
ground that it is cruel and unusual and therefore impermissible punishment.
According to them, nothing that deprives a person of his life can be a usual punishment, and it is cruel for anyone to have his days ended by a period of waiting to be
hanged, electrocuted or gassed. So however effective it is as a means of preventing
crime, execution is wrong and must be avoided.

—TOM SORELL, *Moral Theory and Capital Punishment* (1987), p. 102

2. We also reject petitioners' argument that we should invalidate capital punishment of 16- and 17-year-old offenders on the ground that it fails to serve the legitimate
goals of penology. According to petitioners, it fails to deter because juveniles, possessing less developed cognitive skills than adults, are less likely to fear death; and it fails
to exact just retribution because juveniles, being less mature and responsible, are also
less morally blameworthy.

—JUSTICE ANTONIN SCALIA, for the U.S. Supreme Court, *Stanford v. Kentucky*, 492 U.S. 361
(1989)

3. We believe that informal logic is best understood as the normative study of
argument. It is the area of logic which seeks to develop standards, criteria and procedures for the interpretation, evaluation and construction of arguments and the argumentation used in natural language.

It follows that various studies of argumentation, from the sociological, linguistic,
psychological, literary and political points of view may have pertinence for, but will be
distinct from, informal logic. It also follows that to the extent that it is appropriate to
require the inferences in certain kinds of argument to be deductively valid, informal
logic will make reference to formal deductive logic.

—J. ANTHONY BLAIR and RALPH H. JOHNSON, "The Current State of Informal Logic," *Informal
Logic* 9, Spring & Fall 1987, p. 148

4. [T]here are strong reasons to doubt that an "explosion in heroin abuse" will
soon "boom out of control" and "end up rivaling the . . . cocaine crisis," as Mr.
[Charles B.] Rangel suggests. Public intolerance of drugs is very high at the moment,
so no dangerous drug is likely soon to become "fashionable," the cultural atmosphere
ordinarily surrounding new epidemics. And heroin's particular properties (it is recognized as a "dirty," highly addictive and isolating drug) tend to dampen its potential.

—HERBERT D. KLEBER, letter to the editor, *The New York Times*, 10 September 1990, p. A14

■   *5.* [I]f we can cause animals to suffer, then what we do to them not only can hurt
them, it can harm them; and if it can harm them, than [*sic*] it can detract from the
experiential quality of their life, considered over time; and if it can do that, then we
must view these animals as retaining their identity over time and as having a good or
ill of their own.

—TOM REGAN, *The Case for Animal Rights* (1983), p. 96

6. Now it is self-evident, since some men live in idle luxury, that a laborer normally produces more than he consumes, and that this surplus goes to support idleness.
—BERTRAND RUSSELL, *German Social Democracy* (1965), p. 25

7. Education is as old as man, for in all ages and all societies some provision has always been made to pass on to succeeding generations the knowledge and the values which were fundamental to the culture. Always there have been difficulties, for no society has ever perfected an educational system which fully and completely satisfied its dual needs—the conservation of sound traditional values, and the encouragement of innovation and the creation of new concepts sufficient to serve the needs of a growing, changing culture.
—HAROLD BENJAMIN, "The Problems of Education"

8. Judges, like legislators, cater to competing interests by compromise rather than by the application of a neutral calculus. Therefore, the view that courts are less suited for legislative decision-making because of their institutional nature is unsound. The inference left for the student to draw is that there is little that a court cannot do.
—ALEXANDER TROY, "Learning the Law at Harvard," *The Wall Street Journal,* 6 August 1982, p. 31

9. In peacetime they [satellites] provide both the U.S. and the U.S.S.R. with prompt and virtually irreplaceable intelligence about each other's military forces and operations. As a consequence they are essential to many aspects of military planning, and they are indispensable to the verification of compliance with strategic arms-control agreements.
—RICHARD L. GARWIN, KURT GOTTFRIED, and DONALD L. HAFNER, "Antisatellite Weapons," *Scientific American,* June 1984, p. 45

■ **10.** If you want your computer to be able to handle a bit of data within a nanosecond [a nanosecond is a billionth of a second], no signal path can be much longer than 15 centimeters, because that is roughly the distance an electrical signal can travel in a billionth of a second. So your computer will have to be tiny.
—"Science and Technology," *The Economist,* 3 April 1982, p. 96

11. Shielding against radiation is not the only prerequisite for an adequate shelter. Once the attack has occurred, people must remain inside the shelters until the outside fallout decays to a safe level, a period that may exceed one month if the intensity of fallout has been great. Therefore, the shelter must have adequate ventilation and sanitation facilities, and it must be stocked with sufficient food, water, and other supplies.
—ARTHUR J. VANDER, "The Delusion of Civil Defense," *LSA,* Spring 1983, p. 10

12. There is no possibility, it would seem, of controverting the committed Marxist. His Marxism makes him invulnerable to argument since, among other things, it enables him to assume that those who disagree with him do so because they are, as the editors write, spokesmen for "narrow political interests and biases. . . ."
—STEPHEN MILLER, review of Bertell Ollman and Edward Vernoff, eds., *The Left Academy: Marxist Scholarship on American Campuses,* in *The Public Interest,* Spring 1983, p. 140

13. Legal employment is growing rapidly (43 percent in five years), but it cannot continue to grow at this rate. A country full of lawyers is simply not possible. Nor can they can be exported. The rest of the world is too smart to shift to our contentious adversarial legal system.

—LESTER C. THUROW, "A Non-Industrial Revolution," *Newsweek*, 9 January 1984, p. 79

14. When the government runs a deficit, it has to borrow money to pay its bills. Since the Treasury automatically goes to the head of the credit queue, this tends to crowd out private borrowers and push up interest rates.

—ROBERT S. BOYD, "The Federal Debt," *The Honolulu Advertiser,* 5 June 1982, p. D-7

■ ***15.*** . . . bodies become heavier with increasing speed, thus requiring more force to accelerate them further; in the end an infinitely strong force would be required to make them reach the speed of light. Therefore no object can be accelerated to that speed, let alone beyond.

—RUDOLF PEIERLS, review of Abraham Pais, "Subtle is the Lord . . .": *The Science and the Life of Albert Einstein,* in *The New York Review of Books* 30, 28 April p. 21.

16. Over the decade 1961 average smoke concentrations in urban areas in Britain fell by 60 percent, and SO_2 (sulfur dioxide) concentrations fell by 30 percent, despite increasing population and industrial output. And these are averages of all urban areas, so they include those towns that have not yet taken advantage of the powers conferred on them under the Clean Air Acts to introduce smokeless zones. Hence, the reduction in air pollution in some major cities, such as London and Sheffield, has been much greater than the above figures indicate.

—WILFRED BECKERMAN, *Two Cheers for the Affluent Society* (1974), p. 115

17. A disease entity is defined by signs and symptoms generated by objective— that is, organic—determinants. Thus . . . illness is organic. Since mental disturbances are not organic, mental illness is not illness.

—Attributed to DR. THOMAS SZASZ in *Taking Sides: Clashing Views on Controversial Bio-Ethical Issues,* ed. Carol Levine (1984), p. 181

18. The lower strata of the middle class—the small tradespeople shopkeepers, and retired tradesmen generally, the handicraftsmen and peasants—all these sink gradually into the proletariat, partly because their diminutive capital does not suffice for the scale on which Modern Industry is carried on, and is swamped in the competition with the large capitalists, partly because their specialised skill is rendered worthless by new methods of production. Thus the proletariat is recruited from all classes of the population.

—KARL MARX and FRIEDRICH ENGELS, *The Communist Manifesto,* 1848, pp. 59–60

19. Don't go to the hospital unless you have absolutely no choice. The director of the Center for Disease Control says two million of the people who enter hospitals each year catch infections unrelated to their original conditions. Eighty thousand die from these infections. This makes hospitals more lethal than highways, and that's not even counting victims of botched surgery.

—CHARLES PETERS, "Tilting at Windmills," *The Washington Monthly* 14 May 1982, p. 5

■ ***20.*** The death penalty does not deter criminals because at the time the crime is done they do not expect to be arrested. Also, since many offenders are mentally unbalanced, they do not consider the rational consequences of their irrational activities.

—PIERRE C. HABER, letter to the editor, *Newsweek* 31 October 1983, p. 6

21. While savings may be hoarded rather than channeled into productive invest-
ments, the demand generated by increased consumption necessarily induces
increased investment, and hence promotes the greatest possible utilization of a society's resources. Hence, rather than encouraging individual thrift, the appropriate economic role for government is to generate consumption through such devices as public works programs, which put more money in the hands of the poorer classes (whose
lack of surplus wealth gives them a greater "propensity to consume" than the wealthy).
— ROBERTA SCHAEFER and DAVID SCHAEFER, "The Political Philosophy of J. M. Keynes," *The Public Interest*, Spring 1983, p. 53

22. In talking to the public, the best economists don't need jargon to say what
they mean. They understand their material well enough to put it simply and exactly in
ordinary language. This has some advantages even for the specialists themselves. For
jargon can limit, distort or even poison the thinking of those who use it habitually. It
can easily degenerate into fakery and display.
— LEONARD SILK, *Economics in Plain English* (1978), p. 46

23. Energy in its various forms, from heat to gasoline, plays a larger part in the
budgets of poor families than well-to-do families. This is because energy is largely used
for essentials. For families in the lowest ten percent of households, energy accounts
for a full third of household expenditures; whereas for households in the top ten percent, it absorbs only five percent of household expenses. Therefore, a jump in energy
costs will penalize the poor much more severely than the rich.
— ROBERT HEILBRONER and LESTER THUROW, *Five Economic Challenges* (1981), p. 123

24. Pacifists unencumbered by papal pronouncements are able more openly to
oppose deterrence. To take only the most celebrated recent example, in *The Fate of the
Earth* Jonathan Schell makes the case the bishops would like to make, and stripped of
any theological trappings. In its secular version it goes like this: biological existence is
the ultimate value; all other values are conditional upon it; there can be neither liberty nor democracy nor any other value in defense of which Western nuclear weapons
are deployed, if mankind itself is destroyed; and after nuclear war the earth will be "a
republic of insects and grass." Therefore nothing can justify using nuclear weapons.
— CHARLES KRAUTHAMMER, "On Nuclear Morality," *Commentary* 76, October 1983, p. 49

■ *25.* While the dollar will eventually return to more reasonable levels, the damage
to industrial America is permanent. Once a major international competitor such as
Caterpillar loses foreign and domestic sales because of an overvalued dollar it won't
easily get them back. Foreign competitors will have established the contacts and service networks they do not now have and customers will have little reason to change
suppliers unless there is a substantial period when the dollar is grossly undervalued. A
return to parity won't repair the damage done.

Consequently, the Reagan administration is making a major mistake when it refuses to
intervene in foreign-exchange markets to force the dollar back to levels where
American companies can compete on world markets.
— LESTER C. THUROW, "A Strong Dollar's Price," *Newsweek*, 29 November 1982, p. 89

26. Hunting was a valuable adaptation to the environment since meat could supply more calories and protein than a vegetarian diet. Peking man was evidently able to

compete successfully with large carnivores as a hunter. An abundance of fossil bones of mammals of various sizes found in the cave indicates that Peking man not only hunted small game but also was capable of killing large animals.

—WU RUKANG and LIN SHENGLONG, "Peking Man," *Scientific American* 248, June 1983, p. 93

27. . . . American higher education is facing a crisis that will probably continue through the 1980's. At bottom, the crisis is one of effective demand for higher education. The problem is partly demographic, for we are entering a period of reduced university-age populations. In addition, there are serious economic stringencies. Family budgets are shrinking, while costs of higher education continue to rise.

—FRITZ RINGER, "Academic Grievance and Collective Bargaining," *Academe*, February 1980, p. 41

28. All antisatellite weapons currently deployed or undergoing field tests have a maximum altitude of several thousand kilometers or less. Hence they could attack satellites only in low orbits or in highly elliptical ones. Since the early-warning, navigation, attack-assessment and communications satellites essential to the U.S. strategic forces are all in very high orbits, they are not at risk in the near term. The U.S.S.R. faces a somewhat greater potential threat, since some of its essential communications satellites and all its early-warning satellites are currently in high elliptical Molniya orbits.

—RICHARD L. GARWIN, KURT GOTTFRIED, and DONALD L. HAFNER, "Antisatellite Weapons," *Scientific American,* June 1984, p. 47

29. . . . nuclear warheads are not weapons, as one normally understands the term. No nation can use them to achieve a political end, since if its bluff were called, it would be left with the option of capitulating or committing national suicide. Nuclear warheads are unusable to halt a conventional attack since their use would almost certainly lead to an all-out nuclear exchange and the destruction of all that we were trying to protect. Nuclear weapons are useful only in a canceling-out process—to deter the other side from using them.

—GEORGE W. BALL, "Sovietizing US Policy," *The New York Review of Books 31*, 2 February 1984, p. 34

■ **30.** In inflationary times it is obviously advantageous to borrow money at normal interest rates because dollars will be cheaper and more plentiful when it comes time to repay the loan. Therefore businesses seek to borrow funds—but banks are loath to lend, for exactly the same reasons.

Two results follow. First, interest rates go ever higher to compensate banks for the falling value of the dollars they will receive. . . .

Second, banks refuse to lend for more than short periods of time. The result is that business has to take on short term loans at high interest rates.

—ROBERT HEILBRONER and LESTER THUROW, *Five Economic Challenges* (1981), p. 28

31. Recently, the EEC (European Economic Community) has been deliberating over sanctions against Israel. The nations of the Common Market are reportedly dismayed and angered not only by Israel's continuing refusal to recognize or negotiate with the Palestine Liberation Organization, but more immediately Israel's invasion and occupation of southern Lebanon. The EEC has already shelved a concessionary credit agreement for $40 million, and there has been talk of trade sanctions and an arms embargo.

The motivations behind this set of sanctions are puzzling. The Western European concern doesn't appear to be humanitarian; if it were, the Common Market presumably would have placed sanctions on Libya, Syria, and Iraq in 1975, when those nations assisted in dismembering Lebanon, or it would have agitated for an arms embargo against Syria when that nation occupied Lebanon with a 25,000 man "peace-keeping force." The sanctions would not seem to be a defense of democratic rights, for Israel is the only nation in the region remotely resembling a democracy. And it would be difficult to construe the Common Market's insistence that Israel negotiate with the PLO as a matter of principle, since the PLO has never agreed that Israel has any right to exist.

> —ERIC M. BREINDEL and NICK EBERSTADT, "Western Europe's Use of Economic Sanctions," *The Wall Street Journal*, 16 November 1982, p. 28

32.   In physics, we deal with what have been characterized as "limiting cases"—situations that can be so highly idealized and simplified that they can be subjected to predictive law. We can talk about "the" electron, because each electron is like every other electron. But since no two living things are exactly alike, biological laws are statistical; and since biological systems are so complex the laws are usually nonpredictive. This makes biology a science with goals, methods, and a philosophy very different from those of physics.

> —JEREMY BERNSTEIN, "The Evolution of Evolution," *The New Yorker*, 23 January 1984, p. 98

33.   The free-market remedy for inflation is mass unemployment. This remedy imposes severe economic, social and political costs. It is also cruelly inequitable, since it places the burden of the struggle against inflation on those least able to bear it. It is also unavailing, since mass unemployment will inevitably create a demand for reflation, and with reflation prices and interest rates will shoot up again.

> —ARTHUR SCHLESINGER, JR., "Should Conservatives Embrace Big Government?" *The Wall Street Journal*, 3 February 1983

34.   The language being considered on the labels [of cigarette packages] would require warning of the increased danger of heart disease, lung cancer and emphysema; of hazards to pregnant women of miscarriage and birth deformities; and of the risk of addiction.

The tobacco industry, in a real triumph of doubletalk, is still arguing against strict labeling on the grounds that (a) you don't need it because everyone knows the dangers connected with smoking and (b) you should not have tougher labels because there is no established causal link between smoking and disease, only some statistical "questions."

If you believe either of these arguments you probably also believe in the Easter Bunny, but since some 32 percent of the public still smokes, there obviously are a lot of people who don't or won't recognize the dangers or who do believe in the Easter Bunny.

> —JUDY MANN, "'Sure' Way to Cut Number of Smokers," *Washington Post Service*, 2 April 1982

■ *35.*   ". . . You appeared to be surprised when I told you, on our first meeting, that you had come from Afghanistan."

"You were told, no doubt."

"Nothing of the sort. I *knew* you came from Afghanistan. From long habit the train of thoughts ran so swiftly through my mind that I arrived at the conclusion without being conscious of intermediate steps. There were such steps, however. The train of reasoning ran, 'Here is a gentleman of a medical type, but with the air of a military man. Clearly an army doctor, then. He has just come from the tropics, for his face is dark, and that is not the natural tint of his skin, for his wrists are fair. He has undergone hardship and sickness, as his haggard face says clearly. His left arm has been injured. He holds it in a stiff and unnatural manner. Where in the tropics could an English army doctor have seen much hardship and got his arm wounded? Clearly in Afghanistan.' The whole train of thought did not occupy a second. I then remarked that you came from Afghanistan, and you were astonished."

"It is simple enough as you explain it," I said, smiling.

—A. CONAN DOYLE, *A Study in Scarlet,* Chapter 2

1.6   DEDUCTION AND INDUCTION

Arguments are traditionally divided into two types, *deductive* and *inductive.* Every argument involves the claim (noted in section 1.2) that its premises provide grounds for the truth of its conclusion; but only a deductive argument involves the claim that its premises provide *conclusive* grounds for its conclusion. When the reasoning in a deductive argument is correct, we call that argument *valid;* when the reasoning of a deductive argument is incorrect, we call that argument *invalid.*

We may therefore define *validity* as follows: A deductive argument is valid when its premises, if true, do provide conclusive grounds for the truth of its conclusion. In a deductive argument (but not in an inductive argument) premises and conclusion are so related that it is impossible for the premises to be true unless the conclusion is true also.

In every deductive argument, either the premises succeed in providing conclusive grounds for the truth of the conclusion, or they do not succeed. Therefore, every deductive argument is either valid or invalid. This is a point of some importance: If a deductive argument is not valid, it must be invalid; if it is not invalid, it must be valid. But note that the terms "valid" and "invalid" do not apply to inductive arguments; for inductive arguments other terms of appraisal will be required.

An inductive argument claims not that its premises give conclusive grounds for the truth of its conclusion, but that its premises provide *some* support for that conclusion. Inductive arguments, therefore, cannot be "valid" or "invalid" in the sense in which these terms are applied to deductive arguments. Of course, inductive arguments may be evaluated as better or worse, according to the degree of support given to their conclusions by their premises. Thus, the greater the likelihood, or probability, which its premises confer upon its conclusion, the greater the merit of an inductive argument. But that likelihood, even when the premises are true, must fall short of certainty. The theory of induction is presented in chapters 5 through 7 of this book.

The distinction between deductive and inductive arguments is sometimes drawn in a different way—centering upon the relative generality of their premises and conclusions. Deductive inferences, it is sometimes said, move from the general to the particular, while inductive inferences move from the particular to the general.[54] This way of distinguishing them proves unsatisfactory upon analysis.

In that tradition, the classical example of a deductive argument

All humans are mortal.
Socrates is human.
Therefore, Socrates is mortal.

does indeed have a particular conclusion,[55] inferred validly from two premisses, of which the first is a general or universal proposition. It is also true that a very common form of inductive argument is one in which a general or universal conclusion is inferred from a group of premisses, all of which are particular, as in this example:

Socrates is human and mortal.
Xanthippe is human and mortal.
Sappho is human and mortal.
Therefore, probably all humans are mortal.

But this method of distinguishing between deduction and induction does not always work. The difficulty lies in the fact that a valid deductive argument may have universal propositions for its conclusion as well as for its premisses, as in

All animals are mortal.
All humans are animals.
Therefore, all humans are mortal.

And a valid deductive argument may have particular propositions for its premises as well as for its conclusion, as in

If Socrates is human, then Socrates is mortal.
Socrates is human.
Therefore, Socrates is mortal.

Moreover, an inductive argument need not rely only upon particular premises, but may have universal (i.e., general) propositions for its premises as well for its conclusions, as in

All cows are mammals and have lungs.

---

[54] William Whewell, in *The Philosophy of the Inductive Sciences*, long ago put it thus: ". . . in Deduction we infer particular from general truths, while in Induction we infer general from particular. . . ."

[55] The term "particular" is used by Whewell, and other logicians in his tradition, to refer to propositions about a single thing (e.g., Socrates) as well as to propositions about some but not necessarily all members of a given class (e.g., some humans). More recent logical practice uses the phrase "particular propositions" to refer only to the latter group. At this point we are examining Whewell's view, and therefore follow his usage.

All whales are mammals and have lungs.
All humans are mammals and have lungs.
Therefore, probably all mammals have lungs.

And further, an inductive argument may have a particular proposition as its conclusion, as in

Hitler was a dictator and was ruthless.
Stalin was a dictator and was ruthless.
Castro is a dictator.
Therefore, Castro is probably ruthless.

These examples show that it is not satisfactory to characterize deductive arguments as those in which particular conclusions are inferred from general premisses; nor is it satisfactory to characterize inductive arguments as those in which general conclusions are inferred from particular premisses.

The fundamental difference between these two kinds of argument lies in the claims that are made about the relations between premisses and conclusion. Deductive arguments are those in which a very strict or close relationship is claimed to hold between their premisses and conclusions. If a deductive argument is valid, then, given the truth of its premisses, its conclusion *must* be true no matter what else may be the case.

For example: If it is true that all humans are mortal, and if it is true that Socrates is a human, then it must be true that Socrates is mortal no matter what else may be true in the world and no matter what other premisses are added or other information discovered. If we find that Socrates is ugly, or that angels are immortal, or that cows give milk, it affects the validity of the argument not one bit; the conclusion that Socrates is mortal follows from any enlarged set of premisses with deductive certainty, just as it did from the two premisses originally given. If an argument is valid, nothing additional in the world can make it *more* valid; if a conclusion is validly inferred from some set of premisses, there is nothing that can be added to the set that would make that conclusion follow more validly or more strictly or more logically.

But the relation between premisses and conclusion claimed for an inductive argument, even the best of that kind, is much less strict, and different in kind. Consider the following inductive argument:

Most corporation lawyers are conservatives.
Barbara Shane is a corporation lawyer.
Therefore, Barbara Shane is probably a conservative.

This is a good inductive argument; its first premiss is true, and if its second premiss is true also, its conclusion is more likely true than false. But in this case, by adding new premisses to the original pair, the resulting argument may be substantially weakened, or (depending on the premisses added) strengthened. Suppose we add the premiss that

Barbara Shane is an officer of the American Civil Liberties Union (ACLU).

and also add the (true) premiss that

Most officers of the ACLU are not conservatives.

Now the conclusion (that Barbara Shane is a conservative) no longer seems probable; the original inductive argument has been weakened by the presence of this additional information about Barbara Shane. Indeed, if the final premiss were transformed into the universal proposition

No officers of the ACLU are conservatives.

the opposite of the original conclusion would now follow deductively; that is, validly, from the set of premises affirmed.

On the other hand, if we enlarge the original set of premises by adding the following additional premises instead:

Barbara Shane served in the cabinet of President George Bush.

and

Barbara Shane has long been an officer of the National Rifle Association,

then the original conclusion follows with a greater likelihood from this enlarged set of premises than it did from the original set.

The strength of the *claim* about *the relation between the premises and the conclusion* of the argument is the nub of the difference between deductive and inductive arguments. We characterize the two types of argument as follows. A *deductive* argument is one whose conclusion is claimed to follow from its premises with necessity, this necessity not being a matter of degree and not depending in any way upon whatever else may be the case. In contrast, an *inductive* argument is one whose conclusion is claimed to follow from its premises with probability, this probability being a matter of degree and dependent upon what else may be the case.

1.7 TRUTH, VALIDITY, AND SOUNDNESS

Truth and falsehood may be predicated of propositions (see section 1.2), but never of arguments. And the attributes of validity and invalidity can belong only to deductive arguments, never to propositions. There is a connection between the validity or invalidity of an argument and the truth or falsehood of its premises and conclusion, but the connection is by no means a simple one. Indeed, it is so complex that substantial portions of traditional logic textbooks are devoted to the problem of determining the validity or invalidity of deductive arguments. So only a brief preliminary discussion of validity will be presented in this section.

It is important to realize that an argument may be valid while one or more of its premises is untrue. This point was made forcefully by Abraham Lincoln, in one of his debates with Judge Stephen Douglas, in 1858. Lincoln was attacking the Dred Scott decision, which obliged the return of slaves who had escaped into northern states, to their owners in the south.

> [W]hat follows as the short and even syllogistic argument from it [i.e., from the Dred Scott decision]? I think it follows, and submit to the consideration of men capable of arguing, whether as I state it in syllogistic form the argument has any fault in it:
>
> Nothing in the Constitution or laws of any State can destroy a right distinctly and expressly affirmed in the Constitution of the United States.
>
> The right of property in a slave is distinctly and expressly affirmed in the Constitution of the United States.
>
> Therefore nothing in the Constitution or laws of any State can destroy the right of property in a slave.
>
> I believe that no fault can be pointed out in that argument; assuming the truth of the premises, the conclusion, so far as I have capacity at all to understand it, follows inevitably. There is a fault in it as I think, but the fault is not in the reasoning; but the falsehood in fact is a fault of the premises. I believe that the right of property in a slave is *not* distinctly and expressly affirmed in the Constitution, and Judge Douglas thinks it *is*. I believe that the Supreme Court and the advocates of that decision [the Dred Scott decision] may search in vain for the place in the Constitution where the right of property in a slave is distinctly and expressly affirmed. I say, therefore, that I think one of the premises is not true in fact.[56]

Arguments may exhibit differing combinations of true and false premises and conclusions. Here follow seven examples; their contents are trivial and contrived, but that will put the special features of each example in sharp relief. Using these examples we may formulate important principles concerning the relations of truth and validity.

Some valid arguments contain only true propositions, as, for example:

> All whales are mammals.
> I.   All mammals have lungs.
> Therefore, all whales have lungs.

But an argument may also consist entirely of false propositions and nevertheless be valid, as, for example:

> All spiders have ten legs.
> II.   All ten-legged creatures have wings.
> Therefore, all spiders have wings.

This argument is valid because if its premises were true its conclusion would have to be true also—even though in fact they are false.

---

[56]   Abraham Lincoln, *The Collected Works of Abraham Lincoln*, ed. Roy R. Basler (1953), Vol. 3, p. 231.

Moreover, an argument may have premisses that are true, and have a true conclusion, and nevertheless be invalid, as in the following example:

If I owned all the gold in Fort Knox then I would be wealthy.
III. I do not own all the gold in Fort Knox.
Therefore, I am not wealthy.

The premisses could be true and the conclusion false—as is clear when one considers that if I were to inherit ten million dollars, the premisses would remain true, although the conclusion would become false. Of course the argument would remain invalid.

This point is further illustrated by the following argument, which has precisely the same form as Example III:

If Rockefeller owned all the gold in Fort Knox, then Rockefeller would be wealthy.
IV. Rockefeller does not own all the gold in Fort Knox.
Therefore, Rockefeller is not wealthy.

The premisses of this argument are true, and its conclusion is false. Such an argument cannot be valid, because it is impossible for the premisses of a valid argument to be true while its conclusion is false.

Arguments with false premisses and true conclusions may be valid or invalid. Here is an example of a valid argument with false premisses and a true conclusion:

All fishes are mammals.
V.   All whales are fishes.
Therefore, all whales are mammals.

And here is an example of an invalid argument with false premisses and a true conclusion:

All mammals have wings.
VI. All whales have wings.
Therefore, all whales are mammals.

Finally, there are invalid arguments whose premisses and conclusions are false, as, for example:

All mammals have wings.
VII. All whales have wings.
Therefore, all mammals are whales.

It is clear from these seven examples that there are valid arguments with false conclusions (Example II), as well as invalid arguments with true conclusions (Examples III and VI). Hence it is clear that the truth or falsity of an argument's conclusion does not by itself determine the validity or invalidity of that argument. And the fact that an argument is valid does not guarantee the truth of its conclusion (Example II).

By laying out these seven examples of deductive arguments on the two following charts, we may better appreciate their variety. The first chart, of *invalid* arguments, shows that there are invalid arguments with every combination of true and false premisses and conclusions.

| | *Invalid Arguments* | |
	True conclusion	*False conclusion*
True premisses	Example III	Example IV
False premisses	Example VI	Example VII

The second chart, of *valid* arguments, shows that valid arguments have only three of those combinations of true and false premisses and conclusions:

| | *Valid Arguments* | |
	True conclusion	*False conclusion*
True premisses	Example I	
False premisses	Example V	Example II

The blank position on the second chart exhibits graphically a point of the most fundamental importance: *If an argument is valid and its conclusion is false, not all of its premisses are true.* And also: *If an argument is valid and its premisses are true, its conclusion is true.* Some valid arguments have false conclusions—but any such argument must have at least one false premiss.

When an argument is valid, *and* all of its premisses are true, we call it *sound.* The conclusion of a sound argument obviously must be true. If a deductive argument is not sound—which means either that it is not valid or that not all of its premisses are true— it fails to establish the truth of its conclusion.

To test the truth or falsehood of premisses is the task of common sense or science in general, since premisses may deal with any subject matter at all. The logician is not so much interested in the truth or falsehood of propositions as in the logical relations between them, where by the "logical" relations between propositions we mean those which determine the correctness or incorrectness of arguments in which they may occur. Determining the correctness or incorrectness of arguments falls squarely within the province of logic. The logician is interested in the correctness even of arguments whose premisses might be false.

A question might be raised about the value of this last point. It might be suggested that we ought to confine ourselves to arguments that have true premisses, ignoring all others. But as a matter of fact, we are interested in, and must often depend upon, the correctness of arguments whose premisses are not known to be true. Examples of such situations suggest themselves readily. A scientist who is interested in verifying scientific theories by deriving testable consequences from them does not know beforehand which theories are true. Were that known, there would be no need for verification. In our everyday affairs, we must often choose between alternative courses of action. Where these courses are genuine alternatives that cannot all be adopted, we may try to reason about which should be chosen. Such reasoning generally involves figuring out the consequences of each of the actions among which we must choose. One might reason as follows: Suppose I choose the first alternative; then such and such will be the case. On the other hand, assuming that I choose the second alternative, then something else will follow. In general, we are inclined to choose among alternative courses of action on the basis of which set of consequences we prefer to have realized. In each case, we are interested in reasoning correctly, lest we deceive ourselves. Were we interested only in arguments that have true premisses, we should not know which line of argument to consider until we knew which of the alternative premisses were true. And if we knew which premiss was true, we should not be interested in the arguments at all, because our purpose in considering the arguments was to help us *decide* which alternative premiss to *make* true. To confine our attention to arguments with true premisses would be self-defeating and stultifying.

So far we have been speaking only about propositions and the arguments that contain them as premisses and conclusion. As has been explained (in section 1.2), these are not linguistic entities such as sentences, but what sentences may be uttered to assert. Whether the actual process of thinking or reasoning requires language is an open question. It may be that thinking requires the use of symbols of some sort, words or images or whatnot. We all feel a certain sympathy with the youngster who was told to think before speaking, and replied, "But how can I know what I think until I hear what I say?" Perhaps all thinking requires words or some other kind of symbols, but that is not a question that concerns us here. It is obvious that the communication of any proposition or any argument requires symbols and involves language. In the rest of this book, we are concerned with *stated* arguments, those whose propositions are formulated in language.

The use of language, however, complicates our problem. Certain accidental or misleading features of their formulations in language may make more difficult the task of investigating the logical relations among propositions. It is part of the task of the logician, therefore, to examine language itself, primarily from the point of view of discovering and describing those aspects of it which tend to obscure the difference between correct and incorrect argument. It is for this reason that chapters 1 through 4 of this book are devoted to language.

1.8   THE USE OF REASON IN PROBLEM SOLVING

A great deal of what we do is a matter of habit. As we go to work or school, we usually move along a well-established route, with surroundings so familiar that we scarcely notice them. But if our normal progress is interrupted by some obstacle, an excavation or a barricade, *that* captures our attention. Our progress becomes problematic.

We must think about what to do next. We recognize that we have a problem. We must consider what to do about it.

It has been argued very plausibly that every problem, however abstract, arises from some kind of conflict between a belief and a situation to which the belief seems inappropriate. From this collision between situations and beliefs that do not "fit" them, there arises the discomfort of doubt. And it is doubt that stimulates inquiry. As Charles Sanders Peirce wrote: "The irritation of doubt causes a struggle to attain a state of belief. I shall term this struggle *Inquiry.* . . ."[57]

In section 1.1 we remarked that the skills included in "logical ability" are useful in solving problems. The most fruitful and dependable kind of inquiry is the application of reason to solving problems. This involves all aspects of what Peirce called inquiry: examining and reexamining the problematic situation from every point of view that occurs to us; marshaling all relevant information that is available; and seeking as persistently as we can for some new insight into the situation or some new combination of possible beliefs that will enable us to dispel the discomfort or irritation of doubt.

As William James (1842–1910) put it:

> The individual has a stock of old opinions already, but he meets a new experience that puts them to a strain. Somebody contradicts them; or in a reflective moment he discovers that they contradict each other; or he hears of facts with which they are incompatible; or desires arise in him which they cease to satisfy. The result is an inward trouble to which his mind till then had been a stranger; and from which he seeks to escape by modifying his previous mass of opinions. He saves as much of it as he can, for in this matter of belief we are all extreme conservatives. So he tries to change first this opinion, and then that (for they resist change very variously), until at last some new idea comes up which he can graft upon the ancient stock with a minimum of disturbance of the latter, some idea that mediates between the stock and the new experience and runs them into one another most felicitously and expediently.[58]

John Dewey's (1859–1952) formulation of this important concept is the following:

> . . . thinking takes its departure from specific conflicts in experience that occasion perplexity and trouble. Men do not, in their natural estate, think when they have no troubles to cope with, no difficulties to overcome. A life of ease, of success without effort, would be a thoughtless life, and so also would a life of ready omnipotence.[59]

The serious problems of human life, broadly speaking, have to do with the avoidance of suffering and the achievement of happiness. To achieve these goals we try to learn about causes and effects. Traditional medical investigators sought to discover the causes of specific diseases in order that patients might be cured and that diseases might be wiped out by eliminating their causes. With more recent emphasis on "wellness," that is, on health maintenance and promotion, inquirers seek to identify those aspects of

---

[57]   Charles Sanders Peirce, "The Fixation of Belief," *Readings on Logic,* 2d ed., ed. Irving M. Copi and James A. Gould (1972), p. 62.

[58]   William James, *Pragmatism* (1907), pp. 59–60.

[59]   John Dewey, *Reconstruction in Philosophy* (1957), pp. 138–39.

diet, hygiene, and exercise that produce physical and mental strength and vigor. Today's science and technology have enormously advanced our understanding and control of the world around us. The scientific laws discovered, the scientific hypotheses and theories devised, the machinery and instruments invented, all represent so many problems solved, so much effective thinking and productive reasoning. These topics are treated at length in chapters 6 and 7.

Up to now in this chapter, we have focused our attention on identifying and analyzing other people's arguments. When you solve a problem, however, you must draw your own inferences; you must construct your own arguments. Some of the premises used describe the problematic situation you confront. Other premises contain information that you believe to be relevant to the problem's solution. If the problem is at all difficult, you may find in the course of your thinking that the situation has been misdescribed. Or you may find that the information at hand is not sufficient for solving the problem. Here, as anywhere else, practice makes perfect.

A useful kind of exercise to help strengthen one's problem-solving abilities is the logical puzzle, or "brain-teaser." In this kind of exercise the problematic situation is presented as a mass of more or less unrelated data or propositions given as true in the statement of the puzzle. A specific question or group of questions is posed, the answer to which will constitute the solution to the problem. There is a good deal of plausibility to some of these puzzles. From such information or data a detective or police inspector might have the challenging task of reconstructing the anatomy of a crime in sufficient detail to permit the apprehension and arrest of the felon responsible for it. Or a newspaper reporter might be required to analyze and rearrange such data to produce an intelligible and thus printable journalistic story. Or a scientist might accept the task of explaining the apparently unrelated data by appealing to scientific laws and theories from which just those data might have been predicted to emerge in the circumstances that gave rise to them.

From the given data in puzzles of this sort, a few inferences can perhaps be drawn immediately. And in some particularly elementary puzzles, that might be sufficient to establish the answer to the question posed. For example, consider the following illustration:

> In a certain flight crew the positions of pilot, copilot, and flight engineer are held by Allen, Brown, and Carr, though not necessarily in that order.
> The copilot, who was an only child, earns the least.
> Carr, who married Brown's sister, earns more than the pilot. What position does each person hold?

We can immediately draw several inferences that tell us Carr's position. Since Carr earns more than the pilot, Carr is not the pilot. And since Carr earns more than the pilot, and the copilot earns the least, it follows that Carr is not the copilot either. Hence Carr must be the flight engineer.

Next we can infer that since Brown has a sister, Brown was not an only child and therefore Brown is not the copilot. And we can infer that Brown is not the flight engineer from our identification of Carr as the flight engineer. Hence Brown must be the pilot. And by elimination Allen must be the copilot.

There is no fixed pattern of inference and argument that will lead to the solution of every puzzle of this sort, just as there is no fixed pattern that will lead to the resolution of every problem. But in cases like the flight crew puzzle, where the question is to match persons with positions, and in cases where the puzzle is a little more complicated than the one just considered, it might be useful to construct a diagram or matrix.

Consider the following puzzle:

Alonzo, Kurt, Rudolf, and Willard are four creative artists of great talent. One is a dancer, one a painter, one a singer, and one a writer, though not necessarily in that order.

1. Alonzo and Rudolf were in the audience the night the singer made his debut on the concert stage.
2. Both Kurt and the writer have had their portraits painted from life by the painter, who has never done a self-portrait.
3. The writer, whose biography of Willard was a best-seller, is planning to write a biography of Alonzo, whom he has never met.
4. Alonzo has never heard of Rudolf.

What is each man's artistic field?

To keep track in one's mind of this many facts and the several conclusions that might be inferred from them would be confusing and difficult. Even writing them down in the form of notes might simply produce more clutter. A good method of keeping track of this information and the intermediate inferences or subconclusions drawn, in a way that will be useful and suggestive of further inferences, is to draw an array or diagram in which there is room to represent every possibility. In the present case we would construct a four-row-by-four-column rectangular array as follows:

	Dancer	Painter	Singer	Writer
Alonzo				
Kurt				
Rudolf				
Willard				

Now if we are led to the conclusion that the individual whose name is at the left cannot be the artist whose field heads one of the columns, we can write an "N" (for "No") in the cell or box to the right of that individual's name and in the column headed by the field in question. For example, if we decide that Rudolf is not the singer, we write an "N" in the third box from the left in the third column. Or if we decide that Rudolf is the dancer, we write a "Y" (for "Yes") in the box in the row headed by his name and in the column headed by the category *Dancer*.

In the present puzzle we can infer from (1) that neither Alonzo nor Rudolf is the singer, so we write "N" opposite their names in the third column. From (2) we know that Kurt is neither the painter nor the writer, so we write "N" opposite his name in the second and fourth columns. From (3) we see that the writer is neither Alonzo nor Willard, so we enter "N" opposite their names in the fourth column. Our matrix now looks like this:

	Dancer	Painter	Singer	Writer
Alonzo			N	N
Kurt		N		N
Rudolf			N	
Willard				N

By elimination it is now clear that Rudolf is the writer, so we insert a "Y" in the box opposite his name in the column headed *Writer,* and place an "N" in the remaining boxes in his row. Next we notice that, according to (2), the writer (whom we now know is Rudolf) has had his portrait painted from life by the painter, whereas according to (4), Alonzo does not know Rudolf, from which it follows that Alonzo is not the painter, so we enter an "N" in the box under *Painter* in the row to the right of Alonzo's name. By elimination, again, we know that Alonzo is the dancer, and we write a "Y" in the box next to his name. But then neither Kurt nor Willard can be the dancer, so we write "N" next to each of their names in the first column. This leaves *Singer* as the only category possible for Kurt, and in the remaining empty box in his row we duly write a "Y." We then write an "N" under *Singer* in the row opposite Willard's name, and (again by elimination) we conclude that Willard must be the painter and write a "Y" in the last empty box in the matrix, which now looks like this:

	Dancer	Painter	Singer	Writer
Alonzo	Y	N	N	N
Kurt	N	N	Y	N
Rudolf	N	N	N	Y
Willard	N	Y	N	N

From these entries we can read off that Alonzo is the dancer, Kurt the singer, Rudolf the writer, and Willard the painter.

It must be remarked that real problems in the real world are not as neat and tidy as these logical puzzles. In the first place, many real problems are not accurately described in the first instance, and their misdescription could be sufficiently misleading to prevent *any* solution from being correct. To solve them might require that some part or parts of the initial description be rejected or replaced. But that would be totally inappropriate in seeking to solve a logical puzzle. In the second place, to solve *some* real problems might require us to make important scientific discoveries, to invent and use previously unimagined instruments or equipment, or to search as yet unexplored territories. The information contained in the statement of a logical puzzle, however, must be sufficient for it to be solved—needing no supplementation beyond such items of common knowledge as that an only child has no siblings and that a man must be older than his children. Finally, real problems do not come with an explicitly formulated question whose answer would certify that the problem has been solved. Many real problems are identified as such, initially at least, only by the obscure feeling that something is wrong, rather than by an explicit question whose answer cannot immediately be supplied. Despite these differences, however, such exercises are useful in studying informal logic.

EXERCISES

The following problems require reasoning for their solution. To prove that an answer, once achieved, is correct requires an argument whose premises are contained in the statement of the problem and whose conclusion is the answer to it. If the answer is correct, a valid argument can be constructed. In working at these problems, readers are urged to concern themselves not merely with discovering the answers, but also with formulating arguments to prove those answers correct.

■   *1.* In a certain mythical community, politicians never tell the truth, and non-politicians always tell the truth. A stranger meets three natives and asks the first of them, "Are you a politician?" The first native answers the question. The second native then reports that the first native denied being a politician. The third native says that the first native *is* a politician.

How many of these three natives are politicians?

2. Of three prisoners in a certain jail, one had normal vision, the second had only one eye, and the third was totally blind. All were of at least average intelligence. The jailer told the prisoners that from three white hats and two red hats he would select three and put them on the prisoners' heads. Each was prevented from seeing what color hat was placed on his own head. They were brought together; and the jailer offered freedom to the prisoner with normal vision if he could tell what color hat was on his head. The prisoner confessed that he couldn't tell. Next the jailer offered freedom to the prisoner with only one eye if he could tell what color hat was on his head. The second prisoner confessed that he couldn't tell. The jailer did not bother making the offer to the blind prisoner; but agreed to extend the same terms to him when he made the request. The blind prisoner then smiled broadly and said

I do not need to have my sight;
From what my friends with eyes have said,
I clearly see my hat is——!

How did he know?

3. Mr. Short, his sister, his son, and his daughter are fond of golf and often play together. The following statements are true of their foursome:

a. The best player's twin and the worst player are of opposite sex.

b. The best player and the worst player are the same age.

Which one of the foursome is the best player?

4. The members of a small loan company are Mr. Black, Mr. White, Mrs. Coffee, Miss Ambrose, Mr. Kelly, and Miss Earnshaw. The positions they occupy are manager, assistant manager, cashier, stenographer, teller, and clerk, though not necessarily in that order. The assistant manager is the manager's grandson; the cashier is the stenographer's son-in-law; Mr. Black is a bachelor; Mr. White is twenty-two years old; Miss Ambrose is the teller's stepsister; and Mr. Kelly is the manager's neighbor. (Assume that one must be married in order to have children and that a twenty-two year old cannot have grandchildren.)

Who holds each position?

■ *5.* Benno Torelli, genial host at Hamtramck's most exclusive nightclub, was shot and killed by a racketeer gang because he fell behind in his protection payments. After considerable effort on the part of the police, five suspects were brought before the District Attorney, who asked them what they had to say for themselves. Each of them made three statements, two true and one false. Their statements were

Lefty: I did not kill Torelli. I never owned a revolver in all my life. Spike did it.

Red: I did not kill Torelli. I never owned a revolver. The others are all passing the buck.

Dopey: I am innocent. I never saw Butch before. Spike is guilty.

Spike: I am innocent. Butch is the guilty one. Lefty did not tell the truth when he said I did it.

Butch: I did not kill Torelli. Red is the guilty one. Dopey and I are old pals.

Whodunit?

6. Ms. Adams, Ms. Baker; Ms. Catt, Ms. Dodge, Ms. Ennis, and Ms. Fisk all went shopping one morning at the Emporium. Each woman went directly to the floor carrying the article that she wanted to buy, and each woman bought only one article. They bought a book , a dress, a handbag, a necktie, a hat, and a lamp.

All the women except Ms. Adams entered the elevator on the main floor: Two men also entered the elevator. Two women—Ms. Catt and the one who bought the necktie—got off at the second floor. Dresses were sold on the third floor. The two men got off at the fourth floor. The woman who bought the lamp got off at the fifth floor; leaving Ms. Fisk all alone to get off at the sixth floor.

The next day Ms. Baker, who received the handbag as a surprise gift from one of the women who got off at the second floor, met her husband returning the necktie that one of the other women had given him. If books are sold on the main floor, and Ms. Ennis was the sixth person to get out of the elevator, what did each of these women buy?

7. Five men who were buddies in the last war are having a reunion. They are White, Brown, Peters, Harper, and Nash, who by occupation are printer, writer, barber, neurologist, and heating contractor. By coincidence, they live in the cities of White Plains, Brownsville, Petersburg, Harper's Ferry, and Nashville, but no man lives in the city having a name similar to his, nor does the name of his occupation have the same initial as his name or the name of the city in which he lives.

The barber doesn't live in Petersburg, and Brown is neither heating contractor nor printer—nor does he live in Petersburg or Harper's Ferry. Mr. Harper lives in Nashville and is neither barber nor writer. White is not a resident of Brownsville, nor is Nash, who is neither a barber nor a heating contractor.

If you have only the information just given, can you determine the name of the city in which Nash resides?

8. Daniel Kilraine was killed on a lonely road, two miles from Pontiac, at 3:30 A.M., March 17, 1952. Otto, Curly, Slim, Mickey, and the Kid were arrested a week later in Detroit and questioned. Each of the five made four statements, three of which were true and one of which was false. One of these persons killed Kilraine. Whodunit? Their statements were

Otto: I was in Chicago when Kilraine was murdered. I never killed anyone. The Kid is the guilty one. Mickey and I are pals.

Curly: I did not kill Kilraine. I never owned a revolver in my life. The Kid knows me. I was in Detroit the night of March 17.

Slim: Curly lied when he said he never owned a revolver. The murder was committed on St. Patrick's Day. Otto was in Chicago at this time. One of us is guilty.

Mickey: I did not kill Kilraine. The Kid has never been in Pontiac. I never saw Otto before. Curly was in Detroit with me on the night of March 17.

The Kid: I did not kill Kilraine. I have never been in Pontiac. I never saw Curly before. Otto erred when he said I am guilty.

9. A woman recently hosted a political meeting to which she invited five guests. The names of the six people who sat down at the circular table were Abrams, Banjo, Clive, Dumont, Ekwall, and Fish. One of them was deaf; one was very talkative; one was terribly fat; one simply hated Dumont; one had a vitamin deficiency; and one was the hostess. The person who hated Dumont sat directly opposite Banjo. The deaf one sat opposite Clive, who sat between the one who had a vitamin deficiency and the one who hated Dumont. The fat one sat opposite Abrams, next to the deaf person and to the left of the one who hated Dumont. The person who had a vitamin deficiency sat between Clive and the one who sat opposite the person who hated Dumont. Fish, who was a good friend of everyone, sat next to the fat person and opposite the hostess.

Can you identify each of these people?

■ **10.** Nine men—Brown, White, Adams, Miller, Green, Hunter, Knight, Jones, and Smith—play the several positions on a baseball team. (The battery consists of the pitcher and the catcher; the infield consists of the first, second, and third basemen and the shortstop; the outfield consists of the right, left, and center fielders.) Determine, from the following data, the position played by each man.

   a. Smith and Brown each won $10 playing poker with the pitcher.
   b. Hunter is taller than Knight and shorter than White, but each of them weighs more than the first baseman.
   c. The third baseman lives across the corridor from Jones in the same apartment house.
   d. Miller and the outfielders play bridge in their spare time.
   e. White, Miller, Brown, the right fielder, and the center fielder are bachelors; the rest are married.
   f. Of Adams and Knight, one plays outfielder position.
   g. The right fielder is shorter than the center fielder.
   h. The third baseman is brother to the pitcher's wife.
   i. Green is taller than the infielders and the battery, except for Jones, Smith, and Adams.
   j. The third baseman, the shortstop, and Hunter made $150 each speculating in U.S. Steel.
   k. The second baseman is engaged to Miller's sister.
   l. The second baseman beat Jones, Brown, Hunter, and the catcher at cards.
   m. Adams lives in the same house as his own sister but dislikes the catcher.
   n. Adams, Brown, and the shortstop lost $200 each speculating in copper.
   o. The catcher has three daughters, the third baseman has two sons, but Green is being sued for divorce.

   11. In a certain bank there are eleven distinct positions, namely, in decreasing rank, President, First Vice-President, Second Vice-President, Third Vice-President, Cashier, Teller, Assistant Teller, Bookkeeper, First Stenographer, Second Stenographer, and Janitor. These eleven positions are occupied by the following, here listed alphabetically: Mr. Adams, Mrs. Brown, Mr. Camp, Miss Dale, Mr. Evans, Mrs. Ford, Mr. Grant, Miss Hill, Mr. Jones, Mrs. Kane, and Mr. Long. Concerning them, only the following facts are known:

   a. The Third Vice-President is the pampered grandson of the President but is disliked by both Mrs. Brown and the Assistant Teller.
   b. The Assistant Teller and the Second Stenographer shared equally in their father's estate.
   c. The Second Vice-President and the Assistant Teller wear the same style of hats.
   d. Mr. Grant told Miss Hill to send him a stenographer at once.
   e. The President's nearest neighbors are Mrs. Kane, Mr. Grant, and Mr. Long.
   f. The First Vice-President and the Cashier live at the exclusive Bachelor's Club.
   g. The Janitor, a miser, has occupied the same garret room since boyhood.
   h. Mr. Adams and the Second Stenographer are leaders in the social life of the younger unmarried set.
   i. The Second Vice-President and the Bookkeeper were once engaged to be married to each other.

    j.   The fashionable Teller is the son-in-law of the First Stenographer.

    k.   Mr. Jones regularly gives Mr. Evans his discarded clothing to wear, without the elderly Bookkeeper knowing about the gift.

Show how to match correctly the eleven names against the eleven positions occupied.

    12.   Five terminal cancer patients are in a poker game: Brown, Perkins, Turner, Jones, and Reilly. Their brands of cigarettes are Luckies, Camels, Kools, Old Golds, and Chesterfields, but not necessarily in that order. At the beginning of the game, the number of cigarettes possessed by each of the players was twenty, fifteen, eight, six, and three, but not necessarily in that order.

    During the game, at a certain time when no one was smoking, the following conditions obtained:

    a.   Perkins asked for three cards.

    b.   Reilly had smoked half of his original supply, or one less than Turner smoked.

    c.   The Chesterfield smoker originally had as many more, plus half as many more, plus $2\frac{1}{2}$ more cigarettes than now.

    d.   The player who was drawing to an inside straight could taste only the menthol in his fifth cigarette, the last one he smoked.

    e.   The player who smokes Luckies had smoked at least two more than anyone else, including Perkins.

    f.   Brown drew as many aces as he originally had cigarettes.

    g.   No player had smoked all the cigarettes possessed by that player originally.

    h.   The Camel smoker asked Jones to pass Brown's matches.

How many cigarettes did each player have to begin with, and of what brand?

    13.   Alice, Betty, Carol, and Dorothy were either a lifeguard, a lawyer, a pilot, or a professor. Each wore a white, yellow, pink, or blue dress.

    The lifeguard beat Betty at canasta, and Carol and the pilot often played bridge with the women in pink and blue dresses. Alice and the professor envied the woman in the blue dress, but this was not the lawyer, as she always wore a white dress.

    What was each woman's occupation and dress color?

    14.   In the same mythical community described in Exercise 1, a stranger meets three other natives and asks them: "How many of you are politicians?" the first native replied, "We are all politicians." The second native said, "No, just two of us are politicians." The third native then said, "That isn't true either." Was the third native a politician?

  ■ **15.**   On a certain train, the crew consists of the brakeman, the fireman, and the engineer. Their names listed alphabetically are Jones, Robinson, and Smith. On the train are also three passengers with corresponding names: Mr. Jones, Mr. Robinson, and Mr. Smith. The following facts are known:

    a.   Mr. Robinson lives in Detroit.

    b.   The brakeman lives halfway between Detroit and Chicago.

    c.   Mr. Jones earns exactly $20,000 a year.

    d.   Smith once beat the fireman at billiards.

e. The brakeman's next-door neighbor, one of the three passengers mentioned, earns exactly three times as much as the brakeman.

f. The passenger living in Chicago has the same name as the brakeman.

Who is the engineer?

2

Language

2.1 FUNCTIONS OF LANGUAGE

Language is so subtle and complicated an instrument that we often lose sight of its many uses. Here, as in other situations, there is danger in our tendency to oversimplify.

A common complaint of those who take too narrow a view of the uses of language concerns the way in which words are "wasted" at social or political gatherings. "So much talk, and so little said!" sums up this kind of criticism. And more than one person has been heard to remark, "So-and-so always asks me how I am. What a hypocrite! He doesn't care in the least how I am!" Such remarks reveal a failure to understand the complex purposes for which language is used. It is shown also in the deplorable conduct of those bores who, when asked how they are, actually proceed to tell about the state of their health—usually at great length and in much detail. But people do not usually talk at parties or political rallies to instruct each other. And ordinarily "How are you?" is a friendly greeting, not a request for a medical report.

The philosopher George Berkeley (1685–1753) remarked long ago in his *Treatise Concerning the Principles of Human Knowledge* that

> . . . the communicating of ideas . . . is not the chief and only end of language, as is commonly supposed. There are other ends, as the raising of some passion, the exciting to or deterring from an action, the putting the mind in some particular disposition; to which the former is in many cases barely subservient, and sometimes entirely omitted, when these can be obtained without it, as I think does not infrequently happen in the familiar use of language.

More recently, philosophers have elaborated in great detail the variety of uses to which language can be put. In his *Philosophical Investigations*, Ludwig Wittgenstein (1889–1951) insisted that there are "countless different kinds of use of what we call 'symbols,' 'words,' 'sentences.'" Among the examples suggested by Wittgenstein are giving orders, describing the appearance of an object or giving its measurements, reporting an event, speculating about an event, forming and testing a hypothesis, presenting the results of an experiment in tables and diagrams, making up a story, play-acting, singing catches, guessing riddles, making a joke and telling it, solving a problem in practical arithmetic, translating from one language into another, asking, thinking, cursing, greeting, and praying.

Not everyone agrees with Wittgenstein that there are literally "countless different kinds of use" of language. One philosopher who has taken exception to Wittgenstein's remarks is John Searle (1932–), who writes:

> [T]his rather skeptical conclusion ought to arouse our suspicions. No one I suppose would say that there are countless kinds of economic systems or marital arrangements or sorts of political parties; why should language be more taxonomically recalcitrant than any other aspect of human social life?[1]

Despite this disagreement, Wittgenstein and Searle agree that language is complex, versatile, puzzling, and, for precisely these reasons, philosophically interesting.

Some order can be imposed on the variety of language uses by dividing them into four general categories. This fourfold division of the functions of language is admittedly a simplification, perhaps an oversimplification, but it has been found useful by many writers on logic and language.

Informative

The first of these four uses of language is to communicate information—to tell people how things are. Ordinarily this is accomplished by formulating and affirming (or denying) propositions. Language used to affirm or deny propositions, or to present arguments, is said to serve the *informative* function. In this context we use the word "information" to include misinformation: false as well as true propositions, incorrect as well as correct arguments. Informative discourse is used to describe the world and to reason about it. Whether the alleged facts are important or unimportant, general or particular, does not matter; the language used to describe or report them is being used informatively. Of the importance of this use of language there can be no doubt. One commentator has written:

> Despite abuse and all that has been done to language and committed in its name, it is the most extraordinary piece of equipment forged by men and women for their better understanding of themselves, one another, and the world in which they live. Words describe and give names to what [people] feel, think, see, and do; and so command of them is of paramount importance.[2]

Expressive

Just as science provides us with the clearest examples of informative discourse, so poetry furnishes us the best examples of language serving an *expressive* function. The following lines of Burns

---

[1]   John R. Searle, *Expression and Meaning: Studies in the Theory of Speech Acts* (1979), p. vi.
[2]   Arnold Wesker, *Words as Definitions of Experience* (1976), p. 17

> O my Love's like a red, red rose
>   That's newly sprung in June:
> O my Love's like the melodie
>   That's sweetly play'd in tune!

are definitely not intended to inform us of any facts or theories concerning the world. The poet's concern is not with knowledge but with feelings and attitudes. The passage was not written to report any information but to express certain emotions that the poet felt very keenly and to evoke similar feelings in the reader. Language serves the expressive function whenever it is used to vent or to attempt to arouse feelings or emotions.

It should be noted that we are using the term "express" in a somewhat narrower way than usual. It is perfectly natural to speak of expressing a feeling, an emotion, or an attitude. But one ordinarily speaks also of expressing an opinion, a belief, or a conviction. To avoid confusing the informative and expressive functions of language, we shall speak instead of *stating* or *declaring* an opinion, a belief, or a conviction, and reserve the term "express" in this chapter for revealing or communicating feelings, emotions, and attitudes.

Not all expressive language is poetry, however. We express sorrow by saying "That's too bad" or "Oh my," and enthusiasm by shouting "Wow!" or "Dynamite!" The lover expresses delicate passion by murmuring "Darling!" or "Sweetheart!" The poet expresses complex and concentrated emotions in a sonnet or some other verse form. A worshipper's feeling of awe and wonder at the vastness and mystery of the universe may be expressed by reciting the Lord's Prayer of the twenty-third Psalm of David. These uses of language are not intended to communicate information but to express emotions, feelings, or attitudes. Expressive discourse *as expressive* is neither true nor false. For a person to apply only the criteria of truth or falsehood, correctness or incorrectness, to expressive discourse like a poem is to miss its point and lose much of its value. The student whose enjoyment of John Keats's (1795–1821) sonnet "On First Looking into Chapman's Homer" is diminished by knowing that it was Balboa rather than Cortez who discovered the Pacific Ocean is a "poor reader" of poetry. The purpose of the poem is not to teach history, but something else entirely. This is not to say that poetry can have no literal significance. Some poems do have an informative content that may be an important ingredient in their total effect. Some poetry may well be "criticism of life," in the words of a great poet. But such poems are more than *merely* expressive, as we are using the term here. Such poetry may be said to have a "mixed usage" or to serve a multiple function. This notion will be discussed further in the following section.

Expression may be analyzed into two components. If one curses when alone, or writes poems that are shown to no one, or prays in solitude, the language used functions to express the attitude of the speaker or writer, but it is not intended to evoke a similar attitude in anyone else. On the other hand, when an orator seeks to inspire an audience not to action but to share enthusiasm, when a lover uses poetic language in courtship, when the crowd cheers its athletic team, the language used not only expresses the attitudes of the speakers but is intended to evoke the same attitudes in the hearers. Expressive discourse, then, is used either to *express* the speaker's feelings or to attempt to *evoke* certain feelings on the part of the auditor. Of course it may do both.

Directive

Language serves the *directive* function when it is used for the purpose of causing (or preventing) overt action. It is an attempt to get people to do things. The clearest examples of directive discourse are commands and requests. When a parent tells a child to wash up for dinner, the intention is not to communicate any information or to express or evoke any particular emotion. The language is intended to get results, to cause action of the indicated kind. When a shopper asks a shopkeeper to deliver certain merchandise, the language is again being used directively, to produce *action*. To ask a question is ordinarily to request an answer and is also to be classified as directive discourse. The difference between a command and a request is a rather subtle one, for almost any command can be translated into a request by adding the word "please," or by suitable changes in tone of voice or in facial expression. Other directives are orders, pleas, advice, instructions, prayers, threats, warnings, entreaties, motions, prescriptions, permissions, and decrees.

In its nakedly imperative form, directive discourse is neither true nor false. A command such as "Close the window" cannot be either true or false in any literal sense. Whether the command is obeyed or disobeyed does not make it true or false, for it cannot be either. We may disagree about whether a command has been obeyed; but we never disagree about whether a command is true or false, for those terms simply do not apply to it. However, the reasonableness or propriety, the unreasonableness or impropriety of commands are attributes analogous to the truth or falsehood of informative discourse. In section 1.2 it was noted that reasons can be given for an action to be performed. When the statement of those reasons accompanies the command, their combination can be regarded as an argument. That amounts to regarding the command as a proposition in which the hearers (or readers) of the command are told that they must, should, or ought to perform the action commanded. Explorations of these issues have led some writers to develop a "logic of imperatives," but to discuss it is beyond the scope of this book.[3]

Commissive

The fourth function of language is to commit the user to doing or refraining from doing something. When a parent says to a child, "I promise to take you to Six Flags Over Texas next summer," he or she has made a commitment to the child—one that the youngster is not likely to forget! When Glenn writes in his diary on New Year's Day, "I resolve to kick my smoking habit," he has undertaken to refrain from smoking. There are many kinds of commissive besides promises and resolutions—for

---

[3]   For an introduction to this topic, the interested reader can consult I. M. Copi and J. A. Gould, *Contemporary Philosophical Logic* (1978); or Nicholas Rescher, *The Logic of Commands* (1966).

example, vows (avowals), oaths, pledges, covenants, contracts, agreements, affirmations, renunciations, abjurations, and threats. The utility of commissives is obvious; in fact, one philosopher, John Locke, considered them the bonds of human society.[4] As we shall see in section 2.2, a given use of language—for example, a threat—can both commit the speaker to a course of action and try to change the behavior of others.

There are interesting similarities and differences among the four uses of language. Informatives, as we saw, are put forward as descriptions of the world, so we can say that their *direction of fit* is word to world.[5] That is to say, the speaker tries to get the word to match the world. Just the opposite is true of directives and commissives, for there the aim is to change the world by getting it to conform to one's words. If I say "Close the door" (in most contexts a directive use of language), I am trying to get the door closed. If I say "I do solemnly swear that I will uphold the Constitution of the United States" (a commissive use of language), I commit myself to upholding the Constitution. Expressives have no direction of fit; strictly speaking, they are neither attempts to describe nor attempts to change the world.

Another dimension by which the four language uses can be classified is their *sincerity condition*. Each use of language has an associated mental state. For informatives it is belief. For directives it is desire or wanting; for commissives intention; and for expressives whatever emotion, feeling, or attitude is being expressed. Thus, when I utter an informative, sincerity requires that I believe what I say. If I utter a directive, sincerity requires that I desire what I am trying to get done. If I utter a commissive, I would be insincere if I did not intend to do what I say I shall do.[6] And if I use language expressively, sincerity requires that I actually feel the emotion or attitude being expressed. People are said to be fakes or frauds when they do not.

Finally, we can classify the uses of language by the conditions for their success, or what are called *felicity conditions*. An informative "goes well" or is successful when it is true—that is, when it describes what it purports to describe—or, alternatively, when it is believed or accepted by the person to whom one is speaking. A directive goes well when the person to whom it is addressed complies with it; a commissive goes well when its utterer complies with it; and an expressive is successful when it facilitates the release of whatever feeling, attitude, or emotion is being expressed (or, since expressives can be evocative, when a certain feeling, attitude, or emotion is evoked in one's audience). As you can see, the conditions under which a particular use of language is successful vary considerably. This provides additional support for our claim at the outset of this section that language is complex and versatile.

---

[4]   As Locke put it, "Nothing can make any Man [a member of a commonwealth], but his actually entering into it by positive Engagement, and express Promise and Compact." John Locke, *Two Treatises of Government*, rev. ed., ed. Peter Laslett (1965), p. 394 (second treatise, chapter VIII, section 122).

[5]   The terms "direction of fit," "sincerity condition," and "felicity condition" are taken from Searle in the work cited in a previous footnote. J. L. Austin introduced the notion of a felicitous utterance. See J. L. Austin, *How to Do Things with Words*, 2d ed., eds. J. O. Urmson and Marina Sbisà (1975), p. 14. The remaining paragraphs of this section are indebted to Searle's analysis.

[6]   This explains what is known as a "lying promise." The person who makes a lying promise does not intend to do what he or she promises to do.

The following chart summarizes the dimensions just described:

Use or Function	Direction of Fit	Sincerity Condition	Felicity Condition
Informative	Word to world	Belief	Truth or acceptance
Expressive	None	Whatever is expressed	Release or evocation
Directive	World to word	Desire/want	Hearer's compliance
Commissive	World to word	Intention	Speaker's compliance

2.2 DISCOURSE SERVING MULTIPLE FUNCTIONS

In the preceding section the examples presented were chemically pure specimens, so to speak, of the four basic kinds of communication. The fourfold division proposed is illuminating and valuable, but it cannot be applied mechanically, because almost every ordinary communication exemplifies more than one use of language. Thus a poem, which is primarily expressive discourse, may have a moral and be in effect a command to the reader (or hearer) to lead a different kind of life, and may also convey a certain amount of information. On the other hand, although a sermon may be predominantly directive, seeking to cause certain appropriate action by members of the congregation (whether to abandon their evil ways, or to contribute money to the church, or what-not), it may express and evoke sentiments, thus serving the expressive function, and may also include some information, such as the glad tidings of the Gospels. A scientific treatise, essentially informative, may express something of the writer's own enthusiasm, thus serving an expressive function, and may also, at least implicitly, serve some directive function or other; perhaps bidding the reader to verify independently the author's conclusion. Less esoterically, if, while on a crowded bus, I whisper through clenched teeth to a nearby passenger, "You're standing on my foot," I have (1) informed the passenger of something, (2) expressed pain (and perhaps anger), and (3) directed the passenger to remove his or her foot—all in the same utterance. Most ordinary uses of language are mixed.

It is not always the result of confusion on the part of the speaker when language serves mixed or multiple functions. It is rather the case that effective communication demands certain combinations of functions. Few of us stand to each other in the relation of parent to child or employer to employee. And outside the context of such formal relationships as these, one cannot simply issue an order with any expectation of having it obeyed. Consequently a certain indirection must be employed: A bald command might arouse antagonism or resentment and be self-defeating. Ordinarily one cannot cause action merely by voicing an imperative; it is necessary to use a more subtle method of stimulating the desired action.

Action may be said to have complex causes. Motivation is more properly to be discussed by psychologists than logicians, but it is common knowledge that actions usually involve both desires and beliefs. People who desire to eat food will not touch what is on their plates unless they believe it to be food; and even though they believe it to be food, they will not touch it unless they desire to eat. This fact is relevant to our present discussion because desires are a special type of what we have been calling attitudes.

Consequently, actions may be caused by evoking appropriate attitudes and communicating relevant information. Assuming your listeners to be benevolent, you may cause them to contribute to a given charity by informing them of its effectiveness in accomplishing benevolent results. In such a case your use of language is ultimately directive, since its purpose is to cause action. But a naked command would be far less effective in this situation than the informative discourse used. Suppose, on the other hand, that your listeners already are persuaded that the charity in question does accomplish benevolent results. Here again you cannot simply command with any great hope of being obeyed, but you may succeed in causing them to act in the desired fashion by somehow arousing a sufficiently benevolent feeling or emotion in them. The discourse you use to realize your end is expressive discourse; you must make a "moving appeal." Thus your language will have a mixed use, functioning both expressively and directively. Or, finally, let us suppose that you are seeking a donation from people who have neither a benevolent attitude nor a belief that the charity serves a benevolent purpose. Here you must use both informative and expressive language. In such a case the language used serves three of the four functions, being directive, informative and expressive all at once, not accidentally as a mere mixture that just happens to occur, but essentially, as necessary for successful communication.

We can easily imagine a single utterance that combines all four language functions. Suppose I tell a group of children that lying is wrong. I have simultaneously (1) told them how things are (the informative function), (2) tried to get them to do or refrain from doing something (the directive function), (3) expressed a negative attitude toward something or someone (the expressive function), and (4) committed myself to doing or refraining from doing something (the commissive function). Specifically, I have (1) told the children that lying is wrong, (2) tried to get them not to lie (or to tell the truth, or both), (3) expressed a negative attitude toward lies and liars, and (4) committed myself to not lying (or to telling the truth, or both). Moral judgments such as this appear to perform a variety of functions, which may explain their continuing attraction to philosophers.[7]

Another interesting and important mixed use of language is that which often has been called the *ceremonial.* Included within this category are many different kinds of phrases, ranging from relatively trivial words of greeting to the more portentous discourse of the marriage ceremony, phrasings of state documents, and the verbal rituals performed on holy days in houses of worship. These can all be regarded as mixtures of expressive, directive, and commissive discourse rather than as some altogether different and unique kind. For example, the usual ceremonial greetings and chitchat at social gatherings serve the purpose of expressing and evoking goodwill and sociability. Perhaps for some speakers they are intended also to serve the directive purpose of

---

[7] For a sophisticated analysis of moral judgments along these lines, see R. M. Hare, *The Language of Morals* (1952).

causing their hearers to act in certain definite ways, to patronize the speaker's business, to offer employment or an invitation to dinner. At the other extreme, the impressive language of the marriage ceremony is intended to emphasize the solemnity of the occasion (its expressive function) and also to cause the bride and groom to perform in their new roles with heightened appreciation of the seriousness of the marriage contract (its directive function). Moreover, the words uttered by the parties ("I do") serve to commit them to each other and to various courses of conduct.

Not all ceremonial uses of language are recognized as such. Thus, John Kenneth Galbraith (1908–) wrote in *The Affluent Society:*

> In some measure the articulation of the conventional wisdom is a religious rite. It is an act of affirmation like reading aloud from the Scriptures or going to church. The business executive listening to a luncheon address on the virtues of free enterprise and the evils of Washington is already persuaded, and so are his fellow listeners, and all are secure in their convictions. Indeed, although a display of rapt attention is required, the executive may not feel it necessary to listen. But he does placate the gods by participating in the ritual. Having been present, maintained attention, and having applauded, he can depart feeling that the economic system is a little more secure. Scholars gather in scholarly assemblages to hear in elegant statement what all have heard before. Yet it is not a negligible rite, for its purpose is not to convey knowledge but to beatify learning and the learned.

It has been suggested that the language used in legal contracts performs a similar ceremonial function—specifically, the function of impressing on the parties the solemnity and importance of their joint undertaking.[8]

There is still another use of language that is somewhat akin to the ceremonial. When the minister or justice of the peace says at the end of the marriage ceremony, "I now pronounce you husband and wife," though the words may seem merely to report what the speaker is doing, their utterance actually constitutes the doing of it. Here is an instance of the performative use of language. A *performative utterance* is one that is uttered in appropriate circumstances to do precisely what it appears to report or describe. Such performative utterances involve what may be called performative verbs, where a *performative verb* is one that denotes an action that in appropriate circumstances is typically accomplished by using that verb in the first person. Obvious examples of performative verbs are "accept," "advise," "apologize," "christen," "congratulate," "offer," "promise," and "suggest." The performative function of language is only one among others, but perhaps it merits special mention because it seems to fit less well than the others into our fourfold division of language functions.[9]

This section would be incomplete without at least a mention of nonverbal symbols—those that are not in words.[10] Just as the sentence "Watch out for the divers" can function, in appropriate circumstances, to inform (that there are divers in the vicini-

---

[8]   See Lon L. Fuller, "Consideration and Form," *Columbia Law Review* 41 (1941).

[9]   The notions of performative utterance and the performative verb were first developed by J. L. Austin; see his *How to Do Things with Words*, 2d ed., eds. J. O. Urmson and Marina Sbisà (1975).

[10]   The word "verbal" is sometimes used to mean "oral" or "spoken," as in, "We made a verbal agreement." In this context we use it more broadly, to mean "in or of words." Thus, there are two kinds of verbal communication: that which is oral and that which is written.

ty), direct (people to stay clear), and express (concern for the safety of the divers), so can the nonverbal symbol "▱." Not all of our communication is in words. Other symbols that function in one or more of the ways discussed in this and the previous section are stop signs (as well as other traffic-control devices), the universal negation symbol "⊘," honking horns, clenched fists, and the ubiquitous pointed finger. As an exercise, describe a common nonverbal symbol, fill in the context, and state the symbol's function or functions in that context.

2.3   FORMS OF DISCOURSE

Textbooks of grammar commonly define a sentence as the unit of language that expresses a complete thought and divides sentences into four categories, usually called declarative, interrogative, imperative, and exclamatory. As traditionally understood, a declarative sentence is one in which the subject appears first, followed by the verb (and sometimes an object). An example is "Cecil Fielder hit the baseball over the fence." An interrogative sentence contains an inverted subject and verb, as in "Did Cecil Fielder hit a home run?" and typically ends with a question mark. An imperative sentence is one in which the subject is omitted—for example, "Wash the dishes before you go to bed." An exclamatory sentence ends with an exclamation mark.[11]

These four grammatical categories do not coincide with those of assertions, questions, commands, and exclamations. We may be tempted to identify form with function—to think that declarative sentences and informative discourse coincide, and that exclamatory sentences are suitable only for expressive discourse. Regarding questions as requests for answers, we may be led further to think that directive discourse consists exclusively of sentences in the interrogative and imperative moods. Were such identifications possible, it would immensely simplify the problem of communication, for then we should be able to tell the intended use or function of a passage by its form, which is open to direct inspection. Some people apparently do identify form with function, but these are not sensitive readers, for the identification often makes them misunderstand what is said or done, and they miss the point of much that is to be communicated.

It is a mistake to believe that everything in the form of a declarative sentence is informative discourse, to be valued if true and rejected if false. "I had a very nice time at your party" is a declarative sentence, but its function need not be informative at all, but rather ceremonial or expressive, expressing a feeling of friendliness and appreciation. Many poems and prayers are in the form of declarative sentences, despite the fact that their functions are not informative. To consider them as simply informative and to evaluate them as simply true or false would be to shut oneself off from many valuable aesthetic and religious experiences. Again, many requests and commands are stated indirectly—perhaps more gently—by means of declarative sentences. The declarative sentence "I would like some coffee" should not be taken by a waiter to be a mere report of the psychological fact it apparently asserts about the customer, but as

[11]   For a discussion of these and other grammatical categories, see Jerrold M. Sadock, *Toward a Linguistic Theory of Speech Acts* (1974), pp. 111–46; and F. R. Palmer, *Semantics,* 2d ed. (1981), pp. 149–54.

an order, a request for action. Similarly, the declarative sentence "I'll stop by after work" does more than inform; it functions as a commissive. Were we invariably to judge the truth or falsehood of declarative sentences such as "I'd appreciate some help with this" or "I hope you'll be able to meet me after class at the library," and do no more than register them as information received, we should soon be without friends. These examples should suffice to show that the declarative form is no certain indication of the informative function. Declarative sentences lend themselves to the formulation of every kind of discourse.

It is the same with other forms of sentences. The interrogative sentence "Do you realize that we're almost late?" is not necessarily a request for information but may be a command to hurry. The interrogative sentence "Isn't it true that Russia and Germany signed a pact in 1939 that brought on the Second World War?" may not be a question at all but either an oblique way of communicating information (what is known as a rhetorical question) or an attempt to express and evoke a feeling of hostility toward Russia, functioning informatively in the first instance and expressively in the second. Even a grammatical imperative, as in official documents beginning "Know all men by these presents that . . .," may not be a command but rather informative discourse in what it asserts and expressive discourse in its use of language to evoke the appropriate feelings of solemnity and respect. In spite of its close affinity to the expressive, an exclamatory sentence may serve a quite different function. The exclamation "Good Lord, it's late!" may really communicate a command to hurry. And the exclamation "What a beautiful view!" uttered by a realtor to a potential customer may be intended to function much more directively than expressively.

It should be remembered that some discourse is intended to serve two, three, or possibly all four functions of language at once. In such cases each aspect or function of a given passage is subject to its own proper criteria. One having an informative function may have that aspect evaluated as true or false. The same passage serving a directive function may have that aspect evaluated as proper or improper, right or wrong—and as we saw in section 2.1, it may be either complied with or not complied with. The same is true of commissives. And if there is an expressive function served by the passage in question, that component may be evaluated as sincere or insincere, as valuable or otherwise. To evaluate a given passage properly requires knowledge of the function or functions it is intended to serve.

Truth and falsehood, and the related notions of correctness and incorrectness of argument, are more important in the study of logic than the others mentioned. Hence, as students of logic, we must be able to differentiate discourse that functions informatively from that which does not. And we must be able further to disentangle the informative function a given passage serves from whatever other functions it may also be serving. To do this "disentangling," we must know what different functions language can serve and be able to tell them apart. The grammatical structure of a passage may serve as a clue to its function, but, as we have seen, there is no *necessary* connection between function and grammatical form. Nor is there any strict relation between the function and the content of a sentence—in the sense of what might seem to be asserted by a passage. This is shown by an example of Leonard Bloomfield's (1887–1949) in his chapter entitled "Meaning": "A petulant child, at bedtime, says *I'm hungry,* and his mother, who is up to his tricks, answers by packing him off to bed. This is an example of displaced speech."[12] The child's speech is directive—even though it does not succeed in procuring the wanted diversion. By the function of a passage we mean the intended function. But that, unfortunately, is not always easy to determine.

When a passage is quoted in isolation, it often is difficult to determine what language function the passage is primarily intended to serve. The reason for the difficulty is that context is extremely important in determining the answer to such a question. What is imperative or flatly informative, by itself, may in its proper context function expressively, as part of a larger whole whose poetic effect is derived from all its parts in their arrangement. For example, in isolation,

> Come to the window.

is an imperative serving the directive function; and

> The sea is calm tonight.

is a declarative sentence serving an informative function. But both are from Matthew Arnold's (1822–88) poem "Dover Beach," and in that context contribute to the poem's expressive function.

It is important also to distinguish between the proposition that a sentence formulates and some fact about the speaker for which the utterance of that sentence is evidence. When a person remarks, "It is raining," the proposition asserted is about the weather, not about the speaker. Yet, because the sincerity condition of an informative is belief, making the assertion is evidence that the speaker believes it to be raining, which is a fact about the speaker. It also may happen that people make statements that are ostensibly about their beliefs, not for the sake of giving information about themselves, but simply as a way of saying something else. To say "I believe that gold is valuable" is ordinarily not to be construed as a psychological or autobiographical report on the beliefs of the speaker, but simply a way of saying that gold is valuable. Similarly, since the sincerity condition of a directive is desire, voicing a command usually is evidence that the speaker has a certain desire; and under appropriate circumstances to assert that one has such and such a desire is to give a command. To utter an exclamation of joy gives evidence that the speaker is joyful, although the speaker makes no assertion in the process. On the other hand, to present a psychological report that affirms that the speaker is joyful is to assert a proposition, something quite different from exclaiming joyously.

In section 1.4 the problem of recognizing arguments was discussed. The difference between an argument and an explanation was noted, and it was remarked that their difference depended, to a considerable extent, on the intentions of the speaker or writer. We can now look a little more deeply into the matter. Consider the following letter to the editor that was published in *The Honolulu Advertiser* (6 March 1984, p. A-9):

---

[12]   Leonard Bloomfield, *Language* (1933).

I oppose the idea of holding prayer in our public schools. First of all, parents have ample opportunity to hold prayer in their homes, if this is what they wish to do. Also, they are free to send their children to a religious school of their choice.

It is doubtful that a prayer could be composed that would be acceptable to all the various religious groups in our community, and in any case, it is not a proper function of the state to devise prayers that its citizens are obligated to use.

It would be equally inappropriate if the Sunday schools were to attempt to teach the "three R's." The public schools and the religious schools were each designed with a specific purpose in mind and each should confine itself to its own area of expertise. Our Constitution has wisely declared that there should be no connection between church and state. For the sake of everyone's freedom, let's keep it that way.

The letter begins with the statement "I oppose the idea of holding prayer in our public schools." This is not a simple autobiographical report of what the writer supports or opposes, as would be appropriate if she were being interviewed as a public figure whose likes and dislikes might be a matter of popular concern, or as a subject having a psychological profile constructed by a social scientist. If it were, the rest of the letter could be taken as explaining why she opposes school prayer. Instead, the beginning statement is the writer's way of saying that *it is a bad idea to hold prayer in our public schools* or that *we should oppose it.* One can tell that by the several judgmental remarks in what follows the first sentence, such as "it is not a proper function of the state to . . .," "It would be equally inappropriate . . .," "each [of the public schools and the religious schools] should confine itself to its own area of expertise," and the final exhortation "let's keep it that way." The letter is *not* an explanation of why the writer opposes school prayer, but an argument intended to persuade her readers that school prayer is a bad thing. Her intention is not to explain her own feelings but to persuade others to share them.

This is not to accuse the writer of any kind of deception or subterfuge. Her language is entirely appropriate. The first sentence of her letter is a perfectly legitimate method of announcing the conclusion of the extended argument that her letter contains.

In formal logic there are certain techniques that can be applied mechanically to arguments for the purpose of testing their validity. But there is no mechanical technique for recognizing the *presence* of an argument. That is to say, *there is no mechanical method for distinguishing language that is informative and argumentative from language that serves other functions.* This requires thought and demands an awareness of and sensitivity to the flexibility of language and the multiplicity of its uses. It is a skill that people would do well to inculcate in themselves and others.

EXERCISES

I. What language functions are *most probably intended* to be served by each of the following passages? Give reasons for your answers.

■ *1.* Minister: "Do you take this woman to be your lawfully wedded wife?" Groom: "I do."

—Traditional marriage ceremony

2. Heat engines, which convert heat into useful mechanical work, are of two broad types: those in which combustion operates directly on a piston and those in which it operates indirectly by way of an intermediary known as the working fluid.

—JEARL WALKER, "The Amateur Scientist," *Scientific American* 262, January 1990, p. 140

3. As Europe is transformed politically, we must also redraw the military map of the continent and lift some of the shadows and fears that we and our allies have lived with for nearly half a century.

—GEORGE BUSH, quoted in Michael R. Gordon, "Arms Control Catching Up," *The New York Times* 5 October 1990, p. A9

4. Oil. Wherever it is, we'll find it.

—Advertisement for Agip, an Italian oil company

■ **5.** The mystic chords of memory, stretching from every battle-field, and patriot grave, to every living heart and hearthstone, all over this broad land, will yet swell the chorus of the Union, when again touched, as surely they will be, by the better angels of our nature.

—ABRAHAM LINCOLN, first inaugural address, 4 March 1861, in *Abraham Lincoln: Mystic Chords of Memory*, ed. Larry Shapiro (1984), pp. 41–42

6. The atrocious crime of being a young man, which the honorable gentleman has with such spirit and decency charged upon me, I shall neither attempt to palliate nor deny; but content myself with wishing that I may be one of those whose follies may cease with their youth, and not of that number who are ignorant in spite of experience.

—WILLIAM PITT, speech in the House of Commons

7. The only thing necessary for the triumph of evil is for good men to do nothing.

—EDMUND BURKE, letter to William Smith

8. Pleasure is an actual and legitimate aim, but if anyone says that it is the only thing men are interested in, he invites the old and legitimate reply that much of the pleasure they actually get would have been impossible unless they had desired something else. If men have found pleasure in fox-hunting, it is only because for the time they could forget about hunting pleasure, and hunt foxes.

—BRAND BLANSHARD, *The Nature of Thought*

9. Human history becomes more and more a race between education and catastrophe.

—H. G. WELLS, *The Outline of History*

■ **10.** We must all hang together or assuredly we shall all hang separately.

—BENJAMIN FRANKLIN, to the other signers of the Declaration of Independence

11. A little philosophy inclineth man's mind to atheism; but depth in philosophy bringeth man's mind about to religion.

—FRANCIS BACON, *Essays*

12. You'll never have a quiet world until you knock the patriotism out of the human race.

—GEORGE BERNARD SHAW, *O'Flaherty*, V.C.

13. The story of the whale swallowing Jonah, though a whale is large enough to do it, borders greatly on the marvelous; but it would have approached nearer to the idea of miracle if Jonah had swallowed the whale.

—THOMAS PAINE, *The Age of Reason*

14. That all particular appetites and passions are toward *external things themselves,* distinct from the *pleasure arising from them,* is manifested from hence—that there could not be this pleasure were it not for that prior suitableness between the object and the passion; there could be no enjoyment or delight from one thing more than another, from eating food more than from swallowing a stone, if there were not an affection or appetite to one thing more than another.

—JOSEPH BUTLER, sermon "Upon the Love of Our Neighbor"

■ *15.* Of this man Pickwick I will say little; the subject presents but few attractions; and I, gentlemen, am not the man, nor are you, gentlemen, the men, to delight in the contemplation of revolting heartlessness, and of systematic villainy.

—CHARLES DICKENS, *Pickwick Papers*

16. We do ask that you fasten your seatbelts.

—FLIGHT ATTENDANT

II. For each of the following passages, indicate what propositions they may be intended to assert, if any; what overt actions they may be intended to cause, if any; what commitments the speaker is making, if any; and what they may be regarded as providing evidence for about the speaker, if anything.

■ *1.* The government in its wisdom considers ice a "food product." This means that Antarctica is one of the world's foremost food producers.

—GEORGE F. WILL, "Government, Economy Linked"

2. Of what use is political liberty to those who have no bread? It is of value only to ambitious theorists and politicians.

—JEAN PAUL MARAT

3. While there is a lower class I am in it, while there is a criminal element I am of it, and while there is a soul in prison I am not free.

—EUGENE DEBS

4. There are three classes of citizens. The first are the rich, who are indolent and yet always crave more. The second are the poor, who have nothing, are full of envy, hate the rich, and are easily led by demagogues. Between the two extremes lie those who make the state secure and uphold the laws.

—EURIPEDES, *The Suppliant Women*

■ *5.* I am convinced that turbulence as well as every other evil temper of this evil age belong not to the lower but to the middle classes—those middle classes of whom in our folly we are so wont to boast.

—LORD ROBERT CECIL, *Diary in Australia*

6. I would rather that the people should wonder why I wasn't President than why I am.

—SALMON P. CHASE

7. He [Benjamin Disraeli] is a self-made man, and worships his creator.

—JOHN BRIGHT

8. Even a fool, when he holdeth his peace, is counted wise; And he that shutteth his lips is esteemed as a man of understanding.

—Proverbs 17:28

9. A word fitly spoken is like apples of gold in settings of silver.

—Proverbs 25:11

■ *10.* When people who are tolerably fortunate in their outward lot do not find in life sufficient enjoyment to make it valuable to them, the cause generally is, caring for nobody but themselves.

—JOHN STUART MILL, *Utilitarianism*

III. Think of four sentences—one declarative in form, one interrogative in form, one imperative in form, and one exclamatory in form—that, in appropriate circumstances, can be used informatively. Do the same for each of the other three language functions: expressives, directives, and commissives. The result will be a four-by-four diagram containing sixteen sentences.

2.4 EMOTIVE WORDS

We already have seen that a single sentence can serve an informative as well as an expressive function. For the sentence to formulate a proposition, its words must have descriptive or cognitive meaning, referring to objects or events and their attributes or relations. When it expresses an attitude or feeling, however, some of its words also may have an emotional suggestiveness or impact. A word or phrase can have both a descriptive meaning and an emotional impact. It has become customary to speak of the latter as "emotive significance" or "emotive meaning." There is a high degree of independence between the descriptive and emotive meanings of a word. For example, the terms "bureaucrat," "government official," and "public servant" have almost identical descriptive meanings. But their emotive meanings are different. The term "bureaucrat" tends to express resentment and disapproval, while the term "public servant" is an honorific one, that tends to express favor and approval. The phrase "government official" is more neutral than either of the others.

As John Kenneth Galbraith put it in *The Affluent Society,*

The notion of a vested interest has an engaging flexibility in our social usage. In ordinary intercourse it is an improper advantage enjoyed by a political minority to which the speaker does not himself belong. When the speaker himself enjoys it, it ceases to be a vested interest and becomes a hard-won reward. When a vested interest is enjoyed not by a minority but by a majority, it is a human right.

It is important to realize that one and the same thing can be referred to by words that have different emotive impacts. It might be thought that the emotive impact of a word is always connected with some quality of its referent. As William Shakespeare (1564–1616) wrote,

What's in a name? That which we call a rose
By any other name would smell as sweet.

It is true that the fragrance of roses would be the same through any change of name we might assign them. But our attitude toward them would very likely change if we began to refer to roses as, say, "skunkweeds." An illustration of this kind of connection between attitude and vocabulary was reported by Harold J. Laski (1893–1950) in a letter to Bertrand Russell (1872–1970):

> I find that when one presents the student-mind with syndicalism or socialism namelessly they take it as reasonable and obvious; attach the name and they whisper to the parents that nameless abominations are being perpetrated.

Changes in the other direction are familiar: Purveyors of canned horse mackerel sell much more of their product now that they call it tunafish. As a popular syndicated columnist recently wrote:

> Americans have a genius for inventing new phrases to replace old ones with which we are no longer comfortable. Undertakers became morticians. Janitors became maintenance men. Old people became senior citizens. Lie detector experts are in the process of becoming truth verifiers. The reality doesn't change; only our way of describing it.[13]

Not only Americans have this "genius." In Harold Nicolson's (1886–1968) diary during World War II, he made the following entry:

> I notice that when we get on both sides of an enemy, that enemy is described as "surrounded," but when the enemy gets on both sides of us, we are told that we have driven "a wedge" between his two armies.[14]

More recently, when the United States invaded Grenada in 1983, the campaign was described by the Pentagon as a "pre-dawn vertical insertion."[15]

This flight from less comfortable terms to more comfortable ones can have only the most temporary success. As Germaine Greer (1939–) wrote in *The Female Eunuch,*

> It is the fate of euphemisms to lose their function rapidly by association with the actuality of what they designate, so that they must be regularly replaced with euphemisms for themselves.

The story is told that some of her friends told President Harry Truman's (1884–1972) wife that she should try to stop him from saying "manure," to which she replied that it had taken her forty years to get him to *start* saying "manure."

---

[13]   Ernest Conine, *Los Angeles Service,* 6 April 1975.
[14]   Harold Nicolson, *The War Years,* Volume II of *Diaries and Letters,* ed. Nigel Nicolson (1967).
[15]   Lloyd Shearer, "Intelligence Report," *Parade,* 24 September 1989 (quoting William Lutz, author of *Doublespeak*).

It has been said that language has a life of its own independent of the facts it is used to describe. In our terminology, words can have exactly the same descriptive meanings and yet be either moderately or completely opposite in their emotive suggestiveness or meaning. Certain physiological activities pertaining to reproduction and elimination can be unemotionally described, using a medical vocabulary, without offending the most squeamish taste; but all of these terms have certain four-letter synonyms whose usage shocks all but the most hardened listeners. A writer has reported

> the illuminating story of a little girl who, having recently learned to read, was spelling out a political article in the newspaper. "Father," she asked, "what is Tammany Hall?" And her father replied in the voice usually reserved for the taboos of social communication, "You'll understand that when you grow up, my dear." Acceding to this adult whim of evasion, she desisted from her inquiries; but something in Daddy's tone had convinced her that Tammany Hall must be connected with illicit *amour,* and for many years she could not hear this political institution mentioned without experiencing a secret non-political thrill.[16]

The emotive meaning of a word may be acquired by association, but these associations need not always be with the word's referent.

An instructive joke based on the contrast between descriptive and emotive meaning was made by the philosopher Bertrand Russell when he "conjugated" an "irregular verb" as

> I am firm: you are obstinate;
> he is a pig-headed fool.

The London *New Statesman and Nation* subsequently ran a contest soliciting such irregular conjugations and picked among the winners the following:

> I am righteously indignant; you are annoyed;
> he is making a fuss about nothing.
> I have reconsidered it; you have changed your mind;
> he has gone back on his word.

In his lively book entitled *How to Think Straight,* Robert Thouless (1894–1984) made an experiment designed to show the importance of emotively colored words in poetry. There he examined two lines from Keats's "The Eve of St. Agnes":

> Full on this casement shone the wintry moon,
> And threw warm gules on Madeline's fair breast.

He proposed to show that their beauty arises primarily from the proper choice of emotionally colored words, by showing how that beauty is lost completely if those words are

---

[16] Margaret Schlauch, *The Gift of Tongues* (1942).

replaced by neutral ones. Selecting the words "casement," "gules," "Madeline," "fair," and "breast," Thouless wrote:

> *Casement* means simply a kind of window with emotional and romantic associations. *Gules* is the heraldic name for red, with the suggestion of romance which accompanies all heraldry. *Madeline* is simply a girl's name, but one calling out favorable emotions absent from a relatively plain and straightforward name. *Fair* simply means, in objective fact, that her skin was white or uncolored—a necessary condition for the colors of the window to show—but also fair implies warm emotional preference for an uncolored skin rather than one which is yellow, purple, black, or any of the other colors which skin might be. *Breast* also has similar emotional meanings, and the aim of scientific description might have been equally well attained if it had been replaced by such a neutral word as *chest*.
>
> Let us now try the experiment of keeping these two lines in a metrical form, but replacing all the emotionally-colored words by neutral ones, while making as few other changes as possible. We may write:
>
> Full on this window shone the wintry moon,
> Making red marks on Jane's uncolored chest.
>
> No one will doubt that all of its poetic value has been knocked out of the passage by these changes. Yet the lines still mean the same in external fact; they still have the same objective meaning. It is only the emotional meaning which has been destroyed.[17]

To the extent that humorous impact is to be included in emotive meaning, the revised lines of "poetry" have considerable emotive meaning, though very different from that possessed by the original verses.

EXERCISES

1. Give five original "conjugations of irregular verbs" where the same activity is given a laudatory description in the first person, a neutral one in the second person, and a derogatory one in the third person.

2. Select two brief passages of poetry and perform Thouless's "experiment" on them.

2.5   KINDS OF AGREEMENT AND DISAGREEMENT

The "irregular verb" conjugations mentioned in the preceding section make one thing abundantly clear. The same state of affairs can be described in different words that express widely divergent attitudes toward it. And to the extent that anything can

---

[17]   Robert H. Thouless, *How to Think Straight* (1939).

be described by means of alternative phrases—one of which expresses an attitude of approval, another an attitude of disapproval, still another a more or less neutral attitude—there are different kinds of agreement and disagreement that can be communicated about any situation or activity.

Two people may disagree as to whether something is or was the case, and when they do they may be said to have *disagreement in belief.* On the other hand, they may agree that an event has actually occurred, thus agreeing in belief, and yet they may have strongly divergent or even opposite attitudes toward it. One who approves of it will describe it in language that expresses approval; the other may choose terms that express disapproval. There is disagreement here, but it is not disagreement in belief as to what occurred. The disagreement is rather a difference in feeling about the matter, a *disagreement in attitude.*[18]

With respect to any matter, two persons may agree in belief and disagree in attitude, or they may agree in both belief and attitude. It is also possible for people to agree in attitude despite disagreeing in belief. One may believe that so-and-so has reconsidered a question and changed his position and so praise him for "listening to the voice of reason"; whereas the other may believe that he has *not* changed his mind and praise him for "refusing to be swayed by blandishment." This third kind of situation often occurs in politics; people may support the same candidate for different and even incompatible reasons. A fourth possibility exists in which the disagreement is complete. One speaker, believing that so-and-so has changed her mind, may strongly approve of her for having wisely reconsidered the matter, whereas the second speaker, believing that she has *not* changed her mind, may just as vigorously disapprove of her for being too pigheaded to admit her mistake. Here we have disagreement in belief and also disagreement in attitude.

If we are interested in the problem of resolving disagreements, it is vitally important to realize that agreement and disagreement may relate not only to the facts in a given case, but to attitudes toward those facts. Different methods are applicable to the resolution of different kinds of disagreement, and if we are unclear as to what kind of disagreement exists we shall be unclear as to what methods should be utilized. If the disagreement is in belief, it can be resolved by ascertaining the facts. In the preceding instances, the factual question is whether so-and-so at one time held a certain view and at a later time held a different view, or whether at the later time he or she still maintained the earlier view. To decide the question—were it of sufficient importance—the usual techniques for verification could be utilized: Witnesses could be questioned, documents consulted, records examined, and so on. Theoretically, the facts could be established and the issue decided, and this would resolve the disagreement. The methods of scientific inquiry are available here, and it suffices to direct them squarely at the question of fact about which there is disagreement in belief.

On the other hand, if there is disagreement in attitude rather than disagreement in belief, the techniques appropriate to settling it are rather different, being more varied and less direct. To call witnesses, consult documents, or the like, to the end of

---

[18]   We are indebted to Professor Charles L. Stevenson for the terms agreement and disagreement "in belief" and agreement and disagreement "in attitude," and also for the notion of persuasive definition, which will be discussed in chapter 4. See his *Ethics and Language* (1944).

establishing either that the person held two different views on two different occasions or that he or she held the same view on the two occasions, would be fruitless in the case of this type of disagreement. What may be regarded as the facts of the case are not at issue; the disagreement is not over what the facts *are* but over how they are to be valued. A serious attempt to resolve this disagreement in attitude may involve reference to many factual questions—but not the one mentioned so far. Instead, it may be fruitful to consider what results or consequences follow from the action in question and what would have resulted from this or that alternative course of action. Questions of motive and of intention are of great importance here. These are factual questions, to be sure, but none of them is identical with what would be the issue if the disagreement were in belief rather than in attitude. Still other methods are available to resolve a disagreement in attitude. Nonrational persuasion may be attempted, with its extensive use of expressive discourse. Rhetoric may be of paramount utility in unifying the will of a group, in achieving unanimity of attitude. But of course it is wholly worthless in resolving a question of fact.

A word of warning is appropriate here. Such words as "good," "bad," "right," and "wrong" occur frequently in the writings of moral philosophers. There is no doubt that these terms, in their strictly ethical uses, tend to have very strong emotive impacts. It could scarcely be denied that to characterize an action as *right*, or a situation as *good*, is to express an attitude of approval toward it, whereas to characterize it as *wrong* or as *bad* is to express an attitude of disapproval. Some writers on ethics deny that these terms have any literal or cognitive meaning; only emotive meaning is allowed them. Other writers on ethics vigorously insist that they have cognitive meaning, and refer to objective characteristics of what is being discussed. In this quarrel the student of logic need not take sides. It must be insisted, however, that not every attitude of approval or disapproval implies a moral judgment. Besides moral values there are aesthetic values, and beyond these two important categories there are surely other types, personal preferences that reflect only matters of taste. A negative attitude, say toward a particular style of dress or dessert, need not involve either ethical or aesthetic judgment. Yet such attitudes exist and often are given verbal expression.

Where disagreement is in attitude rather than in belief, the most vigorous—and, of course, genuine—disagreement may be expressed in statements that are literally true, at least so far as their informative content is concerned. An illuminating example of this is reported by Lincoln Steffens (1866–1936) in his autobiography. Shortly after the turn of the century, Steffens, in his capacity as a muckraker, went to Milwaukee to prepare an exposé of "that demagogue," Robert La Follette (1855–1925), then governor of Wisconsin. Steffens called first on a banker, who said that La Follette was "a crooked hypocrite who stirred up the people with socialist anarchist ideas and hurt business." Steffens asked the banker for evidence and described what ensued as follows:

> . . . the banker set out to demonstrate . . . hypocrisy, socialism-anarchism, etc., and he was going fast and hot till I realized that my witness had more feeling than facts; or if he had facts, he could not handle them. He would start with some act of La Follette and blow up in a rage. He certainly hated the man, but I could not write rage.[19]

---

[19]   Lincoln Steffens, *The Autobiography of Lincoln Steffens* (1931).

Steffens's conversation with the banker was interrupted by the arrival of an attorney, who was prepared to present the "evidence" against La Follette. Steffens's account proceeds:

> When I told him how far we had got, the banker and I, and how I wanted first the proofs of the dishonesty alleged, he said: "Oh, no, no. You are getting off wrong. La Follette isn't dishonest. On the contrary, the man is dangerous precisely because he is so sincere. He's a fanatic."

We may remark that the third possibility mentioned previously is perfectly exemplified in the present example. There was disagreement in belief between the banker and the lawyer on the question of La Follette's honesty. But this factual question was completely overshadowed by that of attitude. Here there was vigorous agreement. Both disapproved of La Follette and his actions: curiously enough, the banker because the governor was "a crooked hypocrite," the lawyer because the governor was "so sincere." Then the lawyer got down to cases. His motive here was to achieve agreement with Steffens. The report continues:

> The attorney, with the banker sitting by frowning, impatient, presented in good order the charges against La Follette, the measures he had furthered, the legislation passed and proposed, his political methods. Horrified himself at the items on his list and alarmed over the policy and the power of this demagogue, he delivered the indictment with emotion, force, eloquence. The only hitch was that Bob La Follette's measures seemed fair to me, his methods democratic, his purposes right but moderate, and his fighting strength and spirit hopeful and heroic.

What happened here was that the lawyer's statement of the facts, which presumably Steffens agreed with the lawyer in believing, was not sufficient to produce the kind of agreement in attitude that the lawyer desired. Steffens's attitude toward those facts was altogether different from the lawyer's. Adducing more evidence that the facts actually were as described would not have brought the two men a hair's breadth nearer to agreement—in attitude. The lawyer's "emotion, force, eloquence" were relevant but not sufficient. What the lawyer regarded as newfangled innovations and radical departures from established order, Steffens tended to regard as progressive improvements and the elimination of antiquated prejudice. Both would agree on the fact that change was involved. But their evaluations were different. The reverse was the case with the lawyer and the banker. Their evaluations were the same, even though they disagreed on the factual question of whether La Follette was hypocritical or sincere.

The lesson we may draw from these considerations is simple but important. When two parties appear to disagree and formulate their divergent views in statements that are logically consistent with each other, both being perhaps true in fact, it would be a mistake to say that the parties do not "really" disagree or that their disagreement is "merely verbal." They are not merely "saying the same thing in different words." They may, of course, be using their words to affirm what is the same fact, but they also may be using their words to express conflicting attitudes toward that fact. In such a case their disagreement, although not *factual,* is nevertheless *genuine.* It is not "merely verbal," because words function expressively as well as informatively. And if we are interested in resolving disagreements, we must be clear about their nature, since the techniques appropriate to the resolution of one kind of disagreement may be hopelessly beside the point for another.

Here is an example that shows the complexity of what appears to be a simple disagreement. Suppose Kyle and Kendra are having a discussion of the morality of killing after having learned that one of their townspeople, Jones, killed another, Smith. Kyle says: "Killing is wrong unless it's done in self-defense, and since Jones was acting in self-defense at the time of the killing, Jones did not act wrongly." Kendra responds: "Killing is always wrong, even if done in self-defense; therefore, despite the fact that Jones acted in self-defense, Jones acted wrongly."

Let us assume, to simplify the analysis, that Kyle and Kendra are being sincere— that each of them believes what he or she says. (Otherwise we have no basis for determining what they believe!) To what extent do Kyle and Kendra agree and disagree in belief? First, Kyle believes (because he says) that killings done in self-defense are not wrong; Kendra denies this, for her expressed belief is that even killings done in self-defense are wrong. So Kyle and Kendra have a disagreement in belief concerning the wrongness of self-defense killings. As to other killings, however, they agree; both believe that such killings are wrong. Second, both Kyle and Kendra believe that Jones killed Smith in self-defense; they have an agreement in belief on this factual matter. Third, Kyle believes that Jones did not act wrongly in killing Smith, but Kendra disagrees, believing that Jones did act wrongly. As this example shows, two people can have a partial agreement in belief on the same general subject.

Moving on to agreements and disagreements in attitude, we must make another assumption: that to describe an action as wrong or a person as having acted wrongly is to express a negative attitude, to take an attitude of disapproval toward the action or person. Kyle says (and, given the assumption of sincerity, believes) that killings done in self-defense are not wrong, so he has either a favorable attitude or a neutral attitude toward that class of killings. Kendra, on the other hand, believes that killings done in self-defense are wrong, so she has a negative attitude toward them. Hence, Kyle and Kendra have a disagreement in attitude toward killings done in self-defense. As for other killings, however, Kyle and Kendra agree that they are wrong, so each has a negative attitude toward them. To that extent they have an agreement in attitude. Finally, since Kyle believes that Jones did not act wrongly, he has either a positive attitude or a neutral attitude toward both Jones and Jones's action. Kendra, meanwhile, believes that Jones acted wrongly, so, given our assumption, she has a negative attitude toward both. It follows that Kyle and Kendra have a disagreement in attitude concerning Jones, Jones's action, or both. In principle, every disagreement, moral or otherwise, can be analyzed in this fashion.

Knowledge of the different uses of languages is an aid in discerning what kinds of disagreements may be involved and is thus an aid in resolving them. Drawing the indicated distinctions does not by itself solve the problem or resolve the disagreement, of course. But it clarifies the discussion and reveals the kind and locus of the disagreement. And if it is true that questions can be answered only when they are understood, then the study of the different uses of language is of considerable practical value.

EXERCISES

Identify the kinds of agreement and disagreement exhibited by the following pairs. Give reasons for your answers.

■ *1.* *a.* Look before you leap.
    b. He who hesitates is lost.

2. *a.* It's the principle of the thing.
    b. You're cutting off your nose to spite your face.

3. *a.* Opportunity knocks but once.
    b. It's never too late to mend.

4. *a.* A stitch in time saves nine.
    b. Better late than never.

■ *5.* *a.* Absence makes the heart grow fonder.
    b. Out of sight, out of mind.

6. *a.* The race is not to the swift, nor the battle to the strong.

—ECCLESIASTES 9:11

    b. But that's the way to bet.

—JIMMY THE GREEK

7. *a.* Answer a fool according to his folly, lest he be wise in his own conceit.

—PROVERBS 26:5

    b. Answer not a fool according to his folly, lest thou also be like unto him.

—PROVERBS 26:4

8. *a.* For when the One Great Scorer comes
    To write against your name,
    He marks—not that you won or lost
    But how you played the game.

—GRANTLAND RICE

    b. Winning isn't everything. It's the only thing.

—VINCE LOMBARDI

9. *a.* For that some should rule and others be ruled is a thing not only necessary, but expedient; from the hour of their birth, some are marked out for subjection, others for rule. . . . It is clear, then, that some men are by nature free, and others slaves, and that for these latter slavery is both expedient and right.

—ARISTOTLE, *Politics*

    b. If there are some who are slaves by nature, the reason is that men were made slaves against nature. Force made the first slaves, and slavery, by degrading and corrupting its victims, perpetuated their bondage.

—JEAN JACQUES ROUSSEAU, *The Social Contract*

■ *10.* *a.* War alone brings up to its highest tension all human energy and puts the stamp of nobility upon the peoples who have the courage to face it.

—BENITO MUSSOLINI, *Encyclopedia Italiana*

b. War crushes with bloody heel all justice, all happiness, all that is God-like in man. In our age there can be no peace that is not honorable; there can be no war that is not dishonorable.

—CHARLES SUMNER

11. a. Next in importance to freedom and justice is popular education, without which neither freedom nor justice can be permanently maintained.

—JAMES A. GARFIELD

b. Education is fatal to anyone with a spark of artistic feeling. Education should be confined to clerks, and even them it drives to drink. Will the world learn that we never learn anything that we did not know before?

—GEORGE MOORE, *Confessions of a Young Man*

12. a. Belief in the existence of god is as groundless as it is useless. The world will never be happy until atheism is universal.

—J. O. LA METTRIE, *L'Homme Machine*

b. Nearly all atheists on record have been men of extremely debauched and vile conduct.

—J. P. SMITH, *Instructions on Christian Theology*

13. a. I know of no pursuit in which more real and important services can be rendered to any country than by improving its agriculture, its breed of useful animals, and other branches of a husbandman's cares.

—GEORGE WASHINGTON, letter to John Sinclair

b. With the introduction of agriculture mankind entered upon a long period of meanness, misery, and madness, from which they are only now being freed by the beneficent operation of the machine.

—BERTRAND RUSSELL, *The Conquest of Happiness*

14. a. How does it become a man to behave towards the American government today? I answer, that he cannot without disgrace be associated with it.

—HENRY DAVID THOREAU, *An Essay on Civil Disobedience*

b. With all the imperfections of our present government, it is without comparison the best existing, or that ever did exist.

—THOMAS JEFFERSON

■ **15. a.** Our country: in her intercourse with foreign nations may she always be in the right; but our country, right or wrong!

—STEPHEN DECATUR, toast at a dinner in Norfolk, Virginia, April 1816

b. Our country, right or wrong. When right, to be kept right; when wrong, to be put right.[20]

—CARL SCHURZ, speech in the Senate, January 1872

16. a. It makes but little difference whether you are committed to a farm or a county jail.

—HENRY DAVID THOREAU, *Walden*

---

[20]   On this kind of disagreement G. K. Chesterton (1874–1936) wrote in *The Defendant* that "'My country, right or wrong' is like saying 'My mother, drunk or sober.'"

> ***b.*** I know few things more pleasing to the eye, or more capable of affording scope and gratification to a taste for the beautiful, than a well-situated, well-cultivated farm.
>
> —EDWARD EVERETT

17. ***a.*** Thought, like all potent weapons, is exceedingly dangerous if mishandled. Clear thinking is therefore desirable not only in order to develop the full potentialities of the mind, but also to avoid disaster.

—GILES ST. AUBYN, *The Art of Argument*

> ***b.*** Reason is the greatest enemy that faith has: it never comes to the aid of spiritual things, but—more frequently than not—struggles against the divine Word, treating with contempt all that emanates from God.
>
> —MARTIN LUTHER, *Table Talk*

2.6   *Emotively Neutral Language*

In the preceding discussion it has been insisted that the expressive use of language is just as legitimate as the informative. There is nothing wrong with emotive language, and there is nothing wrong with language that is nonemotive, or neutral. Similarly, we can say that there is nothing wrong with pillows and nothing wrong with hammers. True enough, but it does not mean that we should be successful in attempting to drive nails with pillows or comfortable in trying to sleep with our heads resting on hammers. A great deal of value was lost in Thouless's translation of Keats's lines into neutral language—although the literal meaning was preserved. Here is a case in which emotively colored language is preferable to neutral language. Are there any circumstances in which neutral language is preferable to emotively colored language?

Clearly, when we are trying to "get at the facts," to follow an argument, or to learn the truth about something, anything that distracts us from that goal tends to frustrate us. It is a commonplace that the passions tend to cloud reason, and this view is reflected in the usage of "dispassionate" and "objective" as near synonyms. It follows that when we are attempting to reason about facts in a cool and objective fashion, referring to them in strongly emotive language is a hindrance rather than a help.

Thus William James, in his essay "The Dilemma of Determinism," explained his "wish to get rid of the word 'freedom'" on the grounds that "its eulogistic associations have . . . overshadowed all the rest of its meaning." He rightly preferred to discuss the issue using the words "determinism" and "indeterminism," because "their cold and mathematical sound has no sentimental associations that can bribe our partiality either way in advance." We should do well to follow James's example.

If we are interested in calculating, for example, what economic consequences in terms of productivity and efficiency would follow from various degrees of government economic direction, we shall find our task made more difficult if we insist upon referring to the phenomena in question by words as emotionally charged as "freedom" and "bureaucratic interference" on the one hand and "license" and "irresponsibility" on the other. Much less are we likely to make progress on this issue if the emotively charged words "capitalism," "socialism," and "communism" are used.

The use of such stereotypes is properly frowned upon, not merely because of their lack of literary value, but because of the way in which the hackneyed emotional reactions stirred by them get in the way of any objective appraisal of the facts to which they refer. This danger is familiar to those who have studied public opinion polls, such as George Gallup's (1901–84) and Elmo Roper's (1900–71). In seeking to discover people's views, interviewers must be careful not to prejudice the issue by phrasing their questions in such a way as to influence the answers. An interesting report on this problem is given by Stuart Chase (1888–1985) in his book *The Proper Study of Mankind.*

> In 1946 Roper ran an interesting semantic test. He matched two groups of people so they were practically identical samples. He proved it by asking various questions and getting percentage results which were very close. He then asked each group a similar series of questions except that for one group a new and ugly word was introduced, the word "propaganda."
>
> The general topic was the usefulness of foreign broadcasts by the State Department. Group A was asked to select from three alternative positions, one of which read: "Some people say it is better to explain our point of view as well as give the news." The answer came back "yes," 42.8 percent. Group B got the following wording, and *observe it is precisely the same question:* "Some people say it is better to include some propaganda as well as give the news." The "yes" reaction was almost cut in half, to 25.7 percent! It would be hard to find a better example of what an emotion-stirring word will do to people's opinions![21]

It may be doubted whether it is "precisely the same question" that was asked the two groups. As often used today, at least part of the descriptive meaning of the word "propaganda" concerns the use of nonrational methods to cause acceptance of a point of view. To propagandize is surely a different thing from simply explaining our point of view. Not all emotive differences between closely related words are independent of their descriptive meanings; some are directly derived from them. The differences in our attitudes toward *education* and *indoctrination,* for example, are based on real differences between the two activities, as well as on whatever emotive differences may attach to the words.

The point, however, is this. If our purpose is to communicate information, and if we wish to avoid being misunderstood, we shall find most useful that language which has the least emotive impact. If our interest is scientific, we shall do well to avoid emotional language and to cultivate as emotively neutral a set of terms as we can. This has been done most extensively in the physical sciences. Older and more emotively exciting terms—such as "noble" and "base" characterizing metals—have either been displaced by a special jargon or have come through the passage of time to be completely divorced from their former honorific or derogatory associations. This has been a contributing factor to scientific progress.

Thus if we are concerned to investigate the truth or falsity of a view and to discover its logical implications, our task will be facilitated if we translate any highly emotive formulation concerning it into as nearly neutral a description as possible. Suppose, for example, we are interested in the question of national compulsory health insurance.[22] In the course of our investigations we shall come across certain highly emotive phrase-

---

[21] Stuart Chase, *The Proper Study of Mankind* (1948).
[22] A more burning issue today, for various reasons, than when President Truman proposed it in the late 1940s!

ology, as in the text of the statement by Dr. Elmer L. Henderson, chair of the board of trustees of the American Medical Association, on President Truman's proposed national compulsory health insurance program. Dr. Henderson stated that

> There is a great deal of double talk in the President's message, but what he actually proposes is a national compulsory health insurance system which would regiment doctors and patients alike under a vast bureaucracy of political administrators, clerks, bookkeepers and lay committees.[23]

Can this passage be translated into more nearly neutral language without doing violence to its informative content? No more information is presented by Dr. Henderson in the passage cited than in the following:

> There is some ambiguity in the President's message, but its intended meaning is the proposal to set up a national compulsory health insurance system in which contact between doctors and patients would be regulated by an administrative agency of large size, which would employ government officials, clerks and bookkeepers, and committees not composed exclusively of M.D.s.

The facts may be as Dr. Henderson sees them, but when they are formulated with such a liberal sprinkling of emotively explosive words, like "double talk," "regimentation," "vast bureaucracy," and "*political* administrators," and when there is the hint that "doctors and patients alike" would be *under* clerks and bookkeepers (as though no doctor ever employed a clerk or bookkeeper to keep his or her office records straight), then it requires a disproportionate amount of effort to cut through to the actual information presented.

Emotive language is not in itself bad, but when it is information we are after, we shall do well to choose words whose emotive meanings do not distract and hinder us from dealing effectively with what they describe. As students of logic, we must examine critically what happens if the preceding directive is ignored. The careless use of language in argument often results in fallacies, which will occupy our attention in the following chapter.

In political campaigns today almost every rhetorical trick is played to make the worse seem the better cause. And this playing on emotion, rather than appealing to reason, is even more flagrant in commercial advertising, where the aim is to motivate rather than to persuade, convince, or inform. To be reasonable we must be continually on guard against being manipulated by the torrent of emotively charged language pouring out of Washington and Madison Avenue.

EXERCISES

I. Select a brief passage of emotive writing from a newspaper or periodical and translate it in such a way as to retain its informative content while reducing its expressive significance to a minimum.

---

[23]   *The Journal of the American Medical Association* 140, 7 May 1949, p. 114.

II. Select a brief passage of nonemotive writing from a newspaper report or scientific journal and translate it in such a way as to retain its informative content while *increasing* its expressive significance.

3

Fallacies

3.1 THE NATURE AND CLASSIFICATION OF FALLACIES

The typical reason for constructing an argument is to establish that its conclusion is true. It can fail in this purpose in either of two ways. One is by assuming a false proposition as one of its premises. It was remarked in chapter 1 that an argument involves the claim that the truth of its conclusion follows from, or is implied by, the truth of its premisses. So if even one of an argument's premisses is false, the argument fails to establish its conclusion. To test the truth or falsehood of premisses is not the special responsibility of the logician or philosopher, but rather the task of inquiry in general, because premisses may deal with any subject matter whatever.

The other way an argument can fail to establish its conclusion is for its premisses not to imply its conclusion. Here we have the special province of the logician, who is not so much interested in the truth or falsity of propositions as in the logical relations between and among them. An argument whose premisses do not imply its conclusion is one whose conclusion *could* be false *even if* all of its premisses are true. An argument that fails in this second way is said to be fallacious, or to be a fallacy. People are said to commit fallacies when they reason this way.

The word "fallacy," like many others, is used differently in different contexts. One familiar use of the term is to designate any mistaken idea or false belief, as in the "fallacy" of believing that all people are honest. But logicians use the term in a narrower sense to mean an error in reasoning or argument. People make many kinds of mistakes when they reason and argue. Each fallacy, as we shall use the term in this book, is a type of incorrect argument. Since it is a *type* of incorrect argument and not a particular argument, we can say of two different arguments that they contain or commit the same fallacy. Some arguments, of course, are so obviously incorrect as to deceive no one; for example:

The sky is blue.
  Therefore,
2 + 2 = 4.

These propositions may be true, but the second is not true *because* of the first.

It is customary in the study of logic to reserve the term "fallacy" for arguments that are *psychologically* persuasive but *logically* incorrect; that *do* as a matter of fact persuade but, given certain argumentative standards, *shouldn't*. We therefore define "fallacy" as a type of argument that *seems* to be correct but that proves, on examination, not to be so. There is profit in studying such arguments, for familiarity and understanding help keep us not only from committing fallacies but from being misled by them. To be forewarned is to be forearmed.

Most textbooks of logic and critical thinking contain discussions of fallacies, but their treatments differ, sometimes radically. One reason for this diversity is that there is no universally accepted classification of fallacies. This is not surprising, for as the early modern logician Augustus De Morgan (1806–71) once said, "There is no such thing as a classification of the ways in which [people] may arrive at an error: it is much to be doubted whether there ever *can be*." Just as people keep inventing new and useful technologies, they keep "inventing" new ways to fall into error. The latter, of course, is unintended, for nobody sets out to commit an error.

The first logician Aristotle (384–322 B.C.) listed only thirteen fallacies in his work *Sophistical Refutations,* which has been vastly influential. Fifty-one fallacies are "named, explained, and illustrated" by W. Ward Fearnside and William B. Holther in their book *Fallacy: The Counterfeit of Argument* (1959). The most comprehensive—or at least voluminous—list of fallacies is given by David Hackett Fischer in *Historians' Fallacies: Toward a Logic of Historical Thought* (1970). The index of Fischer's book lists 112 fallacies, although in the book itself he names and discusses many more than that. C. L. Hamblin in *Fallacies* (1970) gives a historical, critical, and theoretical treatment of the topic. Howard Kahane provides an insightful criticism of the usual methods of classifying fallacies in "The Nature and Classification of Fallacies," published in the anthology *Informal Logic* (1980). A more recent and penetrating discussion of fallacies is presented by John Woods and Douglas Walton in *Argument: The Logic of the Fallacies* (1982). We recommend all of these books to readers who wish to pursue the subject of fallacies at greater length and in more depth.

As we said, there is no universally accepted classification scheme for fallacies. One distinction that almost every logician makes, however, is between formal and informal fallacies. A *formal* fallacy is one that can be detected merely by examining the form (hence the name) or structure of the argument. An *informal* fallacy is one that cannot be detected merely by examining the form or structure of the argument but must be detected in some other way. Because of the way these types of fallacy are defined, the categories are mutually exclusive and exhaustive. They are mutually exclusive in that no fallacy is *both* formal and informal; they are exhaustive in that every fallacy is *either* formal or informal. This is analogous to distinguishing blue and nonblue objects (objects that are not blue). Because of the nature of the categories, nothing is in both categories at the same time (how could something be both blue and not blue at the same time?) and everything—this coffee cup, the mayor of Omaha, Madison Square Garden—is in one or the other of the categories (if something is in the blue category, then, by that very fact, it is not in the nonblue category).

This chapter contains a discussion of twenty informal fallacies—those that, in the opinion of the authors, are most often committed in ordinary situations. By definition these fallacies cannot be detected merely by examining the form or structure of the argument in which they occur. How, then, can they be detected? There are two ways. One is by examining the *context* in which the argument is made. Who, for example, is trying to establish the claim, and for what purpose(s)? Who is the audience for the argument? What assumptions do the parties share? Are there any ground rules for the discussion? The context (con-text) is the complete set of circumstances in which the argument (the "text") is made.

The second way is by examining the *content* or substance of the argument. This requires attention to the way the argument is expressed in language, to the meaning of words, and to such things as ambiguity, vagueness, and nonliterality. Content has to do with *what* is being said and *how* it is being said, not the form of what is said. In short, sometimes we reason fallaciously because our arguments are structurally defective (formal fallacies); sometimes we commit fallacies because we violate contextual rules of argument (the first type of informal fallacy); and sometimes we commit fallacies because we misunderstand or misuse language (the second type of informal fallacy).

The presentation, with minor exceptions, proceeds as follows. Each of the twenty informal fallacies is named, characterized, illustrated, and discussed. Since every fallacy by definition is psychologically persuasive but not logically cogent, we will, where it is not obvious, diagnose or explain the psychological appeal of each fallacy and justify our claim that the argument is unreasonable (noncogent). As the logician Howard Kahane (1928-   ) has pointed out, three factors explain the psychological persuasiveness of fallacies:

(1) strong emotions (needed to push us to *act* when action is necessary, but clouders of rational clarity);
(2) strong desires that certain propositions be true (leading to self-deception, or wishful thinking); and
(3) limitations on our ability to reason cogently even when strong emotions or desires do not intrude.[1]

We will also distinguish between the correct versions of each type of argument and those that are incorrect. Exercises follow every fifth fallacy. The chapter concludes with a long section of exercises.

---

[1]   Howard Kahane, "The Nature and Classification of Fallacies," in *Informal Logic: The First International Symposium,* ed. J. Anthony Blair and Ralph H. Johnson (1980), p. 33 (emphasis in original).

3.2   COMMON INFORMAL FALLACIES

Equivocation

As every user of dictionaries knows (that should include all of us), most words have more than one literal meaning. Such words are said to be *ambiguous*. Good dictionaries distinguish these various meanings. The word "pen," for example, means either an instrument for writing, an enclosure for animals, a female swan, or a penitentiary.[2] When we keep these meanings distinct in our minds, no difficulty arises. But when we confuse the different meanings a single word or phrase has, and use it in different senses in the same context, we are said to equivocate (or commit an equivocation). If the context happens to be an argument, we commit the *fallacy of equivocation*. For example, the following argument might look valid at first glance—despite its ridiculous conclusion:

1. Power tends to corrupt.
2. Knowledge is power.
Therefore,
3. Knowledge tends to corrupt.

To reveal the invalidity of this argument we have only to note that the word "power" in the first premiss means "the possession of control or command over people," whereas in the second premiss it means "the ability to control *things*." Another way to put the point is that the first premiss is true only if "power" means "possession of control over people," whereas the second premiss is true only if "power" means "ability to control things." Unfortunately for the arguer, there is no single sense of "power" in which both premisses are true; hence the argument fails to establish its conclusion.

Here is another example of the fallacy of equivocation, one that is more likely to persuade:

Bankers must be very responsible people. Whenever anything goes wrong in the economy, we [bankers] seem to be responsible.[3]

The word "responsible" in the first sentence (which states the conclusion) means "reliable in business or other dealings; showing reliability," whereas the same word in the second sentence (which states the premiss) means "chargeable with being the author, cause, or occasion of something." The arguer has shifted from one sense to the other and as a result committed a fallacy. Where the different meanings are closely related, as in this case, an argument in which they are confused can be psychologically appealing, thus satisfying the definition of "fallacy."

There is a special kind of equivocation that deserves mention here. This has to do with so-called relative terms that have different meanings depending on the class of

---

[2] See, for example, the *Oxford American Dictionary* (1980), p. 493.
[3] Irwin L. Kellner, "Don't Blame the Bankers," *Newsweek*, 16 May 1983, p. 10.

objects to which they are being compared. The meaning of the term is said to be relative (as opposed to absolute). Take the word "tall." A tall mouse is not a tall animal, although all mice are animals. So it would be fallacious to infer "X is a tall animal" from "X is a tall mouse." Even if X *is* a tall mouse, it does not follow that X is a tall animal. Compared to the class of animals, a mouse is short. The meaning of "tall" and other relative terms depends on a comparison class, and one cannot therefore *automatically* shift from one class to another. Consequently, inferences of the form "Object O is an (relative term) X; therefore, O is a (same relative term) Y" must be carefully scrutinized. Some such inferences are legitimate; some are not.

Another example of this type of equivocation concerns the evaluative word "good." It may be true that all lawyers are people, but it does not follow from the fact that X is a good lawyer that X is a good person. X may be a good lawyer but a *bad* person, or, conversely, a bad lawyer and a *good* person. The criteria of goodness in lawyers and people may differ to such an extent that goodness cannot be transferred from one class to the other. Only an investigation into the criteria of goodness for lawyers and people allows one to tell, which is what makes this an informal rather than a formal fallacy. Other relative terms are "bad," "large," "small," "fast," "slow," "short," "fat," "skinny," "smooth," "rough," "hot," "cold," "old," "young," "high," "low," "normal," and "successful." Whenever one reasons or argues using words such as these, one must be careful.

Amphiboly

The *fallacy of amphiboly* can be viewed as a special case of the fallacy of equivocation, because it, too, is generated by ambiguity. It differs from other fallacies of equivocation in that the ambiguity is caused by *grammar* rather than by the meaning of terms. One person utters a sentence, either orally or in writing, that, because of its grammatical construction, creates an ambiguity in meaning. The utterer intends one of the meanings, not the other. A second person, hearing or reading the utterance, draws an inference from the *un*intended meaning. The second person, not the first, commits the fallacy, although the grammatically poor sentence made the error possible.

Consider the following example. Years ago, during the presidency of Jimmy Carter, a UPI news reporter described ongoing peace talks between Egypt and Israel in which the United States was an intermediary. Egyptian President Anwar Sadat had just ended two days of negotiations with President Carter when the two held a joint news conference. The reporter wrote, "Sadat stood aside while Mr. Carter made his brief statement and said nothing."[4] The sentence is poorly constructed. The reporter's intention is clear: *Sadat* is the person who "said nothing." But a reader might conclude from the way the sentence was constructed that it was *Carter* who, although speaking, "said nothing" (or said nothing important). If that inference were drawn, it would be fallacious.

Grammar includes punctuation as well as the organization of words and phrases in sentences. Occasionally, farfetched as it may seem, mispunctuating a sentence cre-

---

[4]   As reported in *The Detroit News,* 6 February 1978.

ates an ambiguity that leads to a fallacy. For example, compare the sentences "We are opposed to taxes, which slow economic growth" and "We are opposed to taxes which slow economic growth." The only difference is the presence or absence of a comma. The first sentence implies that *all* taxes slow economic growth, while the second sentence implies that some taxes do and some taxes do not slow economic growth. The meaning differs quite drastically! Suppose the speaker opposes all taxes on grounds that they slow economic growth but uses the sentence without the comma. A listener may infer or conclude from this that the speaker opposes only certain taxes (those that do in fact slow economic growth). But that would be to commit a fallacy of amphiboly, for we are assuming something that is not the speaker's intent. As this example shows, one must be careful in using punctuation, because it can make a significant difference to the meaning of what is said and can therefore generate fallacious inferences.

Begging the Question

Suppose two people are having a discussion when they reach a disagreement about a particular issue. Let us call the issue on which they disagree "the question." Suppose the question is whether God exists. Person A thinks God exists; person B thinks God does not exist. A, not content to leave it at this, sets out to persuade B that God does in fact exist. There are many ways for A to proceed, of course, but suppose A goes on as follows: "God exists because the Bible says God exists." B, the atheist, is unimpressed. "Why should I give any credence to what *the Bible* says; it's only a book." A responds by saying "Because the Bible is the authoritative word of God." At this point A has committed the *fallacy of begging the question,* which consists in assuming the very proposition one is attempting to establish by argument. The issue (question) on the table between A and B is *whether* God exists, but in the course of resolving this, A asks B to concede *that* God exists. A is said to beg (ask B to concede) the question (issue).

The fallacy of begging the question requires at least two individuals, one of whom (in this case A) is trying to persuade the other (B) to accept or believe a proposition. An argument of this sort can never generate real persuasion, because either B already accepts the conclusion of A's argument or does not. If B already accepts the conclusion (that God exists), then no argument for that conclusion is necessary and it would be misleading to say that B has been *persuaded* by A. On the other hand, if B does *not* already accept the conclusion that God exists, then A's assumption that the Bible is the authoritative word of God is not sufficient to induce belief in B. B will refuse to concede the point and accuse A of failing to carry the self-imposed burden of persuasion.

Not every instance of the fallacy of begging the question is transparent like this one, which is why such inferences are often psychologically persuasive. Sometimes the fallacy occurs in long argumentative passages (chain arguments) in which it is difficult to keep track of the various premises and conclusions. The recipient may not realize that he or she has conceded the very point that is in issue. For instance, one may argue that Shakespeare is a greater writer than Judith Krantz (1928-) because people with good taste in literature prefer Shakespeare to Krantz. If asked how one identifies individuals with good taste in literature, the arguer might reply that such persons are to be identified by their preferring Shakespeare to Krantz. This argument is circular in the worst way, for it presupposes the truth of the proposition to be established.

To avoid confusion, it should be pointed out that the phrase "beg the question" often is used to mean something quite different than what we mean by it here. It often means "raise the question." If S is conversing with T about foreign policy, S may at one point tell T that what T just said "begs an interesting question: whether the United States *should* be the police officer of the world." All S means by this is that the conversation has raised an issue that is worth discussing on its own merits. In this book we use the phrase in the technical way only, to mean "assume what one is trying to prove." It is only in that sense that there is a *fallacy* of begging the question.

Complex Question

Asking questions of others is a frequent and, in most contexts, legitimate use of language. Sincere questions, as opposed to rhetorical questions (those in which a statement is being made), are attempts to elicit responses from those to whom they are addressed. They are directive uses of language, as we saw in chapter 2. But some questions are *loaded* in the sense that they presuppose answers to *other* questions that have not been asked. These so-called complex questions must be answered carefully, if at all. For instance, suppose that S, hoping to trap a neighbor into making a damaging admission, asks the neighbor why she plays her music so loudly. This question conversationally implies that the neighbor *does* play her music loudly, and that may be false. The neighbor may, and perhaps should, contest S's presupposition.

Other loaded questions are of the yes-no variety; for example, the notorious "Are you still abusing your spouse?" The question conversationally implies (presupposes) that the person *has* been abusing his or her spouse. To see this, consider each response the person might make, "yes" and "no." If the person says "yes" in response to the question, then he or she has made the damaging admission straightaway. If the person says "no," the implication is that he or she *was* abusive, but has stopped, which is equally damning. It's a no-win situation for the respondent. All one can do when confronted with a complex question is deny the presupposition, which requires that it be made explicit. The so-called *fallacy of complex question* occurs when the person asking the question draws an inappropriate inference from the other person's unwitting response. If the question about abuse is answered "no" and the person asking it says "Aha; then you *were* abusive!," the inquirer and not the respondent has committed the fallacy.

False Dichotomy

A dichotomy, in both ordinary English and the study of logic, is a division of a thing into two parts or kinds. Often a person will attempt to establish a conclusion by stating a dichotomy in which one of the two propositions is false or otherwise unacceptable, thus leaving the second proposition to be believed. If the dichotomy is "true"— that is, if there *really are* just two alternatives—this is an effective and legitimate form of argument. It is called a disjunctive syllogism.[5] But sometimes the dichotomy is false, which is to say that there are in fact more than the two asserted alternatives. When this occurs the arguer is said to have committed the *fallacy of false dichotomy*.

Advertisers often commit this fallacy in their attempts to induce consumers to buy their products. An advertisement for an antiseptic mouthwash (which we will call "L") says

> Pick one. GINGIVITIS (An early, reversible form of gum disease) OR L (To help prevent and reduce plaque and gingivitis).

The implication of this ad is that there are only two choices: *Either* you, the consumer, purchase and use L *or* you succumb to the dreaded disease of gingivitis. If these *were* the only two choices, it might be reasonable for the consumer to purchase the product; but of course they are not the only two choices. An obvious third alternative is to purchase and use a *different* gingivitis-fighting product, of which, when last we checked, there is no dearth on the market.

The oft-heard injunction "If you're not part of the solution, you're part of the problem" commits the fallacy of false dichotomy, for it ignores the possibility that a particular person is *neither* part of the solution *nor* part of the problem. So does the demagogue's rallying call "You're either with us or against us." Perhaps those in the crowd should shout "Can't I be neutral?" Sometimes, of course, there really *are* only two alternatives. For example, everything in the universe—literally, *every thing*—is either red or not red. There is no third possibility. People can quibble about what counts as red, or about whether a particular object (such as Jones's car) falls into the red category or the nonred category, and things can change color over time, but there can be no doubt that every object at a given time falls into one category or the other. This is a true dichotomy, and it could serve as the premiss of a sound argument.

When presented with a dichotomy, one must examine it carefully to determine whether it is true (states only two alternatives) or false (allows for a third alternative). Suppose a legislator says "Either we raise taxes or we lower taxes." This is a false dichotomy, for taxes can remain as they are. But what if the legislator had said "Either we raise taxes or we don't"? That is a true dichotomy. When making an argument that employs a disjunction (an either-or statement), one should be sure that the dichotomy is true rather than false; otherwise, one runs the risk of committing the fallacy of false dichotomy.

EXERCISES

Each of the following passages arguably exemplifies one of the fallacies discussed in the preceding section. Name and analyze the fallacies being committed. If a particular fallacy has more than one variety, specify which variety is being committed.

■   *1.* Advertisement: Aren't your kids worth Crest (a brand of toothpaste)?

---

[5]   The disjunctive syllogism has the form "Either P or Q; not P; therefore, Q", where "P" and "Q" stand for propositions. A syllogism, as we use the term, is an argument with exactly two premisses.

2. How often is worry about rape on most women's minds? About a third of women say they worry about being raped once a month or more often—many indicated more than once a day—and when they think about it, they feel terrified and somewhat paralyzed.

> —MARGARET T. GORDON and STEPHANIE RIGER, *The Female Fear: The Social Cost of Rape* (1991), p. 21

3. It is impossible to exist apart from God; it is impossible to be neutral towards Him. He who is not for Him is against Him.

> —EMIL BRUNNER, *The Divine Imperative*, trans. Olive Wyon (1947), p. 120

4. . . . we must accept the traditions of the men of old time who affirm themselves to be the offspring of the gods—that is what they say—and they must surely have known their own ancestors. How can we doubt the word of the children of the gods?

> —PLATO, Timaeus

■ *5.* Most liberals say that the death penalty does not deter murderers. I don't know why. There is not a case on record where a killer who has been executed has killed again. It certainly deters him. The graveyards of this nation are inundated with the bodies of second and third victims of killers who via escape, furlough or parole have lived to kill again.

> —B. M. LYBRAND, letter to the editor

6. The only people not required to be protected by seat belts are our school-bus-riding children and commercial bus and train riders. They say it's too expensive. Where is the logic in this? Why is a bus passenger more expendable than a car or airline passenger?

> —ELIZABETH K. BARNES, letter to the editor

7. Fallaci wrote her: "You are a bad journalist because you are a bad woman.
> —ELIZABETH PEER, "The Fallaci Papers," *Newsweek*, 1 December 1980

8. Hypothetical advertisement for Roughcut Chain Saws: You can buy a Roughcut or you can throw your money away.

9. She says that she loves me and she must be telling the truth, because she certainly wouldn't lie to someone she loves.

■ *10.* [What follows is a synopsis of the Lewis and Clark expedition by Dayton Duncan. The reader should know that the only member of the expedition who died during the expedition was Sergeant Charles Floyd.] There were the men who braved constant hardships and perils, yet lost only one of their number: the black slave, York, who intrigued the Indian tribes and who became such an accepted equal during the journey that he was allowed to vote with the other men in deciding where to build their fort on the Pacific Coast; Shannon, the young private who was twice separated from the main party for extended periods; Drouillard, whose hunting skills impressed even the Indians and were credited by Clark as crucial to the expedition's survival; the Field brothers, Reuben and Joseph, who were selected for virtually every mission of importance or danger; the one-eyed French boatmen [sic] Cruzatte who entertained the troupe with his fiddle playing and nearly ended Lewis's life by mistaking him for an elk during a hunt; even the Newfoundland dog that survived the withering heat of the Plains summers and had a moment of glory by chasing out a buffalo bull that had rampaged into camp one night.

—DAYTON DUNCAN, *Out West: American Journey Along the Lewis and Clark Trail* (1988), pp. 162–63 (thanks to David Cortner for bringing this passage to our attention)

Missing the Point

Argumentation is a purposive activity involving two or more individuals. One seeks to persuade the other(s) to accept a conclusion by showing that it is supported or entailed by other propositions (the premises) that the other individual(s) already accept(s). So every argument has a point: to establish a particular conclusion. Unfortunately, we sometimes *miss* the point when we argue. Sometimes we set out to establish proposition P, but state reasons that support some other, possibly related, proposition Q. When this occurs we are said to commit the *fallacy of missing the point*. The psychological persuasiveness of this type of argument derives from the fact that the intended conclusion differs only subtly from the asserted conclusion. The inference rests, in other words, on confusion.

Suppose A and B are discussing the issue of handguns. A believes that individuals have a moral right to possess handguns; B believes there is no such right. B tries to persuade A to share B's view. But suppose B goes about this by discussing cases in which gunowners have harmed themselves with their weapons, either accidentally or intentionally. A might accuse B of missing the point, for the issue, by hypothesis, is not whether handguns are harmful to their owners or to others; it is whether, *even if* handguns are harmful, individuals have a moral right to possess them. In other words, (a) what should be done about handguns as a matter of social policy, and (b) what rights individuals have with respect to handguns, are separate issues, although they concern the same topic. If only one of these issues is on the table, so to speak, it would be a fallacy to make an argument that resolves the other issue. When making an argument, one should keep the intended conclusion clearly in mind and not confuse it with other issues.

Red Herring

The *red-herring fallacy* occurs when, in an argumentative dialogue, one person intentionally distracts the other from the main point of the argument. There is disagreement about the origin of the term "red-herring fallacy," with two theories contending for acceptance. One theory is that the name derives from fox hunting. A bag of herrings, which supposedly have a powerful smell, is dragged across the trail of a fox to try to distract the dogs. Only the best dogs are able to resist the distraction and continue chasing the fox. It's not clear why someone would try to distract dogs in this way; perhaps the aim is to separate the good hounds from the not-so-good hounds. Nor does this theory explain the adjective "red" in the name; surely any type or color of herring would suffice to distract hounds. Another theory is that prisoners at a certain institution would smear themselves with red herrings prior to an escape attempt in hopes of foiling the hounds that they expected to come after them. It's not clear where prisoners would get herrings or why smearing them on one's body would not *increase* the likelihood of capture (because of the strong scent), but that's another matter.

Each of us has experienced the red-herring fallacy either as perpetrator or victim, for it takes intelligence, discipline, and good will to keep a conclusion firmly in mind and refrain from resorting to distractions when it appears that one's argument is weak. Consider the following example:

> O. J. Simpson is not guilty of murdering his wife. How could he be guilty? The man was a fantastic running back and is now a member of the Pro Football Hall of Fame. Everyone loves him.

The conclusion of this argument is expressed in the first sentence. Instead of marshaling support for the conclusion, however, the arguer distracts the reader/listener by changing the subject to Simpson's football exploits and celebrity. Logically speaking these have nothing to do with whether Simpson committed the crime. To see this, consider what premisses would have to be added to those stated to make the argument valid. One such premiss is that famous and successful athletes never commit crimes, or never commit heinous crimes, which is demonstrably false. A second premiss is that people who are widely loved, admired, or respected never commit murder. Unfortunately, that too is false.

The fallacies of missing the point and red herring are related in that in both cases the stated premisses are *irrelevant* to the conclusion. That is to say, even if the stated premisses were true, they would not increase the likelihood of the conclusion being true. The difference between the fallacies is that in missing the point, the error is caused by confusion. Often the arguer does not even *notice* that the stated conclusion differs from the intended conclusion. Red herring, in contrast, is intentional, or at least reckless. It is an attempt to "win" a debate by distracting one's audience—by in effect changing the subject. The red-herring fallacy is psychologically persuasive because although one has been distracted from the main point of the argument, the distraction is on the same general subject as the argument. The reader/listener may not notice that the subject has been changed, especially if the distraction generates strong emotion.

Straw Person

Suppose S makes the following argument in the course of a discussion of pornography:

> Pornography degrades women. It portrays them as willing participants in violent, sadistic activities in which others—mainly men—take pleasure. In doing this, pornography lowers women's status in society vis-à-vis that of men. It treats women as something other than equals. Since an important function of the law in our society is to prevent one group of people from subjugating another, it is morally permissible for the state, using the criminal law, to prohibit and punish pornography.

Leave aside the merits of this argument. Suppose T comes along, listens to S's argument, and says the following:

> That's ridiculous. S is saying that because a few women are offended by skin magazines, it's okay to censor them. Censorship is prohibited by the First Amendment, which protects all of us. If something could be banned just because it offends someone, somewhere, at some time, there would be nothing left for any of us to view, read, or listen to.

T has misstated S's argument in such a way that it appears weaker than it is. S's argument does *not* rest on the offensiveness of pornography to women or to anyone else; it makes use of the concepts of degradation and inequality, which T, in his or her haste to attack the argument, doesn't so much as mention. T proceeds to "knock down" the misstated argument and concludes that the original itself is a bad argument. This is an example of the *straw-person fallacy*. The name derives from the fact that a straw person, if there were one, would be much easier to knock down than a real, flesh-and-blood person. A straw person is so light and flimsy, in fact, that it can be knocked down with the slightest touch.

To avoid committing this fallacy, one must take care whenever one reconstructs and criticizes an argument. Admittedly, this is hard to do in the heat of discussion and debate, but that doesn't make it any the less required. Imagine how you would feel if your well-thought-out, carefully constructed argument were misconstrued and knocked down, the implication being that your argument is bad? If you would not want *your* argument treated in this way, perhaps you should not treat the arguments of others that way. The conscientious critic occasionally goes so far as to ask questions of the arguer, if feasible, in order to understand the argument. Only then will he or she move into the critical mode. This, incidentally, is sometimes called the principle of charity in interpretation. It says that one should first get the argument straight (accurate); then, if possible, proceed to criticize it.

Division

Occasionally as we go about our business we wish to draw inferences from collections of things to one or more members of those collections, or from wholes to one or more of their parts. There is no hard-and-fast rule as to when an inference of this sort is legitimate and when it is not. One must examine the content of the argument in order to make the determination. Ultimately it is a matter of making a judgment, which can of course be done well or poorly. For example, suppose S reasons as follows:

> My automobile is heavy; therefore, every part of my automobile is heavy.

This is a fallacious inference. It is fallacious not because one can *never* draw an inference from whole to part, as is being done here, but because heaviness (weight) is not the *sort* of characteristic that can be transferred in this way. Weight, as everyone knows, is cumulative, so it is possible for a thing to be heavy even though each of its parts, or many of its parts, are not heavy. But consider the following parallel argument:

My automobile is in the garage; therefore, every part of my automobile is in the garage.

This argument is *not* fallacious; indeed, it might persuade someone who doubts the conclusion but accepts the premiss. The reason this argument is not fallacious is that spatial location is relevantly different from weight. Because of the nature of the whole-part relation, at least when dealing with physical objects, all parts of a thing necessarily are located within that thing, spatially. So if S knows that his or her car is in the garage, S can safely conclude that all of its parts are in the garage. It follows that if S's car is in the garage and a particular object, X, is not, then at least *at that time* X is not part of the car.

For our purposes in this chapter there are two types of characteristic: those that can be transferred from whole to part (or from collection to member) and those that cannot be so transferred. The *fallacy of division* occurs whenever one transfers a characteristic from the latter class. As indicated above, one cannot determine this merely by examining the form of the inference, which is what makes this an informal rather than a formal fallacy. One must look at the content of the argument and make a judgment about transferability. In other words, every fallacy of division has one of the following two forms, depending on whether it concerns a whole or a mere collection of objects:

Whole to part:
1. Object W has characteristic C.
Therefore,
2. Every part (or some particular part) of W has C.

Collection to member:
1. Collection O has characteristic C.
Therefore,
2. Every member (or some particular member) of O has C.

While every fallacy of division has one of these two forms, not every argument having one of these forms is fallacious. As we saw in the case of the automobile in the garage, some are quite reasonable.

The reader may be wondering what distinguishes a whole from a collection, either in general or for purposes of understanding this fallacy. The difference is that a whole is more than the collection of its parts (although it is at least that). It is an *organized* collection of parts—a collection that is arranged in such a way as to be useful or functional. A chimney, for example, is more than a collection of bricks; it is a collection of bricks that have been put together to serve a purpose or to function in a certain way. By the same token, a rabbit is more than a collection of bodily organs and a clock is more than a collection of springs, gears, and pulleys. For each instance of the fallacy of division, one can in principle determine whether it proceeds from whole to part or from collection to member.

Composition

This fallacy, known as the *fallacy of composition,* is very much like that of division, except that it proceeds from part to whole (or member to collection) rather than from whole to part (or collection to member). In other words the direction of inference is reversed. Again, not every transfer of a characteristic from part to whole or from member to collection is fallacious. Some are and some are not. In order to decide one must examine the characteristic in question, as well as the context in which the argument is made. Here is an example of a *fallacious* inference:

> Every player on the team is good; therefore, the team is good.

Anyone who has played a team sport, and that probably includes most of us, knows why this inference is fallacious. Team sports require teamwork. Without it even the best players will not win games. Put differently, goodness in players is not sufficient (it may not even be necessary) for goodness in teams of players. This is an example of the part-to-whole version of the fallacy of composition, because a team is a functioning whole rather than a mere collection of individuals. A fallacious example of the *member-to-collection* version would be:

> Each book in my collection has a spine; therefore, my collection of books has a spine.

Sometimes it is reasonable and not fallacious to transfer a characteristic from part to whole, as in this instance:

> Each and every part of my watch is made of plastic; therefore my watch is made of plastic.

The reason this inference is not fallacious is that the characteristic of being made of plastic, or any other material, is such that it can be transferred. Being made of plastic just *means* that all of a thing's parts, if more than one, are made of plastic. To complete the list of illustrations, suppose that each member of a randomly selected group of college students has a grade-point average of 3.4. It follows that the group or collection of such students has a grade-point average of 3.4. This is an example of a nonfallacious inference from member to collection. It is nonfallacious because of the nature of averages, of which a grade-point average is a special case.

Every fallacy of composition has one of the following two forms, depending on whether it concerns a whole or a mere collection of objects:

Part to whole:
1. Every part of object W has characteristic C.
Therefore,
2. W has C.

Member to collection:
1. Every member of collection O has characteristic C.
Therefore,
2. O has C.

Whether a particular inference is fallacious depends, as in the case of the fallacy of division, on whether the characteristic in question is of a sort that can be transferred.

EXERCISES

Each of the following passages arguably exemplifies one of the fallacies discussed in the preceding sections. Name and analyze the fallacies being committed. If a particular fallacy has more than one variety, specify which variety is being committed.

■   *1.*   S says: The national economy is improving. Interest rates fell one percent in the last quarter of the year and the unemployment rate fell half of one percent. T responds: That's a terrible argument! Just because some people got jobs, it doesn't mean everyone did. I know dozens of people who *lost* jobs in the last quarter. How can you say that the national economy is improving?

2.   I'm tired of these anti-war protesters who say the USA's invasion of Iraq was wrong. The United States was *more* than justified in attacking Iraq. Didn't it make you proud to have all of that awesome firepower at our disposal? Smart bombs, Patriot missiles, impenetrable tanks . . . I'm proud to be an American. My country, right or wrong!

3.   The average height of the first-year law-school class is five feet, four inches. Cecilia, who is a member of that class, must therefore be five feet, four inches tall.

4.   X is being tried for robbery. The issue before the court is whether X committed the crime. The prosecuting attorney argues at length to the jury that robbery is a heinous crime and that individuals convicted of robbery should be severely punished.

■   *5.*   . . . the universe is spherical in form . . . because all the constituent parts of the universe, that is the sun, moon, and the planets appear in this form.
—NIKOLAUS COPERNICUS, "The New Idea of the Universe"

6.   An atheist sets out to prove to a believer that God does not exist. The atheist argues as follows: "Religious belief is based on fear and hope, not fact; therefore God does not exist."

7.   Every bus in the fleet has tires; therefore, the fleet of buses has tires.

8.   S says: Most of the people I've talked to in this neighborhood are Republicans, so probably most people in the neighborhood are Republicans. T responds: Just because the handful of people you've *talked to* are Republicans doesn't mean *all* of them are.

9.   Speech by a legislator: The issue before us today is whether to pass the President's health-care bill, a copy of which I have in my hand. I want you to know that

I dislike the way the First Lady has gotten involved in this process. Who elected her, anyway?

■ *10.* The United States Senate is a powerful decision-making body, so every United States Senator is powerful.

Appeal to the People

Is it ever permissible to infer the truth of a given proposition from the fact that many, most, or all people believe it is true (or accept it as true)? Sometimes. It is important to know precisely when and why this inference is permissible in order to avoid committing the *fallacy of appeal to the people.* The first point to keep in mind is that believing something does not, in and of itself, make it true. S's belief that there is a planet beyond Pluto does not make it *true.* S may be mistaken—even when S is convinced that he or she is not. After all, not all beliefs are true and not all true propositions are believed. In most contexts, to say that a proposition is true is to say that it correctly describes the way things are; to believe a proposition, on the other hand, is to affirm to oneself that it is true and perhaps to act accordingly. Unfortunately, our mental states do not always map onto reality.

It would seem to follow from these considerations that even if *everyone* believed that there is a planet beyond Pluto, that fact alone would not make it the case that there *is* a planet beyond Pluto. All of us may be mistaken. In fact, it appears that at one time everyone or almost everyone believed the world to be flat, but we now know that that is false. Nonetheless, it may seem unlikely in this day and age for everyone to be mistaken. What are the chances that everyone is mistaken in the same way at the same time? But there may be an explanation for the prevalence of the belief other than it being the truth: It may be caused by an emotion or feeling common to all (fear or hope, for example); or the same unreliable process may have led everyone to the same conclusion; so unanimity of belief may not be evidence that something is true.

Does this mean that it is *never* reasonable to infer truth from prevalent belief? No. In some cases it is reasonable. For example, suppose S has been on a monthlong kayak trip in the wilderness and is wondering whether his or her favorite baseball team, the Detroit Tigers, won the World Series, which S missed. When S reaches civilization S asks a dozen people whether the Tigers won and all twelve say they did. Unless S has reason to think these individuals are lying, or are merely guessing, or are confused by the question, S will infer that the Tigers won the World Series. That is, S infers the *truth* of the proposition that the Tigers won from the fact that everyone S asked *believes* (and says) they won. In the circumstances, this is a reasonable inference.

But suppose S reasons as follows:

I need a new pickup truck and I want to buy the best truck on the market. Unfortunately I don't know which truck—Ford or Chevy—is best. I saw an advertisement the other day which claimed that Ford trucks outsell Chevy trucks, so Ford must be best. I'll buy a Ford.

All of us have seen advertisements like this. By citing comparative sales figures, the manufacturer hopes to persuade consumers to buy its product. The suggested inference is that because more people buy product A than product B, A is superior to B. To put it in the form with which we're concerned, the inference is:

> Most people believe that Ford is superior to Chevy; therefore, Ford is superior to Chevy.

There are many problems with this inference. First, the manufacturer has said *nothing* about people's beliefs. It has made a claim about people's *actions* (purchasing trucks). It may be that those who purchased Ford trucks did so because they liked their appearance, not the way they perform on the road, the factor about which, by hypothesis, prospective buyers are concerned. It may also be that those who purchased Ford trucks believe that they are equivalent, not superior, to Chevy trucks and preferred them for reasons of brand loyalty, or because a distant relative works for Ford, or for some other reason having nothing to do with quality. Second, people have different criteria of quality in pickups, as in anything else. Unless consumer S knows that those who purchased Ford trucks have the same criteria as S, it is *irrelevant* (to S) that more people bought Fords than Chevys. Indeed, almost all of the relevant questions go unanswered in the advertisement.

There is, alas, no mechanical decision procedure for determining whether one commits the fallacy of appeal to the people. Whether one does so depends on factors such as the following: (a) how widely held the belief is; (b) whether the believers are expert or at least competent in the field, or on the particular proposition believed; (c) whether the believers have good reasons for their belief; and (d) whether the belief is caused or influenced by strong emotion or feeling (in other words, whether it can be explained by something other than the truth of what is believed). Only if these questions are answered in a certain way is it reasonable (as opposed to fallacious) to infer "P is true" from "many, most, or all people believe P." It is almost always safer to study the matter for oneself and form a belief accordingly.

Appeal to Authority

In attempting to make up one's mind on a complicated question, one may seek to be guided by the judgment of an acknowledged expert who has studied the matter thoroughly. One may argue that such-and-such a conclusion is true because it is the best judgment of such an expert. In many cases this type of argument is perfectly legitimate. It has the form:

> 1. S (an alleged authority) says that p.
> Therefore,
> 2. p is true.

If laypeople are disputing some question of physical science and one of them appeals to the testimony of Albert Einstein (1879–1955) on the matter, Einstein's testimony is not only relevant but important. Although it does not *prove* the point in the sense of establishing it to a certainty, it does support it. This is a relative matter, however, for if experts rather than laypeople are disputing a question in the field in which they are experts, their appeal would be only to the facts and to reason; any appeal to the authority of another expert would be without value as evidence.

Occasionally however we appeal to individuals who are not expert on the matter at hand. We may *think* they are authorities but in fact they are not. When this occurs the arguer is said to have committed the *fallacy of appeal to authority*. The form of the argument is the same as before, but this time S, the person to whom the appeal is made, is not really expert on the question or in the field from which the question is drawn. If in an argument over religion one of the disputants appeals to the opinions of Charles Darwin (1809–82), a great authority in biology, the appeal is fallacious. Similarly, an appeal to the opinions of a great physicist like Einstein to settle a political or economic dispute would be fallacious. The claim might be made that people brilliant enough to achieve the status of authorities in advanced and difficult fields such as biology or physics must have correct opinions in fields other than their specialties. But the weakness of this claim is obvious when we realize that, in this day of extreme specialization, to obtain thorough knowledge of one field requires such concentration as to restrict the possibility of achieving authoritative knowledge or skill in others.

The ultimate question is whether the person being appealed to as an expert is indeed an expert on the disputed proposition. What makes someone an expert? Actually, the question is not whether so-and-so *is* an expert but whether the person to whom the argument is being made *accepts* that person as an expert. Suppose S is a follower of Karl Marx and takes Marx, although long dead, to be an expert on questions of economic and social theory. Someone may argue to S as follows:

Marx said that the value of a commodity is a function solely of the labor it takes to produce it; therefore the value of this computer, which is a commodity, is a function solely of the labor it took to produce it.

The relevant question is not whether Karl Marx *really is* an expert on questions of economic value; that surely is a matter of contention. The question is whether S, the person to whom the argument is being made, *accepts* him as an authority, and since, by hypothesis, S does, no fallacy is being committed. That does not mean S is compelled to accept the arguer's conclusion, of course, because S may challenge the claim that Marx said what he is alleged to have said (the first premiss), or S may agree that Marx said this but interpret it differently than does S's interlocutor. The fallacy of appeal to authority consists in citing as an authority someone whom one's interlocutor does not accept as an authority on the matter at hand. An argument of that nature can never persuade because it can never get started.

In addition to the fallacious appeal to authority there is what might be called a fallacious appeal to *non*authority. This occurs where one infers the *falsity* of a proposition from the fact that S says it, on grounds that S is not an authority on the matter at hand, when in fact S *is* an authority. It has the form:

1. S (an alleged nonauthority) says that P.
Therefore,
2. P is false.

Many years ago a group of Catholic bishops issued a pastoral letter in which they criticized the people and government of the United States for creating and allowing significant disparities in wealth. They argued that the prevailing distribution of resources is unjust. The letter was roundly condemned. One common criticism was that the bishops had "ventured into a realm beyond their competence"[6]—namely, economics. In other words, because the bishops were not expert in economics (or so it was assumed), what they had to say about the United States economy was false, or at least not to be believed.

The problem with this inference is that the argument the bishops made was a *moral* argument, not an argument about economic matters that might have required economic training or expertise. Presumably the bishops, like anyone else, were capable of making and supporting moral judgments. The bishops argued, in effect, that it is unjust, unfair, and morally wrong for the United States government to allow significant disparities in wealth. One may disagree with this conclusion, of course, but *it is not false simply because the bishops are not professional economists*. The bishops made a moral claim, not an economic claim, and moral claims as such need no particular economic knowledge or skill.

This example raises the question whether there are any *moral* authorities. The answer is that it depends on the person who is considering the matter. Some people accept others—their religious leaders, for example, or wise friends—as authorities on questions of right and wrong, good and bad, just and unjust. Others insist on judging these matters for themselves without any appeal to the views or sayings of others. There is no single answer to the question. But keep in mind that if one bases one's moral conclusion on the authority of some person or text (such as the Bible or the Koran), one's argument will fail to persuade anyone who does not accept that person or text as an authority. Appeals to authority must be made from *within* the circle of those who accept the authority; outside of that circle they are futile.

Appeal to Ignorance

We saw in section 1.7 that there can be an invalid (hence unsound) argument with a true conclusion. Here is an example:

1. Sophie is a dog.
2. All spaniels are dogs.
Therefore,
3. Sophie is a spaniel.

---

[6]   Editorial, "Justice Without Liberty," *The Arizona Republic,* 14 November 1986.

This argument is invalid, as we define the term, because it is logically possible for the premisses to be true without the conclusion being true.[7] But the conclusion, as a matter of fact, *is* true (Sophie is the animal companion of one of the authors). The problem is that the conclusion, while true, doesn't *follow from* the premisses; the person making the argument has therefore failed to prove his or her conclusion. But we must be careful, for we may not infer from the absence of proof that the person's conclusion is *false*. If we did, we would commit the *fallacy of appeal to ignorance,* which has the form:

1. P hasn't been proved true.
Therefore,
2. P is false.

Notice the movement of thought this inference exhibits. From a state of ignorance, or lack of proof, one affirms knowledge. But how can knowledge derive from ignorance? It would seem that one must know *something* in order to acquire (other) knowledge.

Sometimes, in fact, we *do* know other relevant things that allow us to draw a conclusion from the absence of proof. Suppose A knows that persons S, T, and U are experts in the field of ballistics, which is the scientific study of the flight characteristics of projectiles. These individuals set themselves the task of proving some propositon—say, that a particular bullet came from a particular gun a criminal suspect allegedly used. S, T, and U, let us assume, are working independently of one another. If after trying to prove the proposition for some time, S, T, and U report that they cannot, it is reasonable for A to conclude that the bullet did *not* come from the gun. The inference goes something like this:

> If the bullet came from the gun, then S, T, and U, who are experts on such matters, would be able to prove it; but after several attempts, none of them has proved it; therefore, the bullet did not come from the gun.

The reasonableness of this inference depends on the plausibility of the first premiss. If we have reason to believe that the first premiss is true, then it is reasonable to believe the conclusion; otherwise not. More particularly, one's confidence in the truth of the conclusion can be no greater than one's confidence in the truth of the premisses.

Every appeal to ignorance has an implicit premiss of the sort just stated. In cases where the implied premiss is implausible, one commits the fallacy of appeal to ignorance. In cases where the premiss is plausible, one does not commit the fallacy. As with every informal fallacy, one must examine the circumstances of the case in order to make the determination. Factors to keep in mind include (a) how many individuals are attempting the proof; (b) whether those individuals are expert, or at least competent, on the matter at hand; (c) whether those attempting the proof are motivated (have an incentive) to prove the matter; (d) whether those attempting the proof have

---

[7]   As an exercise, replace the terms "Sophie," "dog(s)," and "spaniel(s)" with terms that make both premisses true and the conclusion false. This will show that it is *possible* for both premisses to be true while the conclusion is false, and hence demonstrate the invalidity of the argument.

the technology and other resources necessary to conduct the inquiry and make the proof; and (e) for how long a time the individuals have tried to prove the proposition. The more experts there are and the longer they try unsuccessfully to prove the truth of the proposition, the greater is the likelihood that the proposition in question is false, and the more reasonable it then becomes to believe that it's false.

A variation on this type of argument goes as follows:

1. P hasn't been proved false.
Therefore,
2. P is true.

Everything we have said about the other version of the argument applies here, with appropriate changes. If all we know is that a particular proposition has not been proved false, it would be fallacious, not to say rash, to infer that it is true. Those attempting the disproof may have been unmotivated, underfunded, undersupplied, rushed, or just plain incompetent.

Appeal to Emotion

Every person has both rational and emotional, or both cognitive and affective, capacities. Reason without emotion would be sterile and useless; it would make us glorified computers rather than the complex, feeling beings we are. But emotion without reason would be equally deficient, for we would then be unable to negotiate the deadfall and debris in the swirling, unpredictable river of life. Some philosophers have not only distinguished the rational and emotional sides of the human being but ranked the rational capacity as superior to the emotional. They say that in cases of conflict between reason and emotion, reason must govern, as a parent governs his or her children. We take no side in this ancient dispute. Our position is simply that no person would be complete without *both* a functional cognitive life and a rich affective capacity.

That said, it is important to understand that emotions or passions, by their nature, can become so powerful as to overwhelm one's rational capacity. They can cloud perception, blind one to what should be obvious facts, induce one to exaggerate claims, and hinder ordinary thought processes. For that reason one must keep a watchful eye on the emotions, so to speak—not because they are intrinsically bad, because they are not, but because they sometimes have bad consequences. They need to be moderated. Occasionally, people with a point to prove exploit this capacity of human emotions to run wild. They try to move us to act rather than persuade us to believe, thus failing to respect our rational capacity. When this occurs, the person in question is said to commit the *fallacy of appeal to emotion*.

The fallacy of appeal to emotion consists not in trying to alter belief or behavior, because every argument does that, but in trying to alter belief or behavior by riling the emotions to the point where they interfere with one's ability to reason. As one student of the subject has written, "The emotional appeal targets the person's unthinking reactions, and so attempts to bypass the critical questioning and logical assessment normally characteristic of reasonable dialogue."[8] The fallacy is like a red herring in that it

---

[8]   Douglas N. Walton, *Informal Logic: A Handbook for Critical Argumentation* (1989), p. 82.

attempts to distract the reader or listener from the point at issue. The difference is that in an appeal to emotion the distraction is generated by powerful emotion rather than cognitive confusion.

There are, in the human being as in certain nonhuman animals, many emotions that can be exploited by a person intent on inducing action. Hence, there are many varieties of the fallacious appeal to emotion. Among these emotions are fear, love, hope, pity, guilt, anger, hatred, reverence, and enthusiasm. Suppose S has a scholarship that requires for its renewal a cumulative grade-point average of 3.00. S needs a grade of B or better in a particular course to maintain this average but is in danger of receiving a C. Naturally, S is worried, so S goes to see the instructor of the course and says the following:

> I hope you understand my predicament. I tried as hard as I could to get a B or better, but unfortunately the effort wasn't enough. It's very important to me to retain my scholarship, as I'm sure you can appreciate, having been through college yourself. If I lose the scholarship I may have to drop out of school to work, and then I'll never achieve my goal of becoming a veterinarian.

Every instructor has heard such stories; some are poignant. The implicit argument is that S should be given a grade of B or better because S's circumstances are pitiable. In other words, S appeals to the instructor's *emotion* of pity to get a grade that S has not, by hypothesis, earned in the course. This is fallacious. It would *not* be fallacious, however, if S's argument had been as follows:

> The grading procedure, as described on the syllabus for the course, provides that anyone who ends up with a score of eighty or higher is entitled to a B. I ended up with a score of eighty or higher for the course. Therefore, I'm entitled to a B. Therefore, you, the instructor, should give me a B.

This argument, like the previous one, is designed to get the instructor to do something—namely, give S a grade of B. But unlike the earlier argument it does not try to exploit the instructor's emotions or feelings. It appeals rather to the instructor's reason and to the principle of fairness. Whether the instructor finds the argument persuasive, ultimately, is another matter. The student may, for example, have misunderstood the syllabus or miscalculated his or her score.

Advertisers are notorious for appealing to the emotions of prospective consumers. Let us give just one example. An advertisement for a chocolate bar is emblazoned with an image of the United States flag and reads "A Free Star-Spangled Offer from The Great American Chocolate Bar." The aim is obviously to arouse the patriotic sentiments of the reading public in hope that these positive feelings are transferred to the product. If one feels good about a product, it stands to reason that one is more likely to purchase it. Presumably the chocolate bar has certain qualities the audience finds desirable and that constitute a reason to buy it, but the advertiser chooses not to emphasize these qualities. Instead, it tries to move people to act by bypassing their rational faculty. The advertiser exploits the widely held sentiment of patriotism in order to preclude or bypass critical thought about the product.

Attack on the Person

When confronted with an argument that has an unsavory conclusion, it is tempting to dismiss the argument on grounds that it is made by a bad or disreputable person. But this is to confuse the argument with the person making it.[9] The fact is, good people can make bad arguments and bad people can make good arguments. One commits the *fallacy of attack on the person* whenever one infers that an argument is bad (unsound) from the mere fact that the person making the argument is bad. That would be as unreasonable as inferring that a table is defective because it was made by a liar, or that a lawsuit is unmeritorious because it was filed by a corrupt attorney. To avoid committing this fallacy, one must keep one's focus on the *argument* and ignore the qualities of the *person* who happens to be making it.

Every fallacious attack on the person has the form:

1. S is a bad/defective person.
Therefore,
2. S's argument is bad/defective.

There are, of course, different types of personal badness, each of which can be the basis of a fallacy. We will discuss four of the main types, but want to emphasize that there are others. The first type of personal badness is *hypocrisy*, or saying one thing and doing another. "Practice what you preach!" one often hears. This is a demand that one live by one's stated principles. Suppose S, a minister, gives a sermon in which he or she condemns adultery, citing as reasons the harmful effects of adultery on children and on the nonadulterous spouse. If S (perhaps unbeknownst to the congregation) is himself or herself an adulterer, then S is a hypocrite, and that, we assume, is bad. Hypocrisy is a character defect to be condemned.

But what effect, if any, does S's hypocrisy have on S's *argument?* The answer is "none." S's argument can and should be evaluated on its merits. Whether the argument's premises are true has nothing whatsoever to do with S's behavior. Whether the argument's conclusion follows logically from its premises has nothing at all to do with S's behavior. The fact is, *even hypocrites can, and sometimes do, make sound arguments.* It would therefore be fallacious to dismiss S's argument solely on grounds that S is a hypocrite. Put differently, one should not reject standards, moral or otherwise, simply because the person who asserts them fails to live up to them. The standards themselves may be perfectly acceptable and defensible.

A second type of personal badness is *irrationality*. An irrational person, for our purposes, is someone with inconsistent beliefs—who believes or accepts both P and Q when P and Q cannot logically both be true. For example, suppose person S is an avowed libertarian, politically speaking. S claims to accept the libertarian doctrine that government should do no more than protect individuals from each other and provide for the common defense. Suppose S argues in favor of government wage and price controls on grounds that such controls will halt inflation, which (it is suggested) will

---

[9]   This, incidentally, explains the psychological persuasiveness of the argument type. Arguments don't present themselves; they are presented by people. But people are not arguments.

in turn promote economic growth. A critic might respond to S as follows: "But you're a *libertarian,* and libertarians *reject* this sort of government interference. Your argument is therefore without merit."

The critic has dismissed S's argument solely because S is inconsistent (irrational). But that's fallacious, because S's argument may very well be cogent despite the fact that one or more of its premises clashes with S's libertarian principles. The fact that *S* has contradictory beliefs does not mean that S's *argument* is defective or that its *conclusion* is false. Perhaps the argument is fine and libertarianism is false or unacceptable. Or perhaps the critic is wrong and there is no inconsistency, despite appearances. The point is that an argument can be sound—can be valid and have true premises— even though the person making the argument cannot consistently maintain its premises.

A third type of personal badness is *selfishness or greediness.* Occasionally an argument is dismissed on grounds that the person making it does so only because he or she is likely to benefit from the changed beliefs or behavior of those to whom the argument is directed. As an example, consider the recently enacted but much criticized forfeiture provision of federal law, which requires that the property of individuals accused of violating drug laws be forfeited to the government before trial. Imagine an attorney arguing as follows:

> The Sixth Amendment of the United States Constitution guarantees that every criminal defendant have assistance of counsel. By taking the tangible property and bank accounts of those accused of violating the drug laws, the federal forfeiture law prevents these individuals from hiring counsel of their own choosing. Therefore, the federal forfeiture law is unconstitutional.

This argument, *as an argument,* is open to challenge at several points. It may or may not be sound. But one may not dismiss it solely because the attorney making the argument represents individuals charged with drug offenses and therefore stands to gain if the forfeiture law is held unconstitutional. In other words, even if it were *true* that the attorney making the argument is selfish or greedy, it would not follow that the attorney's argument is bad. Selfish and greedy individuals, like hypocritical individuals, can and sometimes do make good arguments. This version of the fallacy of attack on the person is known as *poisoning the well,* because the mere suggestion that the arguer is improperly motivated "poisons" everything he or she subsequently says. As a result, it may be difficult for anyone to focus on and evaluate the argument. This is a common but nonetheless fallacious argumentative tactic.

The fourth and final type of personal badness we discuss is *moral badness.* Suppose S makes an argument the conclusion of which is that T has acted wrongly. T may respond that S has done the same, or something equivalent. In other words, T may respond to S's argument by saying that S is just as bad as, if not worse than, T. This is known as *tu quoque,* from the Latin "you're another." As an example, consider the argument that it is wrong to kill animals for food. A critic may respond by saying that the arguer is just as bad as the respondent because he or she wears leather products, such as a belt, which necessitated killing an animal.

Does this undermine the argument? The answer is "no." For one thing, it could be that *both* people are correct; both have acted wrongly. In other words, even if the arguer has acted wrongly, it doesn't follow that the other person *has not* acted wrongly. It can be wrong to kill and eat animals even though S, the person making the argument, wears a leather belt. Perhaps the animal from which the belt came was not killed in order to make the belt, whereas animals *are* killed in order for their flesh to be consumed. Or perhaps the belt-wearer is weak-willed or hypocritical. That, as we saw, does not mean that his or her argument against meat-eating is defective.

It is easy to see why each of these arguments is fallacious. Suppose the person making the argument is bad in one or more of the respects we have described. It is possible for someone else who is not bad in this way, or not bad at all, to make *the same argument.* The criticism would then lack a target. S, a leather belt-wearer, may be a hypocrite when S argues that it is wrong to kill and eat animals; but if someone else comes along who does not eat meat or wear animal products, the charge of hypocrisy loses its force. It was directed at *S,* not S's argument. The moral of the story is that one should always focus on the argument and not be distracted by the personal characteristics of the person making it. This is difficult to do, especially in an era in which personal attacks are accepted (perhaps expected) in politics; but it must be done in order to avoid committing a fallacy.

It should be pointed out that one does not commit a fallacious attack on the person merely by accusing someone of being hypocritical, irrational, selfish/greedy, or morally bad. Each of these character traits is objectionable; perhaps people who exhibit them should be made aware of it and held accountable for their character and behavior. The fallacy occurs only when, from the *alleged fact* of hypocrisy, irrationality, selfishness/greediness, or moral badness, one infers that a person's *argument* is defective. The fallacy, in short, consists in *transferring* badness from the person to his or her argument. Since the criteria of goodness and badness in persons and arguments differ significantly, this is unacceptable.

EXERCISES

Each of the following passages arguably exemplifies one of the fallacies discussed in the preceding section. Name and analyze the fallacies being committed. If a particular fallacy has more than one variety, specify which variety is being committed.

■   *1.*   The solution to teen-age pregnancy depends on related segments of society: family, church, schools, government, economy. In focusing on the "too-soon parent," we must not abandon her "too-soon child" to the quick fix of abortion.
            —WILLIAM V. DOLAN, M.D., letter to the editor, *The Arizona Republic,* 3 June 1987

2.   Nobody has proved that UFOs *don't* exist, so there is good reason to believe that they do.

3.   There must be a god. Belief in God has been a feature of every society at every time in human history. How could all of those people be wrong?

4.   I've yet to hear a convincing argument that black holes exist, so I'm going to remain skeptical of their existence.

■   **5.** According to R. Grunberger, author of *A Social History of the Third Reich*, published in Britain, the Nazis used to send the following notice to German readers who let their subscriptions lapse: "Our paper certainly deserves the support of every German. We shall continue to forward copies of it to you, and hope that you will not want to expose yourself to unfortunate consequences in the case of cancellation."

—*Parade*, 9 May 1971

6. Everyone who saw the accident said (and presumably believed) that the driver of the van swerved into the path of the oncoming sports car, so probably that's what happened.

7. It was interesting to hear Justice Thurgood Marshall characterize President Bush's nomination of David Souter as politically motivated. How would Justice Marshall term his nomination to the high court as an attorney with neither judicial nor elective experience prior to his appointment?

—BILL BOWERS, letter to the editor, *The Dallas Morning News*, 7 August 1990, page 8A

8. In that melancholy book *The Future of an Illusion*, Dr. Freud, himself one of the last great theorists of the European capitalist class, has stated with simple clarity the impossibility of religious belief for the educated man of today.

—JOHN STRACHEY, *The Coming Struggle for Power*

9. Politician during the Persian Gulf War: "Every citizen of the United States should support the war effort in the Persian Gulf. Let's not fail to support United States troops as many citizens did during the Vietnam War. Those people should be ashamed of themselves. They are guilty of abandoning our soldiers in a time of great need."

■   **10.** The reluctance to extend protection [of rape laws] to married women is attributable partly to the feelings of self-preservation on the part of married American male legislators.

—MARGARET T. GORDON and STEPHANIE RIGER, *The Female Fear: The Social Cost of Rape* (1991), p. 62

The Genetic Fallacy

In one sense, to say that a thing is genetic is to say that it is inherited. The *genetic fallacy* employs the word in this sense. It consists in dismissing an idea or belief on the basis of how it originated. The disreputableness of the idea's origin—how it came to be held by one or more people—is inherited by or transferred to the idea itself. The fallacy has the form:

1. S's belief (P) has a disreputable origin.
Therefore,
2. P is false.

The problem with this inference is that beliefs can be true even though they originate in odd or unreliable ways. (By the same token, beliefs can be false even though they originate in reliable ways.) For example, suppose S forms the belief, as she sits in her Texas home, that it is raining in Tucson, Arizona. Suppose moreover that S arrives at this belief by consulting tea leaves. This method of belief-formation is inherently unreliable, but S's belief still may be *true*. If so, it would be true by accident, so to speak; and S could not be said to *know* that it is raining in Tucson. Or suppose S believes that the government is corrupt because a stranger said so. The mere fact that S obtains this belief in an unusual or disreputable way does not entail that it is false. Whether it is false has to be determined by other means, such as by empirical investigation.

This is not to say that any method of belief-formation or idea-acquisition is as good, reliable, or useful as any other. Undoubtedly, some are better than others. Some—such as astrology and crystal-ball gazing—are patently *un*reliable. Others—such as using the senses and employing inductive or deductive reasoning—are reliable even though not infallible. If one's belief derives from an unreliable process, the most one can say is that the belief is unreasonable, unjustified, or unwarranted; it does not follow that it is false. So if the question concerns someone's justification for believing P, it is relevant how he or she came to believe it. The inquiry in such a case centers on the reliability of the belief-formation process. But if the question concerns the *truth* of P, the origin of the person's belief in P is irrelevant and there is danger that a fallacy is being committed. One should not judge ideas, any more than people, by their origins.

Hasty Generalization

To generalize is to say something about a class of objects on the basis of one's knowledge or experience of only some members of that class. There is nothing intrinsically wrong with such a procedure. Indeed, we use it all the time and could not function without it. If it were illegitimate to use this procedure, many of the everyday inferences on which we rely would be illegitimate, an unacceptable result. Occasionally, however, we generalize without adequate knowledge or experience. When this occurs we are said to commit the *fallacy of hasty generalization*.

Every generalization, hasty or otherwise, has the form:

1. All observed Xs are Ys.
Therefore,
2. All Xs are Ys.

From the fact that certain objects within our experience have characteristic Y, we infer that all such objects have Y. The problem with this inference is that the objects with which one has experience may be *unrepresentative* of the class. They may be unusual or peculiar in some way. Consider the following example:

My lawyer did almost no work on my case and ended up charging me a huge sum of money for the "effort." Lawyers are crooks, I tell you.

This inference is fallacious if the lawyer in question is not representative of lawyers generally. For all we know, this lawyer is one of the corrupt ones. It might *not* be fallacious, however, if instead of one lawyer there were several, and they had been randomly selected. In general, the more representative the class of observed objects, the stronger is the inference that all objects and not just those observed have the characteristic in question.

It is often said that one cannot generalize from one, two, or a mere handful of instances. For example, some people complain that national polls are based on only a thousand respondents. But if there is a problem with such a procedure, it is not that there are only a thousand respondents; it is that the thousand respondents are not representative of the nation as a whole (or whatever group about which a claim is being made). As long as the instances, however many, are *representative,* the inference is acceptable (nonfallacious). Indeed, if we knew that a particular person, S, was representative of Americans, we could infer from the fact that S has characteristic C that all Americans have C! There is, unfortunately, no guarantee in a given case that a sample *is* representative, which is why pollsters use randomization techniques. Randomization increases the likelihood of representativeness, which in turn strengthens the inference from the observed objects to all objects.

Racism, sexism, and other "isms" can be understood as fallacies of hasty generalization, for in each case someone bases a conclusion or judgment about an entire group—members of a certain race, members of a certain sex, and so on—on characteristics associated with particular individuals in those classes. The problem is that in many or most cases the particular individuals are not representative of the class. This is not to say that racism, sexism, and other "isms" are nothing more than fallacies; but to the extent that they rest on a cognitive error, they can be *analyzed* as fallacies of hasty generalization.

Nor does our discussion suggest that it is always improper to generalize about human beings or particular classes of human beings. If it were improper to do this, much of modern social science would be called into question. What we are saying is that, in order to avoid the fallacy of hasty generalization, one should take pains to insure that the class of individuals from which one draws an inference is representative of the whole. Randomization is a useful tool in this process.

False Cause

The topic of causation, like so many others in the natural and social sciences, continues to perplex philosophers. Scientists worry less about the philosophical complexities of causation than about ascertaining actual causal connections in the world. In chapters 6 and 7 we take up some of the problems that arise both in our understanding of causation and with various scientific methods for ascertaining causes. For the moment let us focus on a particular fallacy that needs to be avoided as one reasons about causal connections.

To say that event E causes event F is to say, at a minimum, that E occurs at the same time as or before F. E cannot cause F if E comes after F in time; that would be absurd. But the opposite assertion is not true. Just because E and F occur together, temporally, it does not follow that one of them causes the other. For one thing, there may be some other event, G, that causes *both* E and F. G is then said to be a common cause. The measles virus, for example, causes both red spots and coughing. It would be a mistake to conclude that either the red spots cause the coughing or that the coughing causes the red spots just because they occur simultaneously. A possibility other than having a common cause is that the two events, E and F, just happen to occur at the same time. They are (merely) coincidental. Suppose a car horn sounds outside just as S sneezes. If S infers from this simultaneity that the sneeze *caused* the sounding of the horn (or vice versa), S would be committing what is known as the *fallacy of false cause*.

One variety of false-cause fallacy occurs so often that it has its own name, the Latin *post hoc ergo propter hoc* (literally, "after this therefore because of this"). This is the fallacy of inferring causation from temporal succession alone, or, schematically:

1. F comes after E ("post hoc").
Therefore ("ergo"),
2. F comes because of E ("propter hoc").

Suppose a black cat runs in front of S and moments later S twists his or her ankle. If S infers that the cat's running in front of S caused the accident solely because the one happened after the other, S commits the post hoc ergo propter hoc fallacy. Many superstitions originate(d) in this way.

Not all post hoc fallacies are trivial, as this one is. Some are practically significant, which makes it all the more important to be able to identify and diagnose them. Some people conclude from the fact that the economy improves or deteriorates following a presidential election that the new president caused the improvement or deterioration. The president is praised or blamed accordingly. Presidents do affect the national economy, but precisely what the effects are and how they are related to one another must be ascertained by careful examination. The *mere fact* that the economy did X after S was elected does not establish that S caused X.[10] We could not put the point any better than the Scottish philosopher David Hume, who wrote nearly 250 years ago:

> [N]or is it reasonable to conclude, merely because one event, in one instance, precedes another, that therefore the one is the cause, the other the effect. Their conjunction may be arbitrary and casual.[11]

In all likelihood, the psychological persuasiveness of the fallacy of false cause stems from a confusion of necessary and sufficient conditions for causation. It is *necessary*, in order for E to cause F, that E occur before or at the same time as F. But neither of these temporal relations is *sufficient* for causation. The succession or coincidence may be either accidental or based on a common cause. Whenever one reasons about causation, one must be on guard against this fallacy.

Slippery Slope

There are two types of *slippery-slope fallacy*, one logical and the other causal. We will address them in turn, beginning with the latter. Suppose S asserts that doing A will cause B, which will cause C, which will cause D; and suppose furthermore that D is bad

---

[10]   We are not suggesting that causation is necessary for presidential (or, more generally, political) responsibility. That is a matter of substantive debate. It may be that presidents are responsible for *whatever happens,* good or bad, during their administrations. This is analogous to what is called "strict liability," or liability without fault, in the law.

[11]   David Hume, *An Enquiry Concerning Human Understanding,* ed. Eric Steinberg (1977), p. 27 (originally published 1748).

or objectionable in some way. S may conclude that one should not do A. The claim is not that A itself is bad, but that doing A will set in motion a chain of causes the outcome of which (D) is bad. The name slippery slope fallacy derives from the image such an argument calls to mind. Imagine a slope at the bottom of which is a toxic substance (or some other dangerous thing). If the slope is slippery, one would be well advised not to take even one step onto it, for, given the slipperiness, doing so will cause one to slide into the toxic substance. On the other hand, if the slope is *not* slippery, one can turn around at any point and make it back to the top. Whether it is prudent to step onto the slope, therefore, depends crucially on whether it is slippery; that is, on whether there is *in fact* a causal process that cannot be interrupted once set in motion.

The general form of a slippery-slope argument is as follows:

1. If one does A, then one sets in motion a causal process which culminates in event D occurring. (In other words, there is a slope and it is slippery.)
2. D is bad/objectionable.
Therefore,
3. One should not do A.

Some arguments of this form are both psychologically and logically persuasive, and hence nonfallacious. These are the arguments in which both premises are true; in which the slope really is slippery and the bottom really is bad or objectionable. But other arguments of this form are only psychologically persuasive, and hence fallacious. These are the arguments in which either or both of the premises are false—in which either the slope is not slippery or the bottom is not bad or objectionable. One must examine the situation—the context and content of argument—to determine which is the case.

Here is an example of the first or causal version of the slippery-slope argument. We leave it to the reader to determine whether it is fallacious.

> There is no question in my mind that the government is seeking an all-out prohibition on cigarettes. And once we've let them achieve their goal they'll be free to pursue other targets. They'll go for liquor and fast food and buttermilk and who knows what else. There's a line of dominoes a mile long.[12]

For obvious reasons, the slippery-slope argument often is called the domino argument.[13]

The second version of the slippery-slope fallacy is logical rather than causal. In the first type of fallacy what made the slope slippery was *causation*. In the second type of fallacy what makes the slope slippery is *logic*, or more specifically the principle of noncontradiction.[14] The philosopher R. M. Hare gives the following example of the second type:

---

[12] Archie Anderson, opinion piece, "brought to you in the interests of an informed debate by the R.J. Reynolds Tobacco Company," *The Dallas Morning News*, 27 June 1994, p. 9A.

[13] It is also called the "camel's nose in the tent" argument, the "wedge" argument, and the "foot in the door" argument.

[14] The principle (or law) of noncontradiction asserts that no proposition is both true and not true. So if proposition P is known to be true, then its contradictory, nonP, is not true; and if P is known to be not true, then P is true.

[I]f the hotel manager allows the old lady to have her Pekinese on her lap in the lounge, then there will be no stopping people bringing in Great Danes and Wolfhounds and knocking over the tables; so he makes it a matter of principle to allow no dogs in the lounge.[15]

The argument has the form:

1. Situations A and B (and perhaps others) are relevantly alike.
Therefore,
2. If one allows or brings about A, then, on pain of logical contradiction, one must allow or bring about B (and perhaps others).
3. But allowing or bringing about A and B (and perhaps others) is unacceptable.
Therefore,
4. One must not allow or bring about A.

There are instances in which this type of argument is sound. But there are other instances in which it is unsound. The unsound or fallacious version occurs when, contrary to what is asserted in the first premiss, the situations are not relevantly alike. In the case of the dogs, one relevant difference between Pekinese and Great Danes is that Pekinese are smaller and less likely to disrupt the guests. One would not therefore be inconsistent in allowing the former but disallowing the latter.[16] As with the first or causal version of the slippery-slope argument, one must examine the argument's content and context and not just its form to determine whether a fallacy is being committed.

Weak Analogy

An analogy is a comparison of two or more objects. Often analogies are used in argument. The arguer points out that two objects, X and Y, are alike in certain respects and that one of the objects, X, has some further characteristic. He or she concludes that Y has that characteristic as well. There is nothing intrinsically fallacious about arguments by analogy, but some are weaker and less persuasive than others. The *fallacy of weak analogy* occurs when the further characteristic is causally unrelated to the characteristics the objects under consideration are known to possess. For example, suppose S reasons as follows:

I had a good time traveling in the Western states—Montana, Idaho, Washington, and Oregon—in 1989. So I'll probably have a good time this summer, too, because I'm going to the same states.

The fact that the vacations are in the same part of the country is indeed relevant to S's having a good time, and that gives the argument a degree of persuasiveness.

---

[15]   R. M. Hare, *Freedom and Reason* (1963), p. 43.
[16]   The propositions "No dogs are allowed" and "This dog, a Pekinese, is allowed" are contradictory. But the propositions "No large dogs are allowed" and "This *small* dog, a Pekinese, is allowed" are not contradictory.

Presumably S enjoys the terrain, the people, or the history of the area, and these are not likely to have changed in just a few years.

But what if there were companions along on S's 1989 vacation and S plans to go alone this summer? That is a relevant difference between the cases, because, as everyone knows, the number and identity of one's companions can make or break a vacation. Or what if the 1989 vacation was in the autumn, when campgrounds and roads were not crowded with tourists, but S plans to go during peak tourist months this summer? Again, that is a pertinent difference between the cases that weakens S's conclusion. Or what if S had stayed in motels in 1989 but plans to sleep in a tent this year? Each of these differences is relevant because it is causally related to S's having a good time. Each relevant difference weakens S's inference, and the weakening is cumulative.

There is no formula for determining whether an analogical argument is strong or weak; nor is there a mathematical threshold past which an argument can be said to be strong. Strength is a matter of degree, not kind. It is a matter of judgment, not mechanical application of a rule. Perhaps all one can say of an analogical argument such as S's is that it is weaker than it might have been had certain relevant differences not existed. This cautions us not to assign too great a probability to the conclusion. The subject of analogy, including more detail about the form and evaluation of analogical arguments, will be covered in chapter 5.

EXERCISES

Each of the following passages exemplifies one of the fallacies discussed in the preceding section. Name and analyze the fallacies being committed. If a particular fallacy has more than one variety, specify which variety is being committed.

■   *1.* I've had two female bosses in my lifetime and both of them have been incompetent. Women should stay out of management positions.

2. It could be a statistical oddity, but the fact is, the Super Bowl victor has predicted the market's yearly performance with a 90.5% accuracy rate.

How it works:

If a National Football Conference team wins the Super Bowl, expect the market to post a gain for the year.

If an American Football Conference team wins, prepare for a down year.

If the winner is an AFC team whose roots are in the old National Football League— the Cleveland Browns, Pittsburgh Steelers and Indianapolis (formerly Baltimore) Colts—it still counts for an up year. . . .

The predictor has gained such a following that even nonbelievers brace for a rally or a rout on Monday morning, depending on who won the trophy on Super Bowl Sunday.

—ANNE KATES, "Redskins' Win Could Bring Bull Back," USA Today, 29 January 1988, p. 3B

3. You say taxation is theft, but you're just mouthing one of the doctrines of the Libertarian Party, which repeats that slogan ad nauseam.

4. Memory is what makes us who we are. If we lost all our memory whenever we fell asleep at night, it would be the same as if we died and a new person woke up in our body the next morning. History is the memory of a nation—and that memory is being erased in schools and colleges across the country. Worse, fantasies are being recorded over the facts in that memory.

—THOMAS SOWELL, syndicated column, 2 January 1994

■ *5.* [E]ven if it could be established that women as a group are defamed by pornography, a group defamation approach would open the floodgates to all manner of lawsuits. If women can sue the creators and purveyors of pornography for depicting and describing women as sexually warped masochists, then women can sue the producers of television commercials that portray women as unintelligent housewives who agonize over which laundry detergent to use. If women can initiate such suits, industrialists can sue leftists who claim "all capitalists are bloodsuckers," and Latin-Americans can sue the producers of "Miami Vice" for conveying the impression that most Latinos spend their weekends shipping cocaine to the homes of the rich and the famous. And so on, ad infinitum, until everyone is suing someone and our courts collapse under the strain.

—ROSEMARIE TONG, *Feminist Thought: A Comprehensive Introduction* (1989), pp. 115–16

6. I had a disturbing dream last night. I dreamed that my friends, Pat and Chris, had fallen out of love and been divorced from one another. But dreams are notoriously unreliable, so I'm sure Pat and Chris are still happily married.

7. While General Grant was winning battles in the West, President Lincoln received many complaints about Grant's being a drunkard. When a delegation told him one day that Grant was hopelessly addicted to whiskey, the President is said to have replied: "I wish General Grant would send a barrel of his whiskey to each of my other Generals!"

8. One hundred names and telephone numbers were chosen at random from the Seattle telephone directory. All one hundred people whose numbers were chosen were interviewed. Forty of those interviewed reported having more than one automobile in the household. Therefore, forty percent of Seattle residents have more than one automobile in their households.

9. If we as a society allow terminally ill individuals to die at their own request, it is only a matter of time before we are *killing* such individuals. The next step will be killing individuals who are sick and in pain but *not terminally ill.* Then we'll find ourselves killing anyone we as a society deem *unacceptable,* such as the elderly, the poor, the infirm, and the homeless. We must not allow this to happen, so we should curb voluntary euthanasia.

■ *10.* The world of science is like the world of music. Professional music is as full of political intrigue and personal rivalry as professional science. Musical and scientific entrepreneurs are equally obsessed with money and power. The average musician is, like the average scientist, pursuing a difficult vocation under difficult circumstances, sustained by a network of intense professional friendships. Why should we expect scientists to be more virtuous than musicians? Why are we more tolerant of waywardness in musicians than in scientists?

—FREEMAN J. DYSON, "Science in Trouble," *The American Scholar* 62 (Autumn 1993):516

3.3   PASSAGES FOR ANALYSIS

Each of the following passages arguably exemplifies one of the twenty fallacies discussed in this chapter. If a particular passage does exemplify a fallacy, name and analyze it. Be specific. If a particular passage does not exemplify a fallacy explain why the inference in it is reasonable.

■   *1.* In a motion picture featuring the famous French comedian Sacha Guitry some thieves are arguing over division of seven pearls worth a king's ransom. One of them hands two to the man on his right, then two to the man on his left. "I," he says, "will keep three." The man on his right says, "How come you keep three?" "Because I am the leader." "Oh. But how come you are the leader?" "Because I have more pearls."

2. If nation N is allowed to annex nation O, it's only a matter of time before N annexes P, then Q, then R. Pretty soon N will have annexed all of the subcontinent, which is unacceptable. So N must not be allowed to annex O.   *[handwritten: slippery slope (causal)]*

3. Until someone proves to me that there was no conspiracy to kill John F. Kennedy, I'm going to believe that there was.   *[handwritten: appeal to ignorance p. 114–116]*

4. To press forward with a properly ordered wage structure in each industry is the first condition for curbing competitive bargaining; but there is no reason why the process should stop there. What is good for each industry can hardly be bad for the economy as a whole.   *[handwritten: Fallacy of composition 109]*

—*Twentieth Century Socialism*

■   *5.* According to a recent poll, 80 percent of United States citizens think that taxes are too high. Doesn't that prove the point?

6. Given that [human] consciousness is intimately related to [human] physiology and anatomy, that mammalian animals are most like [humans] physiologically and anatomically, and that consciousness has an adaptive value and has evolved from less complex forms of life—given all this, and, as a work in moral philosophy may do, setting to one side skeptical doubts about human consciousness, it is reasonable to conclude that mammalian animals are likewise conscious.

—TOM REGAN, *The Case for Animal Rights* (1983), p. 29

7. S is trying to persuade T that capital punishment is unjustified in principle; that is, no matter how quickly or painlessly the death is brought about. In doing so, however, S goes on at length about how a particular murderer had to be given several lethal injections and was in obvious pain until death occurred. "It was horrible," S says; "capital punishment is wrong."   *[handwritten: Missing the point 105]*

8. But can you doubt that air has weight when you have the clear testimony of Aristotle affirming that all the elements have weight including air, and excepting only fire? *appeal to authority*

—GALILEO GALILEI, *Dialogues Concerning Two New Sciences*

9. No man will take counsel, but every man will take money: therefore money is better than counsel.

—JONATHAN SWIFT

■ *10.* Jimmy Connors to a tennis official during a match: "How could you even *think* about missing that call?"

11. S argues that deer hunting is morally acceptable because, although it involves death and some suffering, it strengthens the deer herd. T responds: "S claims that deer hunting is okay because deer don't mind being killed; but that's absurd; every organism, human and animal alike, strives to continue living."

12. . . . since it is impossible for an animal or plant to be indefinitely big or small, neither can its parts be such, or the whole will be the same.

—ARISTOTLE, *Physics*

13. Suppose the issue is whether teachers should inculcate moral values such as honesty in their students. S argues as follows: "In order for teachers to inculcate moral values in their students, they must themselves *have* moral values. But many teachers lack such values. Those teachers should be fired."

14. A press release from the National Education Association (NEA) distributed in November begins with the following statement: "America's teachers see smaller classes as the most critical element in doing a better job, a survey by the NEA indicates. . . ."

But the NEA, of course, is interested in having as many teachers in the schools as possible. For example, in a 3,000-pupil school system with 30 pupils assigned to each class, the teaching staff would be approximately 100. But if class size were changed to 25 the total number of teachers would rise to 120. And in a time of shrinking enrollments, that is a way to keep teachers on the public payroll. . . .

It is unfortunate that an organization with the professional reputation the National Education Association enjoys should be so self-serving.

—CYNTHIA PARSONS, *Christian Science Monitor* Service, February 1976

■ *15.* My Schwinn bicycle has given me years of maintenance-free use. My friend Dan also has a Schwinn, and his bike too has functioned well without maintenance. Schwinn bikes must be among the best made.

16. S says "I shot a rat in my underwear". T responds: "What was a rat doing wearing your underwear?"

17. Professor Jones came up with that theory while in the shower. How can you take it seriously?

18. Immigration and Naturalization Service district director Ronald Chandler says he could find no "compelling" reasons to stop Salvadoran refugee Vince Quezada from deportation. Perhaps he should have looked into the eyes of four children and a wife who likely now will be forced to accept welfare subsidies.

—KAREN KUTACH, letter to the editor, *The Dallas Morning News,* October 7, 1989

19.   We have to put up with racial and other epithets, much as we detest them. The only alternative is to silence everyone, but that would be too much of an infringement of individual liberty.

■ **20.**   The following is quoted from F. L. Wellman, *The Art of Cross Examination* (New York: Macmillan Publishing Co., 1946). The conclusion here, it should be noted, is implied rather than explicitly drawn.

A very well-known doctor had given important testimony in a case where his most intimate friend appeared as opposing counsel. These two men—doctor and lawyer—stood equally high in their respective professions, and had been close friends for many years and were frequent dinner companions at one another's homes, with their wives and children. In fact, they had practically grown up together. The lawyer knew that his friend had testified to his honest opinion, which no amount of cross-examination could weaken. He therefore confined himself to the following few interrogations; and, fearing that he could not keep a straight face while he put his questions, he avoided facing the witness at all, keeping his face turned toward a side window.

> Q: "Doctor, you say you are a practicing physician. Have you practiced your profession in the City of Chicago for any length of time?"
> A: "Yes, I have been in practice here in Chicago now for about forty years."
> Q: "Well, Doctor, during that time I presume you have had occasion to treat some of our most prominent citizens. Have you not?"
> A: "Yes, I think I have."
> Q: "By any chance, Doctor, were you ever called as a family physician to prescribe for the elder Marshall Field?"
> A: "Yes, I was his family physician for a number of years."
> Q: "By the way I haven't heard of him lately. Where is he now?" (Still looking out of the window.)
> A: "He is dead."
> Q: "Oh—I'm sorry. Were you ever the family physician to the elder Mr. McCormick?"
> A: "Yes, also for many years."
> Q: "Would you mind my asking where he is now?"
> A: "He is dead."
> Q: "Oh—I'm sorry."

Then he proceeded in the same vein to make inquiries about eight or ten of the leading Chicago citizens whom he knew his friend had attended, all of whom were dead, and having exhausted the list he sat down quietly amid the amused chuckles of the jurors with the comment: "I don't think it is necessary to ask you any more questions. Please step down."

4

Definition

4.1 PURPOSES OF DEFINITION

To Increase Vocabulary

Language is a complicated and versatile instrument. People learn to use it in much the same way as they learn to use other tools, such as automobiles or kitchen equipment. Youngsters who do much riding with their parents or friends seldom need formal instruction in driving a car; they acquire their knowledge by observation and imitation. In the same way, those who spend much time in the kitchen learn to use complicated kitchen appliances. The case is similar with language: Certainly in childhood, and for many of us throughout our lives, we learn the proper use of language by observing and imitating the linguistic behavior of the people we meet.

There are, however, limits to this informal learning. The rising devastation from traffic accidents has made it imperative for drivers to be given some formal training over and above the learning by imitation that used to suffice. And the need to supplement home training has long been recognized by including courses in home economics in most high school and some college curricula. The situation is similar in language study. When the usual methods of observation and imitation do not suffice, formal instruction, that is, deliberate explanation of the meanings of terms, is required. To explain the meaning of a term is to give a definition of it. To give a definition is not the primary method of instruction in the proper use and understanding of language; it is, rather, a supplementary device for filling the gaps the primary method leaves.

In conversation or in reading, one often comes upon unfamiliar words whose meanings are not made clear by their contexts. To understand what is being said, it is necessary to find out what the words mean; here definitions are required. One purpose of definition, then, is to increase the vocabulary of the person for whom the definition is constructed. Dictionaries are useful for this purpose.

To Eliminate Ambiguity

Another purpose definition serves is to eliminate ambiguity. Perhaps most words have two or more distinct meanings or senses, and usually no trouble arises from this fact. In some contexts, however, it may not be clear which sense of a given word is intended, and it is said to be ambiguous. Fallacious arguments can result from the unwitting use of ambiguous terms, as was discussed in section 3.2, where they were characterized as fallacies of ambiguity. Such arguments are misleading only if the ambiguity passes unnoticed. When the ambiguity is revealed, the persuasiveness vanishes and the fallacy is exposed. But to reveal the ambiguity, we require definitions to specify the different meanings of the ambiguous word or phrase.

Ambiguous language can lead not only to fallacious argumentation but also to disputes that are merely verbal. Some disagreements turn not on any genuine differences of opinion but rather on different uses of a term. Where the ambiguity of a key term has led to a merely verbal dispute, we often can resolve the dispute by pointing out the ambiguity. That is done by giving the two different definitions of the term so the different meanings can be clearly distinguished and the confusion dispelled. A now-classic example of this method of resolving merely verbal disputes by defining the ambiguous terms involved is due to William James. In the second lecture in *Pragmatism,* James wrote:

> Some years ago, being with a camping party in the mountains, I returned from a solitary ramble to find every one engaged in a ferocious metaphysical dispute. The *corpus* of the dispute was a squirrel—a live squirrel supposed to be clinging to one side of a tree-trunk; while over against the tree's opposite side a human being was imagined to stand. This human witness tries to get sight of the squirrel by moving rapidly round the tree, but no matter how fast he goes, the squirrel moves as fast in the opposite direction, and always keeps the tree between himself and the man, so that never a glimpse of him is caught. The resultant metaphysical problem is this: *Does the man go round the squirrel or not?* He goes round the tree, sure enough, and the squirrel is on the tree; but does he go round the squirrel? In the unlimited leisure of the wilderness, discussion had been worn threadbare. Everyone had taken sides, and was obstinate; and the numbers of both sides were even. Each side, when I appeared, therefore appealed to me to make it a majority. Mindful of the scholastic adage that whenever you meet a contradiction you must make a distinction, I immediately sought and found one, as follows: "Which party is right," I said, "depends on what you *practically mean* by 'going round' the squirrel. If you mean passing from the north of him to the east, then to the south, then to the west, and then to the north of him again, obviously the man does go round him, for he occupies these successive positions. But if on the contrary you mean being first in front of him, then on the right of him, then behind him, then on his left, and finally in front again, it is quite obvious that the man fails to go round him, for by the compensating movements the squirrel makes, he keeps his belly turned towards the man all the time, and his back turned away. Make the distinction, and there is no occasion for any further dispute. You are both right and wrong according as you conceive the verb 'go round' in one practical fashion or the other."
>
> Although one or two of the hotter disputants called my speech a shuffling evasion, saying they wanted no quibbling or scholastic hair-splitting, but meant just plain hon-

est English "round," the majority seemed to think that the distinction had assuaged the dispute.[1]

As James points out, no new "facts" were required to resolve the dispute; none could possibly have helped. What was needed was just what James supplied, a distinction between different meanings of the key term in the argument. This could be accomplished, of course, only by supplying alternative definitions of the term "go round." We can settle merely verbal disputes only by giving definitions of the ambiguous terms involved. The second purpose of definition, then, is to eliminate ambiguity, either to expose fallacies of ambiguity or to resolve disputes that are merely verbal.

An example of defining terms to avoid *potential* ambiguity is the following. Here the definitions of the different senses of the term "ability" are more preventive than corrective. The passage reports that in their work, psychometricians have adopted the eminently sensible practice of using different terms for the different senses distinguished.

> The idea that colleges should choose among applicants on the basis of their "academic ability" appeals to both educators and the public. But "ability" has two distinct meanings, which imply different admissions policies. In one usage academic ability means an *existing* capacity to do academic work. In the other usage academic ability means a *potential* capacity to do such work. To say that an applicant "has the ability to do differential calculus," for example, can mean either that the applicant can already do differential calculus or that the applicant could learn differential calculus given opportunity and motivation. To avoid this ambiguity, psychometricians usually call the ability to learn something an "aptitude" while calling current mastery of a skill or body of knowledge "achievement."[2]

In most (although not all) contexts, it is a good idea to define ambiguous terms in advance to reduce the possibility of fallacious inferences. To achieve this end, one must be aware of the various senses of words, phrases, and sentences.

To Reduce Vagueness

Another occasion for defining a term arises when we desire to use it but are not quite sure of the limits of its applicability, although in a sense we do know its meaning. This motive for wanting a term defined is different from the first one discussed where the motive was to teach the meaning of an unfamiliar term. Here the purpose is to clarify the meaning of a term already known (to some extent). Where the meaning of a term is in need of clarification, we say the term is vague. To clarify its meaning is to reduce its vagueness, and this is accomplished by giving a definition of the term that permits a decision as to its applicability in a given situation where it was previously doubtful. This process sometimes is confused with eliminating ambiguity, because vagueness sometimes is confused with ambiguity. Although the same word can be both vague and

---

[1]   William James, *Pragmatism* (1907), pp. 43–45.
[2]   Christopher Jencks and James Crouse, "Aptitude vs. Achievement: Should We Replace the SAT?" *The Public Interest*, Spring 1982, p. 21.

ambiguous (for example, "light"), vagueness and ambiguity are different characteristics. A term is *ambiguous* in a given context when it has two or more distinct meanings and the context does not make clear which meaning is intended. A term is *vague*, however, when there exist "borderline cases" such that it cannot be determined whether the term applies to them. Most words are vague in the sense indicated. Scientists have been unable to decide whether certain viruses are "living" or "nonliving," not because they do not know whether the virus has the powers of locomotion, reproduction, and so on, but because the word "living" is so vague a term. Perhaps more familiar is the difficulty in deciding whether a certain country is a "democracy" or whether a given novel or motion picture is "obscene."

These "difficulties" may seem trivial, but under certain circumstances they can assume practical importance. Consider the following headline:

> **WHAT IS OBSCENITY?**
> Lack of a Definition
> Stymies a Crackdown
> Against Smut Dealers[3]

Shortly after this headline appeared, the U.S. Supreme Court issued an important ruling on obscenity, one goal of which was to define the term. According to the Court, in determining whether a given work is obscene,

> The basic guidelines for the trier of fact must be: (a) whether "the average person, applying contemporary community standards," would find that the work, taken as a whole, appeals to the prurient interest; (b) whether the work depicts or describes, in a patently offensive way, sexual conduct specifically defined by the applicable state law; and (c) whether the work, taken as a whole, lacks serious literary, artistic, political, or scientific value.[4]

Ironically, in attempting to make the meaning of the word "obscenity" less vague, the Court introduced a number of equally vague, if not more vague, expressions. Among these are "average person," "contemporary community standards," "prurient interest," "patently offensive," "sexual conduct," and "serious literary, artistic, political, or scientific value." This does not show that it is impossible to reduce vagueness by defining key terms, but it does caution us to be careful in doing so.

The indecision attending such borderline cases may be resolved by giving definitions of the vague terms that will make clear whether they are to be applied. Of course the definitions must be "enforceable," which means that the authority of the courts or of legislation must stand behind them. Thus, to decide whether a house trailer is to be taxed as a vehicle or as a dwelling, we must find out how the law defines these terms.

---

[3] *The Wall Street Journal*, 19 August 1970, p. 1.
[4] Justice Warren Burger, for the U.S. Supreme Court. *Miller v. California,* 413 U.S. 15, 24 (1973).

And if the definitions on record are not sufficiently precise to make a decision, the court within whose jurisdiction the question arises must promulgate new definitions that will permit clear application. For example, in 1966 the Supreme Court of North Carolina ruled that a yacht was not a "motor vehicle" for purposes of state law, thus making its sale subject to the state's 3-percent sales tax, and rejecting the contention that as a motor vehicle the craft was subject only to a special 1-percent tax.[5]

The vagueness of "death" has given rise to considerable controversy among lawyers and medical professionals:

> In recent years, there has been much discussion of the need to refine and update the criteria for determining that a human being has died. In light of medicine's increasing ability to maintain certain signs of life artificially and to make good use of organs from newly dead bodies, new criteria of death have been proposed by medical authorities. Several states have enacted or are considering legislation to establish a statutory "definition of death," at the prompting of some members of the medical profession who apparently feel that existing, judicially-framed standards might expose physicians, particularly transplant surgeons, to civil or criminal liability.[6]

A third purpose of giving definitions, then, is to reduce the vagueness of familiar terms, which is a different purpose from the first two mentioned.

To Explain Theoretically

Still another purpose we may have in defining a term is to formulate a theoretically adequate or scientifically useful characterization of the objects to which it is applied. For example, physical scientists have defined the term "force" as the product of mass and acceleration. This definition is not given to increase anyone's vocabulary or to eliminate ambiguity, but to embody part of Newtonian mechanics into the very meaning of the term "force." Although such a definition might well reduce the vagueness of the term being defined, that is not its primary purpose. Another example of a definition intended to serve this theoretical purpose is the chemist's definition of "acid" to mean any substance containing hydrogen as a positive radical. Everything that is correctly called an acid in ordinary usage is denoted by the term as defined by the chemist, but no pretense is made that the chemist's principle for distinguishing acids from other substances is actually applied by cooks or sheet-metal workers. The chemist's definition is intended to attach to the word, as meaning that characteristic which in the context of chemical theory is most useful for understanding and predicting the behavior of those substances that the word denotes.

Social scientists define terms in the same way and with the same purpose, although the data of their theorizing are human actions and institutions rather than natural phenomena. For example, to an economist, "efficiency" means a state of affairs in which resources are allocated to their most highly valued uses. An efficient

---

[5]   *The Wall Street Journal,* 16 March 1966, p. 1.

[6]   Alexander M. Capron and Leon R. Kass, "A Statutory Definition of the Standards for Determining Human Death: An Appraisal and a Proposal," *University of Pennsylvania Law Review* 121, November 1972.

allocation of resources is one in which no value-enhancing transfer is possible.[7] In political science, "state" means "an organized machinery for the making and carrying out of political decisions and for the enforcement of the laws and rules of a government."[8] Psychologists use the word "motivation" in a technical way to mean "a hypothetical internal process that provides the energy for behavior and directs it toward a specific goal."[9] When scientists construct definitions such as these, their purposes are theoretical.

To Influence Attitudes

One often defines a term in order to influence the attitudes or to stir the emotions of one's readers or hearers in certain desired ways. Thus a person may rise to the defense of a friend accused of tactlessness by praising the friend's honesty, defining "honesty" as always telling the truth regardless of circumstances. Here the speaker's purpose is not to give an explanation of the literal meaning of the word "honesty" but to cause his or her listeners to transfer to the friend's behavior the laudatory emotive value that attaches to the term "honesty." The speaker's language is not informative; it is functioning expressively. The emotive value to be transferred need not belong initially to the term being defined but can attach to a word or phrase used in stating the definition. For example, a proponent of socialism may *define* "socialism" to mean *democracy extended to the economic field.* Here the word "socialism" is not being defined to explain its descriptive meaning, but rather to win for it some of the approval usually aroused by the word "democracy." It may be questioned whether rhetorical devices like these should be called definitions, but the word frequently is used in this way, as in newspaper contests for the "best definitions" of various terms.

4.2   TYPES OF DEFINITION

Before distinguishing the various types of definition, it should be remarked that definitions are always of symbols, for only symbols have meanings for definitions to report. We can define the word "chair," since it is a word with a meaning; but although we can sit on it, paint it, burn it, or describe it, we cannot define a chair itself, for a chair is an article of furniture, not a symbol that has a meaning for us to explain. A definition can be expressed in either of two ways, by talking about the symbol to be defined or by talking about its referent. Thus we can equally well say either

The word "triangle" means a plane figure enclosed by three straight lines.

or

A triangle is (by definition) a plane figure enclosed by three straight lines.

---

[7]   See, e.g., Steven E. Rhoads, *The Economist's View of the World: Government, Markets, and Public Policy* (1985), p. 63; and Richard A. Posner, *Economic Analysis of Law,* 3d ed. (1986), p. 9.

[8]   Karl W. Deutsch, *Politics and Government: How People Decide Their Fate,* 2d ed. (1974), p. 115.

[9]   Robert Baron et al., *Psychology: Understanding Behavior,* Concise/Basic Edition (1978), p. 186.

This use of quotation marks to refer to a symbol should not be confused with other uses—for example, to quote people and to indicate unconventional or nonstandard uses of symbols.

Two terms commonly used in discussing definitions may be introduced at this point. The symbol being defined is called the *definiendum,* and the symbol or group of symbols used to state the meaning of the definiendum is called the *definiens.* For example, in the preceding definition the word "triangle" is the definiendum, and the phrase "a plane figure enclosed by three straight lines" is the definiens. The definiens is not the meaning of a definiendum, but another symbol or group of symbols that, according to the definition, has the same meaning as the definiendum.

Stipulative

The first type of definition is that given a term when it is introduced. Anyone who introduces a new symbol has complete freedom to stipulate what meaning is to be given it. The assignment of meanings to new symbols is a matter of choice, and we may call the definitions that propose that assignment *stipulative* definitions. Of course, the definiendum in a stipulative definition need not be a sound or mark or sequence of letters that is absolutely novel. It is sufficient that it be new in the context in which the defining takes place. Traditional discussions are not altogether clear, but it seems that what we are here calling stipulative definitions have sometimes been called "nominal" or "verbal."

New terms may be introduced for a variety of reasons. A commercial establishment with branches in foreign parts may compile a "cable" code in which single words are "short for" lengthy but routine messages. The advantages of introducing such new terms may include the relative secrecy their use achieves and lower costs for transmitting messages by cable or satellite. If such a code actually is to be used for communication, its maker must explain what the new terms are to mean, and to do so will propose stipulative definitions of them. Competitive bicyclists have developed a novel vocabulary to communicate various ideas or messages to one another—both on and off the bicycle. To "bonk," for example, is to experience fatigue by not eating enough food during a long race. Technical terms such as this, designed and used by members of a particular group, are referred to as "jargon."

New terms frequently are introduced into the sciences. There are many advantages to introducing technical symbols defined to mean what would otherwise require long sequences of familiar words to express. By doing so, scientists economize on the space required for writing out reports and theories, and also on the time involved. More importantly, the amount of attention or mental energy required is reduced, for when a sentence or equation grows too long its sense cannot easily be "taken in." Consider the economy achieved on all counts by the introduction of the exponent in mathematics.[10] What is now written quite briefly as

$$A^{12} = B$$

---

[10]   René Descartes (1596–1650), French mathematician and philosopher, generally is credited with introducing exponential notation (as well as the symbol for square roots). His aim, according to a biographer, was "To bring clarity and unity to both [algebra and geometry]." Tom Sorell, *Descartes* (1987), p. 19.

would, prior to the adoption of the special symbol for exponentiation, have had to be expressed either by

$$A \times A \times A \times A \times A \times A \times A \times A \times A \times A \times A \times A = B$$

or by a sentence of ordinary language instead of a mathematical equation.

Still another reason exists for the scientist's introduction of new symbols: The emotive suggestions of familiar words often are disturbing to one interested only in their descriptive meanings. The introduction of new symbols, explicitly defined to have the same descriptive meanings as familiar ones, will free the investigator from the distraction of the latter's emotive associations. This advantage accounts for the presence of some curious words in modern psychology, such as Spearman's "g factor," which is intended to convey the same descriptive meaning as the word "intelligence" but to share none of its emotional significance. Lawyers and judges, who often are accused by laypeople of intentional obfuscation, have developed an arcane vocabulary in part to avoid emotively charged words. For example, in criminal law, the term "mens rea" expresses the idea of a guilty mind, but without the emotional overtones. For the new terminology to be learned and used, the new symbols must have their meanings assigned to them by stipulative definitions.

A symbol defined by a stipulative definition did not have that meaning prior to being given it by the definition. Hence its definition cannot be regarded as a statement or report that the definiendum and the definiens have the same meaning. They actually will have the same meaning for anyone who accepts the definition, but that is something that follows from the definition rather than being asserted by it. A stipulative definition is neither true nor false, but should be regarded as a proposal or resolution to use the definiendum to mean what is meant by the definiens, or as a request or command to do so. In this sense a stipulative definition is directive rather than informative, to use terms introduced in section 2.1. Proposals may be rejected, resolutions quashed, requests denied, commands disobeyed, and stipulations ignored, but none of them are on that account either true or false. So it is with stipulative definitions.

Of course, stipulative definitions may be evaluated on other grounds. Whether a new term serves the purpose or purposes for which it was introduced is a question of fact. The definition may be either so obscure or so complex as to be unusable. It is not the case that any stipulative definition is as "good" as any other, but the grounds for their comparison must clearly be other than truth or falsehood, for these terms simply do not apply. Stipulative definitions are arbitrary only in the sense specified. Whether they are clear or unclear, advantageous or disadvantageous, or the like, are factual questions whose answers depend, ultimately, on our purposes.

Lexical

Where the purpose of a definition is to eliminate ambiguity or to increase the vocabulary of the person for whom it is constructed, the definition is lexical rather than stipulative. A lexical definition does not propose for its definiendum a meaning that it

---

[11]   Eugene Ehrlich et al., *Oxford American Dictionary* (1980), p. 434.

previously lacked, but reports a meaning it already has. Accordingly, a lexical definition may be either true or false. For example, the definition

> The word "mountain" means a mass of land that rises to a great height.[11]

is true; it is an accurate report of how English-speaking people use the word "mountain" (that is, of what they mean by it). On the other hand, the definition

> The word "mountain" means a plane figure enclosed by three straight lines.

is false; it is an inaccurate report of how English-speaking people use the word "mountain." Here is the important difference between stipulative and lexical definitions. Because a stipulative definition's definiendum had no meaning prior to the definition introducing it, that definition cannot be false (or true). But because the definiendum of a lexical definition *does* have a prior and independent meaning, its definition is either true or false, depending on whether that meaning is correctly or incorrectly reported. Although traditional discussions are not altogether clear on this point, it seems that what we are calling lexical definitions sometimes have been referred to as "real" definitions.

One point should be made clear concerning the questions of "existence." Whether a definition is stipulative or lexical has nothing to do with the question of whether the definiendum names any "real" or "existing" thing. The definition

> The word "unicorn" means an animal like a horse but having a single straight horn projecting from its forehead.

is a "real" or lexical definition, and a true one, because the definiendum is a word with long-established usage and means exactly what is meant by the definiens. Yet the definiendum does not name or denote any existing thing, because there are no unicorns.

A qualification must be made at this point, for in asserting that lexical definitions of the kind illustrated are true or false, we are oversimplifying a complex situation. The fact is that many words are used in different ways, not because they have a plurality of standard meanings, but through what we should call error. Not all instances of erroneous word usage are as funny as those of Sheridan's Mrs. Malaprop when she gives the order to "illiterate him . . . from your memory" or uses the phrase "as headstrong as an allegory on the banks of the Nile." Some words are used by many people in ways that might be called erroneous or mistaken but that are perhaps better described as unorthodox. And any definition of a word that ignores the way in which it is used by any sizable group of speakers is not true to actual usage and is therefore not quite correct.

Word usage is a statistical matter, and any definition of a word whose usage is subject to this kind of variation must not be a simple statement of "the meaning" of the term, but a statistical description of the various meanings of the term, as determined by the uses it has in actual speech. The need for lexical statistics cannot be evaded by reference to "correct" usage, for that too is a matter of degree, being measured by the number of "first-rate" authors whose usages of a given term are in agreement. Moreover, literary and academic vocabularies tend to lag behind the growth of living language. Unorthodox usages have a way of becoming catholic, so definitions that report only the meanings countenanced by an academic minority are likely to be misleading. Of course, the notion of statistical definitions is utopian, but dictionaries approximate it more or less by indicating which meanings are "archaic" or "obsolete" and which are "colloquial" or "slang." With the foregoing as qualification, we may repeat that lexical definitions are true or false, in the sense of being or not being true to actual usage.

Precising

Neither stipulative nor lexical definitions can serve to reduce a term's vagueness. A vague term is one for which borderline cases may arise, such that it cannot be determined whether the term should be applied to them. Ordinary usage cannot be appealed to for a decision, because ordinary usage, by hypothesis, is not sufficiently clear on the matter. To reach a decision, then, ordinary usage must be transcended; a definition capable of helping us decide borderline cases must go beyond what is merely lexical. Such a definition may be called a *precising definition*.

A precising definition is different from a stipulative definition because its definiendum is not a new term but one with an established, although vague, usage. Consequently, the makers of a precising definition are not free to assign any meaning they choose to the definiendum. They must remain true to established usage so far as it goes.

Yet they must go beyond that established usage if the vagueness of the definiendum is to be reduced. Exactly how they go beyond, just how they fill the gaps or resolve the conflicts of established usage, is partly a matter of stipulation, but not completely so. Many legal decisions involve precising definitions in which constitutional or statutory terms are clarified so they will specifically cover or specifically exclude the case at issue. We saw an example of this in section 4.1. Jurists usually present arguments intended to justify their decisions in such cases, which shows that they do not regard their precising definitions as mere stipulations even in those areas not covered by precedent or established usage. Instead they seek to be guided in part by the supposed intentions of the framers or legislators who drafted the language and in part by what the jurists conceive to be the public interest. The terms "true" and "false" apply only in a partial fashion to precising definitions, their application signifying that the definition conforms or fails to conform to established usage so far as it goes. In evaluating the way in which a precising definition goes beyond established usage where the latter is unclear, truth and falsehood do not apply. We must speak instead of the definition's convenience or inconvenience or (especially in a legal or quasilegal context) of its wisdom or folly.

Theoretical

It is in connection with theoretical definitions that most "disputing over definitions" occurs. A theoretical definition of a term constitutes an effort to explain the nature of the things to which the definiendum normally applies. Its purpose is to formulate a theoretically adequate or scientifically useful account of the objects to which the term applies. To propose a theoretical definition is tantamount to proposing the acceptance of a theory, and, as the name suggests, theories are notoriously debatable. (For a discussion, see chapter 7.) Here one definition is replaced by another as our knowledge and theoretical understanding increase. At one time physicists defined "heat" to mean a subtle imponderable fluid; now they define it as a form of energy possessed by a body by virtue of the irregular motion of its molecules. Physicists have given different theoretical definitions of "heat" at different times because they accepted different theories of heat at those times.

Those who are acquainted with the writings of Plato will recognize that the definitions he represented Socrates as seeking were neither stipulative, lexical, nor precising, but rather, theoretical. Socrates was not interested in any merely statistical account of how people use the term "justice" (or "courage," or "temperature," or "virtue"), but at the same time he insisted that any proposed definition be consonant with actual usage. Nor was he interested in giving precising definitions of these terms, for borderline cases were not emphasized. To define such terms as "good" and "true" and "beautiful"—or, to put it differently, to analyze the concepts of the good, the true, and the beautiful—is the aim of many philosophers. That they dispute each other's proposed definitions indicates that they are not seeking stipulative definitions. Nor are they after lexical definitions, or recourse to dictionaries or public-opinion polls on word usage could settle the matter. That some philosophers can agree on the application of the term "good" in all circumstances, without being bothered by borderline cases, and still disagree over how the term "good" ought to be defined indicates that they are not seeking a precising definition of the term. Philosophers as well as scientists are most interested in constructing theoretical definitions. Theoretical definitions sometimes are referred to as "analytical" definitions, although this latter term has another sense as well.

Persuasive

The last type of definition to be mentioned is that whose purpose is to influence attitudes. Such definitions are called *persuasive* definitions and their function is expressive. Persuasive definitions are not coordinate with the other types already discussed, however. Because the same language can function both expressively and informatively, it is plausible to suppose that a definition of any one of the other types also can be a persuasive definition if it is phrased in emotive language and is intended to influence attitudes as well as to instruct.

Here, for example, is a report of a precising definition the purpose of which was to influence attitudes:

> [Federal Reserve chairperson] Alan Greenspan, in testimony . . . before the Joint Economic Committee, argued for a definition of recession that is more stringent than the traditional public concept of one. The popular view is that a recession occurs when the gross national product [G.N.P.]—the total value of the new goods and services that the nation is constantly producing—shrinks for six consecutive months.

Mr. Greenspan acknowledged that the economy was very sluggish, so much so that the G.N.P. grew at an annual rate of only 1 percent during the first six months of 1990, including a minuscule four-tenths of 1 percent in the second quarter. Without much change in the public's current sense of malaise, the G.N.P. could easily slip into negative growth for two quarters, he says.

A true recession, Mr. Greenspan argued, is a "cumulative unwinding of economic activity," and not simply a few months of mildly negative G.N.P. growth that might be reversed when the Commerce Department issues its annual revisions of earlier statistics.[12]

Greenspan's proposed definition of "recession" is best characterized as a precising definition, because its definiendum is an established term whose meaning, in his view, is unclear. But he also is trying to influence people's attitudes toward the economy by narrowing the circumstances in which the politically unappealing term "recession" applies; this makes the definition persuasive as well as precising.

Entertaining and illuminating examples of persuasive definitions were published in a Honolulu newspaper during the Hawaiian state legislature's hearings on a proposal to abolish the state's law against abortion. Under the heading "Defining Abortion a Tricky Business" appeared the following story:

Amidst the emotional debate on the abortion issue at the State Legislature, humor still lives.

Anonymous legislative staffers this week drafted and circulated to legislators a proposed "general response to constituent letters on abortion." It goes like this:

"Dear Sir:

"You ask me how I stand on abortion. Let me answer forthrightly and without equivocation.

"If by abortion you mean the murdering of defenseless human beings; the denial of rights to the youngest of our citizens; the promotion of promiscuity among our shiftless and valueless youth and the rejection of Life, Liberty and the Pursuit of Happiness—then, Sir, be assured that I shall never waver in my opposition, so help me God.

"But, Sir, if by abortion you mean the granting of equal rights to all our citizens regardless of race, color or sex; the elimination of evil and vile institutions preying upon desperate and hopeless women; a chance to all our youth to be wanted and loved; and, above all, that God-given right for all citizens to act in accordance with the dictates of their own conscience—then, Sir, let me promise you as a patriot and a humanist that I shall never be persuaded to forego my pursuit of these most basic human rights.

"Thank you for asking my position on this most crucial issue and let me again assure you of the steadfastness of my stand.

"Mahalo and Aloha Nui."[13]

In section 4.1 we discussed five purposes of definition, and in section 4.2 we named five types of definition. The relations between purposes and types are fairly clear. Both

---

[12] Louis Uchitelle, "When Is It a Recession?," *The New York Times,* 26 September 1990, p. C5.

[13] "Defining Abortion a Tricky Business," *The Honolulu Advertiser,* 14 February 1970. The last four words are Hawaiian for "Thanks and Much Love."

stipulative and lexical definitions serve the purpose of increasing the vocabulary of the person for whom the definition is constructed. Lexical definitions also can serve the purpose of eliminating ambiguity, either to expose a fallacy of ambiguity or to resolve a verbal dispute. A precising definition serves the purpose of reducing the vagueness of its definiendum. A theoretical definition serves the purpose of explaining something theoretically; that is, of formulating a theoretically adequate or scientifically useful account of those things to which the definiendum applies. Any of these definitions also can serve the rhetorical purpose of influencing attitudes, and when they do, they are to count also as persuasive definitions.

EXERCISE

Find two examples of each type of definition and discuss the purposes they are intended to serve.

4.3   KINDS OF MEANING

Because a definition states the *meaning* of a term, it is important for us to have clearly in mind the different senses of the word "meaning"—that is, the meaning of "meaning." The distinction between descriptive and emotive meaning was discussed in section 2.4, and we need not repeat what was said. However, a certain further distinction must be drawn in connection with what was there called descriptive meaning, especially in connection with *general terms* or *class terms* applicable to more than a single object. A general term such as "planet" is applicable in the same sense equally to Mercury, Venus, Earth, Mars, and so on. In a perfectly acceptable sense, these various objects to which the term "planet" is applied are meant by the word; the collection of them, or the range of its application, constitutes its meaning. Thus if I assert that all planets have elliptical orbits, part of what I may intend to assert is that Mars has an elliptical orbit; and another part, that Venus has an elliptical orbit; and so on. In one sense the meaning of a term consists of the class of objects to which the term may be applied. This sense of "meaning," its referential sense, traditionally has been called *extensional* or *denotative* meaning. A general or class term *denotes* the objects to which it may correctly be applied, and the collection or class of these objects constitutes the extension or denotation of the term.

However, the foregoing is not the only sense of the word "meaning." To understand a term is to know how to apply it correctly, but for this it is not necessary to know all of the objects to which it may be correctly applied. It is required only that we have a criterion for deciding whether any given object falls within the extension of that term. All objects in the extension of a given term have some common attributes or characteristics that lead us to use the same term to denote them.

The collection of attributes shared by all and only those objects in a term's extension is called the *intension* or *connotation* of that term. General or class terms have both an *intensional* or *connotative* meaning and an extensional or denotative one. Thus, the intension or connotation of the term "skyscraper" consists of the attributes common and peculiar to all buildings over a certain height, whereas the extension or denotation of that term is the class containing the Empire State Building, the World Trade Center, the Wrigley Tower, and so on.

The word "connotation" has other uses, in which it refers to the total significance of a word, emotive as well as descriptive, and sometimes to its emotive meaning alone. If one denies that a person is "human," the word "human" is being used expressively, to communicate a certain attitude or feeling. This expressive function sometimes is equated with, sometimes included in, the "connotation" of a term. But logicians use the word in a narrower sense. In our usage, connotation and intension are part of the informative significance of a term.

Even with this restriction, various senses of "connotation" have yet to be distinguished. There are three different senses of the term "connotation," which have been called the *subjective,* the *objective,* and the *conventional.* The subjective connotation of a word for a speaker is the set of attributes that particular speaker believes to be possessed by the objects comprising that word's extension. It is clear that the subjective connotation of a term may vary from one individual to another. I have met New Yorkers for whom the word "skyscraper" had a subjective connotation that included the attribute of being located in New York City. The notion of subjective connotation is inconvenient for purposes of definition because it varies not merely from individual to individual but even from time to time for the same individual, as new beliefs are acquired or old ones abandoned. We are more interested in the public meanings of words than in their private interpretations; so, having mentioned subjective connotations, we shall eliminate them from further consideration.

The objective connotation or objective intension of a term is the set of characteristics the objects that make up that term's extension actually possess. It does not vary from interpreter to interpreter, for it all planets have the attribute of moving in elliptical orbits, for example, this will be part of the objective connotation of the word "planet" even if no user of the term knows it. But the concept of objective connotation is inconvenient for other reasons. Even in those rare cases where the complete extension of a term is known, it would require omniscience to know all the attributes the objects in that extension share. And because no human being has that omniscience, the objective connotation of a term is not the public meaning in whose explanation we are interested.

Because we do communicate with each other and understand the terms we use, the intensional or connotative meanings involved are neither subjective nor objective in the senses just explained. Those who attach the same meaning to a term use the same criterion for deciding whether any object is part of the term's extension. Thus we have agreed to use *the attribute of being a closed plane curve, all points of which are equidistant from a point within called the center* as our criterion for deciding whether a figure is to be called a "circle." This agreement, tacit though it may be, establishes a convention, and so this meaning of a term is known as its conventional connotation or conventional intension. The conventional connotation of a term is its most important aspect for purposes of definition and communication, because it is both public (unlike subjective connotation) and can be known by people who are not omniscient (unlike objective connotation). In this view, an important part of learning a language is learning the conventional connotations of its terms. For the sake of brevity we shall use the words "connotation" and "intension" to mean "conventional connotation" and "conventional intension" unless otherwise specified.

The extension or denotation of a term has been explained as the collection of objects to which the term applies. There are no troublesome, different senses of extension comparable to those found in the case of intension; however, the notion of extension is not without interest. For one thing, the extension of a term has been alleged to change from time to time in a way that the intension does not. The extension of the term "person" has been said to change almost continually as people die and babies are born. This varying extension does not belong to the term "person," conceived as denoting all persons, the dead as well as the yet unborn, but rather to the term "living person." But the term "living person" has the sense of "person living now," in which the word "now" refers to the fleeting present. Thus the intension of the term "living person" is different at different times. Any term with a changing extension also has a changing intension. So, in spite of the apparent difference, one is as constant as the other; when the intension of a term is fixed, the extension is fixed also.

It is worth mentioning in this connection that extension is determined by intention but not the other way around. The reason for this is that we don't know which objects fall within the term's extension until we know which attributes the term connotes. Thus the term "equilateral triangle" has for its intension or connotation the attribute of being a plane figure enclosed by three straight line segments of equal length. It has as its extension the class of all those objects and only those objects that have this attribute. The term "equiangular triangle" has a different intension, connoting the attribute of being a plane figure enclosed by three straight line segments that intersect each other to form equal angles. But the extension of the term "equiangular triangle" is exactly the same as the extension of the term "equilateral triangle." As this example demonstrates, terms can have different intensions but the same extension, although terms with different extensions cannot possibly have the same intension. (Why is this so?)

Consider the following sequence of terms, each of whose intension is included within the intension of the terms following it: "person," "living person," "living person over twenty years old," "living person over twenty years old having red hair." The intension of each of these terms (except the first, of course) is greater than the intensions of those preceding it in the sequence. The terms are arranged, we may say, in order of *increasing intension,* for a new attribute is added at each step. But if we turn to the extensions of those terms, we find the reverse to be the case. The extension of the term "person" is greater than that of "living person," and so on. In other words, the terms are arranged in order of *decreasing extension.* Consideration of such sequences led some logicians to formulate a "law of inverse variation," asserting that if a series of terms is arranged in order of increasing intension, their extensions will be in decreasing order; or, in other words, that extension and intension vary inversely with each other. This alleged law may have a certain suggestive value, but it cannot be accepted without qualification. That is shown by the following sequence of terms: "living person," "living person with a spinal column," "living person with a spinal column less than one thousand years old," "living person with a spinal column less than one thousand years old who has not read all the books in the Library of Congress." Here the terms are clearly in order of increasing intension, for the same reason as before, but the extension of each of them is the same, not decreasing. The law has been revised to accommodate such cases. In its amended version it asserts that if terms are arranged in order of increasing intension, their extensions will be in nonincreasing order; that is, if the extensions vary at all, they will vary inversely with the intensions.

In a given case, extension may be constant, increasing, or decreasing. The same is true of intension. This produces nine combinations, as depicted on the following chart:

		Extension		
		Constant	Increasing	Decreasing
	Constant	1	2	3
Intension	Increasing	4	5	6
	Decreasing	7	8	9

Only combinations 2, 3, 5, and 9 violate the amended law of inverse variation, for only in those cases is it true that extension varies but false that it varies inversely with intension. Combinations 1, 4, and 7 cannot violate the law because in none of them does extension vary. Combinations 6 and 8 comply with the law. (As an exercise, think of examples—other than those provided in the text—of combinations 1, 4, 6, 7, and 8.)

Finally, we turn to those terms that, although perfectly meaningful, do not denote anything. We use such terms whenever we (correctly) deny the existence of things of a certain kind. When we say that there are no unicorns, we assert that the term "unicorn" does not denote, that it has an "empty" extension or denotation. Such terms show that "meaning" pertains more to intension than to extension. For although the term "unicorn" has an empty extension, it does not follow that the term "unicorn" is meaningless. It does not denote anything because there are no unicorns; but if the term "unicorn" were meaningless, so also would be the statement "There are no unicorns." Far from being meaningless, the statement is true.

Our distinction between intension and extension, and the recognition that extensions may be empty, can be used to resolve the ambiguity of some occurrences of the term "meaning." Thus we can refute the following fallacy of ambiguity:

> The word "God" is not meaningless and therefore has a meaning. But by definition the word "God" means a supremely good and omnipotent being. Therefore, that supremely good and omnipotent being, God, must exist.

The equivocation here is on the words "meaning" and "meaningless." The word "God" is not meaningless, and so there is an intension or connotation that is its meaning in one sense. But it does not follow simply from the fact that a term has connotation that it denotes anything. The distinction between intension and extension is an old one, but it is still valuable and important.[14]

EXERCISES

I. Arrange each of the following groups of terms in order of increasing intension.

■   *1.*   animal, feline, lynx, mammal, vertebrate, wildcat.

2.   alcoholic beverage, beverage, champagne, fine white wine, white wine, wine.

3.   athlete, ball player, baseball player, fielder, infielder, shortstop.

4.   cheese, dairy product, limburger, milk derivative, soft cheese, strong soft cheese.

■   *5.*   integer, number, positive integer, prime, rational number, real number.

II. Divide the following list of terms into five groups of five terms each, arranged in order of increasing intension: aquatic animal, beast of burden, beverage, brandy, cognac, domestic animal, filly, fish, foal, game fish, horse, instrument, liquid, liquor, musical instrument, muskellunge, parallelogram, pike, polygon, quadrilateral, rectangle, square, Stradivarius, string instrument, violin.

4.4   TECHNIQUES FOR DEFINING

Denotative Definitions

We may divide techniques for defining into two groups, the first centering more on denotation or extension, the second on connotation or intension. The obvious and easy way to instruct someone about the denotation of a term is to give examples of objects denoted by it. This technique often is used and often is very effective. It has certain limitations, however, which ought to be recognized.

An obvious but trivial limitation of the method of definition by example is that it cannot be used to define words that have an empty extension, such as the words "unicorn" and "centaur." Having mentioned it, however, let us go on to more serious limitations.

It was observed in the preceding section that two terms with different intensions may have exactly the same extension. If one such term is defined by giving even a complete enumeration of the objects denoted by it, this definition will fail to distinguish it from the other term that denotes the same objects, even though the two terms are not synonyms. This limitation of the method of definition by example is a consequence of the fact that although intension determines extension, extension does not determine intension. Extension is said to "underdetermine" intension.

---

[14]   The useful distinction between intension and extension was introduced and emphasized by St. Anselm of Canterbury (1033–1109), who is best known for his "ontological argument" for the existence of God, to which the preceding fallacious argument has little if any resemblance.

The preceding is a very "academic" limitation, however, because few terms can have their extensions completely enumerated. It is logically impossible to enumerate all the infinitely many numbers denoted by the term "number," and it is practically impossible to enumerate the (probably) finite but literally astronomical number of objects denoted by the term "star." In cases like these we are restricted to giving a partial enumeration of objects denoted, which involves a more serious limitation. Any given object has many, many attributes and therefore is included in the extensions of many, many different terms. Hence any example mentioned in the denotative definition of any one term will be just as appropriately mentioned in the denotative definitions of many other terms. A particular individual, John Doe, can be mentioned as an example in defining "man," "animal," "husband," "taxpayer," or "father." Therefore mentioning him will not help to distinguish between the meanings of any of these terms. The same is true for two examples, or three, or for any number that falls short of the total. Thus three obvious examples to use in defining the term "skyscraper," the Chrysler, Empire State, and Woolworth buildings, serve equally well as examples of the denotation of the terms "buildings," "structures completed since 1911," "objects located in Manhattan," "expensive things," and so on. Yet each of these terms denotes objects not denoted by the others, so definition by partial enumeration cannot serve even to distinguish terms that have different extensions.

Of course, "negative instances" may be brought in to help specify the definiendum's meaning, as in adding to the definition of "skyscraper" that the term does *not* denote such things as the Taj Mahal, the Pentagon Building, Central Park, or the Hope diamond. But because the enumeration of these negative instances must itself be incomplete, the basic limitation remains. Definition by enumeration of examples, whether complete or partial, may have psychological reasons to recommend it, but it is logically inadequate to specify completely the meanings of the terms being defined.

The foregoing remarks have been concerned with denotative definitions in which examples are named or enumerated one at a time. Perhaps a more efficient way to give examples is not to mention the individual members of the class that is the extension of the term being defined, but to mention instead whole groups of its members. Thus to define the word "metal" as meaning gold and iron and silver and tin and the like is different from defining "skyscraper" as meaning the Chrysler and Empire State and Woolworth buildings and the like. This special kind of definition by example— definition by subclasses—also permits complete enumeration, such as when "vertebrate" is defined to mean amphibians, birds, fishes, mammals, and reptiles. In spite of the indicated difference, this second kind of denotative definition has in general the same advantages and limitations as those others that already have been discussed. (Explain why this is so.)

A special kind of definition by example is called *ostensive* or *demonstrative* definition. Instead of naming or describing the objects denoted by the term being defined, as in the ordinary sort of denotative definition, an ostensive definition refers to the examples by means of pointing or some other gesture. An example of an ostensive or demonstrative definition would be "The word 'desk' means *this,*" accompanied by a gesture such as pointing a finger or nodding one's head in the direction of a desk.

Ostensive definitions have all the limitations mentioned in the preceding discussion. In addition, ostensive definitions have limitations peculiar to themselves. Apart from the relatively trivial geographical limitation that one cannot ostensively define the word "skyscraper" in a village or the word "mountain" on the prairie, there is the essential ambiguity of gestures to consider. To point to a desk is also to point to a part of it; and to the color, shape, size, and material of the desk; and also, in fact, to everything that lies in the general direction of the desk, such as the wall behind it or the garden beyond. This ambiguity can be resolved only by adding some descriptive phrase to the definiens, which results in what may be called a quasi-ostensive definition, as, for example, "The word 'desk' means this *article of furniture*" (accompanied by an appropriate gesture).

This addition, however, defeats the purpose that ostensive definitions have been claimed to serve. Ostensive definitions sometimes have been alleged to be the "first" or "primary" definitions, in the sense that all other definitions must assume that some words (those used in the definiens) are already understood and therefore cannot be used unless those words have previously been defined. It has been suggested that this difficulty can be avoided by beginning with ostensive definitions. It is by means of ostensive definitions, some writers have claimed, that we learn to understand our first words. This claim is easily seen to be mistaken, for the meaning or significance of gestures themselves must be learned. If you point with your finger to the side of a baby's crib, the baby's attention, if attracted at all, is as likely to be directed toward your finger as in the direction pointed. And surely one is in the same difficulty concerning the definition of gestures by means of other gestures. The point is this: To understand the definition of *any* sign, some signs already must be understood. This bears out our earlier remark that the primary way of learning to use language is by observation and imitation, not by definition.

It should be acknowledged that these remarks about ostensive definitions are pertinent only to the particular interpretation placed on them here. Some writers on logic have understood the phrase "ostensive definition" to include the process of "frequently hearing the word when the object it denotes is present." But such a process would not be a definition at all, as we have been using the term in the present chapter. It would rather be the primary, predefinitional way of learning to use language.

EXERCISES

I. Define the following terms by example, giving three examples for each term:

- 1. actor
- 4. dramatist
- 7. general (officer)
- 10. poet
- 13. game

- 2. boxer
- 5. element
- 8. harbor
- 11. athlete
- 14. automobile

- 3. composer
- 6. flower
- 9. inventor
- 12. ship
- 15. university

II. For each of the terms in Exercise I, can you find a nonsynonymous term that your examples serve equally well to illustrate?

Connotative Definitions

Before turning to the topic of connotative definition proper, some mention should be made of the frequently used technique of defining a single word by giving another single word that has the same meaning. Two words that have the same meaning are called "synonyms"; so a definition of this type is said to be a *synonymous* definition. Many dictionaries, especially smaller ones, use this method extensively. Thus a pocket dictionary may define "adage" as meaning proverb, "bashful" as meaning shy, and so on. Synonymous definitions almost always are used in textbooks and dictionaries designed to state the meanings of foreign words, where we have foreign words correlated in parallel columns with their English synonyms, as

annonce	advertisement
boîte	box
chat	cat
Dieu	God
élève	pupil

The preceding is an easy and efficient method of defining terms. Its applicability is limited, however, by the fact that many words have no (exact) synonyms. And it cannot be used in the construction of either *precising* or *theoretical* definitions. (Why is this so?)

A new technique for defining recently has come into prominence in the research and writing of scientists. Early in the present century, Einstein's theory of relativity challenged the notions of absolute space and absolute time, which had been defined in abstract terms by Isaac Newton (1642–1727). The success and widespread acceptance of relativity theory led scientists to abandon those abstractions. It was found more fruitful to define space and time by means of the operations used in measuring distances and durations. An *operational definition* of a term states that the term is applied to a given case if and only if the performance of specified operations in that case yields a specified result. For example, the different numerical values of such a quantity as length are operationally defined by reference to the results of specified measuring operations.

An operational definition of a term has a definiens that refers only to public and repeatable operations. Some social scientists have sought to incorporate this new technique of defining into their own disciplines, as when legal theorist John Austin (1790–1859) defined "sovereign" as the person to whom the bulk of society are in the habit of obedience. Others attempted to replace abstract definitions of "mind" and "sensation" by operational definitions referring exclusively to physiology and behavior. In psychology, operational definitions have tended to be associated with behaviorism. Extreme empiricists sometimes have insisted that a term is meaningful only if it is susceptible to operational definition. To evaluate the claims and counterclaims made concerning operational definitions, however, is beyond the scope of this book.[15]

Where a synonymous definition is unavailable or an operational definition inappropriate, often we can use a definition by genus and difference. This method of definition also is called definition by division, analytical definition, definition *per genus et differentiam,* or simply connotative definition. It is regarded by many as the most important kind of definition and by some as the only "genuine" kind. There is scarcely any justification for the latter view, but there is considerable plausibility to the former, because it is more generally applicable than any other technique. The possibility of defining terms by genus and difference depends on the fact that some attributes are complex, in the sense of being analyzable into two or more other attributes. This complexity and analyzability can best be explained in terms of classes or categories.

Classes having members may have their memberships divided into subclasses. For example, the class of triangles may be divided into three nonempty subclasses: scalene triangles (those having no equal sides), isosceles triangles (those having two equal sides), and equilateral triangles (those having three equal sides). The terms "genus" and "species" often are used in this connection: The class whose membership is divided into subclasses is the *genus;* the various subclasses are *species.*[16] As used here, the words "genus" and "species" are *relative* terms, like "parent" and "offspring." Just as the same persons may be parents in relation to their children and offspring in relation to their parents, so one and the same class may be a genus in relation to its own subclasses and a species in relation to some larger class of which it is a subclass. Thus the class of triangles is a genus relative to the species *scalene triangle* and a species relative to the genus *polygon.* The logician's use of the words "genus" and "species" as relative terms is different from the biologist's use of them as absolute terms, and the two should not be confused.

Since a class is a collection of entities having some common characteristic, all the members of a given genus will have some characteristic in common. Thus all members of the genus *polygon* share the characteristic of being closed plane figures bounded by straight-line segments. This genus may be divided into different species or subclasses such that all the members of one subclass have some further attribute in common shared by no member of any other subclass of that genus. The genus *polygon* is divided into *triangles, quadrilaterals, pentagons, hexagons,* and so on. These species of the genus *polygon* are different, and the specific difference between members of the subclass *triangle* and members of any other subclass is that only members of the subclass

---

[15]   The term "operational definition" was first used by Nobel Prize winner P. W. Bridgman in his influential book *The Logic of Modern Physics,* published in 1927. An interesting discussion of his ideas can be found in "The Present State of Operationalism," *The Validation of Scientific Theories,* ed. Phillipp G. Frank (1956), chap. 2.
[16]   These terms give rise to several others. "Genus," for example, spawns "general" (of or affecting all or nearly all, not partial or local or particular); "generic" (of a whole genus or group); and "genre" (a particular kind or style of art or literature); while "species" serves as the root of "specific" (particular, clearly distinguished from others); "special" (of a particular kind, for a particular purpose, not general); and "specimen" (a part or individual taken as an example of a whole or of a class, especially for investigation or scientific examination). Eugene Ehrlich et al., *Oxford American Dictionary* (1980), pp. 271, 272, 655, 656.

triangle have exactly three sides. More generally, although all members of all species of a given genus have some attribute in common, the members of any one species share some further attribute that differentiates them from the members of any other. The characteristic that serves to distinguish them is called the specific difference. Thus having three sides is the *specific difference* between the species *triangle* and all other species of the genus *polygon*.

It is in this sense that the attribute of being a triangle may be said to be analyzable into the attribute of being a polygon and the attribute of having three sides. To someone who did not know the meaning of the word "triangle," or of any synonym of it, but who did know the meanings of the terms "polygon," "sides," and "three," the meaning of the word "triangle" could be explained by means of a *definition by genus and difference:*

The word "triangle" means polygon having three sides (or three-sided polygon).

Here is a more elaborate classification scheme:

Polygon

Quadrilateral				Nonquadrilateral
Parallelogram			Nonparallelogram	
Equiangular (rectangle)		Nonequiangular		
Equilateral (square)	Nonequilateral			
1	2	3	4	5

According to this scheme (sometimes known as a typology or taxonomy), quadrilaterals are members of the genus *polygon*. They are distinguished from other species of the genus (triangles, for example) in having four sides. By the same token, parallelograms are members of the genus *quadrilateral*; rectangles are members of the genus *parallelogram*; and squares are members of the genus *rectangle*. Put differently, a square is a special kind of rectangle (an equilateral one), which is a special kind of parallelogram (an equiangular one), which is a special kind of quadrilateral (one with two pairs of parallel sides), which is a special kind of polygon (a four-sided one).[17]

The ancient definition of the word "human" as meaning rational animal is another example of definition by genus and difference. Here the species *human* is subsumed under the genus *animal,* and the difference between it and other species of that genus is said to be *rationality*. To define a term by genus and difference, one

---

[17]   In which category—1 through 5—does a trapezoid fall? A triangle? A diamond-shaped figure? A pentagon? A figure with four sides, no two of which are parallel? A billboard-shaped figure?

names a genus of which the species designated by the definiendum is a subclass and then names the difference that distinguishes its members from members of other species of that genus. Of course, in the definition of "human" just mentioned, we could regard rational as the genus and animal as the difference, as well as the other way around. The order is not absolute from the point of view of logic, although there may be extralogical reasons (Can you list some?) for considering one as genus rather than the other.

Two limitations of this technique for defining terms may be mentioned briefly. In the first place, the method is applicable only to words that connote *complex* attributes. If there are any simple, unanalyzable attributes, then the words connoting them are not susceptible to definition by genus and difference. Examples that have been suggested of such attributes are the sensed qualities of particular shades of color. Whether there really are such attributes is an open question, but if there are, they limit the applicability of definition by genus and difference. Another limitation has to do with words connoting universal attributes, if they may be called that, such as the words "being," "thing," "entity," "existent," "object," and the like. These cannot be defined by the method of genus and difference because the class of all *entities,* for example, is not a species of some broader genus; entities themselves constitute the highest genus, or *summum genus,* as it is called. The same remark applies to words for ultimate metaphysical categories, such as "substance" or "property." These limitations, although perhaps worth mentioning, are of little practical importance in appraising this method of definition.

Connotative definitions, especially definitions by genus and difference, can serve any of the purposes discussed in section 4.1 and can be of any of the types enumerated in section 4.2.

EXERCISES

I. Give synonymous definitions for each of the following terms.

■ 1. absurd	2. buffoon	3. cemetery
4. dictator	■ 5. egotism	6. feast
7. garret	8. hasten	9. infant
■ 10. jeopardy	11. kine	12. labyrinth
13. mendicant	14. novice	■ 15. omen
16. panacea	17. quack	18. rostrum
19. scoundrel	■ 20. tepee	21. bystander
22. helmet	23. pendant	24. floe
■ 25. tradition		

II. Construct definitions for the following terms by matching the definiendum with an appropriate genus and difference.

Definiendum	*Definiens*	
	Genus	*Difference*
● 1. bachelor	1. body of water	1. female
2. banquet	2. horse	2. male
3. boy	3. man	3. married
4. brook	4. meal	4. unmarried
● 5. brother	5. offspring	5. large
6. child	6. parent	6. small
7. foal	7. sheep	7. young
8. daughter	8. sibling	
9. ewe	9. stream	
● 10. father	10. woman	
11. giant		
12. girl		
13. husband		
14. lake		
● 15. lamb		
16. mare		
17. midget		
18. mother		
19. pond		
● 20. pony		
21. ram		
22. river		
23. sister		
24. snack		
● 25. son		
26. spinster		
27. stallion		
28. wife		

4.5   RULES FOR DEFINITION BY GENUS AND DIFFERENCE

Certain rules traditionally have been laid down for definition by genus and difference. These rules are not a recipe for constructing good connotative definitions without having to think, but are useful as criteria for appraising such definitions once they have been stated. There are five such rules that are intended to apply primarily to lexical definitions.

Rule 1: A definition should state the essential attribute(s) of the species.

As stated, this rule is somewhat cryptic, because in itself a species has just those attributes that it has, and none is more "essential" than any other. But if we understand the rule properly, as dealing with terms, it becomes clear. Earlier we distinguished between the objective connotation of a term and its conventional connotation, the latter being those attributes whose possession constitutes the conventional criterion by which we decide whether an object is denoted by the term. Thus it is part of the objective connotation of "circle" *to enclose a greater area than any other closed plane figure of equal perimeter.* But to define the word "circle" by this attribute would be to violate the spirit or intention of our first rule, because it is not the attribute that people have agreed to mean by that word. The conventional connotation is the attribute of being *a closed plane curve all points of which are equidistant from a given point called the center.* To define it in these terms would be to state its "essence" and thus to conform to this first rule. In our present terminology, perhaps a better way to phrase the rule would be "A definition should state the conventional connotation of the term being defined."

It should be kept in mind that the conventional connotation of a term need not be an intrinsic characteristic of the things denoted by it, but might well have to do with the origin of those things, the relations they have to other things, or the uses to which they are put. Thus the word "Stradivarius," which denotes a number of violins, need not connote any actual physical characteristic shared by all those violins and not possessed by any other, but rather has the conventional connotation of being a violin that was made in the Cremona workshop of Antonio Stradivari (c. 1644–1737). Again, governors are not physically or mentally different from other persons; they simply are related differently to their fellow citizens. Finally, the word "shoe" cannot be defined exclusively in terms of the shapes or materials of the things it denotes; its definition must include reference to the use to which those things are put, as outer coverings for the foot. It should be pointed out, too, that conventionally accepted attributes of objects denoted by a term need not be real attributes of those objects. For example, it may be that people falsely attribute ferociousness to such animals as gorillas and wolves.

Rule 2: A definition should be noncircular.

It is obvious that if the definiendum itself appears in the definiens, the definition can explain the meaning of the term being defined only to those who already understand it. In other words, if a definition is circular, it will fail in its purpose: reporting the meaning of its definiendum. When applied to definition by genus and difference, the rule generally is understood not merely to rule out letting the definiendum appear in the definiens but also to rule out using any synonym of it. The reason for this restriction is that if a synonym is assumed to be understood, one might as well give a synonymous definition instead of using the more powerful but more complicated technique of definition by genus and difference. Rule 2 usually is understood to forbid the use of antonyms as well as synonyms.

Rule 3: A definition should be neither too broad nor too narrow.

This rule asserts that the definiens should denote no more things and no fewer things than the definiendum denotes. This consideration does not apply when we are making a stipulative definition, for in such cases the definiendum has no meaning (in that context) apart from its definition, and rule 3 could not possibly be violated. Of course if the first rule is obeyed, the third one must be also, for if the definiens really names the conventional connotation of the definiendum, the terms are bound to be equivalent in denotation. It follows from this that if rule 3 is violated, so is rule 1.

The story is told that Plato's successors in the Academy at Athens spent much time and thought on the problem of defining the word "man." Finally they decided that it meant featherless biped. They were pleased with the definition until Diogenes (4th century B.C.) plucked a chicken and threw it over the wall into the Academy. Here was a featherless biped, surely, but just as surely it was not a man. The definiens was too broad, for it denoted more than the definiendum did. After additional thought, the Academics added the phrase "with broad nails" to their definiens. Rule 3 is a difficult one to follow.

A violation of this rule in the other direction would be committed by defining the word "shoe" as a leather covering for the foot, for there are wooden, canvas, and plastic shoes as well as leather ones. This definition of the word "shoe" is too narrow, since there are objects denoted by the definiendum that are not denoted by the definiens.

Rule 4: A definition should be expressed in clear, literal, unambiguous language.

Ambiguous terms should be avoided in framing definitions, because if the definiens is itself ambiguous, the definition obviously fails to perform its function of saying what the definiendum means. And since the purpose of definition is to clarify meaning, the use of obscure terms defeats this purpose. Of course, obscurity is a relative matter. Words obscure to children are reasonably clear to most adults, and terms obscure to laypeople are perfectly familiar to specialists in their fields of specialization. Consider the definition of the term "dynatron oscillator" as meaning a *circuit which employs a negative-resistance, volt-ampere curve to produce an alternating current.*[18] To the layperson this definition is terribly obscure. But it is perfectly intelligible to the students of electrical engineering for whom it was written. This definition is not obscure, but justifiably technical. On the other hand, in nontechnical matters, to use obscure language is to attempt to explain the unknown by the still more unknown, a futile procedure. A good example of self-defeating obscurity is found in Herbert Spencer's (1820–1903) definition of "evolution" as "an integration of matter and concomitant dissipation of motion, during which the matter passes from an indefinite, incoherent homogeneity to a definite, coherent heterogeneity, and during which the retained motion undergoes a parallel transformation." Another example of obscurity in definition is Dr. Samuel Johnson's (1709–84) celebrated second definition of the word "net" as meaning "anything made with interstitial vacuities."

A definition that uses figurative or metaphorical language may give some feeling for the use of the term being defined, but it cannot succeed in giving a clear explanation of what the definiendum means. Thus to define "bread" as the staff of life gives very little explanation of the meaning of that word. Often figurative definitions are humorous, as in the definition of "wedding ring" as a *matrimonial tourniquet designed to stop circulation,*

---

[18]   W. G. Dow, *Fundamentals of Engineering Electronics* (1937), p. 331.

or the definition of "discretion" as *something that comes to people after they are too old for it to do them any good.* Sometimes persuasive definitions are highly figurative, as in the liberal's definition of "prejudice" as *being down on what you aren't up on.* But any definition that contains figurative language, however entertaining or persuasive, cannot serve as a serious explanation of the precise meaning of the term to be defined.

> Rule 5: If a definition can be affirmative, it should be affirmative.

A definition is supposed to explain what a term means rather than what it does not mean. This rule is important because, for the vast majority of terms, there are far too many things that they do not mean for any negative definition to cover. To define the word "couch" as meaning *not a bed and not a chair* is to fail miserably to state the meaning of the word, for there are infinitely many things that are not meant by the word "couch." On the other hand, many terms are essentially negative in meaning and so require negative definitions. The word "orphan" means a child who does not have parents living; the word "bald" means the state of not having hair on one's head; and so on. Often the choice between an affirmative and a negative definition is simply a matter of the choice of words. There is not much basis for preferring to define the word "drunkard" as meaning one who drinks excessively rather than as one who is not temperate in drink. It should be emphasized that, even where a negative definition is permissible, the definiens must not be wholly negative, as in the ridiculous definition of "couch" mentioned earlier, but must have an "affirmative" mention of the genus and a negative characterization of the species by rejecting all other species of the genus mentioned. Only in exceptional cases are there few enough species of the given genus for them to be conveniently mentioned and rejected in a negative definition. Because there are only three species of triangle, when that genus is divided according to the relative lengths of the sides, a perfectly adequate definition of "scalene triangle" is a triangle that is neither equilateral nor isosceles. But we cannot define the word "quadrilateral" as *a polygon that is neither a triangle nor a pentagon nor a hexagon nor . . .* because there are too many alternative species of the genus polygon to be excluded. In general, affirmative definitions are superior to negative ones.

EXERCISES

I. Construct a definition by genus and difference for each of the terms in Exercise I on page 154.

II. Criticize the following in terms of the rules for definition by genus and difference. After identifying the difficulty (or difficulties), state the rule (or rules) violated. If the definition is either too narrow or too broad, explain why.

■   *1.*   Freedom is that state where energy and order merge and all complexity is purified into a simple coherence, a fitness of parts and purpose and passions that cannot be surpassed and whose goal could only be to be itself.
                    —A. BARTLETT GIAMATTI, *Take Time for Paradise: Americans and Their Games* (1989), p. 104

2. Let us be very clear what a tax is and what it is not. A tax, for whatever high-minded purpose it is levied, is a penalty laid on honest work and endeavor.

—WILLIAM MURCHISON, "Conflicting Desires Keep Budget a Mess," *The Dallas Morning News*
3 October 1990, p. 27A

3. Knowledge is true opinion.

—PLATO, *Theaetetus*

4. Life is the art of drawing sufficient conclusions from insufficient premises.

—SAMUEL BUTLER, *Notebooks*

■ **5.** "Base" means that which serves as a base.

—CHE'NG WEI-SHIH LUN, quoted in Fung Y-Lan, *A History of Chinese Philosophy*

6. Alteration is a combination of contradictorily opposed determinations in the existence of one and the same thing.

—IMMANUEL KANT, *Critique of Pure Reason*

7. Hypocrisy is the homage that vice pays to virtue.

—FRANÇOIS, DUC DE LA ROCHEFOUCAULD

8. The meaning of a word is what is explained by the explanation of the meaning.

—LUDWIG WITTGENSTEIN, *Philosophical Investigations*

9. War . . . is an act of violence intended to compel our opponent to fulfill our will.

—CARL VON CLAUSEWITZ, *On War*

■ **10.** A hazard is anything that is dangerous.

—*Safety with Beef Cattle,* published by the Occupational Safety and Health Administration, 1976

11. To sneeze [is] to emit wind audibly by the nose.

—SAMUEL JOHNSON, *Dictionary*

12. A bore is a person who talks when you want him to listen.

—AMBROSE BIERCE, *The Devil's Dictionary*

13. Art is a human activity having for its purpose the transmission to others of the highest and best feelings to which men have risen.

—COUNT LYOF TOLSTOI, *What Is Art?*

14. Murder is when a person of sound memory and discretion unlawfully killeth any reasonable creature in being, and under the king's peace, with malice afore-thought, either express or implied.

—EDWARD COKE, *Institutes*

■ **15.** A cloud is a large semi-transparent mass with a fleecy texture suspended in the atmosphere whose shape is subject to continual and kaleidoscopic change.

—U. T. PLACE, "Is Consciousness a Brain Process?" *The British Journal of Psychology,*
February 1956

16. Freedom of choice. The human capacity to choose freely between two or more genuine alternatives or possibilities, such choosing being always limited both by the past and by the circumstances of the immediate present.

—CORLISS LAMONT, *Freedom of Choice Affirmed*

17. Health is a state of complete physical, mental, and social well-being and not merely the absence of disease or infirmity.

—WORLD HEALTH ORGANIZATION

18. By analysis, we mean analyzing the contradictions in things.

—MAO TSETUNG, *Quotations from Chairman Mao*

19. To explain (explicate, *explicare*) is to strip reality of the appearances covering it like a veil, in order to see the bare reality itself.

—PIERRE DUHEM, *The Aim and Structure of Physical Theory*

■ ***20.*** The Master said, Yu, shall I teach you what knowledge is? When you know a thing, to recognize that you know it, and when you do not know a thing, to recognize that you do not know it. That is knowledge.

—CONFUCIUS, *The Analects*

21. Opportunity cost is the economic expression of the familiar idea that you can't have your cake and eat it too.

—DANIEL B. SUITS, *Principles of Economics*

22. The word *body,* in the most general acceptation, signifieth that which filleth, or occupieth some certain room, or imagined place; and dependeth not on the imagination, but is a real part of that we call the universe.

—THOMAS HOBBES, *Leviathan*

III. Evaluate the following definitions.

■ ***1.*** Faith is the substance of things hoped for, the evidence of things not seen.

—Hebrews 11:1

2. "Faith is when you believe something that you know ain't true."

—Definition attributed to a schoolboy by William James in "The Will to Believe"

3. Faith may be defined briefly as an illogical belief in the occurrence of the improbable.

—H.L. MENCKEN

4. Poetry is simply the most beautiful, impressive, and widely effective mode of saying things.

—MATTHEW ARNOLD

■ ***5.*** Poetry is the record of the best and happiest moments of the happiest and best minds.

—PERCY BYSSHE SHELLEY, *The Defence of Poetry*

6. A cynic is a man who knows the price of everything and the value of nothing.

—OSCAR WILDE, *Lady Windermere's Fan*

7. Conscience is an inner voice that warns us somebody is looking.

—H. L. MENCKEN

8. A sentimentalist is a man who sees an absurd value in everything and doesn't know the market price of a single thing.

—OSCAR WILDE, *Lady Windermere's Fan*

9. "The true," to put it very briefly, is only the expedient in the way of our thinking, just as "the right" is only the expedient in the way of our behaving.

—WILLIAM JAMES, "Pragmatism's Conception of Truth"

■ **10.** To be conceited is to tend to boast of one's own excellences, to pity or ridicule the deficiencies of others, to daydream about imaginary triumphs, to reminisce about actual triumphs, to weary quickly of conversations which reflect unfavorably upon oneself, to lavish one's society upon distinguished persons and to economize in association with the undistinguished.

—GILBERT RYLE, *The Concept of Mind*

11. Economics is the science which treats of the phenomena arising out of the economic activities of men in society.

—J. N. KEYNES, *Scope and Methods of Political Economy*

12. Justice is doing one's own business, and not being a busybody.

—PLATO, *Republic*

13. What, then, is the government? An intermediate body established between the subjects and the sovereign for their mutual correspondence, charged with the execution of the laws and with the maintenance of liberty both civil and political.

—JEAN JACQUES ROUSSEAU, *The Social Contract*

14. By good, I understand that which we certainly know is useful to us.

—BARUCH SPINOZA, *Ethics*

■ **15.** Political power, then, I take to be a right of making laws with penalties of death, and consequently all less penalties, for the regulating and preserving of property, and of employing the force of the community in the execution of such laws, and in defense of the commonwealth from foreign injury, and all this only for the public good.

—JOHN LOCKE, *Essay Concerning Civil Government*

16. And what, then, is belief? It is the demi-cadence which closes a musical phrase in the symphony of our intellectual life.

—CHARLES SANDERS PEIRCE, "How to Make Our Ideas Clear"

17. Political power, properly so called, is merely the organized power of one class for oppressing another.

—KARL MARX and FRIEDRICH ENGELS, *The Communist Manifesto*

18. Grief for the calamity of another is pity; and ariseth from the imagination that the like calamity may befall himself.

—THOMAS HOBBES, *Leviathan*

19. We see that all men mean by justice that kind of state of character which makes people disposed to do what is just and makes them act justly and wish for what is just.

—ARISTOTLE, *Nichomachean Ethics*

■ **20.** Inquiry is the controlled or directed transformation of an indeterminate situation into one that is so determinate in its constituent distinctions and relations as to convert the elements of the original situation into a unified whole.

—JOHN DEWEY, *Logic: The Theory of Inquiry*

21.   A fanatic is one who can't change his mind and won't change the subject.

—WINSTON CHURCHILL

22.   Fanaticism consists in redoubling your efforts when you have forgotten your aim.

—GEORGE SANTAYANA, *The Life of Reason*, Vol. 1.

23.   A tragedy is the imitation of an action that is serious and also, as having magnitude, complete in itself; in language with pleasurable accessories, each kind brought in separately in the parts of the work; in a dramatic, not in a narrative form; with incidents arousing pity and fear, wherewith to accomplish its catharsis of such emotions.

—ARISTOTLE, *Poetics*

24.   "Then," I said, "your people don't understand the difference between liberty and license."

He reported my remark, and again there was a long, a very long, general discussion, which the interpreter summed up.

"True," he said, "we don't know the difference between liberty and—what is it?—license. In fact, we never heard of license. We would like you to tell us what is liberty and what is license. And what is the difference?"

"The distinction in America is very important," I said, trying to think quick of a definition, which came to me at last. "Liberty," I defined, "liberty is the right of any proper person—I mean anybody in a good social position—to say anything whatsoever that everybody believes."

The interpreter translated, and I expected his hearers to laugh. But no, they threshed out my definition in all sobriety at great length with never a smile, and the conclusion interpreted was: "Yes. We understand that. And now what is that other thing—license?"

"License," I said, "is not a right. It is an impertinence. License is the impudence of some son-of-a-gun, who has no right to live on earth anyhow, to say some damned thing that is true."

—LINCOLN STEFFENS, *Autobiography*

■ *25.*   Patriotism is loyalty to the civic group to which one belongs by birth or other group bond.

—W. G. SUMNER, *Folkways*

5

Analogy

5.1 USES OF ANALOGY

Argumentative

One of the most common kinds of argument is the argument by analogy, or analogical argument. Two examples of analogical arguments are these:

1. . . . the first industrial revolution, the revolution of the "dark satanic mills," was the devaluation of the human arm by the competition of machinery. There is no rate of pay at which a United States pick-and-shovel laborer can live which is low enough to compete with the work of a steam shovel as an excavator. The modern industrial revolution [high speed electronic computers, so-called "thinking machines"] is similarly bound to devalue the human brain at least in its simpler and more routine decisions. Of course, just as the skilled carpenter, the skilled mechanic, the skilled dressmaker have in some degree survived the first industrial revolution, so the skilled scientist and the skilled administrator may survive the second.[1]

2. We may observe a very great similitude between this earth which we inhabit, and the other planets, Saturn, Jupiter, Mars, Venus, and Mercury. They all revolve round the sun, as the earth does, although at different distances and in different periods. They borrow all their light from the sun, as the earth does. Several of them are known to revolve round their axis like the earth, and by that means, must have a like succession of day and night. Some of them have moons, that serve to give them light in the absence of the sun, as our moon does to us. They are all, in their motions, subject to the same law of gravitation, as the earth is. From all this similitude, it is not unreasonable to think that those planets may, like our earth, be the habitation of various orders of living creatures. There is some probability in this conclusion from analogy.[2]

---

[1]   N. Wiener, *Cybernetics* (1948).
[2]   Thomas Reid, *Essays on the Intellectual Powers of Man,* Essay I, chap. 4.

Most of our own everyday inferences are by analogy. Thus I infer that a new pair of shoes will wear well because I got good wear from other shoes previously purchased from the same store. If a new book by a certain author is called to my attention, I infer that I will enjoy reading it on the basis of having read and enjoyed other books by that author. Analogy is the basis of most of our ordinary reasonings from past experience to what the future will hold. Not an explicitly formulated argument, of course, but something very much like analogical inference is presumably involved in the conduct of the burned child who shuns the fire.

None of these arguments is certain or demonstratively valid. None of their conclusions follows with "absolute logical necessity" from their premises. It is logically possible that what happened to skilled manual workers will not happen to skilled brain workers, that earth is the only inhabited planet, that the new shoes will not wear well, and that I will find my favorite author's latest book to be intolerably dull. It is even logically possible that one fire may burn and another fire not burn. But then, no argument by analogy is *intended* to be mathematically certain. Probability is all that is claimed for them. The point of analogical argument is to extend our knowledge of the world by making comparisons between things that are familiar to us and things that are not so familiar.

Descriptive

In addition to their frequent use in arguments, analogies are often used nonargumentatively, and these different uses should not be confused. Since earliest times writers have made use of analogy for the purpose of lively description. The literary uses of analogy in metaphor and simile are tremendously helpful to the writer who strives to create a vivid picture in the reader's mind. For example,

> . . . the [history] books do not describe change or show the relationship between one kind of event and another. The nineteen-fifties texts are encyclopedias rather than history books. Their vast indexes contain references to everything under the sun, but there is no connection between one thing and another. Events stand isolated below headings of black type, like islands in some archipelago where no one has yet invented the canoe.[3]

Another example is the following:

> Children in school are like children at the doctor's. He can talk himself blue in the face about how much good his medicine is going to do them; all they think of is how much it will hurt or how bad it will taste. Given their own way, they would have none of it.
>
> So the valiant and resolute band of travelers I thought I was leading toward a much hoped-for destination turned out instead to be more like convicts in a chain gang, forced under threat of punishment to move along a rough path leading nobody knew where and down which they could see hardly more than a few steps ahead. School feels

---

[3]   Frances Fitzgerald, "Onward and Upward with the Arts (History Textbooks)," *The New Yorker,* 26 February 1979, pp. 70–71.

like this to children: it is a place where *they* make you go and where *they* tell you to do things and where *they* try to make your life unpleasant if you don't do them or don't do them right.[4]

Descriptive uses of analogy are not designed to establish a conclusion, as in the case of argument; they are designed to create a vivid or memorable picture in the mind of one's audience.

Explanatory

Analogy also is used in explanation, where something unfamiliar is made intelligible through being compared to something else, presumably more familiar, to which it has certain similarities. For example,

> Carbon is a gregarious stuff; the carbon atom has an outer electron shell with four electrons available for making shared-electron-pair, or covalent, bonds—four hands, so to speak, to clasp its neighbors'—where oxygen, say, has but two and hydrogen only one.[5]

Another example of an explanatory analogy is this:

> Quantum mechanics does not say that particles are waves nor even that they bob up and down on some sort of physical wave, like a cork on water. It says that particles can behave like waves—they move according to wave-like principles.
>   The waves are not waves of any substance, but are probability waves. They can be described in an abstract way by a mathematical equation, the solution of which enables precise predictions of relative probabilities to be made. (A rough analogy is a crime wave; if you say a crime wave has hit a neighborhood, what you are really saying is that the probability of a crime being committed is now higher in that area.)[6]

The use of analogies in description and explanation is not the same as their use in argument, though in some cases it may not be easy to decide which use is intended. One should ask whether the author of the passage is attempting to establish the truth of a proposition. If so, the passage is argumentative. If not, the passage is either descriptive or explanatory, depending on whether it is designed to leave a vivid impression in someone's mind (descriptive) or make something unfamiliar intelligible (explanatory). It is ultimately a matter of judgment, so one should be sensitive to contextual factors.

Whether used argumentatively or otherwise, analogy is not difficult to define. To draw an analogy between two or more entities is to indicate one or more respects in which they are similar. Just as there are certain words and phrases that indicate premisses and conclusions (see section 1.2), there are words and phrases that indicate analogies. Among these are

4   John Holt, *How Children Fail*.
5   Horace Freeland Judson, "Annals of Science: DNA," *The New Yorker*, 4 December 1978, p. 103.
6   "Science and Technology," *The Economist*, 3 April 1982, p. 94.

same (as)	similar(ly)
in comparison	like
alike	in like manner
resembles	by the same token
as (in)	just as p, so q
analogously	by analogy
analogue	

Whenever one of these words or phrases is used, one has reason to believe that an analogy is being drawn.

This explains what an analogy is and provides recognition tips, but there is still the problem of characterizing an *argument by analogy*. We may approach this problem by examining a particular analogical argument and analyzing its structure. Let us take the simplest of the examples cited thus far, the argument that my new pair of shoes will wear well because my old shoes, which were purchased from the same store, have worn well. The two things said to be similar are the two pairs of shoes. Three points of analogy are involved: The respects in which the two entities are said to resemble each other are, first, in being shoes; second, in being purchased from the same store; and third, in wearing well. The three points of analogy do not play identical roles in the argument, however. The first two occur in the premises, whereas the third occurs both in the premises and in the conclusion. In general terms, the given argument may be described as having premises that assert first, that two things are similar in two respects, and second, that one of those things has a further characteristic, from which the conclusion is drawn that the other thing also has that characteristic.

Not every analogical argument concerns exactly two things and exactly three characteristics, of course. The argument quoted from Thomas Reid (1710–96) draws analogies among six things (the then known planets) in some eight respects. Apart from these numerical differences, however, all analogical arguments have the same general structure or pattern. Every analogical inference proceeds from the similarity of two or more things in one or more respects to the similarity of those things in some further respect. Schematically, where a, b, c, and d are any entities, and P, Q, and R are any attributes or "respects," an analogical argument may be represented as having the form

Entities a, b, c, and d have attributes P and Q.
Entities a, b, and c have attribute R.
Therefore, entity d probably has attribute R.

In identifying, and especially in appraising analogical arguments, it is helpful to recast them in this form.

As we noted in chapter 1, context and common knowledge must be taken into consideration in deciding whether an argument is present. If an analogy is pointed out or claimed to exist between two situations, and one of them clearly is ridiculous or unwise, the implied but perhaps unstated conclusion is that the other situation is unwise or ridiculous also. Consider for example the following remark:

Lindsay's practice of paying current salaries from long-term borrowing is like a family's taking out a thirty-year mortgage to pay its grocery bill.[7]

Because we know that a family's taking out a thirty-year mortgage to pay its grocery bill is ridiculously unwise, and are told that Lindsay's practice is like it, we can see that the author has presented an argument whose (unstated) conclusion is that Lindsay's practice is unwise and ridiculous.

We can see the same thing in the following remark:

Having heard Argentine diplomats discuss their rights under the Rio Treaty, I want to hear more, just as I once wanted a second bite of abalone to see if the first bite had been as bad as I thought.[8]

Here the inference is that the writer found the Argentine diplomats' discussion of their rights under the Rio Treaty to be incredibly foolish.

It is worth pointing out that lawyers use analogical arguments on a regular basis. In a civil suit, for example, the attorney for the plaintiff (person bringing the suit) typically cites one or more previously decided cases (known as "precedents") in support of his or her claim that the plaintiff ought to prevail. The attorney argues that, because the prior cases share certain features with the current case (the first premiss) and were decided in favor of the plaintiff (the second premiss), the current case should be decided in favor of the plaintiff (the conclusion). Naturally, not all such arguments are persuasive, for reasons to be developed in the next section.

EXERCISES

Each of the following passages contains an analogy. Distinguish those that contain analogical arguments from those that make nonargumentative uses of analogy. If the use is nonargumentative, determine whether it is descriptive or explanatory and give reasons for your answer It may help to circle indicator words.

■   *1.*   Baseball without romance and heroism is like *Hamlet* without poetry or the Prince of Denmark—just words.

—DONALD KAGAN, "George Will's Baseball—A Conservative Critique," *The Public Interest,* Fall 1990, p. 19

2.   Racists violate the principle of equality by giving greater weight to the interests of members of their own race when there is a clash between their interests and the interests of those of another race. Sexists violate the principle of equality by favoring the interests of their own sex. Similarly, speciesists allow the interests of their own species to override the greater interests of members of other species. The pattern is identical in each case.

—PETER SINGER, *Animal Liberation,* 2d ed. (1990), p. 9

---

[7]   Julia Vitullo-Martin, "Sin Will Find You Out," *The New York Review of Books,* 17 May 1979, p. 7.
[8]   George F. Will, "Falklands Evoke Memories of Munich," *Washington Post,* 28 April 1982.

3. [S]pace-time is like a hilly countryside. In the neighbourhood of a piece of matter, there is, as it were, a hill in space-time; this hill grows steeper and steeper as it gets nearer the top, like the neck of a champagne bottle. It ends in a sheer precipice. Now by the law of cosmic laziness . . ., a body coming into the neighbourhood of the hill will not attempt to go straight over the top, but will go round. This is the essence of Einstein's view of gravitation.

—BERTRAND RUSSELL, *The ABC of Relativity,* 3d rev. ed., Felix Pirani (1969), p. 80

4. The best reason for thinking that BSE—mad cow disease—will not infect people is that scrapie—mad sheep disease—never has. Scrapie is BSE, except that it appears in a different species and has been around for at least 250 years. In all that time sheep-eaters exposed to scrapie have been no more demented than the rest of the population. Thus cow-eaters exposed to BSE, the argument goes, will also remain healthy.

—"Science and Technology," *The Economist,* 28 July 1990, p. 69

■ **5.** I'm surprised at someone, especially an elected official from the "Show Me State" [Richard Gephardt], who would suggest we give direct aid to the Soviets. Bill Bradley has it right, "It would be going down a rathole." Supplying the Soviets with direct aid to "get on their feet" in order to get back on track to meet their goal of ruling the world would be like Al Capone receiving aid from Elliott Ness and the G-men. Hopefully we will have enough congressmen and senators who have not been lulled to sleep by Soviet posture at the current time.

—LEROY COPPIC, letter to the editor, *The Dallas Morning News,* 1990

6. The balance of payments is a measure of economic health, not a cause of it; restricting imports to reduce that deficit is like sticking the thermometer in ice water to bring down a feverish temperature.

—MICHAEL KINSLEY, "Keep Trade Free," *The New Republic* 188, 11 April 1983, p. 11

7. The brain secretes thought as the stomach secretes gastric juice, the liver bile, and the kidneys urine.

—KARL VOGT, *Kohlerglaube und Wissenschaft*

8. As in prospecting for gold, a scientist may dig with skill, courage, energy, and intelligence just a few feet away from a rich vein—but always unsuccessfully. Consequently in scientific research the rewards for industry, perseverance, imagination, and intelligence are highly uncertain.

—LAWRENCE S. KUBIE, "Some Unsolved Problems of the Scientific Career," *American Scientist* 42, 1954

9. The famous chemist and biologist, Justus von Liebig, dismissed the germ theory with a shrug of the shoulders, regarding Pasteur's view that microbes could cause fermentation as ridiculous and naive as the opinion of a child "who would explain the rapidity of the Rhine current by attributing it to the violent movement of the many millwheels at Maintz."

—RENÉ DUBOS, *Pasteur and Modern Science*

■ **10.** Thinking is an experimental dealing with small quantities of energy, just as a general moves miniature figures over a map before setting his troops in action.

—SIGMUND FREUD, *New Introductory Lectures on Psychoanalysis*

11. . . . the author goes to great lengths to persuade us that Helms, the CIA's quintessential covert operator, at heart did not approve of covert operations. Which is rather like saying that the Beatles never really *liked* rock and roll and were secretly off in a corner listening to Buxtehude when their concert dates permitted.

—DAVID WISE, *The New Republic,* 3 November 1979, p. 36

12. We have said that normal persons have little motivation to prompt special efforts at self-study. The same thing is true of arithmetic. If motivation were not supplied from parents and school pressure, there would be little learning of mathematics. By analogy, it seems possible that children could be motivated and trained to use their mental skills to solve *emotional* problems. They get almost no training in this important skill at the present time.

—JOHN DOLLARD and NEAL E. MILLER, *Personality and Psychotherapy* (1950)

13. In nearly all of the non-Communist world, socialism, meaning public ownership of industrial enterprises, is a spent slogan. Like promises to enforce the antitrust laws in the United States, it is no longer a political program but an overture to nostalgia.

—JOHN KENNETH GALBRAITH, *The New Industrial State*

14. Perhaps the most startling discovery made in astronomy this century is that the universe is populated by billions of galaxies and that they are systematically receding from one another, like raisins in an expanding pudding.

—MARTIN J. REES and JOSEPH SILK, "The Origin of Galaxies," *Scientific American* 221, August 1969

■ **15.** Suppose that someone tells me that he has had a tooth extracted without an anaesthetic, and I express my sympathy, and suppose that I am then asked, "How do you know that it hurt him?" I might reasonably reply, "Well, I know that it would hurt me. I have been to the dentist and know how painful it is to have a tooth stopped [filled] without an anaesthetic, let alone taken out. And he has the same sort of nervous system as I have. I infer, therefore, that in these conditions he felt considerable pain, just as I should myself."

—ALFRED J. AYER, "One's Knowledge of Other Minds," *Theoria* 19, 1953

16. The atomic model which emerged from the work of Rutherford and others resembled a planetary system, for the force which binds planets to the sun obeys the same general form of law as the force which binds electrons to the nucleus. Both gravity and electricity decrease in strength with the square of distance. From this it follows that the particle-electron, attracted by the positive electricity of the nucleus, should move around it in the same way that a planet moves around the sun.

—BARBARA LOVETT CLINE, *Men Who Made a New Physics*

17. One of the pleasures of science is to see two distant and apparently unrelated pieces of information suddenly come together. In a flash what one knows doubles or triples in size. It is like working on two large but separate sections of a jigsaw puzzle and, almost without realizing it until the moment it happens, finding that they fit into one.

—JOHN TYLER BONNER, "Hormones in Social Amoebae and Mammals," *Scientific American* 221, November 1969

18. It is important that we make clear at this point what definition is and what can be attained by means of it. It seems frequently to be credited with a creative power, but all it accomplishes is that something is marked out in sharp relief and designated by a name. Just as the geographer does not create a sea when he draws boundary lines and says: the part of the ocean's surface bounded by these lines I am going to call the Yellow Sea, so too the mathematician cannot really create anything by his defining.

—GOTTLOB FREGE, *The Basic Laws of Arithmetic*

19. As one expert has explained it, forming a latent image on film is something like filling a leaky bucket with hot molasses. Pour in the thin molasses quickly and you can fill the bucket, but if you pour slowly, the thin fluid refuses to accumulate. If you switch to cold molasses, the thick fluid leaks at a much lower rate. You can fill the bucket with cold molasses by pouring at a much lower rate. The analogy applies to photographic emulsions. Some years ago it was discovered that if an emulsion is refrigerated during exposure, it will accumulate a latent image even under very dim light.

—C. L. STRONG, "The Amateur Scientist," *Scientific American* 221, August 1969

■ *20.* It seemed to us that the synchronous behavior of malaria parasites, all coming to cell division at the same time every 24 hours or a multiple thereof, was remarkably like the behavior of microfilariae, all entering or leaving the peripheral blood at the same time every 24 hours. Microfilariae are carried from one patient to another by mosquitoes, which suck blood mostly at night, and the swarming of the microfilariae in the peripheral blood is arranged to coincide with this time of sucking blood. The biological purpose of the cycle of the microfilariae is clearly to help them encounter mosquitoes and so get transmitted to new patients.

Since malaria is also carried from one person to another by mosquitoes, it seemed to us that the periodic behavior of the malaria parasites in the blood was similarly designed somehow or other to facilitate transmission by mosquitoes.

—FRANK HAWKING, "The Clock of the Malaria Parasite," *Scientific American* 222, 1970

21. The matter stands on the same footing as the making of material tools, which might be argued about in a similar way. For, in order to work iron, a hammer is needed, and the hammer cannot be forthcoming unless it has been made; but, in order to make it, there was need of another hammer and other tools, and so on to infinity. We might thus vainly endeavor to prove that men have no power of working iron. But as men first made use of the instruments supplied by nature to accomplish very easy pieces of workmanship, laboriously and imperfectly, and then, when these were finished, wrought other things more difficult with less labor and greater perfection; and so gradually mounted from the simplest operations of the making of tools, and from the making of tools to the making of more complex tools, and fresh feats of workmanship, till they arrived at making, with small expenditure of labor, the vast number of complicated mechanisms which they now possess. So, in like manner, the intellect, by its native strength, makes for itself intellectual instruments, whereby it acquires strength for performing other intellectual operations, and from these operations gets fresh instruments, or the power of pushing its investigations further, and thus gradually proceeds till it reaches the summit of wisdom.

—BARUCH SPINOZA, *On the Improvement of the Understanding*

22.   . . . professional investment may be likened to those newspaper competitions in which the competitors have to pick out the six prettiest faces from a hundred photographs, the prize being awarded to the competitor whose choice most nearly corresponds to the average preferences of the competitors as a whole; so that each competitor has to pick, not those faces which he himself finds prettiest, but those which he thinks likeliest to catch the fancy of the other competitors, all of whom are looking at the problem from the same point of view. It is not a case of choosing those which, to the best of one's judgment, are really the prettiest, nor even those which average opinion genuinely thinks the prettiest. We have reached the third degree where we devote our intelligences to anticipating what average opinion expects the average opinion to be.

—JOHN MAYNARD KEYNES, *The General Theory of Employment, Interest, and Money*, p. 156

23.   Look around the world: contemplate the whole and every part of it: you will find it to be nothing but one great machine, subdivided into an infinite number of lesser machines, which again admit of subdivisions, to a degree beyond what human senses and faculties can trace and explain. All these various machines, and even their most minute parts, are adjusted to each other with an accuracy, which ravishes into admiration all men, who have ever contemplated them. The curious adapting of means to ends, throughout all nature, resembles exactly, though it much exceeds, the production of human contrivance; of human design, thought, wisdom, and intelligence. Since therefore the effects resemble each other, we are led to infer, by all the rules of analogy, that the causes also resemble; and that the Author of Nature is somewhat similar to the mind of men; though possessed of much larger faculties, proportioned to the grandeur of the work, which he has executed. By this argument a posteriori, and by this argument alone, do we prove at once the existence of a Deity, and his similarity to human mind and intelligence.

—DAVID HUME, *Dialogues Concerning Natural Religion*

24.   Having its origin in the same principle of our nature, *constitution* stands to *government,* as *government* stands to *society;* and, as the end for which society is ordained, would be defeated without government, so that for which government is ordained would, in a great measure, be defeated without constitution.

—JOHN C. CALHOUN, *The Works of John C. Calhoun*, Vol. 1: *A Disquisition on Government and a Discourse on the Constitution and Government of the United States*, ed. Richard K. Crallé (1968), p. 71

■ **25.**   To say that Dorothy (Dodo) Cheney comes from a tennis-playing family is like saying there is water in the ocean.

—ROBERT MCG. THOMAS, JR., letter to the sports editor, *The New York Times*, 17 September 1990, p. B12

5.2   EVALUATING ANALOGICAL ARGUMENTS

Although no argument by analogy is demonstrative, in the sense of having its conclusion follow from its premises with logical necessity, some are more cogent than others. Analogical arguments may be evaluated as establishing their conclusions with more or less probability. In this section we shall discuss some of the standards that are applicable to arguments of this type. Throughout our discussion, we will refer to the argument form displayed on page 166.

1. The first criterion relevant to the evaluation of an analogical argument is the number of entities between (or among) which the analogies are said to hold (represented by the number of lowercase letters in the second premiss). This principle is deeply rooted in common sense. If I advise you not to send your shirts to such and such a laundry because I sent one there once and it came back ruined, you might caution me against jumping to conclusions and urge that they ought perhaps to be given another chance. On the other hand, if I give you the same advice and justify it by recounting four occasions on which the laundry did unsatisfactory work, and report further that our mutual friends Jones and Smith have patronized them repeatedly with similar unhappy results, these premisses serve to establish the conclusion with much higher probability than did the first argument, which cited only a single instance. It should not be thought, however, that there is an exact numerical ratio between the number of instances and the probability of the conclusion. If I have known only one chow dog, and that one was ill-tempered, that gives some probability to the conclusion that the next one I meet will be ill-tempered also. On the other hand, if I have known ten chow dogs, all of them ill-tempered, that gives considerably higher probability to the conclusion that the next one also will be ill-tempered. But it by no means follows that the second argument's conclusion is *exactly ten times* as probable.

2. A second criterion for evaluating analogical arguments is the number of respects in which the things involved are said to be analogous (represented by the number of uppercase letters in the first premiss). Take the example of the shoes again. That a new pair of shoes was purchased at the same store as an old pair that gave good wear is certainly a premiss from which it follows that the new shoes probably will give good wear also. But that same conclusion follows with greater probability if the premisses assert not only that the shoes were purchased from the same store, but that they were manufactured by the same company, that they were the highest-priced shoes in the store, that they are the same style, and that I plan to wear them in the same circumstances and activities. Again, it should not be thought that there is any simple numerical ratio between the number of points of resemblance asserted in the premisses and the probability of the conclusion.

3. A third criterion by which analogical arguments may be evaluated is the strength of their conclusions relative to their premisses (represented by the uppercase letter in the second premiss and the conclusion). If Jones has a new car that gets thirty miles to the gallon, from this Smith can infer with some probability that her new car, of the same make and model as Jones's, also will get good gas mileage. Smith can construct alternative arguments here, with the same premisses but different conclusions. If she draws the conclusion that her car will get more than twenty-five miles to the gallon, that is very probable, or at least more probable than the previous conclusion. If she infers that her car will get more than twenty-nine miles to the gallon, her argument is not so strong; that is, there is less likelihood or probability of her conclusion being true, given the premisses. If she concludes, however, that her own car will get exactly thirty miles to the gallon, she has a much weaker argument.

In this argument, the conclusion was strengthened or weakened *quantitatively*. As the gas mileage referred to in the conclusion increased (in quantity), the strength of the argument decreased. Not every analogical argument is like this. In some of them, the conclusion is *qualitatively* strong or weak relative to the premisses. For example, in exercise 23 of section 5.1, the conclusion drawn by Hume's character, Cleanthes, is that there exists "a Deity." If instead Cleanthes had concluded that a deity of a particular *sort* exists—say, a deity who is all-powerful, all-good, and all-knowing—the argument would be weaker, for it would draw qualitatively more information from the same set of premisses. On the other hand, if Cleanthes had concluded that "something capable of creating the world" exists, his argument would have been strengthened.

4. A fourth criterion used in evaluating analogical arguments has to do with the number of *disanalogies* or points of difference between the instances mentioned only in the premisses and the instance with which the conclusion is concerned (represented by the number of uppercase letters in the first premiss). The conclusion of the preceding argument is made very doubtful if it is pointed out that Jones drives his car for the most part at a steady pace of about twenty-five miles per hour, whereas Smith habitually drives at speeds in excess of sixty miles per hour. This disanalogy between the instance in the premiss and that of the conclusion weakens the argument and greatly reduces the probability of its conclusion.

As mentioned in section 5.1, lawyers use analogical arguments on a regular basis. One of the things law students are taught is to criticize such arguments by pointing out relevant disanalogies. To illustrate the point, suppose that a plaintiff's attorney cites a previously decided case in which the plaintiff, who was injured by a toaster, recovered damages from the manufacturer. The attorney argues that the cases are similar and that, since the plaintiff prevailed in the earlier case, the plaintiff should prevail in the current case. The attorney for the defendant manufacturer will try to identify salient disanalogies (the more the better). If, for example, the plaintiff in the first case had been using the toaster as intended when the injury occurred, but the plaintiff in the second case were misusing it (say, to heat the kitchen), the plaintiff's argument is considerably weakened. It is sometimes said, for obvious reasons, that to be a good litigation attorney one must be "quick with a disanalogy."

5. Of course the larger the number of entities or instances appealed to in the premisses, the less likely it is that they will *all* be disanalogous to the instance mentioned in the conclusion. To minimize disanalogies between the instances of the premisses and the instance of the conclusion, however, we need not enumerate more and more instances in the premisses. The same end can be achieved by taking instances in our premisses that are dissimilar to each other. The less similar the entities mentioned only in the premisses are to each other, the less likely it is for *all* of them to be dissimilar to the conclusion's instance, and hence, by the fourth criterion the more likely it is that the conclusion is true. Our fifth criterion for evaluating an argument by analogy, then, is that the more dissimilar the entities mentioned only in its second premiss (represented by lowercase letters), the stronger is the argument.

This principle is just as often appealed to and just as commonly accepted as any of the others that have been mentioned. The conclusion that Jenny Jones, an entering freshman at State, will successfully finish her college education and receive a degree can be established as highly probable on the grounds that ten other students who graduated from the same high school as Jenny Jones, and received grades there very similar to hers, have entered State as freshmen and have successfully finished their college educations and received degrees. The argument is appreciably stronger if the ten other students mentioned in the premises do not resemble each other too closely. The argument is strengthened by pointing out that those ten other students did not all come from the same economic backgrounds, that they differ from each other in sex, ethnic origin, religious affiliation, and so on. Incidentally, the fifth criterion explains the importance of the first. The greater the number of instances appealed to, the greater the number of disanalogies likely to obtain among them. None of these five criteria is new or in any way startling. Each is constantly used, though for the most part unconsciously, in appraising analogical arguments.

6. The one criterion for evaluating arguments by analogy that remains to be discussed is the most important of all. The examples presented thus far have been fairly good arguments because their analogies have been *relevant*. Thus in support of the conclusion that Smith's new car will get good gas mileage, we adduced as evidence the fact that Jones's new car, which is known to get good gas mileage, is the same make and model; that is, it has the same number of cylinders, the same body weight, and the same horsepower as Smith's. These are all *relevant* considerations. Contrast this argument with one that draws the same conclusion from different premises, from premisses that assert nothing about cylinders, body weight, or horsepower, but affirm instead that the cars have the same color, the same number of gauges on their dashboards, and the same style of upholstery in their interiors. The latter, to say the least, is a much weaker argument. But it cannot be judged so by any of the five criteria mentioned. The two arguments appeal to the same number of instances and the same number of analogies. The reason why the first is a good argument and the second ridiculously bad is that the factors in the first are relevant to gas mileage, whereas those of the second are irrelevant. (To put this in terms of the argument form displayed on page 166, the attributes named by uppercase letters in the first premiss must be relevant to the attribute named by an uppercase letter in the second premiss.)

The question of relevance is crucially important. An argument based on a single *relevant* analogy connected with a single instance will be more cogent than one that points out a dozen *irrelevant* points of resemblance between its conclusion's instance and over a score of instances enumerated in its premisses. Thus a doctor's inference is sound when she reasons that Mr. Black will be helped by a specific drug on the grounds that Mr. White was helped by it when a blood test showed exactly the same type of germs in his system that are now in Mr. Black's. But it would be fantastic for her to draw the same conclusion from premisses that assert that Smith, Jones, and Robinson were all helped by it and that they and Black all patronize the same grocer, drive the same make and model car, have the same number of children, had similar educations, and were born under the same sign of the zodiac. The reason for the weakness of the second argument is that the points of resemblance cited are irrelevant to the matter with which the conclusion is concerned.

Although there may be disagreement about what analogies are relevant for certain conclusions—that is, what attributes are relevant for proving the presence of certain other attributes in a given instance—it is doubtful that there is any disagreement about the *meaning* of relevance. An illustration given by John Wigmore (1863–1943) in one of his legal treatises is the following:

To show that a certain boiler was not dangerously likely to explode at a certain pressure of steam, other instances of nonexplosion of boilers at the same pressure would be relevant, provided the other boilers were substantially similar in type, age, and other circumstances affecting strength.[9]

Here we are given a criterion for relevance itself. An analogy is relevant to establishing the presence of a given attribute (strength, in Wigmore's illustration) provided it is drawn with respect to *other circumstances affecting it.* One attribute or circumstance is relevant to another, for purposes of analogical argument, if the first affects the second; that is, if it has a *causal* or determining effect on that other. The factor of relevance is to be explained in terms of causality. In an argument by analogy, the relevant analogies are those that deal with causally related attributes or circumstances. If my neighbors have their houses insulated and their fuel bills go down, then if I have my house insulated, I can confidently expect my fuel bill to decrease. The analogy is a good one, because insulation is relevant to the size of fuel bills, being causally connected with fuel consumption. Analogical arguments are highly probable whether they go from cause to effect or from effect to cause. They are even probable when the attribute in the premiss is neither cause nor effect of the conclusion's attribute, provided that both are effects of the same cause. Thus from the presence of some symptoms of a given disease, a doctor can predict other symptoms—not that either symptom is the cause of the other, but because they are jointly caused by one and the same infection.

To evaluate analogical arguments, then, requires some knowledge of causal connections. These are discovered empirically, by observation and experiment. The theory of empirical investigation is the central concern of the last two chapters of this book.

The material in this section can be illustrated with a single example. Suppose a friend, Lora, says the following:

> Oliver Stone is directing a new movie about John F. Kennedy. I can't wait until it's released, because I liked Stone's movies *Platoon, Talk Radio,* and *Born on the Fourth of July.*

Lora's analogical argument can be reconstructed as follows:

1. *Platoon, Talk Radio, Born on the Fourth of July,* and the soon-to-be-released movie about John F. Kennedy have several things in common, including being directed by Oliver Stone, being made after 1980, and having big-name stars.
2. I liked *Platoon, Talk Radio,* and *Born on the Fourth of July.*

Therefore, probably,

3. I will like the movie about John F. Kennedy.

The first criterion says that the greater the number of entities referred to in the second premiss, the stronger the argument. Hence, if Lora had listed four movies

---

9   John H. Wigmore, *Wigmore's Code of the Rules of Evidence in Trials at Law* (1942).

instead of three, her argument would have been stronger; had she listed only two, it would have been weaker. The second criterion says that the greater the number of attributes referred to in the first premiss, the stronger the argument. This makes sense, for the more similarities between the earlier movies on the one hand and the soon-to-be-released movie on the other, the more likely it is that the movies have some further attribute—say, Lora's liking it—in common.

The third criterion says that the weaker the conclusion relative to the second premiss, the stronger the argument. Suppose Lora's conclusion had been "I'll love the movie about John F. Kennedy" instead of "I'll like the movie about John F. Kennedy." You can see how this would weaken her argument, for all she said about the earlier movies is that she *liked* them. On the other hand, if she had said in the second premiss that she *loved* the earlier movies, her conclusion that she will *like* the new movie is made more probable. The fourth criterion says that the fewer the dissimilarities between the entities referred to in the second premiss and the entity referred to in the conclusion, the stronger the argument. Suppose the three earlier movies had special effects, but the soon-to-be-released movie does not. That is a dissimilarity that weakens the argument, and a friend would do well to point it out to Lora before she goes to the theater.

The fifth criterion says that the more dissimilar the entities referred to in the second premiss, the stronger the argument. Thus, if *Platoon* and *Born on the Fourth of July* were war movies, but *Talk Radio* was not, Lora's argument would be strengthened; it must be something besides the movie's subject matter that she liked. The sixth criterion requires that all analogies (criterion two) and disanalogies (criterion four) be relevant to the attribute referred to in both the second premiss and the conclusion. It seems clear that the attributes of being directed by Oliver Stone and having big-name stars are relevant to Lora's liking a movie (in each case there is an obvious causal connection), but the attribute of being made after 1980 is doubtful.

EXERCISES

I. Each of the following analogical arguments has six additional premisses suggested for it. For each alternative premiss, decide whether its addition would strengthen the argument, weaken the argument, or leave the argument unaffected. If it strengthens or weakens the argument, state the criterion by which it does so. (The following algorithm or flowchart may be useful for this purpose: First, ask whether the new information is relevant to the argument's conclusion. If not, then the information violates criterion six. If so, ask what effect the new information has on the argument. Does it make the argument stronger? Weaker?)

■   *1.* An investor has purchased one hundred shares of oil stock every December for the past five years. In every case the value of the stock has appreciated about 15 percent a year, and it has paid regular dividends of about 8 percent a year on the price at which she bought it. This December she decides to buy another hundred shares of oil stock, reasoning that she will probably receive modest earnings while watching the value of her new purchase increase over the years.

   a. Suppose that she had always purchased stock in eastern oil companies before and plans to purchase stock in an eastern oil company this year too.

   b. Suppose that she had purchased oil stocks every December for the past fifteen years instead of only five years.

   c. Suppose that the oil stocks previously purchased had gone up by 30 percent a year instead of only 15 percent.

   d. Suppose that her previous purchases of oil stock had been in foreign companies as well as in eastern, southern, and western American oil companies.

   e. Suppose that she learns that OPEC has decided to meet every month instead of every six months.

   f. Suppose that she discovers that tobacco stocks have just raised their dividend payments.

   2. A faithful alumnus, heartened by State's winning its last four football games, decides to bet his money that State will win its next game too.

   a. Suppose that since the last game State's great triple-threat tailback was injured in practice and hospitalized for the remainder of the season.

   b. Suppose that two of the last four games were played away and that two of them were home games.

   c. Suppose that just before the game it is announced that a member of State's Chemistry Department has been awarded a Nobel Prize.

   d. Suppose that State had won its last six games instead of only four of them.

   e. Suppose that it has rained hard during each of the four preceding games, and rain is forecast for next Saturday too.

   f. Suppose that each of the last four games had been won by a margin of at least four touchdowns.

   3. Although she was bored by the last few foreign films she saw, Charlene agrees to go to see another one this evening, fully expecting to be bored again.

   a. Suppose that Charlene also was bored by the last few American movies she saw.

   b. Suppose that the star of this evening's film has recently been accused of bigamy.

   c. Suppose that the last few foreign films seen by Charlene were Italian and that tonight's film is also Italian.

   d. Suppose that Charlene was so bored by the other foreign films that she actually fell asleep during the performance.

   e. Suppose that the last few foreign films she saw included an Italian, a French, an English, and a Swedish film.

   f. Suppose that tonight's film is in color, whereas all of those she saw before were in black and white.

   4. Bill has taken three history courses and found them very stimulating and valuable. So he signs up for another one, confidently expecting that it too will be worthwhile.

   a. Suppose that his previous history courses were in ancient history, modern European history, and American history.

b. Suppose that his previous history courses all had been taught by the same professor who is scheduled to teach the present one.

c. Suppose that his previous history courses all had been taught by Professor Smith, and the present one is taught by Professor Jones.

d. Suppose that Bill had found his three previous history courses the most exciting intellectual experiences of his life.

e. Suppose that his previous history courses all had met at 9 A.M. and that the present one is scheduled to meet at 9 A.M. also.

f. Suppose that, in addition to the three history courses previously taken, Bill also had taken and enjoyed courses in anthropology, economics, political science, and sociology.

■ *5.* Dr. Brown has stayed at the Queen's Hotel every fall for the past six years on her annual visit to New York and has been quite satisfied with her accommodations there. On her visit to New York this fall she goes again to the Queen's Hotel, confidently expecting to enjoy her stay there again.

a. Suppose that when she stayed at the Queen's Hotel before, she had occupied a single room twice, shared a double room twice, and twice occupied a suite.

b. Suppose that last spring a new manager had been put in charge of the Queen's Hotel.

c. Suppose that she had occupied a suite on all of her previous trips and is assigned a suite this time too.

d. Suppose that on her previous trips she had come to New York by train, but this time she flew.

e. Suppose that, when she stayed at the Queen's Hotel before, her quarters had been the most luxurious she had ever known.

f. Suppose that she had stayed at the Queen's Hotel three times a year for the past six years.

II. Analyze the structures of the analogical arguments in the following passages and evaluate them in terms of the six criteria set forth in this section.

■ *1.* If you cut up a large diamond into little bits, it will entirely lose the value it had as a whole; and an army divided up into small bodies of soldiers, loses all its strength. So a great intellect sinks to the level of an ordinary one, as soon as it is interrupted and disturbed, its attention distracted and drawn off from the matter in hand: for its superiority depends upon its power of concentration—of bringing all its strength to bear upon one theme, in the same way as a concave mirror collects into one point all the rays of light that strike upon it.

—ARTHUR SCHOPENHAUER, "On Noise"

2. Every species of plant or animal is determined by a pool of germ plasm that has been most carefully selected over a period of hundreds of millions of years.

We can understand now why it is that mutations in these carefully selected organisms almost invariably are detrimental. The situation can be suggested by a statement made by Dr. J. B. S. Haldane: My clock is not keeping perfect time. It is conceivable that it will run better if I shoot a bullet through it; but it is much more probable that it will stop altogether: Professor George Beadle, in this connection, has asked: "What is the chance that a typographical error would improve *Hamlet*?"

—LINUS PAULING, *No More War!*

3. I think some of our schools should be less rigid than they still are and that teachers should not oppress their pupils in an authoritarian spirit as some of them still do. Yet it is essential for teachers to make clear what they expect of children. This is like giving a vine a pole on which to grow.

—BENJAMIN SPOCK, *Today's Education* 64, January–February 1975

4. All the conspicuous features on the surface of the moon are the result of impacts. These features include not only the craters, which plainly advertise their origin, but also the great maria, or "seas," which are craters that filled with lava following the impact of very massive objects. Most of the impacts took place during a relatively brief period about four billion years ago, when debris left over from the formation of the solar system was swept up by the planets and their satellites. The earth probably received as heavy a pelting as the moon did, and it therefore must have been densely cratered.

—"Science and the Citizen," *Scientific American*, June 1976

■ **5.** To the casual observer porpoises and sharks are kinds of fish. They are streamlined, good swimmers, and live in the sea. To the zoologist who examines these animals more closely, the shark has gills, cold blood, and scales; the porpoise has lungs, warm blood, and hair. The porpoise is fundamentally more like man than like the shark, and belongs, with man, to the mammals—a group that nurses its young with milk. Having decided that the porpoise is a mammal, the zoologist can, without further examination, predict that the animal will have a four-chambered heart, bones of a particular type, and a certain general pattern of nerves and blood vessels. Without using a microscope the zoologist can say with reasonable confidence that the red blood cells in the blood of the porpoise will lack nuclei. This ability to generalize about animal structure depends upon a system for organizing the vast amount of knowledge about animals.

—RALPH BUCHSBAUM, *Animals Without Backbones*

6. There is, however, a great difference between the measurement of time and the measurement of lengths; we can never find again an interval of time that has passed, whilst it is quite easy to find a length and to begin over again the operation of measuring it more carefully and more accurately. This difference, however, is only apparent, for we never find again the *same* length, which has been displaced by the motion of the stars and put out of shape by the molecular motion which never ceases. It is, therefore, only the *approximate* length which we find again, and in an analogous manner we may say that *approximately* we find again the same interval of time. This is what happens when, in the course of several succeeding nights, an astronomer measures the time separating the passage of the meridian by two fixed stars. The astronomer finds that this interval of time is the same, just as we find that the dimensions of a solid body are the same today as they were yesterday. We know very well that the identity cannot be absolute, but the equality is very near, and it is sufficient for the requirements of our science.

—EMILE BOREL, *Space and Time*

7. . . . the population of pure-bred mice, which inhabited the mousery of the Rockefeller Institute, showed that longevity does not depend only on heredity. And that it can be modified at will. These mice lived, on an average, from seventeen to nineteen months. A mouse of twenty months can be arbitrarily compared to a human being sixty years old. Thus, thirty-two months is a very old age. In several groups of the population, no mouse reached this age. In 23,000 animals that were observed during the entire course of their existence, only five were caused to live more than thirty-eight months. One died at forty-two months. The age of thirty-two months in mice may be assumed to be equivalent to about one hundred years in human beings. The experiments demonstrated that as simple a factor as a modification in the diet is capable of augmenting longevity. But the improvements in the food that determined an increase in the stature, in the average duration of life, in the number of the young and the size of the litters, and a decrease in the incidence of pneumonia, did not necessarily promote longevity. On the contrary, the life span increased in groups fed on diets that reduced the size of the animals and caused a higher death-rate during the first month of life. These diets were of great diversity. For instance, fasting, combined with a well-balanced diet, for several generations, increased the longevity of the individuals, their alertness and muscular strength, while diminishing their stature. Strange to say, a deficient diet or certain toxic substances in small amounts also permitted a larger number of animals to reach extreme old age. The life span is far from being a rigid characteristic of a given race. It is probable that a greater longevity could be induced in men, as in mice, by appropriate changes in the diet and mode of living.

—ALEXIS CARREL, *The Mystery of Death*

8. The body is the substance of the soul; the soul is the functioning of the body. . . . The relationship of the soul to its substance is like that of sharpness to a knife, while the relationship of the body to its functioning is like that of a knife to sharpness. What is called sharpness is not the same as the knife, and what is called the knife is not the same as sharpness. Nevertheless, there can be no knife if the sharpness is discarded, nor sharpness if the knife is discarded. I have never heard of sharpness surviving if the knife is destroyed, so how can it be admitted that the soul can remain if the body is annihilated?

—FAN CHEN, *"Essay on the Extinction of the Soul,"* in Fung Yu-Lan, *A History of Chinese Philosophy*

9. If a single cell, under appropriate conditions, becomes a person in the space of a few years, there can surely be no difficulty in understanding how, under appropriate conditions, a cell may, in the course of untold millions of years, give origin to the human race.

—HERBERT SPENCER, *Principles of Biology*

■ *10.* The discovery of this remarkable weapon against disease dates back to 1929. It was purely accidental. Dr. Alexander Fleming, in St. Mary's Hospital, London, was growing colonies of bacteria on glass plates for certain bacteriological researches. One morning he noticed that a spot of mold had germinated on one of the plates. Such contaminations are not unusual, but for some reason, instead of discarding the impurity and starting fresh, Dr. Fleming decided to allow it to remain. He continued to culture the plate, and soon an interesting drama unfolded beneath his eyes. The area occupied by the bacteria was decreasing, that occupied by the mold was increasing, and presently the bacteria had vanished.

Dr. Fleming now took up this fungus for study on its own account. He recognized it as of the penicillium genus, and by deliberately introducing a particle into culture mediums where bacteria were growing, he found that quite a number of species wouldn't grow in its presence. . . . In his laboratory, whenever he wanted to get rid of a growth of gram-positive bacteria, Fleming would implant a little penicillium, and after that the microbes disappeared. . . . So the medical scientists began to speculate. Since the mold destroyed gram-positive organisms on a culture plate, could it be used to destroy gram-positive disease germs in the living body?

—GEORGE W. GRAY, *Science at War*

11.   Just as the bottom of a bucket containing water is pressed more heavily by the weight of the water when it is full than when it is half empty, and the more heavily the deeper the water is, similarly the high places of the earth, such as the summits of mountains, are less heavily pressed than the lowlands are by the weight of the mass of the air. This is because there is more air above the lowlands than above the mountain tops; for all the air along a mountain side presses upon the lowlands but not upon the summit, being above the one but below the other.

—BLAISE PASCAL, *Treatise on the Weight of the Mass of the Air*

12.   While he was attending a group of drug addicts at a sanitarium in Berlin in 1927, it occurred to Dr. Manfred Sakel to try insulin on them. This hormone promotes the utilization of sugar in the body, and on theoretical grounds he believed its effect should relieve the paradox by which a slave of the drug habit requires larger and larger doses of what is essentially a poison. He hoped that through the insulin he might free the victim of dependence on morphine. . . .

Some of the men reacted to the insulin with convulsions, but most of them broke into perspiration and lapsed into deep sleep. When they came out of their seizure, or were awakened after a few hours of coma, their conduct surprised the doctor. He noticed that the morbid fears and anxieties which habitually oppress addicts had diminished. Odd notions of persecution, jumpy nerves, and other psychotic symptoms were gone.

This unexpected outcome set Dr. Sakel to thinking. If insulin improved the mental climate of the drug-crazed men, what would it do for the frankly insane?

—GEORGE W. GRAY, *The Advancing Front of Medicine*

13.   An electron is no more (and no less) hypothetical than a star. Nowadays we count electrons one by one in a Geiger counter, as we count the stars one by one on a photographic plate. In what sense can an electron be called more unobservable than a star? I am not sure whether I ought to say that I have seen an electron; but I have just the same doubt whether I have seen a star. If I have seen one, I have seen the other. I have seen a small disc of light surrounded by diffraction rings which has not the least resemblance to what a star is supposed to be; but the name "star" is given to the object in the physical world which some hundreds of years ago started a chain of causation which has resulted in this particular light-pattern. Similarly in a Wilson expansion chamber I have seen a trail not in the least resembling what an electron is supposed to be; but the name "electron" is given to the object in the physical world which has caused this trail to appear. How can it possibly be maintained that a hypothesis is introduced in one case and not in the other?

—SIR ARTHUR EDDINGTON, *New Pathways in Science*

14. Now if we survey the universe, so far as it falls under our knowledge, it bears a great resemblance to an animal or organized body, and seems actuated with a like principle of life and motion. A continual circulation of matter in it produces no disorder: a continual waste in every part is incessantly repaired; the closest sympathy is perceived throughout the entire system: and each part or member, in performing its proper offices, operates both to its own preservation and to that of the whole. The world, therefore, I infer, is an animal, and the Deity is the *soul* of the world, actuating it, and actuated by it.

—DAVID HUME, *Dialogues Concerning Natural Religion*

■ **15.** In our study we should first start with the fundamental living unit, the cell. Following the fundamental method of physico-mathematical sciences, we do not attempt a mathematical description of a concrete cell, in all its complexity. We start with a study of highly idealized systems, which, at first, may even not have any counterpart in real nature. This point must be particularly emphasized. The objection may be raised against such an approach, because such systems have no connection with reality and therefore any conclusions drawn about such idealized systems cannot be applied to real ones. Yet this is exactly what has been, and always is, done in physics. The physicist goes on studying mathematically, in detail, such nonreal things as "material points," "absolutely rigid bodies," "ideal fluids," and so on. *There are no such things as those in nature.* Yet the physicist not only studies them but applies his conclusions to *real things.* And behold! Such an application leads to practical results—at least within certain limits.

—N. RASHEVSKY, *Mathematical Biophysics*

16. One cannot require that everything shall be defined, any more than one can require that a chemist shall decompose every substance. What is simple cannot be decomposed, and what is logically simple cannot have a proper definition.

—GOTTLOB FREGE, "On Concept and Object"

17. And in truth, I am quite willing it should be known that the little I have hitherto learned is almost nothing in comparison with that of which I am ignorant, and to the knowledge of which I do not despair of being able to attain; for it is much the same with those who gradually discover truth in the sciences, as with those who when growing rich find less difficulty in making great acquisitions, than they formerly experienced when poor in making acquisitions of much smaller amount. Or they may be compared to the commanders of armies, whose forces usually increase in proportion to their victories, and who need greater prudence to keep together the residue of their troops after a defeat than after a victory to take towns and provinces.

—RENÉ DESCARTES, *A Discourse on Method*

18. In the United States, especially, atom-smashing-equipment, such as the Van de Graaff generators and cyclotrons, had been constructed. These machines were already capable of accelerating certain particles used as 'projectiles' up to the enormous energy of nine million volts. Nevertheless, even they had only damaged, without breaking into, the protective walls with which Nature in her wisdom had encircled the atomic nucleus and the tremendous stores of energy it contained. The idea that neutrons, which carried no electrical charge at all, might have been able to accomplish what could not be done with such heavily charged projectiles, was too fantastic to be credited. It was as though one were to suggest to troops which had been vainly shelling an underground shelter with guns of the heaviest calibre for a long time that they should start trying their luck with ping-pong balls.

—ROBERT JUNGK, *Brighter Than a Thousand Suns*

5.3   REFUTATION BY LOGICAL ANALOGY

There is a special kind of argument that uses an analogy to prove the invalidity of another argument. It is intended to refute that other argument, not by showing that at least one of its premises is false (or mistaken), or by showing that it commits one of the fallacies discussed in chapter 3, but by showing that the other argument's premisses do not imply the conclusion that was inferred from them. We have here a basic method of appraising an argument as unsatisfactory from a logical point of view.

Underlying this method of criticizing arguments is the fact that from the point of view of logic, the form of an argument is its most important aspect. This is certainly the case for arguments that are claimed to be absolutely demonstrative. There can be no question but that the world's oldest example of a valid argument is absolutely demonstrative:

All humans are mortal.
Socrates is human.
Therefore, Socrates is mortal.

And any other argument that has exactly the same form (structure, shape, or pattern) is absolutely demonstrative also, as for example:

All dogs are carnivorous.
Fido is a dog.
Therefore, Fido is carnivorous.

This logical fact underlies the method of refutation by logical analogy (sometimes known as the method of refutation by counterexample). If a given argument has true premises but a false conclusion, that is sufficient grounds for classifying it as invalid. But if we do not know whether its component propositions are true or false, we can prove it invalid by constructing a refuting analogy. A refuting analogy for a given argument is an argument of exactly the same form or pattern as the given argument, but whose premises are known to be true and whose conclusion is known to be false. The refuting analogy is thus known to be invalid, and the given argument—since it has the same form—also is known to be invalid.

At the Mad Tea Party in Wonderland, Alice makes a logical mistake. The March Hare tells her:

". . . you should say what you mean."

"I do," Alice hastily replied; "at least—at least I mean what I say—that's the same thing, you know."

"Not the same thing a bit!" said the Hatter. "Why, you might just as well say that 'I see what I eat' is the same thing as 'I eat what I see'!"

"You might just as well say," added the March Hare, "that 'I like what I get' is the same thing as 'I get what I like'!"

"You might just as well say," added the Dormouse, which seemed to be talking in its sleep, "that 'I breathe when I sleep' is the same thing as 'I sleep when I breathe'!"

"It is the same thing with you," said the Hatter, and here the conversation dropped. . . .[10]

Here Alice defended herself by arguing to the conclusion that "I say what I mean" from the premiss that "I mean what I say," on the grounds that they are "the same thing." But they are *not* the same thing, and Alice's premiss does *not* imply her conclusion. That is proved by the obviously invalid analogous arguments so scornfully offered by her disagreeable companions, whom Max Black (1909–88) has characterized as being "infuriatingly logical."[11]

In the present case, what indicates that the Hatter, the March Hare, and the Dormouse are offering refutations by logical analogy is the phrase each of them uses: "You might just as well say." Other phrases often used with refuting analogies are "the same argument proves," "this is about as logical as arguing that," "I could use the same reasoning to claim that," "using the same logic one might also conclude that," "the same methodology would lead to the conclusion that," where the refuting analogy is an argument of the same pattern as the one being refuted but whose premisses are known to be true and whose conclusion is known to be false.

A more serious refutation by logical analogy was given by Abraham Lincoln during the fateful presidential campaign of 1860:

But the South were threatening to destroy the Union in the event of the election of a republican President, and were telling us that the great crime of having destroyed it will be upon us. This is cool. A highwayman holds a pistol to my ear, with "stand and deliver, or I shall kill you, and then you will be a murderer." To be sure the money which he demands is my own, and I have a clear right to keep it, but it is no more so than my vote, and the threat of death to extort my money, and the threat of destruction to the Union to extort my vote, can scarcely be distinguished in principle.[12]

Here the Southern argument is that the North would be responsible for the dissolution of the Union if they elected a Republican president. That argument is answered by Lincoln's refuting analogy of the highwayman who argues that his victim is responsible for murder if he refuses to "deliver" his money to the brigand. Lincoln carefully spells out the parallel between the two kinds of extortion mentioned, relying upon the

---

[10]   Lewis Carroll, *Alice's Adventures in Wonderland,* chap. 7. "Lewis Carroll" was the pseudonym of Charles Lutwidge Dodgson (1832–98), a mathematician and logician at Oxford University.

[11]   Max Black, *Critical Thinking* (1952), p. 43.

[12]   Abraham Lincoln, speech at Dover, New Hampshire, 2 March 1860, *The Collected Works of Abraham Lincoln,* ed. Roy R. Basler (1953), 3:553.

good sense of his listeners to recognize that the extortionist, not the victim, would be the murderer, and the South, not the Republicans, would (try to) destroy the Union.

EXERCISES

Each of the following is a refutation by logical analogy. In each, identify the argument being refuted and the refuting analogy, and decide if they have the same form or pattern.

■   *1.*   Bettelheim . . . is a true believer. 'Psychoanalysis," he writes, "is beyond doubt the most valuable method of psychotherapy"; it is so because it is difficult and time-consuming. The same argument proves that the Model T is the most valuable method of wheeled transportation. . . .
                              —PETER S. PRESCOTT, review of Bruno Bettelheim, *Freud and Man's Soul, Newsweek,* 10 January 1983, p. 64

2.   If widgets can be imported from Asia for a price reflecting labor costs of $1 an hour, then an hour spent making widgets adds a dollar of value to the economy. This is true no matter what American widget makers are being paid. If foreign widgets are excluded in order to protect the jobs of American widget makers getting $10 an hour, $1 of that $10 reflects their contribution to the economy and $9 is coming out of the pockets of other workers who have to pay more for widgets. Nice for widget makers, but perfectly futile from the perspective of net social welfare.

After all, if this economic alchemy really worked, we could shut our borders to all imports, pay one another $1,000 an hour, and we'd all be rich. It doesn't work that way.
                              —MICHAEL KINSLEY, "Keep Trade Free," *The New Republic* 188, 11 April 1983, p. 10

3.   . . . one of the most misleading analogies today is the one that usually turns up for giving the vote to 18-year-olds. This argument asserts that 18-year-olds, being old enough to fight, are old enough to vote. True, only if you believe that fighting and voting are the same kind of thing, which I, for one, do not. Fighting requires strength, muscular coordination and, in a modern army, instant and automatic response to orders. Voting requires knowledge of men, history, reasoning power; it is essentially a deliberative activity. Army mules and police dogs are used to fight: nobody is interested in giving them the right to vote. This argument rests on a false analogy.
                              —RICHARD M. WEAVER, "A Responsible Rhetoric," *The Intercollegiate Review* 12, Winter 1976–77, pp. 86–87

4.   The creationists frequently stress that we cannot explain everything. This comes oddly from a group that many conclude can explain nothing. It would be as foolish to discard evolutionary theory today because it cannot explain everything as it would be to disband the medical establishment because it cannot cure the common cold.
                              —JOHN A. MOORE, "Countering the Creationists," *Academe* 68, March–April 1982, p. 16

■   *5.*   . . . some people argue that there are many things wrong with society—some of which are increasingly conspicuous—and that since we have also had decades of uninterrupted growth the growth must be the cause of the various social and economic ills that we see around us. This is about as logical as arguing that all the ills of society must be caused by the fact that people spend more time these days in cleaning their teeth.

—WILFRED BECKERMAN, *Two Cheers for the Affluent Society* (1974), p. 48

6. In the rush of vitamin and mineral discoveries . . . the food extremists found a scientific argument, which they have pressed ever since. But along with the justification came an error of distortion, which also persists.

The reasoning goes something like this: Funk's pigeons—like other human and animal groups overly dependent on processed grain, such as Eijkman's beriberi sufferers in Indonesia—sickened and died. When the hull of the grain, or an extract of it, was put into their diets, they were healed. Therefore, the hull was seen as the life-giving factor. The heart of the grain was seen as almost worthless. This reasoning is akin to thinking that, because a bad sparkplug is the cause of an auto breakdown, the rest of the car is useless, and one should use sparkplugs for transportation.

—RONALD D. DEUTSCH, *The New Nuts Among the Berries* (1977), p. 157

7. In your thought-provoking cover story about nuclear warfare . . . you said, "Deterrence has worked for 38 years." Has it? I could use the same reasoning to claim that my house has never been struck by lightning because I painted a face on the roof that frightens the lightning away. If something has never happened, we have no way of knowing what prevents it from happening. It is dangerous to award nuclear buildup a credit it may not deserve.

—GEORGE M. HIEBER, letter to the editor, *Newsweek,* 19 December 1983, p. 7

8. Before the end of his freshman year at Cornell, Sullivan had a severe schizophrenic breakdown and he disappeared for two years, probably into the back wards of a state hospital as a catatonic patient. We know that he was overtly schizophrenic because he had the courage to acknowledge the fact in later years. Mrs. Perry has searched assiduously for some external record of his hospitalization but has found none. According to the local gossip of 1909–11 concerning this episode, Sullivan had committed larceny but got off by faking insanity. Mrs. Perry's own conclusion is that the insanity was not faked but that he had in fact committed a criminal act, a conclusion she defends by pointing to his unmistakable empathy for youthful offenders as well as for psychotics. Using the same logic, however, one might also conclude that he was black and female: he was the first social scientist to champion field research on the effects of discrimination on black youth, and a rock of respectful support for intellectually gifted women like Clara Thompson, Ruth Benedict, Hortense Powdermaker, Karen Horney, Frieda Fromm-Reichmann, Margaret Bourke-White, and Katherine Dunham.

—BARBARA LERNER, review of Helen Swick Perry, *Psychiatrist of America: The Life of Harry Stack Sullivan,* in *Commentary* 74, August 1982, pp. 83–84

9. The critics of psychoanalysis argue that people who have been analyzed are "brainwashed" into "believing in" psychoanalysis. But the same could be said of people who have come to a sympathetic understanding of Beethoven's genius through learning to play his piano sonatas.

—JANET MALCOLM, "Annals of Scholarship (Psychoanalysis—Part I)," *The New Yorker,* 5 December 1983, p. 80

■ *10.* [A convicted murderer] . . . may file an infinite number of petitions alleging different violations (or, for that matter, the same ones); every petition, no matter how frivolous, will delay the execution for weeks or months, and its denial will be appealed, which takes even longer. . . .

These nonstop legal proceedings have produced one of the most curious of the abolitionist arguments: death is not a practical sanction, for the inevitable litigation makes prohibitive its cost in time and money. In effect: I have poured glue in the works of your watch; it is therefore worthless, and you ought to throw it away.

—JOSEPH W. BISHOP, JR., review of Ernest van den Haag and John P. Conrad, *The Death Penalty: A Debate, Commentary*, February 1984, p. 70

11. When the film "Gandhi" opened, there was a brief flurry of interest in nonviolence, but even those people who gave the subject more than a moment's thought tended to reject it out of hand. It might have driven the British out of India, but would it suffice against a more brutal regime? One objection, though it was not always spoken, was that nonviolence wouldn't have worked against the Nazis. And that's right— it wouldn't have. The Nazis were brutal enough and strong enough—evil enough—to overwhelm anything save iron and lead. But to toss out an idea on those grounds is to allow Hitler's insanity to continue perverting our earth; one might as well scrap all cars too slow to win the Indy 500, or junk the Cuisinart because it won't chop firewood.

—"The Talk of the Town," *The New Yorker,* 12 December 1983, p. 44

12. U.S. Department of Defense officials and publications have often asserted that the far greater frequency of Russian satellite launches demonstrates that the military space program of the U.S.S.R. is much larger than that of the U.S. The disparity in launch frequency, however, is entirely accounted for by the much shorter lifetime of the Russian satellites. . . . Comparisons based on expenditures devoted to the two military space programs should also be treated with caution; the same methodology would lead to the conclusion that the U.S.S.R. is a more abundant food producer than the U.S.

—RICHARD L. GARWIN, KURT GOTTFRIED, and DONALD L. HAFNER, "Antisatellite Weapons," *Scientific American,* June 1984, p. 46

13. Mr. Clark [William P. Clark, Secretary of the Interior] may be even less qualified to manage America's conservation lands than he was to manage foreign policy: Administration spokesmen have pointed out that Mr. Clark's father and grandfather were forest rangers—a proposition akin to claiming that someone should be Secretary of Transportation because he comes from a long line of cab drivers.

—"What Watt Wrought," *The New Republic,* 26 December 1983, p. 8

14. The American navy has had to pull quite a lot of C–4 missiles out of service from its nuclear submarines, because it suddenly found they weren't working. This is a serious business, since the C–4s carry over a quarter of America's long-range nuclear warheads. It also provides the anti-nuclear people with one good argument, if they had chosen to use it. This renewed evidence that missiles can be unpredictably unreliable makes it even less likely that either Russia or America will launch the crossed-fingers sort of nuclear first strike that depends on having just enough deliverable warheads, x-plus-one, to knock out the other side's missile silos. The argument actually used by some anti-nuclearists is different, and rotten. If the Americans have announced that some of their missiles aren't working, and the Russians haven't taken advantage of it by pushing the button, doesn't this mean—they ask—that the missiles were unnecessary all along?

Apart from the fact that this is rather like saying, if one of your legs goes numb and you don't fall over, that you might as well have it amputated, the question arises of how far those who favour this line of thought think the process could safely go.

—*The Economist,* 25–31 August 1984, pp. 14–15

■ *15.* One of the great scandals of recent and current government rhetoric is that there has been a concerted attempt by the economic leadership to deny that budget deficits lead to inflation (or play anything more than a minimal role in inflation). The government consistently tries to maintain that *price increases* are the cause of inflation. This is like saying that meals cause hunger.

—TOM BETHELL, "Fooling with the Budget," *Harper's,* October 1979, p. 44

16. Father was always a bit sceptical of this story, and of the new flying machines, otherwise he believed everything he read. Until 1909 no one in Lower Binfield believed that human beings would ever learn to fly. The official doctrine was that if God had meant us to fly He'd have given us wings. Uncle Ezekiel couldn't help retorting that if God had meant us to ride He'd have given us wheels, but even he didn't believe in the new flying machines.

—GEORGE ORWELL, *Coming Up for Air*

17. It is urged that motion pictures do not fall within the First Amendment's aegis because their production, distribution, and exhibition is a large-scale business conducted for private profit. We cannot agree. That books, newspapers, and magazines are published and sold for profit does not prevent them from being a form of expression whose liberty is safeguarded by the First Amendment. We fail to see why operation for profit should have any different effect in the case of motion pictures.

—JUSTICE THOMAS CLARK, for the U.S. Supreme Court, *Burstyn v. Wilson,* 43 U.S. 495 (1952)

18. Paton goes on to make the novice's characteristic mistake of arguing that because we expect evolution to produce beings who favor other members of their species, therefore it must be right to favor our own species. (If you find the argument at all plausible, substitute "race" for "species" and see if you still think so.)

—PETER SINGER, "Ten Years of Animal Liberation," *The New York Review of Books,* 17 January 1985, p. 48

19. Dear Ann: I live in North Carolina and I sure wish you would quit trying to put the tobacco industry out of business. A lot of folks down here depend on it for a living.

Don't you know tobacco is a gift from God? He gave us the plant to be used and enjoyed. So lay off, lady. You are getting to be a real bore.

—*Raleigh Reader*

Dear Raleigh: Your argument is ridiculous. God also gave us poison ivy.

—ANN LANDERS, *Honolulu Advertiser,* 24 July 1985, p. C-4

■ *20.* Many find it easier to lie to those they take to be untruthful themselves. It is as though a barrier had been let down. And to Augustine's argument that countering a lie with a lie is like countering sacrilege with sacrilege, they might answer: Such an analogy cannot be stretched to conclude that it is always wrong to repay lies in kind. They might advance another analogy—that between lying and the use of force—and ask: If at times force can be used to counter force, why should lies never be used to counter lies? And they might contend that just as someone forfeits his rights to non-interference by others when he threatens them forcibly, so a liar has forfeited the ordinary right to be dealt with honestly.

—SISSELA BOK, *Lying: Moral Choice in Public and Private Life* (1979), pp. 132–33

6

Causal Connections:
Mill's Methods of Experimental Inquiry

6.1 THE NATURE OF CAUSATION

Necessary and Sufficient Conditions

It is a fundamental axiom in the study of nature that events do not just happen, but occur only under certain conditions. It is customary to distinguish between necessary and sufficient conditions for the occurrence of an event. A *necessary* condition for the occurrence of a specified event is a circumstance in whose absence the event cannot occur. For example, the presence of oxygen is a necessary condition for combustion to occur: If combustion occurs, then oxygen must have been present, for in the absence of oxygen there can be no combustion.

Although it is a necessary condition, the presence of oxygen is not a sufficient condition for combustion to occur. A *sufficient* condition for the occurrence of an event is a circumstance in whose presence the event will occur. The presence of oxygen is not a sufficient condition for combustion because oxygen can be present without combustion occurring. On the other hand, for almost any substance there is some range of temperature such that *being in that range of temperature in the presence of oxygen* is a sufficient condition for combustion of that substance. It is obvious that there may be several *necessary* conditions for the occurrence of an event and that they must all be included in the sufficient condition. For example, each of the following is a necessary condition for the operation of a commercial washing machine: (1) the machine being functional, (2) the electricity being on, (3) the machine being plugged in, (4) coins being inserted, and (5) the lid being closed. Together, conditions (1) through (5) are sufficient for operation of the machine. We could say that conditions (1) through (5) are *individually necessary* and *jointly sufficient* for operation of the machine.

The word "cause" sometimes is used in the sense of necessary condition and sometimes in the sense of sufficient condition. It is most often used in the sense of necessary condition when the problem at hand is the elimination of some undesirable phenomenon. To eliminate it, one need only find some condition that is necessary to its existence and then eliminate that condition. Thus a physician seeks to discover what kind of germ is the "cause" of a certain illness in order to cure the illness by prescribing a drug that will destroy those germs. The germs are said to be the cause of the disease in the sense of a necessary condition for it, since in their absence the disease cannot occur.

The word "cause" is used in the sense of sufficient condition when we are interested not in the elimination of something undesirable but rather in the production of something desirable. Thus a metallurgist seeks to discover the cause of strength in metals in order to create stronger alloys. The process of mixing and heating and cooling is said to be the cause of strengthening, in the sense of a sufficient condition, since such processing suffices to produce a stronger alloy.

In certain practical situations, the word "cause" is used in still a different sense. An insurance company might send investigators to determine the cause of a mysterious fire. If the investigators sent back a report that the fire was caused by the presence of oxygen in the atmosphere, they would not keep their jobs very long. And yet they would be right—in the sense of necessary condition—for had there been no oxygen present, there would have been no fire. But the insurance company did not have *that* sense in mind when it sent them to investigate. Nor is the company interested in the sufficient condition. If after several weeks the investigators reported that although they had proof that the fire was deliberately ignited by the policyholder, they hadn't as yet been able to learn *all* the necessary conditions, and so hadn't been able to determine the cause (in the sense of sufficient condition), the company would recall the investigators and tell them to stop wasting their time and the company's money. The insurance company was using the word "cause" in another sense—what they wanted to find out was the incident or action that, in the presence of those conditions that usually prevail, *made the difference* between the occurrence or nonoccurrence of the event.

We may distinguish two subdivisions of this third sense of "cause." These are traditionally characterized as the *remote* and the *proximate* causes. Where there is a causal sequence or chain of several events, A causing B, B causing C, C causing D, and D causing E, we can regard E as effect of any or all of the preceding events. The nearest of them, D, is the proximate cause of E, and the others are more and more remote causes, A more remote than B, and B more remote than C. In this case the proximate cause was the policyholder's lighting the fire. But that action, and thus the fire, may have been caused by a need for money to cover losses in an investment in a cattle ranch, those losses occasioned by increased expenses brought about by soaring grain prices caused by a crop failure in the Soviet Union. The crop failure was a remote cause of the fire, but the insurance company would not have been interested in hearing that the mysterious fire was caused by a Soviet crop failure.

There are several different senses of the term "cause," as we have seen. We can legitimately infer cause from effect only in the sense of necessary condition. And we can legitimately infer effect from cause only in the sense of sufficient condition. Where inferences are made both from cause to effect and from effect to cause, the term "cause" must be used in the sense of "necessary and sufficient condition." In this usage, cause is identified with sufficient condition, and sufficient condition is regarded as the conjunction of all necessary conditions. It should be clear that there is no single definition of "cause" that conforms to all of the different uses of that word. What we regard as the cause of a given event depends on our interests, aims, or purposes.[1]

Causal Laws

Every use of the word "cause," whether in everyday life or in science, involves or presupposes the doctrine that cause and effect are *uniformly* connected. We admit that a particular circumstance caused a particular effect only if we agree that any other circumstance of that type will—if the attendant circumstances are sufficiently similar—cause another effect of the same kind as the first. In other words, similar causes produce similar effects. Part of the meaning of the word "cause" as used today is that every occurrence of a cause producing an effect is an *instance* or *example* of the causal law that such circumstances are *always* accompanied by such phenomena. Thus we are willing to relinquish a belief that circumstance *C* was the cause of effect *E* in one case if it can be shown that the same (type of) circumstance was present in another situation that was the same as the first except that the effect *E did not occur* in the latter.

Since a causal law is implied by every assertion that a particular circumstance was the cause of a particular phenomenon, there is an element of generality in every such assertion. A causal law—as we shall use the term—asserts that such and such a circumstance is invariably attended by exactly the same kind of phenomenon, no matter when or where it occurs. Now how do we come to know such general truths? The causal relation is not a purely logical or demonstrative relationship; it cannot be discovered by any a priori reasoning. Causal laws can be discovered only a posteriori, by an appeal to experience. But our experiences are always of particular circumstances, particular phenomena, and particular sequences of them. We may observe several instances of a certain kind of circumstance (say, *C*), and every instance *that we observe* may be accompanied by an instance of a certain kind of phenomenon (say, *P*). These observations show us, of course, only that *some* cases of C are cases of P. How are we to get from this evidence to the general proposition that *every* case of *C* is a case of *P*, which is involved in saying that *C* causes *P*?[2]

The method of arriving at general or universal propositions from the particular facts of experience is called *generalization*. From premises that assert that three pieces of blue litmus paper turned red when dipped in acid, we may draw either a particular conclusion about what will happen to a fourth piece of blue litmus paper if it is dipped in acid or a general conclusion about what happens to *every* piece of blue litmus paper that is dipped in acid. If we draw the first, we have an argument by analogy; the second is a generalization. The structure of these two types of argument may be analyzed as follows. The premises report a number of instances in which two attributes (or circumstances or phenomena) occur together. By analogy we infer that a different instance of one attribute also will exhibit the other attribute. By generalization we infer that *all* instances of the one attribute also will be instances of the other. A generalization of the form

---

[1]   For a discussion of this point, see Joel Feinberg, "Sua Culpa," *Doing and Deserving: Essays in the Theory of Responsibility* , pp. 187–221.

[2]   This is a (somewhat crude) formulation of what philosophers refer to as "the problem of induction."

Instance 1 of phenomenon E is accompanied by circumstance C.
Instance 2 of phenomenon E is accompanied by circumstance C.
Instance 3 of phenomenon E is accompanied by circumstance C.

Therefore, every instance of phenomenon E is accompanied by
    circumstance C.

is a generalization by *simple enumeration*. A generalization by simple enumeration is similar to an argument by analogy, differing only in having a general (rather than a particular) conclusion.

Simple enumeration often is used in establishing causal connections. Where a number of instances of a phenomenon are invariably accompanied by a certain type of circumstance, it is only natural to infer the existence of a causal relationship between them. Because the circumstance of dipping blue litmus paper in acid is accompanied in all observed instances by the phenomenon of the paper's turning red, we conclude that dipping blue litmus paper in acid is the *cause* of its turning red. Similarly, from the fact that a number of people have contracted yellow fever after being bitten by mosquitoes that had previously fed on yellow fever patients, we may infer by simple enumeration that the bite of such a mosquito *causes* yellow fever infection. The analogical character of such arguments is quite apparent.

Because of the similarity between argument by simple enumeration and argument by analogy, it should be clear that the same criteria apply to both. Some arguments by simple enumeration may establish their conclusions with a higher degree of probability than others. The greater the number of instances appealed to, the higher the probability of the conclusion. The various instances or cases of phenomenon E accompanied by circumstance C often are called *confirming instances* of the causal law that asserts that C causes E. The greater the number of confirming instances, the higher the probability of the causal law—other things being equal. Thus the first criterion for analogical arguments applies directly to arguments by simple enumeration also.

Generalizations by simple enumeration frequently are made and often are valuable and suggestive. But they are not very trustworthy. For example, consider the following argument:

Tom broke a mirror and cut his hand, which was bad luck.
Jane broke a mirror and then sprained her ankle, which was bad luck.
Sally broke a mirror and then lost her purse, which was bad luck.

Therefore, breaking a mirror *causes* bad luck.

Most of us would be inclined to put little trust in such an argument. Yet it is an argument by simple enumeration, appealing to three "confirming instances." Nevertheless, we should probably say that the three instances reported were coincidences rather than manifestations of a causal law. This is the chief weakness of arguments by simple enumeration. Their very nature prevents them from distinguishing between confirming instances of genuine causal laws, on the one hand, and mere accidents or coincidences, on the other.

Our criticism of the method of simple enumeration can be put in this way. A single negative or disconfirming instance will overthrow an alleged causal law (any exception obviously *disproves* a rule), whereas the method of simple enumeration takes no account of such exceptions. For an exception or negative instance is either one in which *C* is present without *E* or where *E* is present without *C*—but the only legitimate premises in an argument by simple enumeration are reports of instances in which both *C* and *E* are present. In other words, if we were to confine ourselves to simple enumeration arguments, we would look only for confirming instances and would ignore any negative or disconfirming instances that might otherwise be found. For this reason, despite their fruitfulness and value in suggesting causal laws, arguments by simple enumeration are not suitable for *testing* causal laws. For that purpose, other types of argument have been devised, and to these we now turn.

EXERCISES

State the relationship between each of the following pairs of events (or state of affairs). The event in the first column may be (1) necessary (but not sufficient) for the event in the second column, (2) sufficient (but not necessary) for the event in the second column, (3) both necessary and sufficient for the event in the second column, or (4) neither necessary nor sufficient for the event in the second column. Give reasons for your answers.

lying _____	telling a falsehood
shooting _____	killing
hitting a home run _____	hitting a grand slam
rain falling _____	the ground getting wet
being older than twenty _____	being sixty years old
being a dog _____	being an animal
knowing someone _____	loving someone
touching the baseball _____	being charged with an error
being a bachelor _____	being an unmarried adult male
dynamiting the foundation of a building _____	destroying the building

6.2   MILL'S METHODS

Introduction

In late 1992, poultry producers in McCurtin County, Oklahoma, discovered to their dismay that large numbers of chicks were dying. A certain percentage of chick deaths is to be expected in this industry, but nothing approaching what was happening. One farmer said, "I walk in (the chicken houses) and find [the chicks] just laying over dead."[3] Many of the poultry farmers experiencing losses speculated about the cause of death (most assumed that the chicks were dying from the same cause). One farmer thought the cause was overcrowding; another suggested a problem with the feed; still another believed that it was a genetic defect in the chicks. Obviously, there was an urgent need to discover the cause of the deaths, and steps were being taken to do just

---

[3]   "Chicks' Deaths Mystify Farmers," Associated Press report, 10 February 1993. All of the information in the text comes from this report.

that. An official for a large poultry corporation that supplies chicks to farmers for "fattening" advised farmers to "adjust some farming practices and find out what might be causing the deaths."

This sort of puzzle—and other, less urgent ones—have led scientists and scientific-minded philosophers to formulate methods for ascertaining causes. One such philosopher, John Stuart Mill (1806–1873), set out "Four Methods of Experimental Inquiry" in his classic work *A System of Logic Ratiocinative and Inductive,* first published in 1843.[4] (In reality there were five methods, for Mill thought two of them—the methods of agreement and difference—could be combined to create a powerful fifth method.) Mill's aim was to put induction on the same rigorous footing as deduction, which prompted him to make bold (some would say rash) claims for his methods. He concluded that his methods "are the only possible modes of experimental inquiry" and that, along with deduction, they "compose the available resources of the human mind for ascertaining the laws of the succession of phenomena"; in other words, causal laws.[5] As one Mill scholar has put it, all of the methods "have the same purpose and the same basic logic, which is to test a supposed causal connection in a variety of conditions, and to do so by eliminating alternative causal connections."[6]

In this section we discuss Mill's methods of experimental inquiry, each of which is still widely, if not always consciously, used. For each method we do the following: (a) state it in Mill's own words, (b) give at least one of Mill's examples, (c) provide a more recent example of the use of the method, (d) discuss the method's rationale and limitations (if any), and (e) set out five exercises to test the reader's comprehension. The methods will be presented in the order in which Mill discussed them, although this has nothing to do with their importance or status. Our discussion concludes with a summary of the five methods in modern terminology.

Method of Agreement

Like all of Mill's methods, the method of agreement is based on common sense. Suppose something occurs for which we seek the cause—an illness among several people, for example. Assuming that the illness has a common cause, we might begin by trying to find a circumstance that all the sick people share. If we find such a circumstance, and if there is no other circumstance common to those who are ill, that circumstance probably is the cause of the illness. Let us call the event or state of affairs that we find puzzling (in this case the illness) the *phenomenon* and the individuals (in this case people) who exhibit the phenomenon the *instances.* Here is Mill's statement of the method of agreement:

> If two or more instances of the phenomenon under investigation have only one circumstance in common, the circumstance in which alone all the instances agree, is the cause (or effect) of the given phenomenon.

---

[4]   John Stuart Mill, *A System of Logic Ratiocinative and Inductive,* ed. J.M. Robson (1974), p. 388. All quotations are taken from this edition of the text, which is volume VII of the *Collected Works of John Stuart Mill.* Mill's discussion of the four methods can be found in Book III ("Of Induction"), chap. VIII.

[5]   One should not assume that Mill limited himself to causal connections in what are known as "the natural sciences." To the contrary, "his [Mill's] ambition was to analyze and expound [the methods of natural scientists] in the hope that the complex and baffling problems of society would eventually give way before their use." Peter Brian Medawar, *Induction and Intuition in Scientific Thought* (1969), p. 12. In other words, Mill sought a set of methods that could be used by *both* natural and social scientists. The examples and exercises in the text come from both domains.

[6]   Alan Ryan, *J.S. Mill* (1974), p. 80.

Mill's examples of the method of agreement come from natural science, although, as we shall see, the method is not limited to that realm. Here is his second example:

> [L]et the effect [phenomenon] be crystallization. We compare instances in which bodies are known to assume crystalline structure, but which have no other point of agreement; and we find them to have one, and as far as we can observe, only one, antecedent [circumstance] in common: the deposition of solid matter from a liquid state, either a state of fusion or of solution. We conclude, therefore, that the solidification of a substance from a liquid state is an invariable antecedent of its crystallization.

Recently, researchers in Massachusetts were baffled by vitamin D poisoning ("hypervitaminosis D") in a group of eight patients. As most people know, vitamin D is essential to the formation of strong bones and since the 1930s has been added to milk to prevent rickets and other bone diseases. But alas, too much of a good thing can be a bad thing, and in the case of the eight patients suffering from hypervitaminosis D it was a bad thing indeed.

Researchers, motivated by both intellectual and practical considerations, began their inquiry by sending questionnaires to the poisoned patients. These questionnaires elicited information about the patients' diet and use of vitamin supplements. Although the poisoned individuals were different in many respects, such as age (ranging from 15 months to 82 years), sex, diet, and general state of health, they shared one salient circumstance: All drank milk from the same local dairy. As the researchers put it in their report, "The dairy milk was the sole common vehicle for vitamin D that was identified from the responses to the questionnaires."[7] The following table summarizes this information (the numerals "1" through "8" represent the eight individuals; the letter "A" represents the circumstance of having drunk milk from the suspect dairy; the letters "B," "C," "D," and "E" represent other circumstances; and the letter "p" represents the phenomenon to be explained, hypervitaminosis D):

Instances	Circumstances					Phenomenon
1	A	B	C		E	p
2	A		C	D	E	p
3	A		C	D		p
4	A	B		D	E	p
5	A	B	C			p
6	A		C	D		p
7	A	B		D		p
8	A	B	C	D	E	p

[7]   Claire H. Jacobus et al., "Hypervitaminosis D Associated with Drinking Milk," *The New England Journal of Medicine* 326 (30 April 1992):1175; see also *Science* (2 May 1992):295.

When the researchers analyzed milk from the suspect dairy as a way of verifying their conclusion about the cause of the poisoning, they found that the vitamin D concentration in the milk was "up to 580 times the stipulated requirement of 400 [units] per quart for vitamin D-fortified milk."

This case illustrates Mill's method of agreement in that there were "two or more instances of the phenomenon under investigation" (two or more people with hypervitaminosis D) who had "only one circumstance in common" (having drunk milk from the same local dairy). The conclusion therefore follows, by Mill's method, that drinking milk from the dairy caused the poisoning. Subsequent analysis of the milk confirmed this conclusion. The researchers, aware of the possibility of error, framed their conclusion cautiously: "Hypervitaminosis D may result from drinking milk that is incorrectly and excessively fortified with vitamin D." Then, exercising a degree of social responsibility, they added: 'Milk that is fortified with vitamin D must be carefully monitored." By the time the report had been written and published, the Massachusetts Department of Public Health had "halted vitamin D supplementation by the dairy to prevent further vitamin D intoxication."

The rationale for the method of agreement is easy to grasp. In order for event A to be the cause of event B, A must be present whenever B is and B must occur whenever A does. If B can occur without A or A without B, then A is not the cause of B. In terms of our example, if vitamin-D poisoning can occur without drinking milk from the suspect dairy or if drinking milk from the suspect dairy does not lead to vitamin-D poisoning, then drinking milk from the suspect dairy cannot be the cause of hypervitaminosis D. As Mill pointed out, one can verify a causal claim arrived at by the use of the methods by experimentally producing the circumstance alleged to be the cause and watching to see whether that produces the phenomenon. To the extent that verification is possible and the phenomenon occurs, the causal claim is strengthened; to the extent that verification is impossible, it is weakened. Sometimes the main value of the method of agreement is that it *suggests* a cause, which can then be tested by other means (such as the method of difference, to which we will turn momentarily).

Mill was aware, and we too should be, of the limitations of the method of agreement as a mode of experimental inquiry. For one thing, not all of the instances may be present in a given case, and those that are present may not be representative or typical of all of them. For example, the eight people stricken with hypervitaminosis D may have been only a subset of those with the illness, the others of whom did *not* drink milk from the dairy in question. Another problem has to do with the circumstances. Mill wrote: "Unfortunately it is hardly ever possible to ascertain all the antecedents [circumstances], unless the phenomenon is one which we can produce artificially." The problem is that any person or thing has countless characteristics, some of which (such as height) are known and others of which (such as genetic makeup or chemical composition) are unknown. One must do the best one can with what is known. Perhaps the most serious problem with the method of agreement, however, is that even if all the circumstances are known, they may be incorrectly analyzed. This limitation is illustrated by "the case of the scientific drinker."

Consider Pat, who is extremely fond of liquor and as a result gets drunk every night of the week. Pat's health, career, and personal relationships are being ruined by the fondness, so friends and family plead with Pat to stop drinking. Realizing that things cannot go on as they are, Pat resolves to conduct an experiment to discover the cause of the frequent inebriations. For five nights in a row Pat collects instances of the given phenomenon, the antecedent circumstances being, respectively, scotch and soda, bourbon and soda, brandy and soda, rum and soda, and gin and soda. Using Mill's method of agreement, Pat swears a solemn oath never to touch soda again!

The problem with this case is not that Mill's method of agreement was employed incorrectly, for it was employed exactly as specified. As analyzed by Pat, the one circumstance common to the five instances of inebriation was ingestion of soda. The problem, as we know by other means, is that Pat incorrectly analyzed the antecedent circumstances. Had the various liquors not been treated as so many different single circumstances but analyzed into their alcohol contents plus their various other constituents, the method of agreement would have revealed that, besides the soda, *alcohol* was a common circumstance. Then, using Mill's method, the conclusion would have been that *either* the soda or the alcohol, or some combination of the two, caused the intoxication. Another of Mill's methods—most likely the method of difference—could have been used to rule out the soda as the cause.

The moral of this story is that Mill's method of agreement must be used with caution and judgment. Mill himself referred to it as an inferior resource and viewed it as a mere precursor to the use of other, more powerful methods, such as the method of difference. Mill also saw the method of agreement as being useful primarily in cases in which it is impossible to artificially produce the phenomenon the cause of which is sought, for if we could artificially produce the phenomenon we could employ a more powerful method. We would do well to keep these limitations in mind. It may help to think of the method of agreement as one would an automobile. Used properly (that is, with caution and judgment), an automobile can be a valuable means of transportation. Used *improperly,* however, it can lead to disaster. This is true even if the car will never go as fast as a commercial airplane or be as strong as a tank.

EXERCISES

Analyze each of the following passages in terms of instances, circumstances, and phenomena. Show how each passage exemplifies the method of agreement. State the causal connection. It may be useful to construct a diagram or table to portray the information.

■ *1.* Several residents of a dormitory become violently ill, suffering stomach distress and nausea. Half a dozen of the affected students are interviewed to find out what they ate on the day the illness began. The first student ate soup, bread and butter, salad, vegetables, and canned pears; the second student ate soup, bread and butter, vegetables, and canned pears; the third student ate soup, salad, a pork sandwich, and canned pears; the fourth student ate bread and butter, salad, a pork sandwich, vegetables, and canned pears; the fifth student ate soup, salad, vegetables, and canned pears; and the sixth student ate bread and butter, vegetables, and canned pears.

2. It is interesting to note that one of the frequent symptoms of extreme combat anxiety cases is an interference with speech that may run from complete muteness to hesitation and stuttering. Similarly, the sufferer from acute stage fright is unable to speak. Many animals tend to stop vocalizing when frightened, and it is obvious that this tendency is adaptive in preventing them from attracting the attention of their enemies. In the light of this evidence one might suspect that the drive of fear has an innate tendency to elicit the response of stopping vocal behavior.

—JOHN DOLLARD and NEAL E. MILLER, *Personality and Psychotherapy*

3. He [Edward Jenner] kept neatly detailed records of his work, noting how Sarah Portlock, Mary Barge and Elizabeth Wynne, and Simon Nichols, Joseph Merret and William Rodway, had "taken" cowpox and how they showed immunity when he inoculated them with smallpox. He repeated his observations on others, and years passed as he accumulated page upon page of records of cowpox and smallpox. Eventually he was satisfied. He was convinced that the people who had taken cowpox were without exception immune to smallpox.

Jenner's crucial experiment was done in 1796. He took cowpox matter from the hands of Sarah Nelmes, dairymaid, and with it he vaccinated the arm of eight-year-old James Phipps. Two months later, Jenner inoculated Phipps with smallpox on both arms, and several months later he repeated the inoculation. There was neither fever nor pocks, only a trivial sore at the point of inoculation typical of immunity.

—A. L. BARON, *Man Against Germs*

4. A few years ago a small number of people living in various sections of the United States were afflicted with an identical disease. At about the same time the eyes of these individuals developed what the physician calls cataracts—small, irregular, opaque spots in the tissue of the lens. Cataracts interfere with the clear passage of light through the transparent medium of the eye lens. In severe cases they may block vision, visual acuity is lost and the lens must be removed. It turned out that all the individuals who developed these cataracts were physicists and that all of them had been connected with nuclear-energy projects during the war. While they worked with cyclotrons in atomic-energy laboratories they had been the targets of stray neutron rays. They were under medical supervision all during their work, but the density of the neutrons was thought to be entirely harmless. Several years later, however, they developed cataracts.

This case is one of the best examples of the insidiousness of nuclear radiation.

—HEINZ HABER, *Man in Space*

■ **5.** We shall begin our consideration of this material with a fairly detailed examination of one of the more striking studies, that by Heilig and Hoff. This concerns the induction of herpetic blisters (cold-sores) by means of suggested hallucinations. Three psychopathic women were employed as subjects. The typical experimental procedure was as follows: The experimenter recalled to the subject's mind when in deep hypnotic state an extremely unpleasant emotional experience connected with her particular neurosis. Thereupon the patient showed signs of great excitement, such as flushing, tossing about, and groaning in fear. At this juncture the psychiatrist stroked the patient's lower lip and suggested a feeling of itchiness such as the patient had often felt when a cold-sore was starting. Calming suggestions were then given, after which the patient was dehypnotized. During the following twenty-four hours or so the patient reported an itching on the lower lip, at the end of which time there appeared a slight swelling on the lip in question. At the end of forty-eight hours numerous small herpetic blisters appeared, which gradually merged into a large blister. After a few days this dried up, forming a scab, and finally healed. The contents of the fresh blister, when transmitted to the cornea of a rabbit, caused a herpes in the rabbit on the third day, thus providing the technical genuineness of the cold-sore. This picture, with unimportant variations, holds for all three patients.

—CLARK L. HULL, *Hypnosis and Suggestibility*

Method of Difference

If as we suggested the method of agreement is rooted in common sense, then all the more so with the method of difference, which Mill described as "a logical process to which we owe almost all the inductive conclusions we draw in daily life." But there the similarity ends. Whereas the method of agreement requires two *or more* instances (and the more the better), the method of difference requires *exactly* two. The objective of the investigator using the method of difference is to find two instances that are alike in every respect except one; if that solitary difference is correlated with a difference in the presence of the phenomenon, then it is causally related to the phenomenon. Here is how zMill stated the method:

> If an instance in which the phenomenon under investigation occurs, and an instance in which it does not occur, have every circumstance in common save one, that one occurring only in the former; the circumstance in which alone the two instances differ, is the effect, or the cause, or an indispensable part of the cause, of the phenomenon.

Mill gives the following example of the method of difference:

> When a man is shot through the heart, it is by this method we know that it was the gunshot which killed him: for he was in the fullness of life immediately before, all circumstances being the same, except for the wound.

The two instances in this example are (1) the situation immediately before the gunshot and (2) the situation immediately after the gunshot. These instances are alike in every respect but one: the absence or presence of the gunshot. When the gunshot is absent (that is, before the gun is fired), the man is alive; when the gunshot is present (that is, after the gun is fired), the man is dead. So, by the method of difference, we conclude that the gunshot caused the man's death.

It might be objected that we already *know* this, and of course we do. But that is not a criticism of the method, for one of the things Mill was trying to show is that this and the other methods underlie what we call "common sense"—the sense that is common to all. The cause of death in the gunshot case is obvious. But in other cases the cause of a given event is not at all obvious. In those cases the methods can give us new, and often useful, knowledge of causal relationships.

Consider the following application of the method of difference, the results of which run counter to many people's intuition. Criminologists and lawyers have long wondered whether capital punishment—the killing of certain offenders—has a deterrent effect on various forms of homicide (for simplicity I use the word "murder" from now on, although the terms are not synonymous), and if so how strong the effect is. It strikes many people as obvious that if the punishment for murder is death rather than, say, imprisonment for life, there will be a lower murder rate. The thinking seems to be that some individuals who are not deterred by the prospect of life in prison *are* deterred by the prospect of death.

But researchers wanted something more than common sense or intuition on which to rest an important policy judgment such as this, for if capital punishment does not deter prospective murderers, or does not deter many of them, one of the most powerful arguments for capital punishment disappears.[8] On the other hand, if it can be shown by sound research that capital punishment *does* deter prospective murderers or some significant percentage of them, then there is at least one reason to execute those convicted of the crime: It will reduce the murder rate.

Early research on the deterrent effect of capital punishment exemplified Mill's method of difference. Beginning in the 1950s, Thorsten Sellin studied clusters (usually three) of contiguous states, at least one of which capitally punished murderers and at least one of which did not.[9] Sellin was careful to select states that were alike in all other respects, such as population and socioeconomic condition, for his aim was to determine whether the presence of capital punishment and not some other circumstance was causally responsible for a lower murder rate. What he discovered surprised and disturbed many people. For each cluster of states Sellin studied, he found that there was *no significant difference* in the murder rate between states that had capital punishment and those that punished murder with life imprisonment.

Sellin's reasoning was simple and straightforward: The states in each cluster are alike in all respects but one; if capital punishment deters prospective murderers, then states with capital punishment should have a lower murder rate than those without it; but they do not. "The inevitable conclusion," Sellin wrote, "is that executions have no discernable effect on homicide death rates." In other words, contrary to prevailing wisdom, some of which had to that point been reflected in law, the prospect of death does not deter individuals from committing murder.

We said above that Sellin's experiment exemplifies Mill's method of difference. The astute reader will have noticed one minor deviation from the pattern. The method requires exactly *two* instances, whereas typically Sellin's clusters of states consisted of three, at least one of which had and at least one of which lacked capital punishment. But we can bring Sellin's research in line with Mill's method of difference by treating the capital-punishment states (if more than one) as one large state and by treating the non-capital-punishment states (if more than one) as one large state. What Sellin found, in effect, is that the presence of capital punishment is a difference that makes no causal difference with respect to murder rates.[10]

---

[8] We say "one of the most" because there are other arguments in favor of capital punishment. One of these other arguments, known as the retributive argument, contends that by committing murder one forfeits one's right to life and deserves to die. This is true (so the argument goes) even if nobody will be deterred by the execution.

[9] The information in this paragraph comes from Lawrence R. Klein, Brian Forst, and Victor Filatov, "The Deterrent Effect of Capital Punishment: An Assessment of the Evidence," in *The Death Penalty in America*, 3rd ed., ed. Hugo Adam Bedau (1982), pp. 139–40.

[10] The reader should not assume that everyone is content with Sellin's studies. In fact, his studies have been challenged on methodological and other grounds. For a review of these challenges and other, more sophisticated research on the deterrent effect of the death penalty, see Bedau, ed., *The Death Penalty in America*, 3rd ed. (1982), chap. 4.

Sometimes Mill's method of difference leads to the conclusion that there *is* a causal relationship. In research now being conducted in laboratories across the United States, scientists are discovering the roles played by various genes (known as "Hox" genes) in bodily development. The procedure involves disabling or "knocking out" a particular gene in a fruit-fly, mouse, or chicken embryo, then watching to see what effect the intervention has on the developing organism. According to news reports, knocking out a particular gene "halts construction of glands in the head and neck and disrupts tissues of the throat, tongue and other organs"; knocking out another gene "erases most of the ear, eliminates much of the hindbrain—which normally controls heartbeat and stomach secretions—and deletes nerves in the face."[11] One researcher, commenting on the work being done by a colleague, said that the colleague "has developed a technique to specifically knock out individual genes and see what happens. It's the most definitive way to see what a gene does." To date, the researcher "has studied eight of the 38 genes in mice."

Let us reconstruct one of these experiments. Suppose we take two mouse embryos that are alike in every respect. (Perhaps they come from the same litter; or, better yet, suppose they come from the same egg.) One embryo is subjected to a change—namely, a particular Hox gene is knocked out. The embryos are then incubated under similar circumstances. If the mouse with the knocked-out gene develops without ears while the other develops ears, then there is reason to believe that the disabled Hox gene causes ear development. What else can explain the difference? The following table summarizes this information (the letter "B" represents the presence of the Hox gene; the letters "A," "C," "D," and "E" represent circumstances shared by the two embryos; and the letter "p" represents the phenomenon to be explained, the presence of ears):

Instances	Circumstances					Phenomenon
1	A	B	C	D	E	p
2	A		C	D	E	

Since mouse embryos develop comparatively quickly, it doesn't take long to reach a conclusion using Mill's method of difference. This example shows that Mill's method of difference plays a vital role in what is known as "controlled experimentation." Very often, as in this case, the investigator can hold everything constant except one circumstance and watch to see whether a difference appears. If a difference does appear, there is reason to believe that a causal relationship exists; if not, as we saw in the case of capital punishment, there is reason to doubt the existence of such a relationship.

Mill stated the rationale of the method of difference as follows:

> Whatever antecedent cannot be excluded without preventing the phenomenon, is the cause, or a condition, of that phenomenon: Whatever consequent [phenomenon] can be excluded, with no other difference in the antecedents than the absence of a particular one, is the effect of that one.

---

[11]   This information is drawn from a news report by Robert Cooke of *Newsday*.

In terms of our mouse example, the antecedent is the Hox gene that was knocked out and the phenomenon is the presence of ears. Since the Hox gene cannot be "excluded" without preventing the development of ears, the former is either the cause or a condition of the latter. And since the ears can be "excluded" with no difference in the mouse other than the absence of the particular Hox gene, the ears are an effect of that gene.

As with the method of agreement, one must be careful in stating and analyzing circumstances if the method of difference is to work. A more significant limitation on the method of difference is that it cannot always tell the investigator the precise nature of the relationship that has been determined to exist. One event might be the cause of the other, the effect of the other, or an indispensable part of the cause of the other. To illustrate this problem, suppose that you have two cigarette lighters in exactly the same condition except that the flint has been removed from one of them. When struck, only the lighter with flint in it flames. Yet we would not say that the presence of flint was *the* cause, but rather an *indispensable part of the cause* of the lighting. For as we know, the flint works in conjunction with other elements of the lighter to produce flame. In general, when determining whether event A is the cause or the effect of event B, temporal order is crucial. If A occurs before B, then B cannot be the cause of A. We can learn from the past, but we cannot change it. As before, these limitations and problems must be kept in mind while using the method of difference. When used properly, it can be a powerful tool of experimental inquiry.

EXERCISES

Analyze each of the following passages in terms of instances, circumstances, and phenomena. Show how each passage exemplifies the method of difference. State the causal connection. It may be useful to construct a diagram or table to portray the information.

■   *1.*   Identical twins X and Y are separated at birth and raised in different families in different parts of the country. Both, as adults, are over six feet tall. X becomes an alcoholic; Y does not.

2.   The primitive brain, as we saw it in the planaria, served chiefly as a sensory relay—a center for receiving stimuli from the sense organs and then sending impulses down the nerve cord. This is also true of the nereis, for, if the brain is removed, the animal can still move in a coordinated way—and, in fact, it moves about more than usual. If it meets some obstacle, it does not withdraw and go off in a new direction but persists in its unsuccessful forward movements. This very unadaptive kind of behavior shows that in the normal nereis the brain has an important function which it did not have in flatworms—that of *inhibition* of movement in response to certain stimuli.

—RALPH BUCHSBAUM, *Animals Without Backbones*

3.   Nitric oxide, a naturally occurring gas known to cause blood vessels to relax, plays a key role in males' ability to achieve an erection, Johns Hopkins University researchers concluded last week in [the journal] *Science*. The scientists studied rats with electrically induced erections. When the researchers injected the rats with small doses of a substance that inhibits production of nitric oxide, the animals lost their erections. The scientists wrote that their finding could prove useful in the treatment of priapism, a condition of painful, prolonged erections that are not associated with sexual arousal or desire.

—*The Dallas Morning News*, 20 July 1992

4. There is a deep-red dye, well known to analytical chemists, which is used for the analysis of aluminum and to a lesser extent for beryllium and which, on paper, seemed to meet our requirements. This dye is known by the trade name "aluminon," and by the chemical name aurintricarboxylic acid, or simply ATA. In the first test of ATA we injected mice with enough beryllium salt to kill them within a few days. We then injected half the animals with a small dose of ATA and left the others untreated. The results were dramatic: virtually every animal treated with ATA survived and lived on normally, while all of the untreated animals died. We have repeated this experiment with hundreds of animals of different species, with the same high degree of protection.

—JACK SCHUBERT, "Beryllium and Berylliosis," *Scientific American*, Vol. 199, No. 2, August 1958

■ ***5.*** It was assumed for a long time, by analogy with the mosquito and other blood-sucking vectors, that the virus of typhus was injected by the louse when sucking blood. But apparently this is not so. The infection is not in the saliva of the louse, as it probably is with the mosquito, but in the feces. The disease is thought to be spread through the feces coming into contact with scratches or abrasions in the skin, and scratching and louse infection are generally inseparable. This fact was first suggested in 1922 by the two workers who fed infected lice on a monkey, while taking great care that no feces from the lice should come into contact with the monkey's skin. They found that the monkey remained healthy.

—KENNETH M. SMITH, *Beyond the Microscope*

Joint Method of Agreement and Difference

What would you do if it were your responsibility to determine the cause of the chick deaths in the example with which we began this chapter? Many people, with little or no knowledge of Mill's methods but with good instincts, would proceed as follows. First, select a group of chicks—say, one hundred of them. Like any group of individuals, these chicks will be alike in many respects and different in many others; but the experiment will work better if the chicks selected are diverse. They should be drawn from different gene pools, be of different ages and sexes, and have been raised (to that point anyway) under different conditions. Now divide the chicks into two groups. (For the sake of simplicity, place fifty in each group.) The next step is to determine what we want to test. One poultry farmer quoted in the news report speculated that the problem was with the feed, so let us feed one group of chicks feed X and the other group feed Y, and see what happens. Suppose on doing this, we find that all fifty chicks in the group fed X die, while all fifty chicks in the group fed Y continue living. This result provides strong grounds for believing that feed X is the cause of death.

The method we have just used exemplifies what Mill called the joint method of agreement and difference, which he stated as follows:

> If two or more instances in which the phenomenon occurs have only one circumstance in common, while two or more instances in which it does not occur have nothing in common save the absence of that circumstance; the circumstance in which alone the two sets of instances differ, is the effect, or the cause, or an indispensable part of the cause, of the phenomenon.

The joint method, as the name implies, possesses features of both previous methods. The method of agreement is used twice, once positively and once negatively. The only circumstance the chicks that died share is that they ate feed X (the positive use), while the only circumstance the chicks that did not die shared is that they did not eat feed X (the negative use). This explains Mill's comment that the joint method "consists in a double employment of the Method of Agreement, each proof being independent of the other, and corroborating it."

The method of difference is also involved, however, except that instead of there being two *instances* (which, strictly speaking, the method of difference requires) there are two *groups* of instances: the fifty chicks fed X (who died), and the fifty chicks fed Y (who did not die). These groups, *as groups*, differ in only one respect, the presence or absence of feed X. The following table summarizes this information. (To simplify, we have represented only five of each group of fifty chicks; the letter "A" represents the presence of feed X; the letter "p" represents the phenomenon to be explained, death.)

Instances	Circumstances				Phenomenon
1	A	B	C	E	p
2	A		C D	E	p
3	A		C D		p
4	A	B	D	E	p
5	A	B	C		p
6			C D		
7		B	D		
8		B	C D	E	
9			C D	E	
10		B	C	E	

As in the case of the vitamin-D poisoning, chemical analysis of feed X might disclose a toxic substance, which would verify the findings of Mill's joint method.

---

[12]   He also called it the "indirect method of difference," but to avoid confusion we will not use that name.

While scientific researchers rarely use the term "joint method of agreement and difference," it underlies much of their work. Consider the following example. A team of pediatricians and psychobiologists in Irvine, California, sought to determine whether newborn human infants are capable of learning. They selected forty-eight one-day-old infants who differed in the usual ways infants differ (for example, genetic endowment, method of delivery, method of feeding, sex, and race) and divided them at random into two groups. Infants in the experimental group were presented with a citrus odor while being stroked; infants in the control group received either the odor alone, the stroking alone, or the stroking followed by the odor. Everything else was held constant.

The next day all of the infants were presented with the same odor and their reactions observed and recorded. According to the published report, "only those infants who received the . . . pairings of the odor and stroking exhibited conditioned responding (head turning toward the odor)."[13] This was true, amazingly, whether the infants were awake or asleep! The researchers concluded that "infants are capable of olfactory associative learning during the first day after birth," a finding that has obvious practical implications for childrearing and for diagnosing cognitive defects in newborns. Stated in causal language, we can say that positive reinforcement (stroking) causes learning. All of the infants who received reinforcement learned; none of the infants who did not receive reinforcement learned. To paraphrase Mill, the only thing the infants who learned had in common is that they received reinforcement; the only thing the infants who did not learn had in common is that they did not receive reinforcement.

In experiments in which human reactions to various substances or procedures are being tested, researchers must be careful not to introduce secondary agreements and differences that can interfere with the circumstance being studied. For instance, suppose investigator S is testing the effects of a new drug. S selects a sample of subjects, each of whom, for ethical reasons, has given informed consent to the experiment. S divides the subjects randomly into two groups and administers the drug. A problem arises: Those who receive the drug may believe (and come to expect) that a certain result will follow, and this psychological state may itself increase the likelihood of that result obtaining. Since the study (we assume) is designed to test the pharmacological properties of the drug and not its effect on psychological states, the researcher must "control" for this factor. The usual way to do this is to administer a "placebo" or "dummy pill" to those who do not receive the drug. Since no subject in either group knows whether he or she received the drug or the placebo, everyone is in the same psychological state (the technical word is "blind") with respect to it. The use of placebos is widespread in medical and psychological research.[14]

Another methodological problem that arises in research concerns the attitudes of the investigators. It would be nice to think that among scientists, at least, pre-

[13] The information presented in the text, some of it simplified for purposes of exposition, is taken from Regina M. Sullivan et al., "Olfactory Classical Conditioning in Neonates," *Pediatrics* 87 (4 April 1991):511–18. The quotation is from page 511 of this article.

[14] For those who doubt that a placebo could have an effect on a person's physical condition, consider this. "Studies indicate that placebos relieve some symptoms of approximately thirty-five percent of patients who suffer from such conditions as angina pectoris, cough, anxiety, depression, hypertension, headache, and the common cold." Tom L. Beauchamp and James F. Childress, *Principles of Biomedical Ethics,* 3rd ed. (1989), p. 93.

conceptions about the results of the study would not affect the experiment. But this is not the case. Sometimes investigators "see" what they expect to see. If the investigator believes or hopes that the drug will have consequence C, then he or she may be more likely to identify C among the phenomena. To control for this factor, researchers have developed what they call "double-blind" testing. Not only is the subject kept in the dark (single-blind testing), but the person administering the pill and making observations regarding its effects (if any) is kept ignorant of whether the pill is the drug or the placebo. The aim of these measures is to insure to the maximum extent possible that only *one difference* exists between the control group and the experimental group.

Strictly speaking, the joint method of agreement and difference requires that *every* instance in which the phenomenon appears exhibit the circumstance in question and that *every* instance in which the phenomenon does not appear not exhibit that circumstance. There are cases (for example, that just examined) in which this strict requirement is satisfied. But much modern scientific research involves a variation on the Millian theme. What if, in the case of the newborns described above, most but not all of the infants who had been stroked responded to the citrus, whereas a few of those who were not reinforced did respond? While our confidence in a causal connection may be weakened somewhat by these findings, most of us would probably continue to assert a causal connection.

Let us call this the "quantitative" version of the joint method, for what we have is a difference in the *quantity* of agreements rather than complete agreement and complete disagreement. There are two types of quantification. One, which we just described, involves different *percentages* of instances exhibiting the phenomenon. Another involves different *averages* for the control and experimental groups. Here are illustrations of each variation, beginning with the percentage version.

For some time medical researchers have known that women who smoke cigarettes have more difficulty getting pregnant than nonsmokers, but until recently it was not known why this is so. British physicians and epidemiologists claim to have found out. Forty-five otherwise diverse women undergoing in vitro (test-tube) fertilization were divided into two groups. One group (presumably the smokers) had cotinine, a derivative of nicotine, in their eggs; the other did not. Testing was done. Of those in the smoking/cotinine group, the fertilization rate was forty-four percent (that is, forty-four percent of the eggs became fertilized). Of those in the nonsmoking group (without cotinine), the fertilization rate was significantly higher: seventy-two percent. As it turns out, the difference did not have to do with the effect of cotinine on egg *production,* for researchers found that the women produced roughly the same number of eggs, regardless of the presence of cotinine. The difference must therefore have to do with the *fertilizability* of the eggs. Since there was a significantly higher fertility rate in the women without cotinine in their systems than in those with cotinine, researchers concluded that cotinine causes, or is an indispensable part of the cause of, infertility.[15]

Sometimes controlled experimentation shows only that the average for some value differs significantly in the control and experimental groups. This difference suggests a causal connection. Our example this time comes from the field of ecology.

---

[15]   See "Study Finds Infertility, Smoking Tie," Associated Press report, 14 November 1992.

Ecologists and zoologists have long known that body sizes of fish such as carp differ depending on the presence or absence of various predators; but until recently it was not known why this is so. In a study published in 1992, Swedish ecologists Christer Bronmark and Jeffrey Miner undertook a field experiment (meaning it was done "in the field" rather than in a laboratory) in which they divided a small pond into halves, each containing crucian carp. A predatory species, pike, was introduced into one of the halves but not the other. Meanwhile, other things (such as food supply for the carp) were held constant. "After 12 weeks," Bronmark and Miner report, "crucian carp had diverged in body shape; in pond sections with pike, carp tended to have a deeper body."[16] Body shape was represented in the study as a ratio between depth and length. What the researchers found, specifically, is that this ratio differed significantly in the two pond halves.

On the basis of this version of Mill's joint method of agreement and difference (they did not use that term), Bronmark and Miner concluded that predation *causes* changes in the body shape of carp. Since the changes occurred within the same generation of carp, it cannot have been as a result of natural selection in which pike selectively prey on carp of a certain size and shape, leaving only those of other sizes and shapes to reproduce. Rather, the change must be behavioral: Individual carp grow thicker so that pike, who have a limited mouth capacity, cannot swallow them! This allows the carp to survive longer and reproduce more, thus passing on the remarkable body-changing ability to its offspring. Identifying the mechanism through which this occurs, however, called for another study. As the researchers put it, "Our experimental design could not discern the precise cue that triggered the body morphology modifications in crucian carp, but cyprinids [the zoological category to which crucian carp belong] do respond behaviorally to alarm substances released by conspecifics [members of the same species] when attacked by piscivores [predatory fish]." This suggests that body shape is altered by chemical cues emanating from the carp themselves.

A common feature of controlled scientific experimentation is that it suggests further research. One set of findings suggests another experiment, which suggests another, and so on. Knowledge accumulates gradually. Bronmark and Miner followed up their field experiment with a laboratory experiment (also exemplifying Mill's method of agreement and difference) designed to eliminate other possible causes (such as food supply) of the altered body shape. This follow-up study eliminated food supply as a cause and led to the conclusion that "the presence of pike induced a phenotypical change in resource allocation, giving priority to growth in body depth."

The reference to resource allocation has to do with how the carp's energy, of which there is a finite amount, is used. Larger fish require more energy for swimming but are more likely, by virtue of their size, to escape predation than smaller fish. The study showed that when predators are present, carp energy is allocated primarily to bodily growth, whereas when predators are absent carp energy is allocated primarily to swimming. We can only assume that after these studies Bronmark and Miner turned their attention to the chemical cue that triggers changes in body morphology. In all

---

[16]   This quotation and all of the information given in the text is taken from Christer Bronmark and Jeffrey G. Miner, "Predator-Induced Phenotypical Change in Body Morphology in Crucian Carp," *Science* 258 (20 November 1992):1348–50.

likelihood they will make further use of Mill's joint method of agreement and difference—in one or another of its versions.

Let us call the three versions of Mill's joint method, respectively, the "strict" or "qualitative" version, the "percentage" version, and the "average" version (leaving open the possibility that there are others). The following chart summarizes the differences among these methods. (Assume an initial group of twenty diverse instances randomly divided into two groups of ten; let these groups be represented by the letters "A" and "B".)

Version	Features
Strict/ qualitative	All 10 instances in A have p; all 10 instances in B lack p.
Percentage	The percentage of instances with p in A is significantly higher than the percentage of instances with p in B.
Average	The average value of p in A is significantly higher than the average value of p in B.

It is not clear what Mill would have said about these variations on his theme—or about whether the practice of controlled experimentation exemplifies any one or some combination of them. One scholar wrote that "The controlled experiment seems to embody the valuable insights Mill formulated in his famous methods,"[17] however much those experiments may diverge from the letter of the methods. Another scholar, in an essay provocatively entitled "A Sixth Mill's Method,"[18] claims that *none* of Mill's five methods, singly or combined, can incorporate controlled experimentation as we know it, so he concludes that the list of methods should be expanded to six.[19] For our part, we remain uncommitted on this question, preferring to let the variations stand or fall on their own merits; that is, on how well they actually are incorporated by practicing scientists.

EXERCISES

Analyze each of the following passages in terms of instances, circumstances, and phenomena. Show how each passage exemplifies the joint method of agreement and difference. Since there are different versions of this method, identify which version it exemplifies. State the causal connection. It may be useful to construct a diagram or table to portray the information.

---

[17]   Wesley C. Salmon, *Logic*, 2nd ed. (1973), p. 103, n. 9.
[18]   Thomas R. Grimes, "A Sixth Mill's Method," *Teaching Philosophy* 10 (June 1987):123–27.
[19]   According to Grimes, "Though his methods cover a good many cases, Mill seems to have overlooked what is perhaps the most commonly used technique." Ibid., p. 123. Grimes proposes to call the overlooked sixth method "the Split Method of Difference and Concomitant Variations." Ibid., p. 125. We will take up the method of concomitant variations next.

■   *1.*   New research on rats indicates that some memories are stored for a short period in the hippocampus region of the brain before being permanently imprinted elsewhere. Two researchers from the University of California, Los Angeles, gave rats a foot shock while playing a particular tone. Afterward, the rats froze in fear after hearing the tone or when placed in the chamber where they were shocked. The scientists then removed the rats' hippocam[p]us at various times after the shock training. The rats that had their hippocam[p]uses removed just one day after the shock showed no fear when placed in the shock chamber, although they continued to respond to the tone. But other rats that had their hippocam[p]uses removed up to four weeks after the shock training continued to exhibit fear each time they were placed in the chamber.

—*The Dallas Morning News,* 4 May 1992

2.   A new method of cardiopulmonary resuscitation proved more effective than regular CPR in recent hospital tests. The study compared 29 patients resuscitated with a new compression-decompression method to 33 resuscitated with traditional CPR. The new method, developed by Dr. Todd Cohen of the Cornell University Medical College in Manhasset, N.Y., relies on a suction cup device that attaches to a patient's chest. The device both compresses the chest when pushed down, and decompresses it when pulled up. When used in CPR, it successfully resuscitated patients 62 percent of the time. Traditional CPR successfully resuscitated 30 percent of patients who received it.

—*The Dallas Morning News,* 3 January 1994

3.   Eighteen healthy men were placed on a low-cholesterol, mixed natural diet. The men were randomly divided into two groups, one of which received twenty percent of its calories in the form of walnuts. After four weeks, researchers found that "With the walnut diet, the mean [average] total cholesterol level was 22.4 mg per deciliter . . . lower than the mean level with the reference [nonwalnut] diet."

—JOAN SABATE et al., "Effects of Walnuts on Serum Lipid Levels and Blood Pressure in Normal Men," *The New England Journal of Medicine* 328 (4 March 1993):603

4.   Eijkman fed a group of chickens exclusively on white rice. They all developed polyneuritis and died. He fed another group of fowl unpolished rice. Not a single one of them developed the disease. Then he gathered up the polishings from rice and fed them to other polyneuritic chickens, and in a short time the birds recovered. He had accurately traced the cause of polyneuritis to a faulty diet. For the first time in history, he had produced a food deficiency disease experimentally, and had actually cured it. It was a fine piece of work and resulted in some immediate remedial measures.

— Bernard Jaffee, *Outposts of Science*

■   *5.*   Partying may help cut your risk of catching colds, according to new findings by British researchers. Although stress increases the risk of catching a cold, a pint of beer a day may cut that risk by more than half, the researchers reported at the recent meeting of the British Psychological Society. In a study of 400 volunteers conducted at the Common Cold Research Unit near Salisbury, England, researchers found people who were under stress were more prone to colds than those whose lives were relatively stress-free. However, people who consumed more than two units of alcohol daily ran a 15 percent risk of developing a cold after they had been deliberately exposed to the cold virus, while 45 percent of nondrinkers came down with the symptoms. Study author

Andrew Smith says that while alcohol clearly is not a cure for colds, it does appear to switch off the body's mechanisms that increase nasal secretions in cold sufferers.

—*The Dallas Morning News,* 4 January 1993

Method of Residues

The residue of a thing or process is "the remainder, what is left over."[20] The word *residue* is a clue to the nature of Mill's fourth method, which Mill characterized as very simple and which one Mill scholar has described, perhaps pejoratively, as "more like redundant good advice than a method of anything."[21] Occasionally in our investigations of nature we come across a complex phenomenon the cause of which is unknown to us and which we seek to ascertain. Suppose the phenomenon consists of three distinguishable parts and that the causes of two of the three parts are known, perhaps by earlier applications of Mill's methods. Then, assuming that we have identified all of the circumstances, the third part—the "residue" of the complex phenomenon—must be caused by the remaining circumstance. We might say that we have arrived at our conclusion by a process of elimination. Here is Mill's statement of the method:

> Subduct [subtract] from any phenomenon such part as is known by previous induction to be the effect of certain antecedents, and the residue of the phenomenon is the effect of the remaining antecedents.

Mill devoted an entire section of *A System of Logic* to examples of the method of residues, pointing out that it has been used with much success by both chemists and astronomers. For example, at one time it was thought that among celestial bodies only the sun exerts gravitational force on objects around it. To be sure, the sun's presence accounts for a good *part* of the observed orbits of the planets, but it cannot account for all of those orbits. There is a residual phenomenon to be explained. But what else could explain it? The only bodies left are the planets. This fact, together with something like Mill's method of residues, led astronomers to conclude that the planets *themselves,* including the Earth, exert gravitational force on each other. When these additional forces are considered and measured, the planetary orbits are completely accounted for.[22]

Not all applications of the method of residues come from the natural sciences. Consider the following application from a social-scientific context. On average, women in the 1980s earned 64 percent of the income men earned.[23] For anyone concerned with fairness in the job market, this is disturbing as well as puzzling. Why

---

[20] Eugene Ehrlich et al., *Oxford American Dictionary* (1980), p. 575.

[21] Ryan, *J.S. Mill,* p. 80.

[22] At least one of the known planets, Neptune, was discovered in this manner. First its existence was inferred; then an astronomer saw the planet through a telescope. For a narrative of these events, see Edward Arthur Fath, *The Elements of Astronomy* (1934).

[23] The information in this paragraph, except for the concluding quotation, comes from Rosemarie Tong, *Feminist Thought: A Comprehensive Introduction* (1989), p. 59. A more recent study shows that in 1992, women earned 75.4 percent of what men earned, so perhaps the gap is narrowing. See Diana Kunde, "Theories Fail to Explain Women's Lower Pay," *The Dallas Morning News,* 5 January 1994. Kunde is the source of the concluding quotation.

do women as a class earn so much less than men as a class? Let the pay disparity be the phenomenon to be explained. Researchers have discovered that *part* of the pay disparity, but not all of it, is the result of unequal educational preparation; men, generally speaking, have more education than women, which is reflected in higher pay.

Another part of the disparity is caused by differential work experience, with men as a group having more experience than women as a group. Since pay is correlated with commitment to the job and since men traditionally have been more likely than women to stay with the same job (in part because of maternity leaves), this accounts for yet another part of the pay disparity. But these circumstances together do not explain the 36-cent differential in pay; there is a residual phenomenon to be accounted for. What circumstances is left? According to feminist researchers, the remaining circumstance is sexism: discrimination on the basis of sex. Women are paid less than men *simply because* they are women, which in turn seems to reflect a belief that the work women do is less valuable than the work men do. As one social scientist put it after studying the matter, "We can't point to anything but bias."

This example illustrates an important limitation on the method of residues. The method requires that after "subducting" the parts of the phenomenon that have known causes, the investigator attribute the residual or remaining part to the remaining circumstance. But there may be more than one remaining circumstance, in which case the most that can be said is that the residual phenomenon is caused by one *or some combination* of them.[24] Thus, in the pay-disparity case there may be other, as yet-undiscovered factors that explain the residual disparity in pay between men and women. Good researchers must take care to identify all factors that play a role in the existence of the phenomenon. Unless and until they do so, they should state their conclusion tentatively, in keeping with the scientific spirit.

A more mundane use of the method of residues occurs when one weighs a small animal. As everyone knows, the procedure is to step onto the scales while holding the animal, taking note of the weight, and then to weigh oneself without the animal, again taking note. The complex phenomenon to be explained is the quantity of weight the scale's pointer or digital readout reflects—say, 172 pounds. *Part* of this amount can be explained by the weight of the person alone, which we will assume to be 150 pounds. The residue, 22 pounds, is therefore the animal's weight, for by hypothesis there is no other circumstance to which the residual weight can be attributed. A similar procedure is used at weigh stations along interstate highways. The empty weight of a truck is indicated on documents the driver is required to carry. This figure is subtracted from the loaded weight to give the weight of the cargo, which is useful for various purposes (such as taxation).

---

[24]   All of Mill's methods are inductive in the sense that they involve inferences from the known to the unknown. They extend, rather than reconfigure, human knowledge. In the case of the method of residues, what is known is that circumstances A, B, and C together cause complex phenomenon abc. By two applications of other methods we also know that A causes a and that B causes b. We infer from this what was previously unknown, namely, that C causes c. Unfortunately, as Mill pointed out, we do not always know that we have identified all of the circumstances; there may be an unobserved circumstance D. Hence our confidence that C causes c can be no greater than our confidence that A, B, and C are the only circumstances present. See Robert Hoffman, "A Note on Mill's Method of Residues," *The Journal of Philosophy* 59 (30 August 1962):495–97.

Despite its simplicity, which Mill acknowledged, the method of residues has been important in the history of science and will in all likelihood continue to be so. Mill wrote:

> Of all the methods of investigating laws of nature, this [the method of residues] is the most fertile in unexpected results: often informing us of sequences in which neither the cause nor the effect were sufficiently conspicuous to attract of themselves the attention of observers. The agent C may be an obscure circumstance, not likely to have been perceived unless sought for, nor likely to have been sought for until attention had been awakened by the insufficiency of the obvious causes to account for the whole of the effect. And c [the effect of circumstance C] may be so disguised by its intermixture with a and b [effects the causes of which are known], that it would scarcely have presented itself spontaneously as a subject of separate study.

What Mill seems to be saying here is that occasionally in scientific research, unanticipated discoveries are made. To put it in terms of an analogy, by taking a particular road, one may find paths to interesting and valuable destinations. The English word for this is *serendipity*. This suggests that scientists should be both attentive (so that they notice otherwise hidden phenomena) and flexible (so that they can deviate, at least temporarily, from whatever research program they are presently conducting).

EXERCISES

Analyze each of the following passages in terms of circumstances and phenomena. Show how each passage exemplifies the method of residues. State the causal connection.

■ *1.* Changes in the sun's output affect global temperatures, but they do not account for the 1.5-degree warming over the last century, two new studies conclude. Scientists from the Climatic Research Unit in Norwich, England, and the University of Illinois at Urbana-Champaign found that variations in the sun's activity help explain some of the changes in the Earth's surface temperature since 1880. But the sun could not have produced all of the warming, the scientists said. Instead, increased concentrations of greenhouse gases—notably carbon dioxide and methane—are primarily responsible. In the past, global warming skeptics have argued that the sun could account for all of the warming. But the new studies, published last week in the journal *Nature,* challenge that idea.

—*The Dallas Morning News,* 30 November 1992

2. It is no longer open to discussion that the air has weight. It is common knowledge that a balloon is heavier when inflated than when empty, which is proof enough. For if the air were light, the more the balloon was inflated, the lighter the whole would be, since there would be more air in it. But since, on the contrary, when more air is put in, the whole becomes heavier, it follows that each part has a weight of its own, and consequently that the air has weight.

—BLAISE PASCAL, *Treatise on the Weight of the Mass of the Air*

3. [I]t has been said that boys' apparent superiority in quantitative and visual-spatial ability gives them an advantage in mathematics and science and explains why so many more males than females choose to study and work in these areas. Because the differences are so small, the argument misses the point. For example, [Janet S.] Hyde . . ., making the initial assumption that a person would have to be in the top 5 percent of the range of spatial abilities to be qualified for a profession such as engineering, calculated that, if spatial ability were the only determining factor, the ratio of males to females in such professions would be 2 to 1. Since[] the ratio of men to women in engineering has never been less than 20 to 1, gender differences in spatial ability could conceivably explain only a small part of the male dominance of the engineering professions.

—HILARY M. LIPS, "Gender-Role Socialization: Lessons in Femininity," in *Women: A Feminist Perspective*, 4th ed., ed. Jo Freeman (1989), p. 206

4. Hoarders.

Is avarice a natural tendency or an acquired habit? Two Harvard psychologists have been investigating this question with rats. Louise C. Licklider and J.C.R. Licklider provided six rats with all the food they could eat and more. Their food after weaning consisted of pellets of Purina Laboratory Chow. Although none of the rats had ever experienced a food shortage, all immediately started hoarding pellets. Even after they had accumulated a hoard and the food-supply bin was empty, they kept coming back to hunt for more.

This behavior confirmed what previous investigators had found. But the Lickliders refined the experiment to try to unearth the rats' motives for hoarding. They covered half of the pellets with aluminum foil, thus eliminating their value as food. The experimenters discovered that four of the six avaricious rats actually preferred the worthless, inedible pellets in hoarding.

The rats were then put on short rations for six days. After this "deprivation period" they hoarded even more greedily and showed more interest in the plain food pellets, but some still hoarded foil-wrapped pellets and continued to prefer them.

The Lickliders conclude, in a report to the *Journal of Comparative and Clinical Psychology:* "The factors that lead to hoarding and that determine what is hoarded are by no means entirely alimentary. The initiation of hoarding seems to be for the rat, as for the human being, a complex motivational problem to which sensory and perceptual factors, rather than blood chemistry, hold the key."

—"Science and the Citizen," *Scientific American*, Vol. 183, No. 1, July 1950

■ *5.* The radioactivity of every pure uranium compound is proportional to its uranium content. The ores are, however, relatively four times as active. This fact led M. and Mme. Curie, just after 1896, to the discovery that the pitchblende residues, from which practically all of the uranium had been extracted, exhibited nevertheless considerable radioactivity. About a ton of the very complex residues having been separated laboriously into the components, it was found that a large part of the radioactivity remained with the sulphate of barium. From this a product free from barium, and at least one million times more active than uranium, was finally secured in the form of the bromide. The nature of the spectrum and the chemical relations of the element, now named radium, placed it with the metals of the alkaline earths. The ratio by weight of chlorine to radium in the chloride is 35.46:113, so that, on the assumption that the element is bivalent, its chloride is $RaCl_2$ and its atomic weight is 226. With this value it occupies a place formerly vacant in the periodic table.

—JAMES KENDALL, *Smith's College Chemistry*

Method of Concomitant Variations

All four of the methods discussed to this point have been qualitative as opposed to quantitative. That is to say, the qualities claimed to be causally related to one another (the circumstance and the phenomenon) were either present or absent in their entirety. They were not *more or less* present; either they were there or they were not.[25] In the case of the patients with vitamin-D poisoning, which illustrated the method of agreement, those being studied were either poisoned or not poisoned, and each either drank or did not drink milk from the local dairy. No attempt was made to quantify the amount of poisoning or the amount of milk consumed.

In the case of the Hox genes, which illustrated the method of difference, the mice being studied either had or lacked a particular Hox gene, and the subject mice either developed or did not develop ears. In the case of the conditioned newborns, which illustrated the "pure" version of the joint method of agreement and difference, the infants being studied were either given or not given the stimulus, and as a result they either responded to the reintroduction of the stimulus or did not respond. In the pay-disparity case, which illustrated the method of residues, each of several circumstances was eliminated as a cause of the entire complex phenomenon (the pay disparity) by being shown to account for only a part of it, leaving only the circumstance of sexism or bias to account for the residue.

The fifth method of experimental inquiry, which Mill named "the method of concomitant variations," differs from the previous four in being *quantitative* rather than qualitative. While this method is useful primarily when a particular circumstance cannot be experimentally eliminated, it can be used even when the circumstance can be eliminated. The classic example of the use of this method is the investigation into the effect of the moon on the tides, which Mill described as follows:

> Let us . . . suppose the question to be, what influence the moon exerts on the surface of the earth. We cannot try an experiment in the absence of the moon, so as to observe what terrestrial phenomena her annihilation would put an end to; but when we find that all the variations in the *position* of the moon are followed by corresponding variations in time and place of high water, the place being always either the part of the earth which is nearest to, or that which is most remote from, the moon, we have ample evidence that the moon is, wholly or partially, the cause which determines the tides. [Emphasis in original.]

In some cases, as with the moon, it is physically impossible to eliminate the circumstance; in other cases it is physically *possible* to eliminate the circumstance but either is not costworthy or is inconsistent with moral standards. Society *could* eliminate automobiles in order to test the hypothesis that automobiles cause air pollution, but that would be prohibitively expensive; and no one would seriously suggest executing overtime parking offenders in order to test the hypothesis that capital punishment would deter overtime parking—although that would certainly provide interesting data!

Here is how Mill stated the method of concomitant variations:

---

[25] We exclude from our discussion at this point the two quantitative versions of Mill's joint method of agreement and difference. What we say here applies only to Mill's original "pure" version.

Whatever phenomenon varies in any manner whenever another phenomenon varies in some particular manner, is either a cause or an effect of that phenomenon, or is connected with it through some fact of causation.

The word "concomitant" means "accompanying,"[26] so what we are looking for, according to Mill, are two sets of changes, one of which accompanies (or is correlated with) the other. But there are two kinds of accompaniment, in one of which the changes are the same and in the other of which the changes differ. If the circumstance and phenomenon are doing the same thing—either both increasing in quantity or both decreasing in quantity—let us call it a *direct* variation. If the circumstance and phenomenon are doing the opposite thing—one increasing in quantity while the other decreases—let us call it an *inverse* variation. Mill's method covers both kinds of variation.

A recent study of the relation between air pollution and mortality illustrates this method. A team of epidemiologists set out to determine whether fine-particulate air pollution, the sort that can be inhaled deeply into the lungs, causes human beings to contract lethal diseases such as lung cancer. Previous studies affirmed such a relation, but did not "directly control for cigarette smoking and other health risks."[27] The randomly chosen sample, consisted of 8111 adults from six communities in the United States: Watertown, Massachusetts; Harriman, Tennessee; parts of St. Louis, Missouri; Steubenville, Ohio; Portage, Wisconsin; and Topeka, Kansas. These communities were chosen because they were known to have different quantities of fine-particulate air pollution.

When the mortality rate in each city was compared with its pollution level, a surprising correlation appeared. Steubenville, which had the highest mortality rate, also had the highest level of fine-particulate air pollution; Portage, which had the lowest mortality rate, had the lowest level of pollution. As the researchers put it, "we observed significant effects of air pollution on mortality even when we controlled for sex, age, smoking status, education level, and occupational exposure to dust, gases, and fumes." The researchers concluded, by what appears to be the method of concomitant variations, that "exposure to air pollution contributes to excess mortality."

When researchers plotted the study data on a graph, one axis reflecting the mortality rate and the other the level of fine-particulate air pollution, it looked like this:

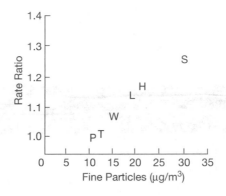

[26]   Ehrlich et al., *Oxford American Dictionary* (1980), p. 131.
[27]   The information in the text comes from Douglas W. Dockery et al., "An Association Between Air Pollution and Mortality in Six U.S. Cities," *The New England Journal of Medicine* 329 (9 December 1993):1753–59.

This shows (graphically!) that there is a near-perfect correlation between the level of pollution and the mortality rate; as one variable increases, so does the other—and at about the same rate. Thus we find a direct variation. A line going from the southwest to the northeast on a graph of this sort represents a direct variation, with the slope or steepness of the line reflecting the strength of the relationship. In the case of an inverse relation between variables, the line goes from northwest to southeast. For example, in classical economic theory the relation between a commodity's supply and its price is inverse; other things being equal, the greater the supply of X, the lower the price for X. That relation is expressed in graph form as follows:

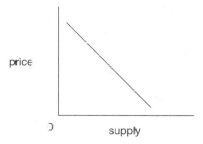

It may help (as Mill suggested) to think of the method of concomitant variations as a special case of the method of difference. When using the method of difference, one finds two instances that are alike in every respect but one. If that difference is correlated with a difference in the appearance of the phenomenon, then the circumstance is causally related to the phenomenon. Similarly, when using the method of concomitant variations, one finds two (or more) instances that are alike in every respect but one. But this time the circumstance isn't present or absent; it's present in *both* instances, but to a different degree. If that difference in degree is correlated with quantitative differences in the phenomenon, then the two are causally related. This is what occurred in the air-pollution case. The researchers used special techniques to hold such circumstances as age, sex, and smoking status constant across the six communities. This allowed them to focus on the only circumstance that was allowed to vary: the level of particulate matter in the air. And this, as we saw, was found to be directly correlated with mortality.

A final note. Four of Mill's five methods (all but the method of residues) are phrased in such a way as to leave open the precise nature of the causal connection claimed to exist. Typically, in his discussions of the methods Mill writes that the circumstance is "the effect, or the cause, or an indispensable part of the cause, of the phenomenon." The reason for this open-endedness in the formulation is that strictly speaking the methods do not tell us *how* the events are related; all they show is *that there is* a causal connection. Logically, there are several possibilities. Event A could be the *cause* of event B; A could be the *effect* of B; or A and B could be *jointly caused* by some other event, C. In each case A and B are correlated with one another. Mill's solution to the problem is that the investigator try to bring about one event by producing the other. If the investigator produces A and finds that B follows, then B cannot be the cause of A, for there is no such thing as backward causation. This is, alas, another limitation on Mill's methods of experimental inquiry. When properly used, they tell us something, perhaps much, about the causal structure of the world; but they cannot tell us everything we might wish to know.

EXERCISES

Analyze each of the following passages in terms of circumstances and phenomena. Show how each passage exemplifies the method of concomitant variations. State the causal connection. It may be useful to construct a diagram or table to portray the information.

■ *1.* At Cornell University in Ithaca, N.Y., Linda D. Youngman and T. Colin Campbell divided 800 rats into three groups: One group was fed lots of protein; the second, a moderate amount; and the third, a low-protein diet. On average over the two-year study, the less protein the rodents ate, the fewer the cancerous tumors they had, the better their immune function, and the longer they lived.
—*The Dallas Morning News,* 23 November 1993

2. Vole populations often fluctuate cyclically, with 3–5 years between peaks. To mimic different points in the natural cycle, we established three replicates each of meadow vole populations held chronically at low, medium and high density in nine field enclosures. Populations averaged about 70, 180 and 380 voles per hectare, respectively ..., maintained at targeted densities by removing subadults. ... Enclosures were closely juxtaposed and therefore experienced similar abiotic and biotic conditions. Avian and mammalian predators were not excluded by the fences. ... ... Females and males on high-density grids became nonreproductive 2–4 weeks earlier in the autumn, and reproductive four weeks later in the spring than voles on medium-density grids. On low-density grids, although there was a reduction in the proportion of voles breeding between October and May, roughly half [of them] bred throughout this period, resulting in continuous recruitment. ... High-density treatments resulted in 2–3 fewer generations per year than medium-density treatments, and up to 5 fewer generations per year than low-density treatments.
—RICHARD S. OSTFELD, CHARLES D. CANHAM, and STEPHEN R. PUGH, "Intrinsic Density-Dependent Regulation of Vole Populations," *Nature* 366 (18 November 1993):259

3. Careful studies have been made of the incidence of leukemia in the survivors of the atomic bombs burst over Hiroshima and Nagasaki. These survivors received exposures ranging from a few roentgens to 1000 roentgens or more.

They are divided into four groups. ... The first group, A, consists of the estimated 1,870 survivors, who were within 1 kilometer of the hypocenter (the point on the surface of the earth directly below the bomb when it exploded). There were very few survivors in this zone, and they received a large amount of radiation.

The second group, B, consists of the 13,730 survivors between 1.0 and 1.5 kilometers from the hypocenter, the third, C, of the 23,060 between 1.5 and 2.0 kilometers, and the fourth, D, of the 156,400 over 2.0 kilometers from the hypocenter.

The survivors of zones A, B, and C have been dying of leukemia during the period of careful study, the eight years from 1948 to 1955, at an average rate of about 9 per year. . . . Many more cases of leukemia occurred in the 15,600 survivors of zones A and B than in the 156,400 survivors of zone D, who received much less radiation. There is no doubt that the increased incidence is to be attributed to the exposure to radiation.

. . . The survivors of zone A received an estimated average of 650 roentgens, those of zone B, 250; those of zone C, 25; and of zone D, 2.5. . . . To within the reliability of the numbers, the incidence of leukemia in the three populations A, B, and C is proportional to the estimated dose of radiation, even for class C, in which the estimated dose is only 25 roentgens.

—LINUS PAULING, *No More War!*

4. First Douglass attempted to get records of rainfall of this district as far back as possible, to test the correlation of moisture and the thickness of tree rings. Fortunately, temperature and rainfall measurements had been made and recorded at Whipple Barracks to the south of Flagstaff since 1867, and they were made available for his study. Then, in January, 1904, he visited the lumber yards of the Arizona Lumber and Timber Company and spent hours in the snow measuring the rings of many of their oldest trees. The president of the company became interested in the singular pastime of this strange hybrid of astronomer and politician, and had sections cut from the ends of scores of logs and stumps sent to Douglass for analysis. These pieces were carefully scraped with razor blades and brushed with kerosene for examination under the microscope. Every ring from the center of the tree to its bark was scrupulously scrutinized. To facilitate the dating of the rings, Douglass would make one pin prick to mark the last year of each decade, two to mark the middle year of each century, and three for the century year. Those cross sections which contained more than a thousand rings had an additional four pin pricks at the thousand-year tree-ring position. Douglass made tens of thousands of measurements, tabulated the data, drew curves and graphs, and as the average age of his trees was 348 years he was able to draw conclusions regarding the rainfall and tree-ring appearance of periods hundreds of years back.

Douglass found a striking correlation between tree growth and the recorded rainfall of the region. So accurate were his measurements and so apparently reliable his method that any marked peculiarity of any year could be identified with surprising ease and clarity in trees which often had grown more than four hundred miles apart. For example, the yellow pine ring of 1851 is small in trees which grew in regions between Santa Fe and Fresno because it represents a drought year. He could illustrate the accuracy of his technique in another way. He would pick out an old pine stump, study its rings, and then declare in what year the tree had been felled, much to the surprise of the owner of the land on which the tree had been cut. His tree time or "dendrochronology" was uncannily accurate.

—BERNARD JAFFE, *Outposts of Science*

■ *5.* Alcohol increases the likelihood that cancer will spread because it thwarts a key immune system cell, studies in rats have shown. Natural killer cells are among the immune system's chief weapons against tumor cells, which can spread from their original site to form new tumors in other parts of the body. In rats injected with breast cancer cells, alcohol reduced natural killer cell activity, and many more tumors formed in the rats' lungs. The higher the alcohol dose, the more tumors formed, researchers from the University of California, Los Angeles, reported last week at the annual meeting of the Society for Neuroscience. The researchers cautioned that more study will be needed to determine whether the same effect occurs in humans.

—The Dallas Morning News, 2 November 1992

SUMMARY

Here is a recapitulation, in plain language, of Mill's five methods of experimental inquiry:

Method of Agreement

One observes that a phenomenon (event to be explained) occurs in more than one case (instance). One examines the instances to determine in what respects they are alike and in what respects they differ. If there is only one respect in which they are alike (that is, if they have only one circumstance in common), that circumstance probably is the cause of the phenomenon. If there is more than one respect in which the instances are alike, then one or some combination of the circumstances probably is the cause; further testing, using another of Mill's methods, may determine which. In short, find a correlation (agreement) and infer causation.

Method of Difference

One notices that a phenomenon occurs in some instances but not in others. One looks for a correlation among the circumstances. If two instances are alike in all respects but one (where the one difference is either naturally or artificially produced), but only one of the instances exhibits the phenomenon, the circumstance in which the instances differ probably is the cause of the phenomenon. In short, find a difference and infer causation.

Joint Method of Agreement and Difference

To determine whether a particular circumstance is causally related to a given phenomenon, select a large and diverse group of instances (the larger and more diverse the better) and divide them into two roughly equal groups. Introduce the circumstance in question into one of the two groups (the experimental group) but not the other (the control group). If all of the instances exhibiting the circumstance also exhibit the phenomenon, while none of the instances lacking the circumstance exhibits the phenomenon, the circumstance is probably the cause, or an indispensable part of the cause, of the phenomenon. (Note: This is the strict or qualitative version of the method. The two *quantitative* versions require, respectively, differences in the percentage of each group that exhibit the phenomenon and differences in the average value of the phenomenon in each group.)

Method of Residues

One notices that part of a complex phenomenon is causally unexplained. One explains as much of the phenomenon as one can with known antecedent circumstances and infers that the residue (the remaining part of the phenomenon) is caused by the remaining circumstance(s). In short, find a residue and infer causation.

Method of Concomitant Variations

One notices that two phenomena vary either directly or inversely with one another. From this one infers that one of the phenomena causes the other, or that they have a common cause. In short, find a concomitant variation and infer causation.

6.3   THE ALLEGED CIRCULARITY OF MILL'S METHODS

Mill's Dilemma

Mill made a number of grandiose claims on behalf of his methods, even describing them at one point as "the only possible modes of experimental inquiry." He claimed that the methods can be used to discover and prove laws of nature. They do this, he said, by experimentally altering the circumstances (or finding variations of circumstances in nature) and making careful observations of the resulting phenomena (or lack thereof). But at least three of Mill's methods—the method of agreement, the method of difference, and the joint method of agreement and difference—run the risk of circularity, which, if established, would cast serious doubt on Mill's assertion that the methods are instruments of discovery and proof. It is important to understand what this risk is, why it poses a dilemma for Mill, and how, if at all, Mill can resolve the dilemma.

Let us begin with the method of agreement, which, as we saw, requires that two or more instances exhibiting the phenomenon have only one circumstance in common. The example we gave concerned vitamin-D poisoning in eight Massachusetts residents. According to our analysis, the only circumstance these individuals had in common was that they consumed milk from a particular local dairy. Researchers inferred from this that the milk caused the poisoning. But was consumption of the milk the *only* common circumstance? Surely not! The poisoned individuals had much more in common than that. All of them, presumably, had consumed water as well as milk. All had slept, breathed, and come into contact with other people in the 24 hours prior to becoming sick. For that matter, all of them were residents of Massachusetts; all had arms; and all were born in the twentieth century. A moment's reflection reveals that the eight individuals had many, perhaps *indefinitely* many, things in common; so strictly speaking Mill's method of agreement does not apply to the situation and cannot be used.

The same is true of the method of difference, which requires that two instances differ in only one respect. One of our examples concerned Hox genes in mice. The only difference between the mouse that developed ears and the mouse that didn't develop ears is that the first had and the second lacked a particular Hox gene, which was inferred to be the cause of the ear development. But surely these mice differed in ways other than the presence of the Hox gene. For one thing, they never occupied the same space at the same time. They breathed different air; they ate different food (even if the same *type* of food); and they were gestated in different, albeit highly similar, environments. In the capital-punishment example the states being compared to one another differed in many ways besides having or lacking the death penalty. They had different populations, differ-ent weather, different histories, different laws, different governmental policies, and different territorial boundaries (just to name a few)[28]

The joint method of agreement and difference is also implicated. One example of this method concerned learning in newborn infants. Each member of the group of infants given the conditioned stimulus learned, while no member of the group of infants not given the conditioned stimulus learned. But to be applicable this method requires not only that the instances that exhibit the phenomenon have only one common circumstance, but that the instances that do not exhibit the phenomenon have nothing in common except the *absence* of the circumstance. We know, however, that the infants who learned had more in common than exposure to the conditioned stimulus (they had eaten, breathed, occupied the same room, and so on), just as we know that the infants who did not learn had more in common than lack of exposure to the conditioned stimulus. In short, the infants were alike and different in *many* respects, not just one.

It might be interjected that the problems being described arise only for the examples chosen—that Mill's examples, which were more carefully selected than ours, avoid the problem. Unfortunately, they do not. Mill illustrated the method of agreement with the case of crystallization. He claimed that the only circumstance the crystalline bodies shared is that they had been transformed from a liquid state. His conclusion was that "the solidification of a substance from a liquid state is an invariable antecedent of its crystallization." But the crystalline bodies had other common circumstances besides that. All had shape and size; all were affected by gravity and other physical laws; and all had a chemical composition. Which of these agreements is the cause? Mill's example of the method of difference fares no better. The man immediately before the gunshot and the man immediately after the gunshot differed in more than one respect. For one thing, the victim occupied different points in space and time (however small). His brain state (and presumably his feelings and thoughts) were different before and after the gunshot. People and objects in the vicinity of the victim changed location. The second hand of the clock moved. Which of these differences is the cause?

It would appear that Mill faces a dilemma.[29] Either his methods are meant to be strictly (that is, mechanically) applied, with no prior knowledge of causation, or they are not. If they *are* meant to be mechanically applied, then they are useless, for as

---

[28]   In a brief filed with the United States Supreme Court in 1974, Solicitor General Robert Bork "faulted [Thorsten] Sellin's work for its failure 'to hold constant factors other than the death penalty that might influence the rate of murders.'" Klein, Forst, and Filatov, "The Deterrent Effect of Capital Punishment," p. 140. In other words, if the states being studied differed in more than one respect, then one could not have cited a particular difference as the cause of differences in the homicide rate.

[29]   A dilemma, in ordinary language, is "a perplexing situation, especially one in which a choice has to be made between alternatives that are equally undesirable." Ehrlich et al., *Oxford American Dictionary*, p. 179. Logicians use the term "constructive dilemma" to refer to an *argument* of the following form: Either P or Q; if P then R; if Q then S; therefore, either R or S. See Robert M. Martin, *The Philosopher's Dictionary* (1991), p. 47.

our discussion suggests, any two instances agree in more than one respect and no two instances differ in only one respect, contrary to what the methods require. If the methods are *not* meant to be mechanically applied, then they are circular, for they presuppose precisely what they are intended to establish—namely, causation. To determine the cause of a particular phenomenon, we must already know that certain circumstances are *not* the cause! But where are we supposed to have acquired this knowledge? The absence of such knowledge is why we are using the methods. Given these assumptions it follows that Mill's methods are either useless or circular, neither of which, to him, is a happy result. *Either* Mill's methods never apply (because the world is not the way they require it to be) *or* they sometimes apply but require prior, independent knowledge about which circumstances can and which cannot cause the phenomenon.

Resolving the Dilemma

Facing a dilemma is like facing a charging bull. Both situations are unpleasant and both can be fatal (in one case literally, in the other, fortunately, only figuratively). Happily, both situations are survivable. Just as there are different ways to avoid being gored by a charging bull, there are different ways to resolve a dilemma. One way is to show that the initial statement of choices is incomplete—that there are more than two alternatives. This, in keeping with the charging-bull metaphor, is known as "escaping between the horns." Another way to resolve a dilemma is to show that one or both of the conditional statements—the statements that draw out the implications of the alternatives—are false. This is known as "grasping the bull by the horns." Since Mill would presumably reject the conclusion of the dilemma, which asserts that the first three of his five methods are either useless or circular, and since the reasoning of the dilemma is valid,[30] *he must adopt one or both of these strategies.* But the statement of alternatives can hardly be denied, for logically speaking Mill's methods are either meant to be or not meant to be mechanically applied; there is no third possibility. So Mill must grasp the bull by the horns. But how?

In all likelihood Mill would agree with the critic that *if* his methods are to be mechanically applied, they are useless. This conclusion is suggested by his discussion of the method of difference, where he writes:

> The two instances which are to be compared with one another must be exactly similar, in all circumstances except the one which we are attempting to investigate. . . . It is true that this similarity of circumstances *needs not extend to such as are already known to be immaterial to the result.* And in the case of most phenomena we learn at once, from the commonest experience, that most of the coexistent phenomena of the universe may be either present or absent without affecting the given phenomenon; or, if present, are present indifferently when the phenomenon does not happen and when it does. [Emphasis added.]

---

[30] By "valid" we mean what we meant in chapter 1, section 7—namely, truth-preserving. *If* there are only two choices; and *if* the first choice has consequence C; and *if* the second choice has consequence D; *then* either C is true or D is true. It is impossible for all three of these assumptions to be true without the conclusion being true.

Mill seems to be admitting that it is rarely (if ever) the case that two instances differ in only one respect. One suspects he would also admit that it is rarely (if ever) the case that two or more instances differ in every respect but one. But this is just to say that his methods of agreement and difference (hence also his joint method of agreement and difference) cannot be applied mechanically. The world is not as these methods require it to be. But that is of no great concern, Mill appears to be saying, because in most cases we can safely rule out certain circumstances as causes.

In the case of the vitamin-D poisoning, for example, common sense tells us that such poisoning cannot be the result of having slept, or of being a resident of Massachusetts, or of having arms. These circumstances, to quote Mill, are "already known to be immaterial to the result." The same is true of the mice in the Hox-gene experiment. It is hard to imagine how taking up different space and breathing different air can have anything to do with the development of ears, so these circumstances can be safely ignored in the investigation. As a matter of fact, scientific researchers make assumptions of causal irrelevance quite often in their work. When they do so, they are not *certain* that the circumstance is causally unrelated (irrelevant); rather, they *assume* its irrelevance in order to investigate the causal role of a different circumstance. If researchers did not make assumptions of causal irrelevance, they would be unable to draw any conclusions at all, and science as we know it would grind to a halt.

This strategy is precisely what we have described as grasping the bull by the horns. Mill, we suspect, would concede that *if* his methods are to be applied mechanically they are useless, but he denies the converse proposition that if his methods are *not* meant to be applied mechanically they are circular. Or rather, he would admit that his methods are circular, but insists that it is a harmless and indispensable kind of circularity rather than a vicious kind. New causal knowledge, he would say, *presupposes* old causal knowledge. Paradoxically, to know anything we must already know something.

Mill's Methods and Modern Science

Every scientific investigation begins with an assumption about possible causes of the phenomenon under investigation. This assumption is known as the hypothesis. It is what guides research.[31] Having formulated a hypothesis, the investigator proceeds to test it by means of one or more of Mill's methods. By systematically eliminating all but one of the circumstances as the cause, the investigator concludes that a particular circumstance *is* the cause (or effect) of the phenomenon. This, Mill would insist, is what the methods of experimental inquiry are designed to show; but they cannot do so in the absence of either common sense or a set of background beliefs about what sorts of event can cause what other sorts of event. In short, Mill's methods are to be used by people who already have a basic understanding of the world and who know generally

---

[31]   As we shall see in chapter 7, unless there is at least a working hypothesis there can be no data. Or to put it differently, what *counts* as a datum depends on the hypothesis with which one is working. The hypothesis allows the investigator to sift relevant from irrelevant data.

how things work; the methods are useless to those who are (or pretend to be) ignorant of everything.[32]

To illustrate the role Mill's methods play in modern science, reconsider the chick deaths discussed at the beginning of this chapter (see page 195). To make headway on discovering the cause of the deaths, one must begin with an assumption or hypothesis about what might be causing them. Suppose one narrows the possible causes to three: the feed (F), overcrowding (O), and genetic defects (G). This can be viewed as one disjunctive hypothesis—"either F or O or G is the cause of the deaths"—or as three separate hypotheses. To test hypothesis F, one may use the joint method of agreement and difference. Suppose one does this and discovers no difference in the quantity of chick deaths. One concludes that F is not the cause. Suppose one conducts the same experiment with hypothesis O and discovers no difference. Then O is not the cause. That leaves G. Assuming that F, O, and G are the only possible causes (our working hypothesis), we conclude that the chick deaths are caused by a genetic defect. Of course, a good researcher will not stop *there*. He or she will conduct a third experiment, perhaps again using the joint method, to determine whether the chick deaths are attributable to genetic defects. This experiment will show either that G is the cause or that G is not the cause. If G is *not* the cause, then either the initial hypothesis which limited the causes to three is false or one or more of the experiments was improperly conducted.

Notice the role being played by the hypothesis. By assuming that only certain circumstances *can* cause the phenomenon, the investigator produces a demonstrative (deductive) inference. In the case of the chicks the inference goes as follows:

1. Either F or O or G causes the chick deaths (hypothesis).
2. F does not cause the chick deaths (by experiment and observation).
3. O does not cause the chick deaths (by experiment and observation).
   Therefore,
4. G causes the chick deaths.

This reasoning is demonstrative because *if* the premisses are true, then so is the conclusion. If we discover upon testing hypothesis G that it does not cause the chick deaths, then, assuming that the reasoning is valid (as it appears to be), one or more of the premisses must be false.[33] That is to say, either the experiments concerning F and O were improperly conducted (premisses 2 and 3) or the initial hypothesis assuming just three possible causes (premiss 1) is false. Demonstrativity is desirable in science, as elsewhere, but to acquire it here one must introduce a questionable premiss (1).

---

[32]   Perhaps Mill would respond to the dilemma as follows. There are two kinds of circularity: harmless and vicious. If "circular" means "viciously circular," then the conclusion ("Either the methods are useless or the methods are circular") and the third premise ("If the methods are not meant to be applied mechanically, then they are circular") are false. The rationale is that one can make causal assumptions in the course of acquiring causal knowledge. If "circular" means "harmlessly circular," on the other hand, then the conclusion is true—not because the methods are useless, but because they are harmlessly circular.

[33]   Why? If you have trouble answering this question, review the discussion of validity in chapter 1.

One hallmark of modern science is its formulation of insightful and fruitful hypotheses—what one philosopher of science has called "bold conjectures."[34] We can now see that Mill's methods are an important element of this procedure. His methods are instruments—although perhaps not the only instruments—for testing scientific hypotheses, about which we will say much more in chapter 7.

EXERCISES

Analyze each of the following passages in terms of circumstances and phenomena. Show how each passage exemplifies either the method of agreement, the method of difference, the joint method of agreement and difference, the method of residues, or the method of concomitant variations. If the passage exemplifies the joint method, specify the version (pure or quantitative). State the causal connection. It may be useful to construct a diagram or table to portray the information.

Set One

■   *1.* Researchers at a Galveston clinic say the drug Depo Provera . . . has helped many male sex offenders they've treated keep from repeating their crimes. . . . The Galveston study involved 61 men, 40 of whom agreed to take Depo Provera and 21 who refused but agreed to participate in the same psychological counseling program as those who received injections. Of the 40 who took the drug, researchers said 17 [42.5 percent] committed new offenses. . . . "Only 18 percent re-offended while on therapy, and 35 percent re-offended after stopping," Dr. [Collier] Cole said. "In contrast, 58 percent who never received the drug re-offended."

—Associated Press report, 1 March 1993

2. The return of the comet predicted by Professor Encke a great many times in succession, and the general good agreement of its calculated place with its observed place during any one of its periods of visibility, would lead us to say that its gravitation toward the sun and planets is the sole and sufficient cause of all the phenomena of its orbital motion; but when the effect of this case is strictly calculated and subducted from the observed motion, there is found to remain behind a *residual phenomenon,* which would never have been otherwise ascertained to exist, which is a small anticipation of the time of its re-appearance, or a diminution of its periodic time, which cannot be accounted for by gravity, and whose cause is therefore to be inquired into. Such an anticipation would be caused by the resistance of a medium disseminated through the celestial regions; and as there are other good reasons for believing this to be a *vera causa* (an actually existing antecedent), it has therefore been ascribed to such a resistance.

—SIR JOHN HERSCHEL, quoted by John Stuart Mill, *A System of Logic*

3. Over in Denmark Johannes Fibiger, a pathologist of the University of Copenhagen, had been working thirteen years on the problem of tuberculosis among laboratory animals. During a series of postmortem examinations of tubercular rats, he

---

[34] See Karl R. Popper, *Conjectures and Refutations: The Growth of Scientific Knowledge* (1963).

found three had suffered from stomach cancers. Fibiger knew enough about cancer to realize that he had come across a singular phenomenon. Rats rarely suffered from tumors of the stomach.

Fibiger made a visit to the dealer who had been supplying him with these rats, and on questioning found that those sent to his laboratory had all come from a sugar refinery. Was there anything peculiar about this refinery which could account for the unusually large percentage of stomach-cancerous rats from this spot? He investigated the place and found nothing unusual except a high infestation with cockroaches, which formed a fairly large part of the diet of its rats. Could he find some connection between roaches, rats, and cancer? Cancer as a disease of filth had been spoken about for years, and vermin were said to be responsible for the so-called "cancer houses," private homes from which emerged many a human cancer victim of the same family.

Fibiger planned a controlled experiment. He collected thousands of the refinery roaches and fed them to rats from another breeding establishment. The rats enjoyed this strange treatment, and for three years—that was the normal life span of his rodents—Fibiger remained skeptical. Then they died, and one by one he opened them up. To his astonishment, he found many stomach cancers. Fibiger made a careful microscopic study of the growths. He discovered that in every case they had formed around a parasitic worm, the same worm to which the roach had been host before it was fed to the rat. The larva of the worm coiled up in the muscles of the rat, later developing into an adult worm in the animal's stomach. Around this the tumorous growth had appeared. Fibiger had actually for the first time produced artificial cancer in a laboratory animal.

—BERNARD JAFFE, *Outposts of Science*

4. Chris has coached five basketball teams, all of which, under Chris's tutelage, had winning records. In fact, each team won more than three-fourths of its games. The teams were remarkably diverse. One was a junior-high team, one a high-school team, one a college team, one a professional team, and one a recreation-league team. Some had losing records when Chris came aboard; others had winning records; at least one had a break-even record. Some played only a dozen games; others played more than fifty. Which of Mill's methods supports the conclusion that Chris's skills as a coach are causally responsible for the success of the teams?

■ *5.* On the 31st of August, 1909, Paul Ehrlich and Hata stood before a cage in which sat an excellent buck rabbit. Flourishing in every way was this rabbit, excepting for the tender skin of his scrotum, which was disfigured with two terrible ulcers, each bigger than a twenty-five-cent piece. Those sores were caused by the gnawing of the pale spirochete of the disease that is the reward of sin. They had been put under the skin of that rabbit by S. Hata a month before. Under the microscope—it was a special one built for spying just such a thin rogue as that pale microbe—under this lens Hata put a wee drop of the fluid from these ugly sores. Against the blackness of the dark field of this special microscope, gleaming in a powerful beam of light that hit them sidewise, shooting backwards and forwards like ten thousand silver drills and augers, played myriads of these pale spirochetes. It was a pretty picture, to hold you there for hours, but it was sinister—for what living things can bring worse plague and sorrow to men?

Hata leaned aside. Paul Ehrlich looked down the shiny tube. Then he looked at Hata, and then at the rabbit.

"Make the injection," said Paul Ehrlich. And into the ear-vein of that rabbit went the clear yellow fluid of the solution of 606, for the first time to do battle with the disease of the loathsome name.

Next day there was not one of those spiral devils to be found in the scrotum of that rabbit. His ulcers? They were drying already! Good clean scabs were forming on them. In less than a month there was nothing to be seen but tiny scabs—it was like a cure of Bible times—no less! And a little while after that Paul Ehrlich could write:

"It is evident from these experiments that, if a large enough dose is given, the spirochetes can be destroyed *absolutely and immediately with a single injection!*"

—PAUL DE KRUIF, *Microbe Hunters*[33]

6.   Having waited for some weeks for favourable weather, [Florin] Perier assembled his team in a convent garden in the town of Clermont [France]. Two identical tubes were tested together in the same mercury bath, and the reading at successive immersions duly noted by the group assembled, amongst which were respected clergy, lawyers and doctors. It was established that no variation occurred between the two tubes. A priest was left in the garden with one of the tubes, instructed to note whether the reading changed at any time during the day. Meanwhile, the others set off up the mountain of Puy-de-Dome, and on its summit (1465 metres) took readings in the open, under cover, and in the different weather conditions experienced on a very changeable day. [The readings varied.] Halfway down they did the same, and on their return checked their tube once more against the control, which of course had not changed. The readings were accurate, . . . and the now familiar facts of atmospheric pressure established clearly and without doubt.

—A.J. KRAILSHEIMER, *Pascal* (1980), p. 19

7.   . . . MacLarty had reasoned that these physiological disorders were most probably caused by some mineral deficiency or mineral unbalance within the trees. Following up this line of reasoning, he injected severely affected apple trees with some thirty different chemicals. In these experiments, the dry test material was packed in holes drilled into the trunks of the trees. The holes were about one-half inch in diameter and two inches deep. After having been filled the holes were sealed with a commercial grafting compound. The dry materials were used because of the convenience of handling and also because greater amounts could be used without injury to the foliage. The following year the crop of two of the injected trees was practically free of the disorders, and it was noted that one of these trees had been injected with boric acid and the other with manganese borate. The trees injected with manganese compounds, other than the borate, showed no change. Following up this lead, forty trees were injected with either boric acid or borax in the fall of 1934. In the summer of 1935 every tree that had been injected the previous fall showed none of the diseases or a very low incidence of them. Because of the great economic losses which many of the growers were suffer-

---

[33] Excerpted from *Microbe Hunters*, copyright 1926, 1954 by Paul de Kruif. Reprinted by permission of Harcourt Brace Jovanovich and Jonathan Cape.

ing that year, the committee decided that it was well worthwhile to make an immediate recommendation that all affected trees be injected with boric acid crystals.

—C. G. WOODBRIDGE, "The Role of Boron in the Agricultural Regions of the Pacific Northwest," *The Scientific Monthly*, Vol. 70, No. 2, February 1950

8. Repeated reports, before and after Kinsey, showed college-educated women to have a much lower than average divorce rate. More specifically, a massive and famous sociological study by Ernest W. Burgess and Leonard S. Cottrell indicated that women's chances of happiness in marriage increased as their career preparation increased. . . .

Among 526 couples, less than ten per cent showed "low" marital adjustment where the wife had been employed seven or more years, had completed college or professional training, and had not married before twenty-two. Where wives had been educated beyond college, less than 5 per cent of marriages scored "low" in happiness. The following table shows the relationship between the marriage and the educational achievement of the wife.

Marriage Adjustment Scores at Different
Educational Levels

Wife's Educational Level	Very Low	Low	High	Very High
Graduate Work	0.0	4.6	38.7	56.5
College	9.2	18.9	22.9	48.9
High School	14.4	16.3	32.2	37.1
Grades Only	33.3	25.9	25.9	14.8

—BETTY FRIEDAN, *The Feminine Mystique*

9. It was Wolfgang Pauli who in 1930 postulated the existence of the neutrino in order to reconcile an apparent contradiction between the quantum-mechanical model of the phenomenon of nuclear beta decay and the observed products of this decay. (The term "beta decay" is used by physicists to describe the spontaneous transformation of a neutron in an unstable atomic nucleus into a proton and an electron; it is also applied to the transformation of a proton into a neutron and a positron, or positive electron.) When experiments measured the total energy of the nuclear system both before and after beta decay, they invariably found a discrepancy in the energy budget. The observed products of the reaction not only varied in total energy from measurement to measurement: they were poorer in energy than the original nuclear system. Faced with the disturbing alternative of declaring a failure in the law of the conservation of energy, Pauli was moved to suggest a less radical solution, namely to postulate the existence of an unobserved particle that carries away the missing energy.

—FREDERICK REINES and J. P. P. SELLSCHOP, "Neutrinos from the Atmosphere and Beyond," *Scientific American*, Vol. 214, No. 2, February 1966

■ **10.** Why do global temperatures change? Researchers have hypothesized that the sun's radiation is a major cause, but obviously the sun cannot be eliminated in order to test the hypothesis. What to do? Two Danish meteorologists have found a striking correlation between the length of the solar cycle (which they assume to be a measure of solar activity) and global climate during the past 130 years. When plotted on a graph, the lines representing cycle length (in years) and temperature anomaly are virtually identical. As the researchers put it, "this agreement supports (although it does not prove) the suggestion of a direct solar activity influence on global temperature."

—E. FRIIS-CHRISTENSEN and K. LASSEN, "Length of the Solar Cycle: An Indicator of Solar Activity Closely Associated with Climate," *Science* 254 (1 November 1991):699

Set Two

■ *1.* Scientists at the University of Texas Health Science Center in Houston have located a gene that causes one type of retinitis pigmentosa, a hereditary eye disorder that often leads to blindness. By studying a large Kentucky family, [all of whose members had the disorder], the researchers found that a gene linked to a form of retinitis pigmentosa must sit on a segment of chromosome 8.

—*The Dallas Morning News,* 14 October 1991

2. Diets high in polyunsaturated fats might increase the risk of breast cancer and help spread the disease, according to a new study by researchers at the American Health Foundation in Valhalla, N.Y. The scientists fed one group of mice a diet high in corn oil—which is rich in polyunsaturated fats—and another group a low-fat diet. After injecting human breast cancer cells into the mice, the scientists found that mice fed the high-fat diet were more likely to develop tumors than those on the low-fat diet. And in the mice that developed mammary tumors, those on the high-fat diet were more likely to have cancer spread to the lungs than those on the low-fat diet.

—*The Dallas Morning News,* 21 October 1991

3. The French historian Roustan asserts that the *philosophes* had a direct and strong influence upon the revolutionary development that exploded in 1789. Poverty, despair, and mistreatment inflamed the masses but without the intellectuals there would have been no revolution: the men of 1789 were not merely escaping starvation which had been an integral part of the national tradition. In 1753, eight hundred people died of hunger in one small community alone—more died in other cities. There were riots, but no revolution—the military won the day. It took almost forty years of education and propaganda on the part of the philosophers before the French could stand up and demand their rights and human dignity: "The spirit of the *philosophes* was the spirit of the Revolution."

—GUNTER W. REMMLING, *Road to Suspicion*

4. A group of psychologists at the University of Florida have worked on a curious riddle concerning the role of age in tolerating sleep loss. In the early 1960s, Wilse B. Webb and his associates at Gainesville placed a group of young rats on a mesh water wheel which rotated slowly and continuously. If the animals fell asleep, they toppled into cold water. The researchers kept expecting the rats to topple, but some of them managed to stay on the water wheel for twenty-seven days. However, when older rats were placed on the wheel they fell off in three to four days. By testing rats of intermediate ages, the experimenters saw that the staying power of the animal was directly correlated with its age. Delicate EEG techniques revealed that the young animals were snatching brief naps of ten to fifteen seconds as they rode the wheel. They would sleep for a few seconds, then move to the end of the wheel and sleep as they rode forward.

— Gay Gaer Luce and Julius Segal, *Insomnia*

■ **5.** M. Arago, having suspended a magnetic needle by a silk thread, and set it in vibration, observed that it came much sooner to a state of rest when suspended over a plate of copper, than when no such plate was beneath it. Now, in both cases there were two *verae causae* (antecedents known to exist) why it *should* come at length to rest, viz., the resistance of the air, which opposes, and at length destroys, all motions performed in it; and the want of perfect mobility in the silk thread. But the effect of these causes being exactly known by the observation made in the absence of the copper; and being thus allowed for and subducted, a residual phenomenon appeared, in the fact, that a retarding influence was exerted by the copper itself; and this fact, once ascertained, speedily led to the knowledge of an entirely new and unexpected class of relations.

—JOHN STUART MILL, *A System of Logic*, Book III, Chapter 9

6. During the first half of the nineteenth century it was firmly believed that animals were unable to manufacture carbohydrates, fats or proteins, all of which had to be obtained in the diet preformed from plants. All organic compounds were believed to be synthesised in plants whereas animals were thought to be capable only of breaking them down. Claude Bernard set out to investigate the metabolism of sugar and in particular to find where it is broken down. He fed a dog a diet rich in sugar and then examined the blood leaving the liver to see if the sugar had been broken down in the liver. He found a high sugar content, and then wisely carried out a similar estimation with a dog fed a sugar-free meal. To his astonishment he found also a high sugar content in the control animal's herpatic blood. He realised that contrary to all prevailing views the liver probably did produce sugar from something which is not sugar.

—W. I. B. BEVERIDGE, *The Art of Scientific Investigation*

7. It has been known to entomologists for many years that if a bright light is used for attracting insects at night, the catches are considerably higher near the period of new moon than near full moon. One of us (C. B. W.) showed that in three successive years, between May and October, the catches in a light trap, both of Lepidoptera alone and of all insects together (chiefly Diptera), reached a peak at, or shortly after, new moon, when the geometric mean catches were three to four times as great as those at full moon.

In spite of the fact that it is generally believed that other methods of catching are also poor at full moon, in the absence of any real evidence for this there was a distinct probability that the low catches in a light trap might be due to a lowered relative luminosity and hence a lowered attractiveness of the trap at full moon.

During the summer of 1950, we carried out continuous trapping of insects at night by means of a 'suction-trap" which draws in the insects by a strong electric fan, and thus is in no way dependent on reaction to light. The insects so caught are mostly Diptera; but many other orders are present.

An analysis of five complete lunar cycles between July and November 1950 shows that the geometric mean catches in the four weeks, that is, three days on either side of (1) full moon, (2) last quarter, (3) new moon and (4) first quarter, were as follows:

204; 589; 1,259 and 562.

Each of these figures is the mean of thirty-five nights.

These results are slightly affected by accidental differences in temperature and wind on the different nights, and when a correction is made for these, the figures become:

240; 490; 1,175 and 589.

Thus the geometric mean catch in the new moon week is nearly five times that in the full moon week. As the records include nights with cloud as well as clear nights, the effect of full moon on a clear night must be greater than this.

Mr. Healy, of the Statistical Department at this station, informs me that the differences between full and new moon are significant at the 2 percent level.

It appears, therefore, that the moonlight must have a definite effect on nocturnal insects, and that the low catches in a light trap at full moon are not merely due to a physical reduction of the efficiency of the trap.

Further repetition and analysis will be carried out during the present year. In the meantime, we would be glad of any other evidence on this problem, particularly long series of night catches of insects by any technique not depending on attraction to light.

—C. B. WILLIAMS and B. P. SINGH, "The Effect of Moonlight on Insect Activity," *Nature*, Vol. 167, No. 4256, May 26, 1951

8.   One of the procedures which showed a high correlation with ulcers involved training the monkeys to avoid an electric shock by pressing a lever. The animal received a brief shock on the feet at regular intervals, say, every 20 seconds. It could avoid the shock if it learned to press the lever at least once in every 20-second interval. It does not take a monkey very long to master this problem; within a short time it is pressing the lever far oftener than once in 20 seconds. Only occasionally does it slow down enough to receive a shock as a reminder.

One possibility, of course, was that the monkeys which had developed ulcers under this procedure had done so not because of the psychological stress involved but rather as a cumulative result of the shocks. To test this possibility we set up a controlled experiment, using two monkeys in "yoked chairs" in which both monkeys received shocks but only one monkey could prevent them. The experimental or "executive" monkey could prevent shocks to himself and his partner by pressing the lever; the control monkey's lever was a dummy. Thus both animals were subjected to the same physical stress (i.e., both received the same number of shocks at the same time), but only the "executive" monkey was under the psychological stress of having to press the lever.

We placed the monkeys on a continuous schedule of alternate periods of shock-avoidance and rest, arbitrarily choosing an interval of six hours for each period. As a cue for the executive monkey we provided a red light which was turned on during the avoidance periods and turned off during the "off" hours. The animal soon learned to press its lever at a rate averaging between 15 and 20 times a minute during the avoidance periods, and to stop pressing the lever when the red light was turned off. These responses showed no change throughout the experiment. The control monkey at first pressed the lever sporadically during both the avoidance and rest sessions, but lost interest in the lever within a few days.

After 23 days of a continuous six-hours-on, six-hours-off schedule the executive monkey died during one of the avoidance sessions. Our only advance warning had been the animal's failure to eat on the preceding day. It had lost no weight during the experiment, and it pressed the lever at an unflagging rate through the first two hours of its last avoidance session. Then it suddenly collapsed and had to be sacrificed. An autopsy revealed a large perforation in the wall of the duodenum—the upper part of the small intestine near its junction with the stomach, and a common site of ulcers in man. Microscopic analysis revealed both acute and chronic inflammation around this lesion. The control monkey, sacrificed in good health a few hours later, showed no gastrointestinal abnormalities. A second experiment using precisely the same procedure produced much the same results. This time the executive monkey developed ulcers in both the stomach and the duodenum; the control animal was again unaffected.

—JOSEPH V. BRADY, "Ulcers in 'Executive' Monkeys," *Scientific American*, Vol. 199, No. 4, October 1958

9. It was not merely the amount of water in circulation which was influenced by temperature. . . . It was the total amount of haemoglobin. The mystery was: "Whence came this outpouring of haemoglobin?" It was not credible that the bone-marrow could have provided the body with new corpuscles at the rate required. Moreover, there was no evidence of increase of immature corpuscles in circulation. . . .

The question then was forced upon us: Has the body any considerable but hidden store of haemoglobin which can be drawn upon in case of emergency? . . . In searching for a locality which might fulfill such a condition one naturally seeks in the first instance for some place where the red blood corpuscles are outside the circulatory system—some backwater outside the arteries, capillaries, and veins. There is only one such place of any considerable size in the body—that place is the spleen.

—JOSEPH BARCROFT, *The Lancet*, February 1925

■ *10.* A series of tests carried out by the Federal Aviation Agency has substantiated the common complaint of air travelers that swift transition through several time zones disturbs their bodily and even their mental functions. The tests may result in changes of schedule for the crews on certain types of international flight. Moreover, the tests have implications for the proposal to build supersonic airplanes that would travel even faster than today's jets.

The tests involved healthy male volunteers, who were carried by jet airplane from the U.S. to such cities as Tokyo, Manila and Rome, passing through as many as 10 time zones. As a control to make sure that the effects resulted from changes of times and not merely from jet travel, there was a flight from Washington, D.C., to Santiago, Chile; it covered a long distance but was all in the same time zone. On the outbound flights that crossed a number of time zones the passengers underwent physiological changes—in heart rate, temperature and perspiration—that persisted for several days. They also showed a deterioration, for about a day, in mental acuity as indicated by difficulty in doing simple problems in arithmetic and by slowed responses to sensory stimuli. Similar effects appeared on the return trips but did not last as long. In contrast, the flight to Chile produced only a sense of fatigue.

The F.A.A. plans to give the tests to some pilots on the New York–Rome run in March. Sheldon Freud, an Air Force psychologist who has worked on the testing, said that the reaction of the passengers made it important to test the crews. "These men are responsible for the lives of millions of passengers every year," he said. Freud also raised a question about supersonic flights, which will be at least twice as fast as today's jet flights: "Will we have to rest twice as long afterward? Is it worthwhile getting over there in such a hurry?"

—"Science and the Citizen," *Scientific American,* Vol. 214, No. 2, February 1966

7

Science and Hypothesis

7.1 VALUES AND DISVALUES OF SCIENCE

Modern science came into existence only a few hundred years ago, yet it has profoundly changed almost every aspect of life in the Western world. Improvements in farming and manufacturing, in communication and transportation, in health and hygiene, and in our standard of living generally, all have resulted from the application of scientific knowledge. Steam, water, and nuclear power have been harnessed to run our machinery. Rivers have been diverted to turn deserts into vineyards. These are but a few of the beneficent uses of science as a tool for ameliorating a hostile environment.

Much the same appraisal is stated in the following passage:

> Science and technology have permitted enormous growth in the world population by improving man's ability to increase food production; to accommodate to harsh climates; to provide transportation and communication for the world's goods, services and ideas; to increase available resources and use them more effectively; and to live longer in better health.[1]

Some of the practical results of science are not so cheerful. The tremendous increase in the destructive power of weapons, together with their proliferation around the globe, has made the risk of nuclear war a menace to civilization itself. As we learned from the Chernobyl incident in the Soviet Union, nuclear power plants constitute a profound risk to the lives and well-being of those around them. And the habitability of our planet is increasingly threatened by industrial, chemical, and automotive pollution. These practical results threaten not just human beings, present and

---

[1]   Chauncey Starr, "The Growth of Limits," *Edison Electric Institute Symposium on Science, Technology and the Human Prospect*, April 1979.

future, but other sentient life on our planet. Whole ecosystems are in danger of being destroyed if we, as individuals and societies, do not monitor and control the technology spawned by science.

Despite these and other unhappy aspects of scientific achievement, it is arguable that science and technology have benefited humanity. (Whether science has been a boon or a bust for other sentient beings is another matter.) Terrible as recent wars have been, their toll of human life has been much smaller than that of the great plagues that formerly swept over Europe, decimating the population. And those plagues have been almost completely wiped out by modern medical science. The *practical* value of science lies in the easier and more abundant life made possible by technological advances based on scientific knowledge. The issue is clearly stated and cogently reasoned in the following passage:

> It's sometimes argued that there's no real progress; that a civilization that kills multitudes in mass warfare, that pollutes the land and oceans with ever larger quantities of debris, that destroys the dignity of individuals by subjecting them to a forced mechanized existence can hardly be called an advance over the simpler hunting and gathering and agricultural existence of prehistoric times. But this argument, though romantically appealing, doesn't hold up. The primitive tribes permitted far less individual freedom than does modern society. Ancient wars were committed with far less moral justification than modern ones. A technology that produces debris can find, and is finding, ways of disposing of it without ecological upset. And the school-book pictures of primitive man sometimes omit some of the detractions of his primitive life—the pain, the disease, famine, the hard labor needed just to stay alive. From that agony of bare existence to modern life can be soberly described only as upward progress, and the sole agent for this progress is quite clearly reason itself.[2]

Its applications are not the only value of science, however. Science generates knowledge, which most people take to be an end in itself. The laws and principles discovered in scientific investigation have a value apart from any practical utility they may possess. This intrinsic value is the satisfaction of curiosity, the fulfillment of the desire to know. That human beings have such a desire has long been recognized. Aristotle wrote that

> . . . to be learning something is the greatest of pleasures not only to the philosopher but also to the rest of mankind, however small their capacity for it. . . .[3]

If we consult the most distinguished of twentieth-century scientists, Albert Einstein, we are told that

> There exists a passion for comprehension just as there exists a passion for music. That passion is rather common in children, but gets lost in most people later on. Without this passion, there would be neither mathematics nor natural science.[4]

---

[2]   Robert M. Pirsig, *Zen and the Art of Motorcycle Maintenance* (1975), p. 121.

[3]   *Poetics* 1448b 14.

[4]   Albert Einstein, "On the Generalized Theory of Gravitation," *Scientific American* 182, April 1950.

Scientific knowledge does not merely give us power to satisfy our practical needs; it is itself a direct satisfaction of a particular desire, the desire to know. It is an end in itself. Some philosophers, to be sure, have denied the second of these values. They have challenged the notion of a purely disinterested desire for knowledge. People have only practical wants, they have said, and science is simply an instrument to be used for the control of nature. There can be no doubt that its utility has profoundly stimulated the development of science. But when the great contributors to scientific progress are consulted about their own motives for research, their answers seldom mention this pragmatic or engineering aspect. Most answers to such questions are like that of Einstein:

> What, then, impels us to devise theory after theory? Why do we devise theories at all? The answer to the latter question is simply: because we enjoy 'comprehending,' i.e., reducing phenomena by the process of logic to something already known or (apparently) evident.[5]

These remarks of Einstein suggest a fruitful conception of the nature of science.

The task of science, as we know, is to discover facts; but a haphazard collection of facts cannot be said to constitute a science. To be sure, some parts of science may focus on this or that particular fact. A geographer, for example, may be interested in the exact configuration of a particular coastline, or a geologist in the rock strata in a particular locality. But in the more advanced sciences, bare descriptive knowledge of this or that particular fact is of little importance. The scientist is eager to search out general truths that particular facts illustrate and for which they are evidence. Isolated facts may be known—in a sense—by direct observation. That a particular released object falls, that this ball moves more slowly down an inclined plane than it did when dropped directly downward, that the tides ebb and flow, all these are matters of fact open to direct inspection. But scientists seek more than a mere record of such phenomena; they strive to *understand* them. To this end they seek to formulate general laws that state the patterns of all such occurrences and the systematic relationships between them. The scientist searches for natural laws that govern particular events and for the fundamental principles that underlie them.

This preliminary exposition of the theoretical aims of science can perhaps be made clearer by means of an example. By careful observation and by applying geometrical reasoning to the data thus collected, the Italian physicist and astronomer Galileo Galilei (1564–1642) succeeded in formulating the laws of falling bodies, which described the behavior of bodies near the earth's surface. At about the same time the German astronomer Johannes Kepler (1571–1630), basing his reasonings on the astronomical data collected by Denmark's Tycho Brahe (1546–1601), formulated the laws of planetary motion describing the elliptical orbits traveled by the planets around the sun. Each of these scientists succeeded in unifying the various phenomena in his own field of investigation by formulating the interrelations between them: Kepler in celestial mechanics, Galileo in terrestrial mechanics. Their discoveries were great

---

[5]   Ibid.

achievements, but they were, after all, separate and isolated. Just as separate particular facts challenge the scientist to unify and explain them by discovering their lawful connections, so a plurality of general laws challenges the scientist to unify and explain *them* by discovering a still more general principle that subsumes the several laws as special cases. In the case of Kepler's and Galileo's laws, this challenge was met by one of the greatest scientific geniuses of all time, Sir Isaac Newton (1642–1727). By his Theory of Gravitation and three Laws of Motion, Newton unified and explained celestial and terrestrial mechanics, showing them to be deducible within the framework of a single more fundamental *theory*.[6] Scientists seek not merely to know what the facts are, but to explain them, and to this end they devise *theories*. To understand exactly what is involved here, we must consider the general nature of explanation itself.

7.2   EXPLANATIONS: SCIENTIFIC AND NONSCIENTIFIC

What Is an Explanation?

In everyday life it is the unusual, startling, or puzzling for which we demand explanations. An office assistant may arrive at work on time every morning without arousing curiosity. But let her come an hour late one day, and her employer will demand an *explanation*. What is wanted when an explanation for something is requested? An example will help to answer this question. The office assistant might reply that she had taken the seven-thirty bus to work as usual, but the bus had been involved in a traffic accident, which entailed considerable delay. In the absence of any other transportation, the assistant had had to wait a full hour for the bus to be repaired. This account probably would be accepted as a satisfactory explanation. It can be so regarded because, from the statements that constitute the explanation, the fact to be explained follows logically and no longer appears puzzling. An explanation is a group of statements or a story from which the thing to be explained can logically be inferred and whose acceptance removes or diminishes its problematic or puzzling character. Of course the inference to the fact to be explained by the explanation might require some "understood" additional premisses.[7] Or the conclusion might follow with probability rather than demonstratively. But, as we remarked in chapter 1, explanation and argument are closely related. They are, in fact, the same process regarded from opposite points of view. Any conclusion that can logically be inferred from a set of (true) premises can be regarded as being explained by them. And given something to be explained, we say that we have found an explanation for it when we have found a set of (true) premises from which it can logically be inferred. As was indicated in our first chapter, "*Q because P*" can express either an argument or an explanation, depending on whether "because" functions as a justification (premiss) indicator or an explanation indicator.[8]

---

[6]   For an interesting account of this progression by a person who was to extend it, see Albert Einstein, "The Mechanics of Newton and Their Influence on the Development of Theoretical Physics," *Ideas and Opinions*, ed. Carl Seelig and trans. Sonja Bargmann (1954), pp. 253–61.

[7]   This complication will be considered further in section 7.6, but for the present it can be ignored.

[8]   See section 1.4.

Of course some proposed explanations are better than others. The chief criterion for evaluating explanations is *relevance*. If the tardy office assistant had offered as explanation for her late arrival the fact that there is a war in Liberia or a famine in Ethiopia, that would have been a poor explanation, or "no explanation at all." Such a story would have had "nothing to do with the case"; it would have been *irrelevant* because from it the fact to be explained *cannot* be inferred. The relevance of a proposed explanation, then, corresponds to the cogency of the argument by which the fact to be explained is inferred from the proposed explanation. Any acceptable explanation must be relevant, but not all stories that are relevant in this sense are acceptable explanations. There are other criteria for deciding the worth or acceptability of proposed explanations.

The most obvious requirement to propose is that the explanation be *true*. In the example involving the office assistant, the crucial part of her explanation was a particular fact, the traffic accident, to which she claimed to be an eyewitness. But the explanations of science are for the most part *general* rather than particular. The keystone of Newtonian Mechanics, for example, is the Law of Universal Gravitation, whose statement is

Every particle of matter in the universe attracts every other particle with a force that is directly proportional to the product of the masses of the particles and inversely proportional to the square of the distance between them.

Newton's law is not directly verifiable in the same way as a bus accident. There is simply no way in which we can inspect *all* particles of matter in the universe and observe that they do attract each other in precisely the way asserted by Newton's Law. Few propositions of science are *directly* verifiable as true. For the most part they concern *unobservable* entities, such as molecules and atoms, electrons and protons, and the like. Many of them concern events that already have taken place. Hence the proposed requirement of truth is not *directly* applicable to most scientific explanations. Before considering more useful criteria for evaluating scientific theories, it will be helpful to compare scientific with nonscientific explanations.

Science is supposed to be concerned with facts, and yet in its further reaches we find it committed to highly speculative notions far removed from the possibility of direct experience. How then are scientific explanations to be distinguished from those that are frankly mythological or superstitious? A nonscientific "explanation" of the regular motions of the planets was the doctrine that each heavenly body was the abode of an "intelligence" or "spirit" that controlled its movement. A certain humorous currency was achieved during World War II by the nonscientific explanation of certain aircraft failures as being due to "gremlins," invisible but mischievous little beings who played pranks on aviators. The role is played today by computer "glitches." The point to note here is that from the point of view of observability and direct verifiability there is no great difference between modern scientific theories and the nonscientific doctrines of mythology or theology. One can no more see or touch a Newtonian "particle," atom, or electron than an "intelligence" or a "gremlin." What, then, is the difference between scientific and nonscientific explanations?

What Makes an Explanation Scientific?

There are two important and closely related differences between the kind of explanation science seeks and the kind superstitions of various sorts provide. The first lies in the attitude taken toward the explanation in question. The typical attitude of one who accepts a nonscientific explanation is *dogmatic.* The nonscientific explanation is regarded as being unquestionably true and beyond all possibility of improvement or correction. During the Middle Ages and the early modern period, the word of Aristotle was the ultimate authority to which scholars appealed for deciding questions of fact. However empirically and openmindedly Aristotle himself may have arrived at his views, they were accepted by some scholastics in a completely different and nonscientific spirit. One of the scholastics to whom Galileo offered his telescope to view the newly discovered moons of Jupiter declined to look, being convinced that none could possibly be seen because no mention of them could be found in Aristotle's treatise on astronomy! Because nonscientific beliefs are absolute, ultimate, and final, within the framework of any such doctrine or dogma there can be no rational method of considering the question of its truth.

The scientist's attitude toward his or her explanations is altogether different. Every explanation in science is put forward tentatively and provisionally. Any proposed explanation is regarded as a hypothesis, more or less probable on the basis of the available facts or relevant evidence. It must be admitted that the scientist's vocabulary is a little misleading on this point. When what was first suggested as a "hypothesis" is confirmed, it is frequently elevated to the position of a "theory." And when, on the basis of a great mass of evidence, it achieves well-nigh universal acceptance, it is promoted to the lofty status of a "law." This terminology is not always strictly adhered to: Newton's discovery is still called the "Law of Gravitation," whereas Einstein's contribution, which supersedes or at least improves on Newton's, is referred to as the "Theory of Relativity." The vocabulary of "hypothesis," "theory," and "law" is unfortunate, because it obscures the important fact that *all* of the general propositions of science are regarded as hypotheses, never as dogmas.

Closely allied with the difference in the way they are regarded is the second and more fundamental difference between scientific and nonscientific explanations or theories: the basis for accepting or rejecting them. Many nonscientific views are mere prejudices that their adherents could scarcely give any reason for holding. Because they are regarded as "certain," however, any challenge or question is likely to be regarded as an affront and met with abuse. If those who accept a nonscientific explanation *can* be persuaded to discuss the basis for its acceptance, there are only a few grounds on which they will attempt to "defend" it. It is true because "we've always believed it" or because "everyone knows it." These all-too-familiar phrases express appeals to tradition or popularity rather than evidence. Or a questioned dogma may be defended on the grounds of revelation or authority. The absolute truth of their religious creeds and the absolute falsehood of all others have been revealed from on high, at various times, to Moses (c. 1392–1272 B.C.), to Paul (?–64), to Mohammed (570–632), to Joseph Smith (1805–44), and to many others. That there are rival traditions, conflicting authorities, and revelations that contradict one another does not seem disturbing to those who have embraced an absolute creed. In general, nonscientific beliefs are held independently of anything we should regard as *evidence* in their favor. Because they are *absolute*, questions of evidence are regarded as having little or no importance.

The case is different in the realm of science. Because every scientific explanation is regarded as a hypothesis, it is regarded as worthy of acceptance *only to the extent that there is evidence for it.*[9] As a hypothesis, the question of its truth or falsehood is open, and there is a continual search for more and more evidence to decide that question. The term "evidence" as used here refers ultimately to experience; *sensible* evidence is the ultimate court of appeal in verifying scientific propositions. Science is *empirical* in holding that sense experience is the *test of truth* for all its pronouncements. Consequently, it is of the essence of a scientific proposition that it be capable of being tested by observation. We shall call this characteristic *empirical testability*.

Direct and Indirect Testing

Some propositions can be tested directly. To decide the truth or falsehood of the proposition that it is now raining outside, we need only glance out the window. To tell whether a traffic light shows green or red, all we have to do is look at it. But the propositions offered by scientists as explanatory hypotheses are not of this type. As indicated above, such general propositions as Newton's Laws or Einstein's Theory are not directly testable in this fashion. They can, however, be tested indirectly. The indirect method of testing the truth of a proposition is familiar to all of us, although we may not be familiar with this name for it. For example, if her employer had been suspicious of the office assistant's explanation for her tardiness, the employer might have checked up on it by telephoning the bus company to find out whether the seven-thirty bus really had had an accident. If the bus company's report checked with the assistant's story, this would serve to dispel the employer's suspicions; whereas if the bus company said that an accident had not occurred, that would probably convince the employer that the office assistant's story was false. This inquiry would constitute an indirect test of the proffered explanation.

The pattern of indirect testing has two parts. First the investigator derives from the hypothesis to be tested one or more other propositions capable of being tested directly. This derivation can be expressed in a hypothetical statement of the form

If hypothesis *H* is true, then (directly testable) proposition *p* is true.

or, more simply,

If *H*, then *p*.

As we saw in section 1.4, a hypothetical statement does not assert that its antecedent (in this case, *H*) is true; nor does it assert that its consequent (*p*) is true. What it asserts

---

[9]   As the Scottish philosopher and historian David Hume put it, "A wise man . . . proportions his belief to the evidence." David Hume, *An Enquiry Concerning Human Understanding*, ed. Eric Steinberg (1977), p. 73 (originally published 1748).

is a relation between them—namely, that the truth of the antecedent *implies* the truth of the consequent. That is, *if* the hypothesis is true, then *p* (a directly testable proposition) is true. Constructing a hypothetical statement is the first step in the process of indirect testing.

The second step is to test the derived proposition, *p*. If, on a direct test, *p* turns out to be false, then by *modus tollens* (see section 3.8) we can conclude that the hypothesis from which *p* was derived (*H*) is false. Formally:

1. If *H,* then *p.*
2. Not *p.*
Therefore,
3. Not *H.*

The hypothetical premiss asserts that *H* implies *p;* but if *p* is false, then so is *H*. This follows with certainty. On the other hand, if, on a direct test, *p* turns out to be true (in which case we say that it is "verified"), the most we can conclude about *H* is that it is *confirmed* or *corroborated*—that is, probably true. We cannot conclude that it is true, for that would commit the fallacy of affirming the consequent (see section 3.8). Formally:

1. If *H,* then *p.*
2. *p.*
Therefore, probably,
3. *H.*

The more one tests a hypothesis without falsifying it, the greater is one's confidence that it is true; but the investigator will never be able to conclude with certainty that it is true.

This account of indirect testing is, alas, oversimplified. The problem is that few hypotheses generate directly testable propositions on their own; almost always, additional premisses are required. The conclusion that the bus company will acknowledge that its seven-thirty bus had an accident does not follow validly from the proposition that the seven-thirty bus had an accident. Additional premisses are needed—for example, that all accidents get reported to the company's office, that the reports are not mislaid or forgotten, and that the company has a policy of acknowledging its accidents. When we conjoin these premisses to the hypothesis, we get the following compound proposition:

> *If* (a) the seven-thirty bus had an accident and (b) all accidents get reported to the company's office and (c) the report is not mislaid or forgotten and (d) the bus company has a policy of acknowledging its accidents, *then* the bus company will acknowledge that its seven-thirty bus had an accident.

The consequent of this hypothetical statement is directly testable. If, when the employer inquires, the company acknowledges that there was an accident, the hypothesis that the bus had an accident is confirmed (though not proved). The inference looks like this:

1. *If* (a) the seven-thirty bus had an accident and (b) all accidents get reported to the company's office and (c) the report is not mislaid or forgotten and (d) the bus company has a policy of acknowledging its accidents, *then* the bus company will acknowledge that its seven-thirty bus had an accident.
2. The bus company acknowledges that its seven-thirty bus had an accident.
Therefore, probably,
3. The seven-thirty bus had an accident, all accidents get reported, etc.

On the other hand, if the bus company does *not* acknowledge that there was an accident, we get a different result:

1. *If* (a) the seven-thirty bus had an accident and (b) all accidents get reported to the company's office and (c) the report is not mislaid or forgotten and (d) the bus company has a policy of acknowledging its accidents, *then* the bus company will acknowledge that its seven-thirty bus had an accident.
2. The bus company does not acknowledge that its seven-thirty bus had an accident.
Therefore,
3. *Either* (i) the seven-thirty bus did not have an accident, (ii) not all accidents get reported to the company's office, (iii) the report was mislaid or forgotten, *or* (iv) the bus company does not have a policy of acknowledging its accidents.

The antecedent of the hypothetical statement is a conjunction, and, as we saw in section 1.4, when one denies a conjunction, one denies at least one of its parts (conjuncts). Since the second premiss denies the consequent of the hypothetical statement, the conclusion denies its conjunctive antecedent. This is an application of *modus tollens*.

So the bus company's failure to acknowledge that an accident occurred would not *prove*, in the sense of *demonstrate*, the office assistant's story (our hypothesis) to be false, for the discrepancy might be due to the falsity of one of the assumptions. The assumptions, however, ordinarily have such a high degree of probability that a negative reply on the part of the bus company would render the office assistant's story doubtful indeed. The most we can say is this: Our confidence in the *truth* of statements (b) through (d) is directly proportional to our confidence in the *falsity* of statement (a) (the hypothesis). The greater our confidence that all accidents get reported, that the report has not been mislaid, that the bus company acknowledges its accidents, and so on, the greater is our confidence that the seven-thirty bus did not have an accident.

It must be admitted that every proposition, scientific or nonscientific, that is a relevant explanation for any observable fact has *some* evidence in its favor, namely, the fact to which it is relevant. Thus the regular motions of the planets must be conceded to constitute evidence for the (nonscientific) theory that the planets are inhabited by "intelligences" that cause them to move in just the orbits that are observed. The motions themselves are as much evidence for that proposition as they are for Newton's or Einstein's theories. The difference lies in the fact that is the *only* evidence for the nonscientific hypothesis. No other directly testable propositions can be inferred from it. On the other hand, a large number of directly testable propositions can be deduced from the scientific explanations mentioned. Here, then, is *the* difference between scientific and nonscientific explanations. A scientific explanation for a given fact will have directly testable propositions deducible from it, in addition to the one stating the fact to be explained. But a nonscientific explanation will have no other directly testable propositions deducible from it. In other words, it is of the essence of a scientific explanation or hypothesis to be empirically testable.

It is clear that we have been using the term "scientific explanation" in a general sense. As here defined, an explanation may be scientific even though it is not part of one of the various special sciences such as physics, biology, or psychology. Thus the office assistant's explanation of her tardiness would be classified as a scientific one, for it is empirically testable, even if only indirectly. But had she offered as explanation the proposition, "God willed me to be late this morning, and God is omnipotent," the explanation would have been nonscientific. For although her being late that morning is deducible from the proferred explanation, no other directly testable proposition is, so the explanation is not empirically testable.

EXERCISE

Criticize the following letter to the editor in light of the discussion in the preceding section:

I see no objection to including evolution as a scientific theory, but for consistency, it should also be treated by the scientific method that requires conclusive proof before a theory can advance to credibility. If the scientists religiously apply this method, they might even conclude that *The Link* is missing because it never existed. But is truth what they really seek?

—ROBERT A. ROWLAND, letter to the editor, *The Dallas Morning News*, 22 July 1990

7.3 EVALUATING SCIENTIFIC EXPLANATIONS

The question naturally arises as to how scientific explanations are to be evaluated—that is, judged as good or bad, or at least as better or worse. This question is especially important because there often is more than a single scientific explanation for one and the same fact. A person's abrupt behavior may be explained either by the hypothesis that the person is shy or by the hypothesis that the person is unfriendly. In a criminal investigation, two different and incompatible hypotheses about the identity of the criminal may equally well account for the known facts. In the realm of science proper, the fact that an object expands when heated is explained by both the caloric theory of heat and the kinetic theory. The caloric theory regarded heat as an invisible weightless fluid, called "caloric," with the power of penetrating, expanding, and dissolving bodies or dissipating them in vapor. The kinetic theory, on the other hand, regards the heat of a body as consisting of random motions of the molecules of which the body is composed. These are *alternative* scientific explanations that serve equally well to explain some of the phenomena of thermal expansion. They cannot both be true, however, and the problem is to evaluate or choose between them.

What is wanted here is a list of conditions that a good explanatory hypothesis can be expected to fulfill. It must not be thought that such a list of conditions will provide a *recipe* by means of which anyone at all can construct good hypotheses. No one has ever pretended to lay down a set of rules for the invention or discovery of hypotheses. It is likely that none could ever be laid down, for that is the *creative* side of the scientific enterprise—the art of science, if you will. Ability to create is a function of imagination and talent and cannot be reduced to a mechanical process. A great scientific hypothesis with wide explanatory powers, like those of Newton or Einstein, is as much the product of genius as a great work of art. There is no formula for discovering new hypotheses, but there are certain rules to which acceptable hypotheses can be expected to conform. These can be regarded as the criteria for evaluating hypotheses.

There are four criteria commonly used in judging the worth or acceptability of a scientific hypothesis. They may be listed as (1) relevance, (2) compatibility with previously well-established hypotheses, (3) predictive or explanatory power, and (4) simplicity. The first criterion, relevance, already has been discussed (in section 7.2), but we shall review it briefly here.

Relevance

No hypothesis is ever proposed for its own sake but is always intended as an explanation of some fact or other. Therefore it must be *relevant* to the fact it is intended to explain; that is, the fact in question must be *deducible* from the proposed hypothesis— either from the hypothesis alone; or from it together with certain causal laws that may be presumed to have already been established as highly probable; or from these together with certain assumptions about particular initial conditions. A hypothesis that is not relevant to the fact it is intended to explain simply fails to explain it and can only be regarded as having failed to fulfill its intended function. A good hypothesis must be *relevant*.

Compatibility with Previously Well-Established Hypotheses

The requirement that an acceptable hypothesis be compatible or consistent with other hypotheses that have been well confirmed is eminently reasonable. Science, in seeking to encompass more and more facts, aims at achieving a *system* of explanatory hypotheses. Of course, such a system must be self-consistent, for no self-contradictory set of propositions could possibly be true—or even intelligible. Ideally, the way in which scientists hope to make progress is by gradually expanding their hypotheses to comprehend more and more facts. For such progress to be made, each new hypothesis must be consistent with those already confirmed. Thus Urbain Leverrier's (1811–77) hypothesis that there was an additional but not yet charted planet beyond the orbit of Uranus was perfectly consistent with the main body of accepted astronomical theory. A new theory must fit with older theories if there is to be orderly progress in scientific inquiry.

It is possible, of course, to overestimate the importance of the second criterion. Although the ideal of science may be the gradual growth of theoretical knowledge by the addition of one new hypothesis after another, the actual history of scientific progress has not always followed that pattern. Many of the most important new hypotheses have been inconsistent with older theories and have in fact replaced them rather than fitted in with them. Einstein's Relativity Theory was of that sort, shattering many of the preconceptions of the older Newtonian theory. The phenomenon of radioactivity, first observed during the last decade of the nineteenth century, led to the overthrow—or at least the modification—of many cherished theories that had almost achieved the status of absolutes. One of these was the Principle of the Conservation of Matter, which asserted that matter could neither be created nor destroyed. The hypothesis that radium atoms undergo spontaneous disintegration was inconsistent with that old, established principle—but it was the principle that was relinquished in favor of the newer hypothesis. Considerations such as these led Thomas Kuhn (1922–   ), an influential historian and philosopher of science, to conclude that

> Cumulative acquisition of unanticipated novelties proves to be an almost nonexistent exception to the rule of scientific development. The [person] who takes historic fact seriously must suspect that science does not tend toward the ideal that our image of its cumulativeness has suggested. Perhaps it is another sort of enterprise.[10]

The foregoing is not intended to give the impression that scientific progress is a helter-skelter process in which theories are abandoned right and left in favor of newer, shinier ones. Older theories are not so much abandoned as corrected. Einstein himself always insisted that his own work was a modification rather than a rejection of Newton's.[11] The Principle of the Conservation of Matter was modified by being absorbed into the more comprehensive Principle of the Conservation of Mass-Energy. Every established theory has been established through having proved adequate to explain a considerable mass of data, of observed facts. And it cannot be dethroned or discredited by any new hypothesis unless that new hypothesis can account for the same facts as well or better. There is nothing capricious about the development of science. Every change represents an improvement, a more comprehensive and thus more adequate explanation of the way in which the world manifests itself in our experience. Where inconsistencies occur between hypotheses, the greater age of one does not automatically prove it to be correct and the newer one wrong. The *presumption* is in favor of the older one if it already has been extensively confirmed. But if the new one in conflict with it *also* receives extensive confirmation, considerations of age or priority are irrelevant. Where there is a conflict between two hypotheses, we must turn to the observable facts to decide between them. Ultimately our last

---

[10]   Thomas S. Kuhn, *The Structure of Scientific Revolutions* (1962), p. 95.

[11]   See, e.g., Albert Einstein, *Ideas and Opinions*, ed. Carl Seelig and trans. Sonja Bargmann (1954), pp. 231, 232, 260. According to Einstein, "The whole evolution of our ideas about the processes of nature, with which we have been concerned so far, might be regarded as an organic development of Newton's ideas." Ibid., p. 261.

court of appeal in deciding between rival hypotheses is experience. What our second criterion, compatibility with previous well-established hypotheses, comes to is this: The totality of hypotheses accepted at any time should be consistent with each other,[12] and—other things being equal—of two new hypotheses, the one which fits in better with the accepted body of scientific theory is to be preferred. The question of what is involved in "other things being equal" takes us directly to our third criterion.

Predictive or Explanatory Power

The predictive or explanatory power of a hypothesis is the range of observable facts that can be derived from it. If one of two testable hypotheses has a greater number of observable facts derivable from it than from the other, it is said to have greater predictive or explanatory power. Thus, Newton's hypothesis of universal gravitation joined together with his three laws of motion had greater predictive power than either Kepler's or Galileo's hypotheses, because all observable consequences of the latter two also were consequences of the former, and the former had many more besides. An observable fact that can be derived from a given hypothesis is said to be explained by it and also can be said to be *predicted* by it. The greater the predictive power of a hypothesis, the more it explains and the better it contributes to our understanding of the phenomena with which it is concerned.

Our third criterion has a negative side that is crucially important. If a hypothesis is inconsistent with any well-attested fact of observation, the hypothesis is false and must be rejected. This was the lesson of section 7.2. Where two hypotheses are relevant to explaining some set of facts and both are testable, and both are compatible with the whole body of already established scientific theory, it may be possible to choose between them by deriving from them incompatible propositions that are directly testable. If H_1 and H_2, two different hypotheses, entail incompatible consequences, it may be possible to set up a *crucial experiment* to decide between them. Thus if H_1 entails that under circumstance C phenomenon P will occur, whereas H_2 entails that under circumstance C phenomenon P will *not* occur, then all we need do to decide between H_1 and H_2 is to produce circumstance C and observe the presence or absence of phenomenon P. If P occurs, this is evidence for H_1 and *against* H_2, whereas if P does not occur, that is evidence against H_1 and for H_2.

This kind of crucial experiment to decide between rival hypotheses may not always be easy to carry out, for the required circumstance C may be difficult or impossible to produce. Thus the decision between Newtonian Theory and Einstein's General Theory of Relativity had to await a total eclipse of the sun—a situation or circumstance clearly beyond our power to produce. In other cases the crucial experiment may have to await the development of new instruments, either for the production of the

---

[12] Scientists may, however, consider and even use inconsistent hypotheses for years while awaiting the resolution of that inconsistency. This is the case today with respect to the wave and the corpuscular theories of light.

required *circumstances* or for the observation or measurement of the predicted phenomenon. Thus proponents of rival astronomical hypotheses must often bide their time while they await the construction of new and more powerful telescopes. That is why the scientific community was so excited by deployment of the Hubble Space Telescope in 1990 (and why it was so disappointed by the telescope's failure to operate as planned). The Hubble telescope permits astronomers to view space from beyond the distortions of the Earth's atmosphere. The topic of crucial experiments will be discussed further in section 7.6.

Simplicity

It sometimes happens that two rival hypotheses satisfy the first three criteria equally well. Historically the most important pair of such hypotheses were those of Ptolemy (c. 90–168) and Nikolaus Copernicus (1473–1543). Both were intended to explain all of the then known data of astronomy. According to the Ptolemaic or geocentric theory, the earth is the center of the universe, and the heavenly bodies move about it in orbits that require a very complicated geometry of epicycles to describe. Ptolemy's theory was relevant and compatible with previously well-established hypotheses, satisfying the first two criteria perfectly. According to the Copernican or heliocentric theory, the sun rather than the earth is at the center, and the earth itself moves around the sun along with the other planets. Copernicus's theory, too, satisfied the first two criteria perfectly. With respect to the third criterion, that of predictive power, there was not a great deal of difference between the two theories. (In the early years of their rivalry, optical instruments were still very crude.) But with respect to the fourth criterion there was a significant difference between the two hypotheses. Although both used the clumsy method of epicycles to account for the observed positions of the various heavenly bodies, fewer such epicycles were required within the Copernican theory. The Copernican system was therefore simpler, and this contributed greatly to its acceptance by all later astronomers.

The criterion of simplicity is a perfectly natural one to invoke. In ordinary life as well as in science, the simplest theory that fits all the available facts is the one we tend to accept. In criminal trials, the prosecutor attempts to develop a hypothesis that includes the guilt of the accused and fits in with all the available evidence. Opposing the prosecuting attorney, the defense attorney may try to set up a hypothesis that includes the innocence of the accused and also fits all the available evidence. Often both sides succeed, and then the case usually is decided—or *ought* to be decided—in favor of the hypothesis that is simpler or more "natural." Simplicity, however, is a very difficult term to define. Not all controversies are as straightforward as the Ptolemaic–Copernican one, in which the latter's greater simplicity consisted merely in requiring a smaller number of epicycles. And, of course, "naturalness" is an almost hopelessly deceptive term—for it seems much more "natural" to believe that the earth is still while the apparently moving sun really does move. The fourth and last criterion, simplicity, is an important and frequently decisive one, but it is difficult to formulate and not always easy to apply.

7.4   THE DETECTIVE AS SCIENTIST

Now that we have stated and discussed the criteria by which hypotheses are evaluated, we are in a position to describe the general pattern of scientific research. It will be helpful to begin by examining an illustration of that method. A perennial favorite in this connection is the detective, whose problem is not quite the same as that of the pure scientist, but whose approach and technique illustrate the method of science very clearly. The classical example of the astute detective who can solve even the most baffling mystery is Arthur Conan Doyle's (1859–1930) immortal creation, Sherlock Holmes. Holmes, his stature undiminished by the passage of time, will be our hero in the following account.

The Problem

Some of our most vivid pictures of Holmes are those in which he is busy with magnifying glass and tape measure, searching out and finding essential clues that had escaped the attention of those stupid bunglers, the "experts" of Scotland Yard. Or those of us who are by temperament less vigorous may think back more fondly on Holmes the thinker,

> . . . who, when he had an unsolved problem upon his mind, would go for days, and even for a week, without rest, turning it over, rearranging his facts, looking at it from every point of view until he had either fathomed it or convinced himself that his data were insufficient.[13]

At one such time, according to Dr. Watson,

> He took off his coat and waistcoat, put on a large blue dressing-gown, and then wandered about the room collecting pillows from his bed and cushions from the sofa and armchairs. With these he constructed a sort of Eastern divan, upon which he perched himself cross-legged, with an ounce of shag tobacco and a box of matches laid out in front of him. In the dim light of the lamp I saw him sitting there, an old briar pipe between his lips, his eyes fixed vacantly upon the corner of the ceiling, the blue smoke curling up from him, silent, motionless, with the light shining upon his strong-set aquiline features. So he sat as I dropped off to sleep, and so he sat when a sudden ejaculation caused me to wake up, and I found the summer sun shining into the apartment. The pipe was still between his lips, the smoke still curled upward, and the room was full of a dense tobacco haze, but nothing remained of the heap of shag which I had seen upon the previous night.[14]

But such memories are incomplete. Holmes was not always searching for clues or pondering solutions. We all remember those dark periods—especially in the earlier stories—when, much to the good Watson's annoyance, Holmes would drug himself with

---

[13]   *The Man with the Twisted Lip.*

[14]   Ibid.

morphine or cocaine. That would happen, of course, between cases. For when there is no mystery to be unraveled, nobody in his right mind would go out to look for clues. Clues, after all, must be clues *for* something. Nor could Holmes, or anyone else, for that matter, engage in profound thought unless he had something to think about. Sherlock Holmes was a genius at solving problems, but even a genius must have a problem before he can solve it. All reflective thinking, and this term includes criminal investigation as well as scientific research, is a problem-solving activity, as John Dewey and other pragmatists have rightly insisted. There must be a problem felt before either the detective or the scientist can go to work.

Of course, the active mind sees problems where the dullard sees only familiar objects.[15] One Christmas season Dr. Watson visited Holmes to find that the latter had been using a lens and forceps to examine

> . . . a very seedy and disreputable hard-felt hat, much the worse for wear, and cracked in several places.[16]

After they had greeted each other, Holmes said of it to Watson,

> I beg that you will look upon it not as a battered billycock but as an intellectual problem.[17]

It so happened that the hat led them into one of their most interesting adventures, but it could not have done so had Holmes not seen a problem in it from the start. A *problem* may be characterized as a fact or group of facts for which we have no acceptable explanation, which seem unusual, or which fail to fit in with our expectations or preconceptions. It should be obvious that *some* prior beliefs are required if anything is to appear problematic. If there are no expectations, there can be no surprises.

Sometimes, of course, problems came to Holmes already labeled. The very first adventure recounted by Dr. Watson began with the following message from Gregson of Scotland Yard:

> My Dear Mr. Sherlock Holmes:
>
> There has been a bad business during the night at 3, Lauriston Gardens, off the Brixton Road. Our man on the beat saw a light there about two in the morning, and as the house was an empty one, suspected that something was amiss. He found the door open, and in the front room, which is bare of furniture, discovered the body of a gentleman, well dressed, and having cards in his pocket bearing the name of "Enoch J. Drebber, Cleveland, Ohio, USA." There had been no robbery, nor is there any evidence as to how the man met his death. There are marks of blood in the room, but there is no wound upon his person. We are at a loss as to how he came into the empty house; indeed, the whole affair is a puzzler. If you can come round to the house any

---

[15]   Another way to put this is that puzzlement is *relative*. What puzzles a scientist (for example) may not puzzle a layperson.
[16]   *The Adventure of the Blue Carbuncle.*
[17]   Ibid.

time before twelve, you will find me there. I have left everything *in statu quo* until I hear from you. If you are unable to come, I shall give you fuller details, and would esteem it a great kindness if you would favour me with your opinion.
Yours faithfully,
Tobias Gregson[18]

Here was a problem indeed. A few minutes after receiving the message, Sherlock Holmes and Dr. Watson

were both in a hansom, driving furiously for the Brixton Road.

Preliminary Hypotheses

On their ride out Brixton way, Holmes

prattled away about Cremona fiddles and the difference between a Stradivarius and an Amati.

Dr. Watson chided Holmes for not giving much thought to the matter at hand, and Holmes replied:

No data yet. . . . It is a capital mistake to theorize before you have all the evidence. It biases the judgment.[19]

This point of view was expressed by Holmes again and again. On one occasion he admonished a younger detective that

The temptation to form premature theories upon insufficient data is the bane of our profession.[20]

Yet for all of his confidence about the matter, on this one issue Holmes was mistaken. Of course one should not reach a *final judgment* until a great deal of evidence has been considered, but this procedure is quite different from *not theorizing*. As a matter of fact, it is impossible to make any serious attempt to collect evidence unless one *has* theorized beforehand. As Charles Darwin (1809–82), the great biologist and author of the modern theory of evolution, observed,

. . . all observation must be for or against some view, if it is to be of any service.

The point is that there are too many particular facts, too many data in the world, for anyone to try to become acquainted with them all. Everyone, even the most patient and thorough investigator, must pick and choose, deciding which facts to study and which to pass over. One must have some preliminary or working hypothesis for or

---

[18]   *A Study in Scarlet.*
[19]   Ibid.
[20]   *The Valley of Fear.*

against which to collect relevant data. It need not be a *complete* theory, but at least the rough outline must be there. Otherwise how could one decide what facts to select for consideration out of the totality of all facts, which is too vast even to begin to sift?

Holmes's actions were wiser than his words in this connection. After all, the words were spoken in a hansom speeding toward the scene of the crime. If Holmes really had no theory about the matter, why go to Brixton Road? If facts and data were all that he wanted, any old facts and any old data, with no hypotheses to guide him in their selection, why should he have left Baker Street at all? There were plenty of facts in the rooms at 221-B Baker Street. Holmes might just as well have spent his time counting all the words on all the pages of all the books there, or perhaps making very accurate measurements of the distances between each pair of articles of furniture in the house. He could have gathered data to his heart's content and saved himself cab fare into the bargain!

It may be objected that the facts to be gathered at Baker Street have nothing to do with the case, whereas those awaiting Holmes at the scene of the crime were valuable clues for solving the problem. It was, of course, just this consideration that led Holmes to ignore the "data" at Baker Street and hurry away to collect those off Brixton Road. It must be insisted, however, that the relevance of the latter could not be *known* beforehand but only conjectured on the basis of previous experience with crimes and clues. It was in fact a *hypothesis* that led Holmes to look in one place rather than another for his facts, the hypothesis that there was a murder, that the crime was committed at the place where the body was found, and that the perpetrator had left some trace or clue. Some such hypothesis is *always* needed to guide an investigator in the search for relevant data, for in the absence of any preliminary hypothesis, there are simply too many facts in this world to examine. The preliminary hypothesis ought to be highly tentative, and it must be based on previous knowledge. But a preliminary hypothesis is as necessary as the existence of a problem for any serious inquiry to begin.

It must be emphasized that a preliminary hypothesis, as here conceived, need not be a complete solution to the problem. The hypothesis that the man was murdered by someone who had left some clues to his identity on or near the body of the victim was what led Holmes to Brixton Road. This hypothesis is clearly incomplete: It does not say who committed the crime, or how it was done, or why. Such a preliminary hypothesis may be very different from the final solution to the problem. It will never be complete: It may be a tentative explanation of only part of the problem. But however partial and however tentative, a preliminary hypothesis is required for any investigation to proceed.

Collecting Additional Facts

Every serious investigation begins with some fact or group of facts that strikes the investigator as problematic and thus initiates the whole process of inquiry. The initial facts that constitute the problem usually are too meager to suggest a wholly satisfactory explanation for themselves, but they will suggest—to the competent investigator—some preliminary hypotheses that lead to the search for additional facts. These additional facts, it is hoped, will serve as clues to the final solution. The inexperienced or bungling investigator will overlook or ignore all but the most obvious of them, but the careful worker will aim at completeness in the examination of those additional facts to which the preliminary hypotheses led. Holmes, of course, was the most careful and painstaking of investigators. He insisted on dismounting from the hansom a hundred yards or so from his destination and approached the house on foot, looking carefully at its surroundings and especially at the pathway leading up to it. When Holmes and Watson entered the house, they were shown the body by the two Scotland Yard operatives, Gregson and Lestrade.

> "There is no clue," said Gregson. "None at all," chimed in Lestrade.

But Holmes had already started his own search for additional facts, looking first at the body:

> . . . his nimble fingers were flying here, there, and everywhere, feeling, pressing, unbuttoning, examining. . . . So swiftly was the examination made, that one would hardly have guessed the minuteness with which it was conducted. Finally, he sniffed the dead man's lips, and then glanced at the soles of his patent leather boots.[21]

Turning his attention to the room itself,

> . . . he whipped a tape measure and a large round magnifying glass from his pocket. With these two implements he trotted noiselessly about the room, sometimes stopping, occasionally kneeling, and once lying flat upon his face. So engrossed was he with his occupation that he appeared to have forgotten our presence, for he chattered away to himself under his breath the whole time, keeping up a running fire of exclamations, groans, whistles and little cries suggestive of encouragement and of hope. As I watched him I was irresistibly reminded of a pure-blooded, well-trained foxhound as it dashes backward and forward through the covert, whining in its eagerness, until it comes across the lost scent. For twenty minutes or more he continued his researches, measuring with the most exact care the distance between marks which were entirely invisible to me, and occasionally applying his tape to the walls in an equally incomprehensible manner. In one place he gathered up very carefully a little pile of gray dust from the floor and packed it away in an envelope. Finally he examined with his glass the word upon the wall, going over every letter of it, with the most minute exactness. This done, he appeared to be satisfied, for he replaced his tape and his glass in his pocket.
> "They say that genius is an infinite capacity for taking pains," he remarked with a smile. "It's a very bad definition, but it does apply to detective work."[22]

One matter deserves to be emphasized very strongly. Steps 2 and 3 are not completely separable but usually are intimately connected and interdependent. True enough, we require a preliminary hypothesis to begin any intelligent examination of facts, but the additional facts may themselves suggest new hypotheses, which may lead to new facts, which suggest still other hypotheses, which lead to still other additional facts, and so on. Thus, having made his careful examination of the facts available in the house off Brixton Road, Holmes was led to formulate a further hypothesis, which

---

[21]   *A Study in Scarlet.*
[22]   Ibid.

required the taking of testimony from the constable who found the body. The man was off duty at the moment, and Lestrade gave Holmes the constable's name and address.

> Holmes took a note of the address.
> "Come along, Doctor," he said: "we shall go and look him up. I'll tell you one thing which may help you in the case," he continued, turning to the two detectives. "There has been murder done, and the murderer was a man. He was more than six feet high, was in the prime of life, had small feet for his height, wore coarse, square-toed boots and smoked a Trichinopoly cigar. He came here with his victim in a four-wheeled cab, which was drawn by a horse with three old shoes and one new one on his off fore-leg. In all probability the murderer had a florid face, and the fingernails of his right hand were remarkably long. These are only a few indications, but they may assist you."
> Lestrade and Gregson glanced at each other with an incredulous smile.
> "If this man was murdered, how was it done?" asked the former.
> "Poison," said Sherlock Holmes curtly, and strode off.[23]

Formulating the Hypothesis

In any investigation the stage will be reached, sooner or later, at which the investigator—whether detective, scientist, or layperson—will begin to feel that all the facts needed for solving the problem are at hand. The investigator has the "2 and 2," so to speak, but the task still remains of "putting them together." At such a time Sherlock Holmes might sit up all night, consuming pipe after pipe of tobacco, trying to think things through. The result or end product of such thinking, if it is successful, is a hypothesis that accounts for all the data, both the original set of facts that constituted the problem and the additional facts to which the preliminary hypotheses pointed. The actual discovery of such an explanatory hypothesis is a process of creation, in which imagination as well as knowledge is involved. Holmes, who was a genius at inventing hypotheses, described the process as reasoning "backward." As he put it,

> Most people if you describe a train of events to them, will tell you what the result would be. They can put those events together in their minds, and argue from them that something will come to pass. There are few people, however, who, if you told them a result, would be able to evolve from their own inner consciousness what the steps were which led up to that result.[24]

Here is Holmes's description of the process of formulating an explanatory hypothesis. Whether his account is right or wrong, when a hypothesis has been proposed, its evaluation must be along the lines that were sketched in section 7.3. Granted its relevance and its compatibility with other well-attested beliefs, the ultimate criterion for evaluating a hypothesis is its predictive power. As a more recent writer put it,

> The formation of hypotheses is the most mysterious of all the categories of scientific method. Where they come from, no one knows. A person is sitting somewhere, mind-

---

[23] Ibid.
[24] Ibid.

ing his own business, and suddenly—flash!—he understands something he didn't understand before. Until it's tested the hypothesis isn't truth. For the tests aren't its source. Its source is somewhere else.[25]

Deriving Further Consequences

A really fruitful hypothesis will explain not only the facts that inspired it, but many others in addition. A good hypothesis will point beyond the initial facts in the direction of new ones whose existence might otherwise not have been suspected. And of course the verification of those further consequences will confirm the hypothesis that led to them. Holmes's hypothesis that the murdered man had been poisoned was soon put to such a test. A few days later the murdered man's secretary and traveling companion was also found murdered. Holmes asked Lestrade, who had discovered the second body, whether he had found anything in the room that could furnish a clue to the murderer. Lestrade answered, "Nothing," and went on to mention a few quite ordinary effects. Holmes was not satisfied and pressed him, asking, "And was there nothing else?" Lestrade answered, "Nothing of any importance," and named a few more details, the last of which was

> "a small chip ointment box containing a couple of pills."

At this information,

> Sherlock Holmes sprang from his chair with an exclamation of delight.
> "The last link," he cried, exultantly. "My case is complete." The two detectives stared at him in amazement.
> "I have now in my hands," my companion said, confidently, "all the threads which have formed such a tangle. . . . I will give you a proof of my knowledge. Could you lay your hands upon those pills?"
> "I have them," said Lestrade, producing a small white box. . . .[26]

On the basis of his hypothesis about the original crime, Holmes was led to predict that the pills found at the scene of the second crime must contain poison. Here deduction has an essential role in the process of any scientific or inductive inquiry. The ultimate value of any hypothesis lies in its predictive or explanatory power, which means that additional facts must be deducible from an adequate hypothesis. From his theory that the first man was poisoned and that the second victim met his death at the hands of the same murderer, Holmes inferred that the pills found by Lestrade must be poison. His theory, however sure he may have felt about it, was only a theory and needed further confirmation. He obtained that confirmation by testing the consequences deduced from the hypothesis and finding them to be true. Having used an inference to make a prediction, his next step was to test it.

---

[25] Pirsig, op. cit.
[26] *A Study in Scarlet.*

Testing the Consequences

The consequences of a hypothesis, that is, the predictions made on the basis of that hypothesis, may require various means for their testing. Some require only observation. In some cases, Holmes needed only to watch and wait—for the bank robbers to break into the vault in *The Adventure of the Red-Headed League,* or for Dr. Roylott to slip a venomous snake through a dummy ventilator in *The Adventure of the Speckled Band.* In the present case, however, an experiment had to be performed.

Holmes asked Dr. Watson to fetch the landlady's old and ailing terrier, which she had asked to have put out of its misery the day before. Holmes then cut one of the pills in two, dissolved it in a wineglass of water, added some milk, and

> . . . turned the contents of the wineglass into a saucer and placed it in front of the terrier, who speedily licked it dry. Sherlock Holmes's earnest demeanor had so far convinced us that we all sat in silence, watching the animal intently, and expecting some startling effect. None such appeared, however. The dog continued to lie stretched upon the cushion, breathing in a laboured way, but apparently neither the better nor the worse for its draught.
>
> Holmes had taken out his watch, and as minute followed minute without result, an expression of the utmost chagrin and disappointment appeared upon his features. He gnawed his lip, drummed his fingers upon the table, and showed every other symptom of acute impatience. So great was his emotion that I felt sincerely sorry for him, while the two detectives smiled derisively, by no means displeased at this check which he had met.
>
> "It can't be a coincidence," he cried, at last springing from his chair and pacing wildly up and down the room: "it is impossible that it should be a mere coincidence. The very pills which I suspected in the case of Drebber are actually found after the death of Stangerson. And yet they are inert. What can it mean? Surely my whole chain of reasoning cannot have been false. It is impossible! And yet this wretched dog is none the worse. Ah, I have it! I have it!" With a perfect shriek of delight he rushed to the box, cut the other pill in two, dissolved it, added milk, and presented it to the terrier. The unfortunate creature's tongue seemed hardly to have been moistened in it before it gave a convulsive shiver in every limb, and lay as rigid and lifeless as if it had been struck by lightning.
>
> Sherlock Holmes drew a long breath, and wiped the perspiration from his forehead.[27]

By the favorable outcome of his experiment Holmes's hypothesis had received dramatic and convincing confirmation.

Application

The detective's concern, after all, is a practical one. Given a crime to solve, he or she has not merely to explain the facts but to apprehend and arrest the criminal. The latter involves applying the theory, and using it to predict where the criminal can be found and how he or she may be caught. The detective must deduce still further consequences from the hypothesis, not for the sake of additional confirmation but for

---

[27] Ibid.

practical use. From his general hypothesis Holmes was able to infer that the murderer was acting the role of a cabman. We already have seen that Holmes had formed a pretty clear description of the man's appearance. He sent out his army of "Baker Street Irregulars," street urchins of the neighborhood, to search out and summon the cab driven by that man. The successful "application" of this hypothesis can be described again in Dr. Watson's words. A few minutes after the terrier's death,

> . . . there was a tap at the door, and the spokesman of the street Arabs, young Wiggins, introduced his insignificant and unsavoury person.
>
> "Please, sir," he said touching his forelock, "I have the cab downstairs."
>
> "Good boy," said Holmes, blandly. "Why don't you introduce this pattern at Scotland Yard?" he continued, taking a pair of steel handcuffs from a drawer. "See how beautifully the spring works. They fasten in an instant."
>
> "The old pattern is good enough," remarked Lestrade, "if we can only find the man to put them on."
>
> "Very good, very good," said Holmes, smiling. "The cabman may as well help me with my boxes. Just ask him to step in, Wiggins."
>
> I was surprised to find my companion speaking as though he were about to set out on a journey, since he had not said anything to me about it. There was a small portmanteau in the room, and this he pulled out and began to strap. He was busily engaged at it when the cabman entered the room.
>
> "Just give me a help with this buckle, cabman," he said, kneeling over his task, and never turning his head.
>
> The fellow came forward with a somewhat sullen, defiant air, and put down his hands to assist. At that instant there was a sharp click, the jangling of metal, and Sherlock Holmes sprang to his feet again.
>
> "Gentlemen," he cried, with flashing eyes, "let me introduce you to Mr. Jefferson Hope, the murderer of Enoch Drebber and of Joseph Stangerson."[28]

Here we have a picture of the detective as scientist, reasoning from observed facts to a testable hypothesis that not only explains the facts but also permits a practical application.

7.5 SCIENTISTS IN ACTION: THE PATTERN OF SCIENTIFIC INVESTIGATION

As the term "scientific" is generally used today, it refers to any reasoning that attempts to proceed from observable facts of experience to reasonable (that is, relevant and testable) explanations for those facts. The scientific method is not confined to professional scientists: Anyone can be said to be proceeding scientifically who follows the general pattern of reasoning from evidence to conclusions that can be tested by experience. The skilled detective is a scientist in this sense, as are most of us—in our more rational moments, at least. The pervasive pattern of scientific inquiry is expressible in terms of the steps illustrated in the preceding section.

---

[28] Ibid.

Those seven steps will be explained further by analyzing an important example of scientific research.[29] During the eighteenth century, the caloric theory of heat had become widely accepted. Heat was believed to be a subtle, highly elastic fluid that could be added to or extracted from a body, thereby causing temperature changes in it. The hypothesized fluid was supposed to be indestructible; its particles were thought to be self-repellent but attracted by ordinary matter; and it was alleged to be ubiquitous. The caloric theory of heat had considerable explanatory power. The expansion of bodies when heated was explained as the natural result of "swelling" caused by the heat fluid being forced into its pores. The production of heat by pounding on a body was explained as being due to the releasing or "jarring loose" of some of the caloric that had been condensed in the body, so that pounding increased the amount of free caloric heat in it. Even the conversion of fuel to power in the early steam engine could be explained on the caloric theory; a given quantity of caloric "falling" from a higher to a lower temperature was analogous to a given quantity of water falling from a higher to a lower level; each was capable of producing mechanical power. By the end of the eighteenth century, the caloric theory of heat as a material substance was generally accepted.

It was against this background that Count von Rumford (Benjamin Thompson) (1753–1814) encountered the problem that guided much of his subsequent research. Rumford described the beginning in these words:

> Being engaged, lately, in superintending the boring of cannon, in the workshops of the military arsenal at Munich, I was struck with the very considerable degree of heat which a brass gun acquires, in a short time, in being bored; and with the still more intense heat (much greater than that of boiling water, as I found by experiment) of the metallic chips separated from it by the borer.
>   The more I meditated on these phaenomena, the more they appeared to me to be curious and interesting.[30]

Here we have the first step in any inquiry: A problem is felt; someone is puzzled. It should be noted that in this case the problem arose from an apparent conflict between the data of experience and accepted scientific theories. The relevant theories were two: first, the caloric theory, which asserted heat to be a material substance; and second, the principle of the conservation of matter, which asserted that material substance could be neither created nor destroyed. The observed fact, on the other hand, was that considerable amounts of heat were produced—without any apparent decrease in the amounts of any other material substances. The production of as much heat as Rumford observed was inexplicable on the basis of the science of his day. The situation was problematic and demanded a solution. It should be clear that the problem would not be felt by someone who was ignorant of the accepted theories. Nor would it be felt by an unobservant individual who took no notice of the facts. Finally, it would not be felt by someone whose mind was not disturbed by gaps or inconsistencies between theory and observation. It may be remarked, then, that the requisite

[29]   The following is freely adapted from F.K. Richtmyer, *Introduction to Modern Physics* (1934).
[30]   Quoted in William Francis Magie, *A Source Book in Physics* (1935).

qualities a person must have to initiate any fruitful inquiry are three: One must be familiar with current theories, observant of new facts, and uncomfortable in the presence of a conflict or gap between fact and theory.

Judging from the experiments he was led to perform, it seems reasonable to suppose that Count Rumford's preliminary hypothesis was something like the following. Because considerable heat was generated without appreciable diminution of other material substances present, perhaps it might be possible to obtain *unlimited* amounts of heat without exhausting the supply of matter at hand. This conjecture was suggested by the original data that posed the problem. Helpful in setting up an experiment to test this hypothesis, or to collect data suggested by it, was Rumford's knowledge that boring with dull tools generates more heat than is obtained by using sharp ones.

On the basis of this knowledge, and being guided by the preliminary hypothesis mentioned, Rumford went about collecting additional relevant data, which he procured by the following experimental setup. He caused a blunt steel boring tool to rotate, under great pressure, against a piece of brass while both were immersed in water. The apparatus was powered by two horses. In just two and one half hours the water boiled, a process that continued as long as the horses kept the machinery in motion. Rumford thus arrived at the additional fact that there was no limit to the amount of heat that could be produced without any decrease in the amount of material substance in the vicinity. This fact was clearly incompatible with the caloric theory of heat, according to which there can be only a finite or limited amount of the heat fluid in any body.

Having gathered these additional data, Count Rumford addressed himself to the task of formulating a hypothesis that would explain the facts encountered. It was with some reluctance that he abandoned the popular caloric theory. But the facts were stubborn and not to be ignored. Rumford wrote:

> . . . anything which any isolated body, or system of bodies, can continue to furnish without limitation cannot possibly be a material substance; and it appears to me to be extremely difficult, if not quite impossible, to form any distinct idea of anything capable of being excited and communicated in the manner heat was excited and communicated in these experiments, except it be motion.[31]

Rumford's hypothesis that heat is a form of motion has come to be called the *mechanical* or *kinetic* theory of heat. On the basis of the facts at his disposal, he rejected the *materialistic* or *caloric* theory.

But in science, as elsewhere, progress must struggle against inertia. The caloric theory had been accepted for a long time, and Rumford's hypothesis was so revolutionary that its acceptance was slow in coming. (Actually, Sir Isaac Newton had anticipated it in Query 18 of his *Opticks* almost one hundred years earlier, but Newton's authority had not been established in this field.) Before the kinetic theory could be widely accepted, further confirmation was necessary. That confirmation was supplied by other scientists.

Here we come to another important aspect of scientific thought. Whatever else it

---

[31] F. K. Richtmyer, op. cit.

may be, science is *social,* an activity of the group rather than of an isolated individual. A scientific structure can be built or created by many investigators, and the well-developed branches of science are joint enterprises. The cooperative nature of scientific research accounts for the "objectivity" (really, intersubjectivity) of science. The data with which scientists traditionally deal are public data, available to any qualified investigator who makes the appropriate observations. In reporting their experiments, scientists include a wealth of detail, not for its intrinsic interest but to enable other investigators to duplicate the experimental setup and see for themselves whether the reported result really does occur. There are many cases in which individuals are mistaken in what they think they see. In a court of law, two witnesses may swear to conflicting versions of an event at which both were present, with no perjury on the part of either. Many times people will see what they expect or what they want to see, rather than what actually occurs. Although the facts of experience are the ultimate court of appeal for scientists, they must be public facts that anyone with normal perceptual faculties can experience under appropriate conditions. When elaborate experiments are repeated by different scientists, it does not betoken suspicion or distrust of the other person's results, but universal agreement that to be decisive facts must be public and repeatable. Repetition and careful checking by qualified observers minimizes the intrusion of subjective factors and helps maintain the objectivity of science.

Sir Humphry Davy (1778–1829) was the next scientist of importance to interest himself in the kinetic theory of heat. From the two theories, Davy deduced testable consequences that were strictly incompatible with each other. He asserted that *if* the caloric theory were true, then two pieces of ice that were initially below the melting point and were kept in a vacuum would not be melted by any amount of friction that could be produced between them.[32] On the other hand, with the kinetic theory of heat as premise he deduced the conclusion that two pieces of ice that were rubbed together would melt no matter what their initial temperatures and regardless of whether the operation was performed in a vacuum. These deductions pointed the way to further experimentation.

The crucial experiment these deductions made possible was then performed by Davy, who reported his procedures in great detail, specifying that he used "two parallelopipedons of ice, of the temperature of 29°, six inches long, two wide, and two-thirds of an inch thick."[33] It was experimentally verified that under the described conditions the ice *did melt.* That result convinced Sir Humphry Davy of the correctness of the kinetic theory of heat and of the untenability of the caloric theory. In Davy's own words,

> It has . . . been experimentally demonstrated that caloric, or the matter of heat, does not exist. . . . Since bodies become expanded by friction, it is evident that their corpuscles must move or separate from each other. Now a motion or vibration of the corpuscles of bodies must be necessarily generated by friction and percussion. Therefore we may reasonably conclude that this motion or vibration is heat, or the repulsive power.

---

[32] His actual deduction involved considerations having to do with the theory of "heat capacity" and the phenomenon of oxidation and is too complex to reproduce here in detail. It can be found in Magie, op. cit., pp. 161–65.
[33] Ibid.

Heat, then, or that power which prevents the actual contact of the corpuscles of bodies, and which is the cause of our peculiar sensation of heat and cold, may be defined as a peculiar motion, probably a vibration, of the corpuscles of bodies, tending to separate them.[34]

Davy's experiment confirmed Rumford's hypothesis. Perhaps even more decisive than Davy's experiments were those of the British physicist James Prescott Joule (1818–89), who made the kinetic theory quantitative by experimentally establishing the mechanical equivalent of heat.

Especially in its quantitative form, the kinetic theory of heat has many applications. Some of these are theoretical: In connection with the kinetic theory of gases, it serves to unify mechanics with the theory of heat phenomena. The almost independent science of thermodynamics has been one result of this unification. As for practical applications of the kinetic theory of heat, the most obvious is in the field of artificial refrigeration, which is only one of the technological results that theory made possible.

EXERCISES

1. Take some detective story and analyze its structure in terms of the seven steps discussed in the preceding sections.

2. Find an account of some specific line of research in a popular or semipopular book on science and analyze its structure in terms of the seven steps discussed in the preceding sections.

7.6   CRUCIAL EXPERIMENTS AND *AD HOC* HYPOTHESES

From the foregoing account, a reader might form the opinion that it is ridiculously easy to make scientific progress. It might appear that, given any problem, all one need do is set down all relevant hypotheses and then perform a series of crucial experiments to eliminate all but one of them. The surviving hypothesis is then "the answer," and we are ready to go on to the next problem. But no opinion could be more mistaken.

It already has been remarked that formulating or discovering relevant hypotheses is not a mechanical process but a creative one: Some hypotheses require genius for their discovery (or invention). It has been observed further that crucial experiments may not always be possible, either because no different observable consequences are deducible from the alternative hypotheses or because we lack the power to arrange the experimental circumstances in which different consequences would manifest themselves. We wish at this time to point out a more pervasive theoretical difficulty with the program of deciding between rival hypotheses by means of crucial experi-

---

[34]   Magie, op. cit. See also E. N. Da C. Andrade, *Nature* 135, 1935, p. 359; and R. L. Weber, ed., *A Random Walk in Science* (1974), pp 40–41.

ments. It may be well to illustrate our discussion by means of a fairly simple example. One that is familiar to all of us concerns the shape of the Earth.

In ancient Greece, the philosophers Anaximenes (c. 570–500B.C.) and Empedocles (493–433 B.C.) held that the earth is flat, and this view, close to common sense, still had adherents in the Middle Ages and the Renaissance. Christopher Columbus (1451–1506), however, insisted that the Earth is round–or rather, spherical. One of Columbus's arguments was that as a ship sails away from shore, the upper portions of it remain visible to a watcher on land long after its lower parts have disappeared from view. Copernicus included a slightly different version of the same argument in his epoch-making treatise *On the Revolutions of the Heavenly Spheres*. In section II of book I of that work, entitled "That the Earth Also Is Spherical," he presented a number of arguments intended to establish the truth of that view. Of the many found there, we quote the following:

> That the seas take a spherical form is perceived by navigators. For when land is still not discernible from a vessel's deck, it is from the masthead. And if, when a ship sails from land, a torch be fastened from the masthead, it appears to watchers on the land to go downward little by little until it entirely disappears, like a heavenly body setting.[35]

As between these rival hypotheses about the earth's shape, we might regard the foregoing as a description of a crucial experiment. The general pattern is clear. From the hypothesis that the earth is flat, H_f, it follows that, if a ship gradually recedes from view, then neither its masthead nor its decks should remain visible after the other has vanished. On the other hand, from the hypothesis that the earth is spherical, H_s, it follows that if a ship gradually recedes from view, its masthead should remain visible after its decks have vanished from sight. The rationale involved here is nicely represented by the diagrams in Figure 1.

 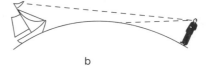

a   b

FIGURE 1

In the figure, *a* represents the situation that would obtain if H_f were true. It is clear that *if* the earth is flat, there is no reason why any one portion of the ship should disappear from sight before any other portion. The figure *b* represents the situation corresponding to H_s. As the ship recedes, the curvature of the earth rises between the observer and the ship, blocking out his or her view of the decks while the masthead remains visible. In each case the rays of light passing from ship to observer are represented by dotted lines. Now the experiment is performed, a receding ship is watched attentively, and the masthead *does* remain visible after the decks have disappeared. Our

---

[35] Nikolaus Copernicus, *On the Revolutions of the Heavenly Spheres,* ed. John Warren Knedler, Jr., *Masterworks of Science, Digests of 13 Great Classics* (1947).

experiment may not have demonstrated the truth of H_s, it can be admitted, but surely it has established the falsehood of H_f. We have as clear an example of a crucial experiment as it is possible to obtain.

But the experiment described is *not* crucial. It is entirely possible to accept the observed facts and still maintain that the earth is flat. The experiment has considerable value as evidence, but it is not decisive. It is not crucial because the various testable predictions were not inferred from the stated hypotheses H_f and H_s alone, but from them plus the additional proposition or hypothesis that "light travels in straight lines." The diagrams show clearly that this additional assumption is essential to the argument. That the decks disappear before the masthead does is not deducible from H_s alone but requires the additional hypothesis that light rays follow a rectilinear path (H_r). And that the decks do *not* disappear before the masthead does is not deducible from H_f alone but requires the same additional hypothesis that light rays follow a rectilinear path (H_r). The latter argument may be formulated as

1. If the earth is flat (H_f) and light rays follow a rectilinear path (H_r), then the decks of a receding ship will not disappear from view before the masthead.
2. The decks of a receding ship do disappear from view before the masthead. Therefore,
3. Either the earth is not flat or light rays do not follow a rectilinear path.

As this argument shows, all we can conclude from the observation that the decks of a receding ship disappear from view before the masthead is that at least one of the hypotheses—H_f or H_r—is false. We are not driven to the conclusion that the earth is spherical. Instead, we can reject the hypothesis that light rays follow a rectilinear path, which is, after all, a contingent proposition, not one that is necessarily true.

Suppose we adopt the contrary hypothesis that light rays follow a curved path, concave upward (H_c). Again, we are not driven to the conclusion that the earth is spherical. The argument can be formulated as follows:

1. If the earth is flat (H_f) and light rays follow a curved path (H_c), then the decks of a receding ship will disappear from view before the masthead.
2. The decks of a receding ship do disappear from view before the masthead. Therefore, probably,
3. The earth is flat and light rays follow a curved path.

a   b

FIGURE 2

Figure 2 explains the reasoning involved here. In this figure, *a* represents the situation when the ship is near the shore, whereas *b* shows that, as the ship recedes, the earth (even though flat) blocks out the view of the decks, while the masthead remains visible. The light rays in this diagram too are represented by dotted lines, but in this case curved rather than rectilinear. The same experiment is performed, the decks do disappear before the masthead, and the observed fact is perfectly compatible with this group of hypotheses that includes H_f the claim that the earth is flat. The experiment, therefore, is *not crucial* with respect to H_f, for that hypothesis can be maintained to be true regardless of the experiment's outcome.[36]

The point is that where hypotheses of a fairly high level of abstractness or generality are involved, no observable or directly testable prediction can be deduced from just a single one of them. A whole group of hypotheses must be used, and if the observed facts are other than those predicted, *at least one* of the hypotheses in the group is shown to be false. But we have not established which one is in error. An experiment can be crucial in showing the untenability of a group of hypotheses. But such a group usually will contain a considerable number of separate hypotheses, the truth of any one of which can be maintained in the teeth of *any* experimental result, however "unfavorable," by the simple expedient of rejecting some *other* hypothesis of the group. A conclusion often drawn from these considerations is that no individual hypothesis can ever be subjected to a crucial experiment.

The preceding discussion may be objected to strenuously. It may be urged that the experiment in question "really does" refute the hypothesis that the earth is flat. It may be charged that the argument to the contrary is guilty of making an *ad hoc* hypothesis to obscure and get around the plain facts of the case. It may be felt that only the invention of *ad hoc* hypotheses right and left can prevent some experiments from being crucial and decisively refuting single hypotheses. This objection deserves careful attention.

The crux of the objection would seem to lie in the phrase "*ad hoc*," which in this context is a highly charged term of abuse. Of its emotive significance there can be little doubt, but its descriptive meaning is somewhat ambiguous. There are three different senses in which the term "*ad hoc*" is used.[37] Its first and etymological meaning would seem to be that an *ad hoc* hypothesis is one that was specially made up to account for some fact *after* that fact had been established. In this sense, however, *all* hypotheses—even the best scientific ones—are *ad hoc,* since it makes no sense to speak of a hypothesis that was not devised to account for some antecedently established fact or other. Hence the first sense does not fit in very well with the derogatory emotive significance of the term. We must consider its other meanings.

The term "*ad hoc*" also is used to characterize a hypothesis that accounts *only* for the particular fact or facts it was invented to explain and has no other explanatory power, that is, no other testable consequences. No *scientific* hypothesis is *ad hoc* in this second sense of the term, although *every* hypothesis is *ad hoc* in the first sense explained. A hypothesis that is *ad hoc* in the second sense is nonscientific; since it is not testable, it has no place in the structure of science. The second sense of "*ad hoc*" fits in perfectly with the derogatory emotive meaning of the term. But it should be

---

[36]   This illustration was first suggested by Professor C. L. Stevenson.

[37]   Literally, the words mean "for this" or "for this purpose," so, for example, an *ad hoc* committee is a committee empaneled for a particular purpose. See Eugene Ehrlich et al., *Oxford American Dictionary* (1980), p. 10.

realized that the auxiliary hypothesis about light rays traveling in curved paths, which was sufficient to save the hypothesis that the earth is flat from being definitely refuted by the experiment described, is *ad hoc* only in the first sense, not the second, for it does have a considerable number of empirically testable consequences.

There is a third sense of the term "*ad hoc*," in which it is used to denote a mere descriptive generalization. Such a descriptive hypothesis will assert only that all facts of a particular sort occur in just some particular kinds of circumstances and will have no explanatory power or theoretical scope. For example, limiting their diet to polished rice was found by Christiaan Eijkman (1858–1930) to cause polyneuritis in the small group of chickens with which he was working (as described in exercise 4 on page 211 in section 6.2). Eijkman's hypothesis to account for this fact was *ad hoc* in the third sense: He simply drew the generalization that a diet limited to polished rice will cause polyneuritis in *any* group of chickens. His hypothesis accounts for more than just the particular facts observed; it is testable by controlling the diets of *other* groups of chickens. But it is descriptive rather than explanatory, *merely* empirical rather than theoretical. The science of nutrition has come a long way since Eijkman's contribution. Both the identification and the analysis of vitamins are required for a more adequate account of the facts Eijkman observed. Science seeks to explain and illuminate rather than merely to describe; hypotheses that consist of mere generalizations of the facts observed are said to be *ad hoc*. The classical example of an *ad hoc* hypothesis in this third sense is the Fitzgerald Contraction Effect introduced to account for the results of the Michelson–Morley experiment on the velocity of light. By affirming that bodies moving at extremely high velocities contract, Fitzgerald accounted for the given data; his account was testable by repetitions of the experiment. But it was generally held to be *ad hoc* rather than explanatory, and not until Einstein's Special Theory of Relativity were the anomalous results of the Michelson–Morley experiment given an adequate, that is, a theoretical, explanation. It should be noted that the auxiliary hypothesis about the curved path of light rays is not *ad hoc* in this third sense either, because it is not a mere generalization of observed facts. (It is, in fact, an essential ingredient in the General Theory of Relativity.)

The general situation seems to be that it is not necessary to invoke *ad hoc* hypotheses—in either the second or third senses of the term, which are the derogatory ones—to prevent experiments from being crucial. Even if we confine our attention to theoretically significant hypotheses and never invoke *ad hoc* hypotheses, no experiments are crucial for individual hypotheses, since hypotheses are testable only in groups.[38] For example, either of the following hypothesis clusters can explain the observation that, when a ship gradually recedes from view, its decks disappear before its masthead does:

Cluster 1 (depicted in Figure 1b):

    a.   The earth is spherical (H_s).

    b.   Light rays follow a rectilinear path (H_r).

---

[38] This view has been argued persuasively by P. Duhem, *The Aim and Structure of Physical Theory*, trans. P. P. Wiener (1954). A challenging objection to it can be found in Adolf Grunbaum, "The Duhemian Argument," *Philosophy of Science* 27, January 1960. See also Sandra G. Harding, ed., *Can Theories Be Refuted? Essays on the Duhem-Quine Thesis* (1976).

Cluster 2 (depicted in Figure 2b):
    a.   The earth is flat (H_f).
    b.   Light rays follow a curved path, concave upward (H_c).

No single experiment can force a choice between H_f and H_s, for, as we saw, the proponent of H_f can save it by rejecting H_r (accepting H_c). Each hypothesis about the shape of the earth is "insulated," if you will, by the associated hypothesis about light rays. It appears that one must reject an entire hypothesis *cluster* in order to reject one of the hypotheses that it contains. How this might be achieved is beyond the scope of this book.

This limitation illuminates the *systematic* character of science. Scientific progress consists in building ever more adequate theories to account for the facts of experience. True enough, it is of value to collect or verify isolated particular facts, for the ultimate basis of science is factual. But the theoretical structure of science grows in a more organic fashion. In the realm of theory, piecemeal progress, one-step-at-a-time advances, can be accomplished, but only within the framework of a generally accepted body of scientific theory. The notion that scientific hypotheses, theories, or laws are wholly discrete and independent is a naive view.

The term "crucial experiment" is not a useless one, however. Within the framework of accepted scientific theory that we are not concerned to question, a hypothesis *can* be subjected to a crucial experiment. If a negative result is obtained—that is, if some phenomenon fails to occur which had been predicted on the basis of the single dubious hypothesis together with accepted parts of scientific theory—then the experiment is crucial and the hypothesis is rejected. But there is nothing absolute about such a procedure, for even well-accepted scientific theories tend to be changed in the face of new and contrary evidence. Science is not monolithic, either in its practices or in its aims.

Perhaps the most significant lesson to be learned from the preceding discussion is the importance to scientific progress of dragging "hidden assumptions" into the open. That light travels in straight lines was assumed in the arguments of Columbus and Copernicus, but it was a hidden assumption. Because they are hidden, there is no chance to examine such assumptions critically and to decide intelligently whether they are true or false. Progress often is achieved by formulating explicitly an assumption that previously had been hidden and then scrutinizing and rejecting it. An important and dramatic instance of this occurred when Einstein challenged the universally accepted assumption that it always makes sense to say of two events that they occurred *at the same time*. In considering how an observer could discover whether two distant events occurred "at the same time," Einstein was led to the conclusion that two events could be simultaneous for some observers but not for others, depending upon their locations and velocities relative to the events in question. Rejecting the assumption led to the Special Theory of Relativity, which constituted a tremendous step forward in explaining such phenomena as those revealed by the Michelson–Morley experiment. It is clear that an assumption must be recognized before it can be challenged. Hence it is enormously important in science to formulate explicitly all relevant assumptions in any hypothesis, allowing none of them to remain hidden.

7.7   CLASSIFICATION AS HYPOTHESIS

It might be objected that hypotheses play important roles only in the more advanced sciences, not in those that are relatively less advanced. It may be urged that although explanatory hypotheses may be central to such sciences as physics and chemistry, they play no such role—at least not yet—in the biological or social sciences. The latter are still in their descriptive phases, and it may be felt that the method of hypothesis is not relevant to the so-called descriptive sciences, such as botany, zoology, and history. This objection is easily answered. An examination of the nature of description will show that *description itself is based on or embodies hypotheses*. Hypotheses are as basic to the various systems of taxonomy or classification in biology as they are in history or any of the other social sciences.

The importance of hypothesis in the science of history is easily shown and will be discussed first. Some historians believe that the study of history reveals the existence of a single cosmic purpose or pattern, either religious or naturalistic, which accounts for or explains the entire course of recorded history. Others deny the existence of any such cosmic design but insist that the study of history reveals certain historical laws that explain the actual sequence of past events and can be used to predict the future. On either of these views, historians seek explanations that must account for and be confirmed by the recorded events of the past. On either of these views, therefore, history is a theoretical rather than a merely descriptive science, and the role of hypothesis must be admitted as central in the historian's enterprise.

There is, however, a third group of historians who set themselves what is apparently a more modest goal. According to them the task of historians is simply to chronicle the past, to set forth a bare description of past events in their chronological order. On this view, it might seem "scientific" historians have no need of hypotheses, since their concern is with the facts themselves, not with any theories about them.

But past events are not as easily chronicled as this view implies. The past itself simply is not available for this kind of description. What *is* available are present records and traces of the past. These range all the way from official government archives of the recent past to epic poems celebrating the exploits of half-legendary heroes, and from the writings of older historians to artifacts of bygone eras unearthed in the excavations of archeologists. These are the only facts available to historians, and from them they must infer the nature of those past events it is their purpose to describe. Not *all* hypotheses are general; some are particular. The historian's description of the past is a particular hypothesis intended to account for present data, for which the present data constitute evidence.

Historians are detectives on a grand scale.[39] Their methods are the same, and their difficulties too. The evidence is scanty, and much of it has been destroyed—if not by the bungling local constabulary, then by intervening wars and natural disasters. And just as the criminal may have left false or misleading clues to throw pursuers off the scent, so many present "records" are falsifications of the past they purport to describe, either intentional, as in the case of such forged historical documents as the "Donation of Constantine," or unintentional, as in the writings of early uncritical historians. Just

---

[39]   See Robin W. Winks, ed., *The Historian as Detective: Essays on Evidence* (1969).

as the detective must use the method of science in formulating and testing hypotheses, so the historian must make hypotheses too. Even those historians who seek to limit themselves to bare descriptions of past events must work with hypotheses: They are theorists in spite of themselves.

Biologists are in a somewhat more favorable position. The facts with which they deal are present and available for inspection. To describe the flora and fauna of a given region, they need not make elaborate inferences of the sort to which historians are condemned. The data can be perceived directly. Their descriptions of these items are not casual, of course, but systematic. They are usually said to *classify* plants and animals rather than merely to describe them. But classification and description are the same process. To describe a given animals as carnivorous is to classify it as a carnivore; to classify it as a reptile is to describe it as reptilian. To describe any object as having a certain attribute is to classify it as a member of the class of objects having that attribute.

Classification, as generally understood, involves not merely a single division of objects into separate groups but further subdivision of each group into subgroups or subclasses and so on. For an example, see the typology of polygons in section 4.4. This pattern is familiar to most of us, if not from our various studies in school, then certainly from playing the old game of "Animal, Vegetable, or Mineral?" or its more recent version, "Twenty Questions." Thomas Jefferson (1743–1826), who is not widely known to have been expert in such matters (but was), described the process of classification as follows in an 1814 letter:

> Nature has, in truth, produced units only through all her works. Classes, orders, genera, species, are not of her work. Her creation is of individuals. No two animals are exactly alike; no two plants, nor even two leaves or blades of grass; no two crystallizations. . . . This infinitude of units or individuals being far beyond the capacity of our memory, we are obliged, in aid of that, to distribute them into masses, throwing into each of these all the individuals which have a certain degree of resemblance; to subdivide these again into smaller groups, according to certain points of dissimilitude observable in them, and so on until we have formed what we call a system of classes, orders, genera and species.[40]

People classify objects for many reasons. For primitive people to live, they were required to classify roots and berries as edible or poisonous, animals as dangerous or harmless, and other tribes as friend or foe. People tend to draw distinctions that are of practical importance to them and to neglect those that play a less immediate role in their affairs. A farmer will classify grains and vegetables carefully and in detail but may call all flowers "posies," whereas florists will classify their merchandise with the greatest of care but may lump all the farmer's crops together as "produce." There are several motives that may lead us to classify things. One is practical, another theoretical. Having only three or four books, one could know them all well and could easily take them all in at a glance, so there would be no need to classify them. But in a public or college library containing many thousands of volumes, the situation is different. If the books there were not classified, the librarian could not find the books that might be wanted, and the collection would be practically useless. The larger the number of

---

[40] Thomas Jefferson, letter to Dr. John Manners, 22 February 1814, *Writings* (1984), pp. 1329–30.

objects (relative to our capacities), the greater is the need for classifying them. A practical purpose of classification is to make large collections accessible. This is especially apparent in the case of libraries, museums, and public records of one sort or another.

In considering the theoretical purpose of classification, we must realize that the adoption of this or that alternative classification scheme is not anything that can be true or false.[41] Objects can be described in different ways, from different points of view. The scheme of classification adopted depends upon the purpose or interest of the classifier. Books, for example, would be classified differently by a librarian, a bookbinder, and a bibliophile. The librarian would classify them according to their contents or subject matter, the bookbinder according to their bindings, and a bibliophile according to their date of printing or perhaps their relative rarity. The possibilities are not thereby exhausted, of course: A book packer would divide books according to their shapes and sizes, and persons with still other interests would classify them differently in the light of those different interests.

What special interest or purpose do scientists have that can lead them to prefer one scheme of classification to another? The scientist's aim is knowledge, not merely of this or that particular fact for its own sake, but knowledge of the general laws to which they conform and their causal interrelations. One classification scheme is better than another, from the scientist's point of view, to the extent that it is more fruitful in suggesting scientific laws and more helpful in the formulation of explanatory hypotheses.

The theoretical or scientific motive for classifying objects is the desire to increase our knowledge of them. Increased knowledge of things is further insight into their attributes, their similarities and differences, and their interrelations. A classification scheme made for narrowly practical purposes may obscure important similarities and differences. Thus a division of animals into dangerous and harmless will assign the wild boar and the rattlesnake to one class and the domestic pig and the grass snake to the other, calling attention away from what we should today regard as more profound similarities in order to emphasize superficial resemblances. A scientifically fruitful classification of objects requires considerable knowledge about them. A slight acquaintance with their more obvious characteristics would lead one to classify the bat with birds, as flying creatures, and the whale with fishes, as creatures that live in the sea. But a more extensive knowledge would lead us to classify bats and whales as mammals, because being warm blooded, bearing their young alive, and suckling them are more important characteristics on which to base a classificatory scheme.

A characteristic is important when it serves as a clue to the presence of other characteristics. An important characteristic, from the point of view of science, is one that is causally connected with many other characteristics, and hence relevant to the framing of a maximum number of causal laws and the formulation of very general explanatory hypotheses. Thus, the best classification scheme is that which is based on the most important characteristics of the objects to be classified. But we do not know in advance what causal laws obtain, and causal laws themselves partake of the nature of hypotheses, as was emphasized in the preceding chapter. Therefore any decision as to which classification scheme is best is itself a hypothesis, which subsequent investigations may

---

[41] Hypotheses, being propositions, are either true or false. So while classification schemes themselves are neither true nor false, the hypotheses that they embody are.

lead us to reject. If later investigations revealed *other* characteristics to be more important, that is, involved in a greater number of causal laws and explanatory hypotheses, it would be reasonable to expect the earlier classification scheme to be rejected in favor of a newer one based on the more important characteristics.

This view of classification schemes as hypotheses is borne out by the actual role such schemes play in the sciences. Taxonomy is a legitimate, important, and still growing branch of biology, in which some classification schemes, like that of Carolus Linnaeus (1707–78), have been adopted, used, and subsequently abandoned in favor of better ones, which are themselves in turn subject to modification in the light of new data. Classification generally is most important in the early or less developed stages of a science. It need not always diminish in importance as the science develops, however. For example, the standard classification scheme for the elements, as set forth in Mendeleeff's Table, is still an important tool for the chemist.

In the light of the foregoing discussion, a further remark can be made on the role of hypothesis in the science of history. It already has been said that the historian's descriptions of past events are themselves hypotheses based on present data. There is an additional, equally significant role that hypotheses play in the descriptive historian's enterprise. It is obvious that no historical era or event of any magnitude can be described in *complete detail*. Even if all of its details could be known, historians could not possibly include them all in their narratives. Life is too short to permit an exhaustive description of anything. Historians must therefore describe the past selectively, recording only some of its aspects. Upon what basis shall they make their selection? Clearly, historians want to include what is significant or important in their descriptions and to ignore what is insignificant or trivial. The subjective bias of this or that historian may lead to laying undue stress on the religious, the economic, the psychological, or some other aspect of the historic process. But to the extent that they can make an objective or scientific appraisal, historians will regard those aspects as important that enter into the formulation of causal laws and general explanatory hypotheses. Such appraisals are, of course, subject to correction in the light of further research.

The first Western historian, Herodotus (c. 485–425 B.C.), described a great many aspects of the events he chronicled, personal and cultural as well as political and military. The so-called first scientific historian, Thucydides (460–400 B.C.), restricted himself much more to the political and the military. For a long time most historians followed Thucydides, but now the pendulum is swinging in the other direction, and the economic and cultural aspects of the past are being given increased emphasis.[42] Just as biologists' classification schemes embody their hypotheses as to which characteristics of living things are involved in a maximum number of causal laws, so historians' decisions to describe past events in terms of one rather than another set of characteristics embody their hypotheses as to which characteristics are causally related to a maximum number of others. Some such hypotheses are required before historians can even begin any systematic description of the past. It is this hypothetical character of classification and description, whether biological or historical, that leads us to regard hypothesis as the all-pervasive method of scientific inquiry.

---

[42]   See, e.g., Gary B. Nash and Cynthia J. Shelton, eds., *The Private Side of American History: Readings in Everyday Life,* 2 vols., 4th ed. (1987).

EXERCISES

In each of the following passages,

    a. What data are to be explained?

    b. What hypotheses are proposed to explain them?

    c. Evaluate the hypotheses in terms of the criteria presented in section 7.3.

■   *1.* The distant universe looks quite different from the nearby universe. To explain this astronomers adopt an evolutionary hypothesis. Distant objects, they believe, are young objects. The signals we get from them, delivered here at the speed of light, were emitted when the objects were in an earlier stage of development than we see in the local region. If, for example, one of MacAlpine's survey objects [quasars—quasi-stellar objects whose light has traveled some billions of years to reach us] were one and one-half billion parsecs away, its light would have originated at a time when our own solar system was still forming and our sun quite young. What was our galaxy like at that time? It is hard to know except to infer that perhaps it looked then like quasars look to us today.

        —BLANCHARD HIATT, *University of Michigan Research News* 30 August–September 1979

2. In the United States, regardless of the way health is measured (mortality, morbidity, symptoms, or subjective evaluation), and regardless of the unit of observation (individuals, city or state averages), *years of schooling usually emerges as the most powerful correlate of good health.* Michael Grossman, an economist who has done extensive research on this question, has tended to interpret this relationship as evidence that *schooling increases the individual's efficiency in producing health,* although he recognizes that some causality may run from better health to more schooling. The way schooling contributes to efficiency in producing health has never been made explicit, but Grossman has speculated that persons with more education might choose healthier diets, be more aware of health risks, choose healthier occupations, and use medical care more wisely.

        —VICTOR R. FUCHS, "The Economics of Health in a Post-Industrial Society," *The Public Interest,*
Summer 1979

3. The central geographical and climatic characteristic of North Africa and the Mideast is its aridity. A current hypothesis is that there exists a feed-back relationship between the plant growth of a marginally arid area and its rainfall. If for some reason—overgrazing, for example—the area is partially denuded of growth, its albedo, or reflectivity, will increase. A greater percentage of sunlight is returned to space, the corresponding heat loss is compensated by sinking air motions; and mean cloudiness, and hence mean rainfall, decreases. Then plant growth decreases still further, and a feed-back, or vicious circle, mechanism is set in motion.

        —MORTON G. WURTELE and JEHUDA NEUMANN, "Some Areas for International Cooperation in
the Geophysical Sciences," *Middle East Review* 10 Spring 1978

4. One of the most challenging problems in all of social science has been untangling the environmental and genetic influences of the family on children's intellectual, occupational, and economic attainments. The educational level of parents correlates fairly well with both school achievement and mental ability test scores of their children. This correlation is usually assumed to indicate the strength of the influence of environment on school success, since parents with more years of schooling tend to expect their children to do well in school and create a richer educational environment in the home than do poorly educated parents. If the causal connection runs from the rich family environment to the academic-ability level of the child, then it makes sense to try to induce all parents to provide more educative environments, as a way of improving school performance of educationally disadvantaged children.

If mental ability is to some extent inherited, however, a different set of causal linkages may be involved: Parents possessing high levels of mental ability will tend to spend more years in school than others do, will pass on some of their ability to their children, *and* will create more educative home environments. In this view, correlation between home environment and the child's academic performance may mask a more important genetic relation between parents' abilities and children's abilities.

— HARRY L. MILLER, "Hard Realities and Soft Social Science," *The Public Interest*, Spring 1980

■ **5.** The mechanism of stimulus and response in geotropism has often been studied. If very young seedlings in which the root and stem are just appearing are fixed in any position whatever, the young root will invariably grow downward and the young stem upward. The English horticulturalist Knight, more than a century ago, suggested that this behavior was due to gravity. He reasoned that if this were so, it should be possible to substitute a stronger force for gravity and thus to change the direction of growth. Knight fastened young plants in various positions to the rim of a wheel, which he revolved rapidly in a horizontal plane, thus subjecting the plants to a "centrifugal force" greater than gravity. Under these conditions the roots grew outward, in the direction of the centrifugal pull, and the stems grew inward, toward the hub, in an exactly opposite direction. Knight thus proved that plant structures orient themselves to this force in just the same way that they do to gravity.

— EDMUND W. SINNOTT and KATHERINE S. WILSON, *Botany: Principles and Problems*

6. On the 7th of January 1610, at one o'clock in the morning, when he [Galileo] directed his telescope to Jupiter, he observed three stars near the body of the planet, two being to the east and one to the west of him. They were all in a straight line, and parallel to the ecliptic, and they appeared brighter than other stars of the same magnitude. Believing them to be fixed stars, he paid no great attention to their distances from Jupiter and from one another. On the 8th of January, however, when, from some cause or other, he had been led to observe the stars again, he found a very different arrangement of them: all the three were on the west side of Jupiter, *nearer one another than before,* and almost at equal distances. Though he had not turned his attention to the extraordinary fact of the mutual approach of the stars, yet he began to consider how Jupiter could be found to the east of the three stars, when but the day before he had been to the west of two of them. The only explanation which he could give of this fact was, that the motion of Jupiter was *direct,* contrary to astronomical calculations, and that he had got before these two stars by his own motion.

In this dilemma between the testimony of his senses and the results of calculation, he waited for the following night with the utmost anxiety; but his hopes were disappointed, for the heavens were wholly veiled in clouds. On the 10th, two only of the stars appeared, and both on the east of the planet. As it was obviously impossible that Jupiter could have advanced from west to east on the 8th of January, and from east to west on the 10th, Galileo was forced to conclude that the phenomenon which he had observed arose from the motion of the stars, and he set himself to observe diligently their change of place. On the 11th, there were still only two stars, and both to the east of Jupiter; but the more eastern star was now *twice as large as the other one,* though on the preceding night they had been perfectly equal. This fact threw a new light upon Galileo's difficulties, and he immediately drew the conclusion, which he considered to be indubitable, "*that there were in the heaven three stars which revolved round Jupiter, in the same manner as Venus and Mercury revolved round the sun.*" On the 12th of January, he again observed them in new positions, and of different magnitudes; and, on the 13th, he discovered a fourth star, which completed the four secondary planets with which Jupiter is surrounded.

—SIR DAVID BREWSTER, *The Martyrs of Science*

7. Again, however solid things are thought to be, you may yet learn from this that they are of rare body: in rocks and caverns the moisture of water oozes through and all things weep with abundant drops; food distributes itself through the whole body of living things; trees grow and yield fruit in season, because food is diffused through the whole from the very roots over the stem and all the boughs. Voices pass through walls and fly through houses shut, stiffening frost pierces to the bones. Now if there are no void parts, by what way can the bodies severally pass? You would see it to be quite impossible. Once more, why do we see one thing surpass another in weight though not larger in size? For if there is just as much body in a ball of wool as there is in a lump of lead, it is natural it should weigh the same, since the property of body is to weigh all things downwards, while on the contrary the nature of void is ever without weight. Therefore when a thing is just as large, yet is found to be lighter, it proves sure enough that it has more of void in it; while on the other hand that which is heavier shows that there is in it more of body and that it contains within it much less of void. Therefore that which we are seeking with keen reason exists sure enough, mixed up in things; and we call it void.

—LUCRETIUS, *On the Nature of Things,* Book I

8. . . . there was something wrong with the atomic model based on the discovery of the nucleus, the model that depicted the atom as a miniature solar system.

According to this model, the electron was attracted to the nucleus of opposite electrical charge. Therefore the electron would move; it would move, like the planets, in an elliptical orbit around the nucleus-sun. But a moving electron was impossible. Why? Because, according to the laws of electricity, a moving charge must produce electromagnetic radiation, light. The electron, always in motion, would produce radiation; all atoms would emit light at all times. But matter under ordinary circumstances does not glow with light.

—BARBARA LOVETT CLINE, *Men Who Made a New Physics*

9. While walking one night with Dr. Frink, we accidentally met a colleague, Dr. P., whom I had not seen for years, and of whose private life I knew nothing. We were naturally very pleased to meet again, and on my invitation, he accompanied us to a cafe, where we spent about two hours in pleasant conversation. To my question as to whether he was married, he gave a negative answer, and added, "Why should a man like me marry?"

On leaving the cafe, he suddenly turned to me and said: "I should like to know what you would do in a case like this: I know a nurse who was named as co-respondent in a divorce case. The wife sued the husband for divorce and named her as co-respondent, and *he* got the divorce." I interrupted him saying, "You mean *she* got the divorce." He immediately corrected himself saying, "Yes, she got the divorce," and continued to tell how the excitement of the trial had affected this nurse to such an extent that she became nervous and took to drink. He wanted me to advise him how to treat her.

As soon as I had corrected his mistake, I asked him to explain it, but, as is usually the case, he was surprised at my question. He wanted to know whether a person had no right to make mistakes in talking. I explained to him that there is a reason for every mistake, and that if he had not told me that he was unmarried, I should say that he was the hero of the divorce case in question, and that the mistake showed that he wished he had obtained the divorce instead of his wife, so as not to be obliged to pay alimony and to be permitted to marry again in New York State.

He stoutly denied my interpretation, but his emotional agitation, followed by loud laughter, only strengthened my suspicions. To my appeal that he should tell the truth "for science's sake" he said, "Unless you wish me to lie, you must believe that I was never married, and hence, your psychoanalytic interpretation is all wrong." He, however, added that it was dangerous to be with a person who paid attention to such little things. Then he suddenly remembered that he had another appointment and left us.

Both Dr. Frink and I were convinced that my interpretation of his *lapsus linguae* was correct, and I decided to corroborate or disprove it by further investigation. The next day, I found a neighbor and old friend of Dr. P., who confirmed my interpretation in every particular. The divorce was granted to Dr. P.'s wife a few weeks before, and a nurse was named as co-respondent. A few weeks later, I met Dr. P., and he told me that he was thoroughly convinced of the Freudian mechanisms.

—A. A. BRILL, *Psychoanalysis: Its Theories and Practical Applications*

■ **10.** Since Venus rotates so slowly, we might be tempted to conclude that Venus, like Mercury, keeps one face always toward the Sun. If this hypothesis were correct we should expect that the dark side would be exceedingly cold. Pettit and Nicholson have measured the temperature of the dark side of Venus. They find that the temperature is not low, its value being only -9˚ F., much warmer than our stratosphere in broad daylight. It is unlikely that atmospheric currents from the bright side of Venus could perpetually heat the dark side. The planet must rotate fairly often to keep the dark side from cooling excessively.

—FRED L. WHIPPLE, *Earth, Moon and Planets*

11. In the different excursions which he [Captain Vancouver] made, particularly about Port Discovery, the skulls, limbs, ribs, and backbones, or some other vestiges of the human body, were scattered promiscuously in great numbers; and, as no warlike scars were observed on the bodies of the remaining Indians, and no particular signs of fear and suspicion were noticed, the most probable conjecture seems to be that this depopulation must have been occasioned by pestilential disease.

—THOMAS ROBERT MALTHUS, *An Essay on Population*

12. ... one of Rutherford's students, given the problem of measuring the ionizing property of the radioactive element thorium (which gave its degree of radioactivity), had run into difficulties. His electroscope gave a different intensity of ionization at different times; he could not arrive at a definite measurement. And curiously enough, the different intensities seemed to depend on whether the door to the laboratory was closed or open.

At this point Rutherford became very interested in the problem. Before long he had explained the capricious measurements with the discovery that the element thorium emits a radioactive gas (now called "thoron"). When the laboratory door was closed, the gas hovered over the element, adding its radioactivity to that of thorium; but when the door was open, the gas was blown about the laboratory by air drafts.

—BARBARA LOVETT CLINE, *Men Who Made a New Physics*

13. Like multiple sclerosis, poliomyelitis in its paralytic form was a disease of the more advanced nations rather than of the less advanced ones, and of economically better-off people rather than of the poor. It occurred in northern Europe and North America much more frequently than in southern Europe or the countries of Africa, Asia or South America. Immigrants to South Africa from northern Europe ran twice the risk of contracting paralytic poliomyelitis than South-African-born whites ran, and the South-African-born whites ran a much greater risk than non-whites. Among the Bantu of South Africa paralytic poliomyelitis was rarely an adult disease. During World War II in North Africa cases of paralytic poliomyelitis were commoner among officers in the British and American forces than among men in the other ranks. At the time various wild hypotheses for the difference were proposed; it was even suggested that it arose from the fact that the officers drank whiskey whereas men in the other ranks drank beer!

We now understand very well the reason for the strange distribution of paralytic poliomyelitis. Until this century poliomyelitis was a universal infection of infancy and infants hardly ever suffered paralysis from it. The fact that they were occasionally so affected is what gave the disease the name "infantile paralysis." With the improvement of hygiene in the advancing countries of the world more and more people missed infection in early childhood and contracted the disease for the first time at a later age, when the risk that the infection will cause paralysis is much greater.

This explains why the first epidemics of poliomyelitis did not occur until this century and then only in the economically advanced countries.

—GEOFFREY DEAN, "The Multiple Sclerosis Problem," *Scientific American* 223, July 1970

14. Indeed, from the commencement of the period during which we possess historic accounts, that is, for a period of about 4000 years, the temperature of the earth has not sensibly diminished. From these old ages we have certainly no thermometric observations, but we have information regarding the distribution of certain cultivated plants, the vine, the olive tree, which are very sensitive to changes of the mean annual temperature, and we find that these plants at the present moment have the same limits of distribution that they had in the times of Abraham and Homer; from which we may infer backwards the constancy of the climate.

—HERMANN VON HELMHOLTZ, "The Conservation of Energy"

■ *15.*   Dr. Konrad Buettner of the University of California at Los Angeles has recently advanced the hypothesis that, during the lifetime of the moon, the everlasting influx of cosmic rays has slowly ground the upper-surface layers of rocks into fine dust. That the moon's skin cannot consist of solid rocks has been demonstrated through temperature measurements during lunar eclipses. As soon as the shadow of the earth creeps over the measuring area the temperature drops steeply, and after half an hour it is over 200° F. lower than it was in the full sun. When the shadow has passed by, the temperature again rises at a similarly steep rate. No solid piece of rock can cool down and heat up so quickly. These drastic temperature changes can be explained only by the existence of a thick layer of heat-insulating dust as fine as face powder. The thickness of the layer must be at least several inches. The sandblasting of meteoric dust also grinds at the moon's surface, but cosmic rays can be expected to do a much better job.

—HEINZ HABER, *Man in Space*

16.   Even more thought-provoking was the unexpected discovery that certain types of bacteria could live without air. According to Pasteur's account, he had once placed under the microscope a drop of sugar solution that was in the process of changing into butyric acid. The drop contained bacteria, which were at first rapidly motile. Then he observed the odd fact that whereas the bacteria in the center of the drop continued to move, those at the periphery soon came to a standstill. From this simple observation he guessed that air was toxic for these bacteria and that they probably lived without oxygen.

—RENE DUBOS, *Pasteur and Modern Science*

17.   The cause of the peculiar affection which we are considering was until recently very obscure. During the months of May and June, 1909, an outbreak (20 cases) of this eruptive disease developed among the crew upon a private yacht docked in the Delaware River. At almost the same time 33 more cases appeared among the crews of 4 other boats. Besides these 53 cases we learned in the course of our investigation of about 70 other cases in 20 different private residences and boarding houses scattered about the city of Philadelphia and its vicinity. In practically every case we were able to determine that the patient had either recently slept upon a new straw mattress or had freely handled the same. The facts elicited by our inquiry enabled us to exclude from consideration the jute or cotton topping or the ticking of the mattresses and we satisfied ourselves that the essential causative factor was connected with the wheat straw. The mattresses were made by 4 of the leading manufacturers, all of whom received a large proportion if not quite all of their straw from the same source in New Jersey.

In order to establish the etiological role of the straw mattresses experimentally, one of us[43] exposed his (left) bare arm and shoulder for one hour between two straw mattresses. At the end of about 16 hours the characteristic itching eruption appeared.

---

[43] This was Goldberger. See R. P. Parsons, *Trail to Light: a Biography of Joseph Goldberger* (1943).

Later 3 volunteers slept upon a mattress during a night and each one developed the eruption at the end of about the same period.

We next took some of the straw and sifted such particles as would pass through the meshes of a fine flour sieve. The sifted particles were divided into two portions and placed in two clean glass Petri dishes. One of these was then applied for one hour to the left axilla of a volunteer. At the end of about 16 to 18 hours the characteristic eruption was present in the area of the left axilla to which the Petri dish of straw siftings had been applied.

Having therefore determined not only by the deduction from the epidemiological facts but by experiment that the straw in the straw mattresses was in some way capable of producing the eruption we next sought in the straw for the responsible factor. First we exposed for an hour the second portion of the siftings in a Petri dish to the vapour of chloroform under a bell jar with a view to killing any insect or acarine that might be present. These siftings were then applied to the right axilla of the volunteer to whose left axilla the untreated siftings were applied. While, as has been stated, the application of the untreated siftings was followed by the appearance of the characteristic eruption, the skin to which the chloroformized siftings were applied remained perfectly normal. We inferred, therefore, that the essential causative factor residing in the straw had been killed by the chloroform fumes. Careful scrutiny of some of the fresh siftings from the straw disclosed the presence of a small almost microscopic mite. Five of these mites were fished out, placed in a clean watch crystal and then applied to the axilla of another volunteer. At the end of about 16 hours following this application 5 of the characteristic lesions appeared on the area to which the mites had been applied.

We established, therefore, that the minute mite which we fished out of the straw siftings was the factor in the straw that was responsible for the production of the eruption. This mite was identified for us by Mr. Nathan Banks, expert in acarina of the United States Bureau of Entomology, as very close to, if not identical with, *Pediculoides ventricosus.*

—J. GOLDBERGER and J. F. SCHAMBERG, "The Epidemic of an Urticarioid Dermatitis Due to a Small Mite (*Pediculoides ventricosus*) in the Straw of Mattresses," *Public Health Reports* 24, 1909

18.   Mosquitoes can carry living bacilli of Hansen's disease in areas where this disease is highly endemic. This capability has been shown for the first time in medical history in a study being conducted in India by Indian and U.S. investigators. Thus, transmission of Hansen's disease from person to person by an arthropod carrier has become more than just a theoretical possibility.

Waldemar F. Kirchheimer, M.D., Ph.D., chief of Laboratory Research Branch, Public Health Service Hospital, Carville, La., and clinical professor of bacteriology, tropical diseases, and medical parasitology, Louisiana State University Medical Center, New Orleans, described the study as follows: . . .

The Jawaharlal Institute for Postgraduate Medical Education at Pondicherry, South India, was selected as the best location for the study, and work began there in August 1969. We tried to determine what species of arthropods in the area around Pondicherry would be most likely to transmit Hansen's disease by virtue of their ability to pierce human skin and inject bacilli. We also sought to learn how often a particular arthropod would become a carrier of Hansen's bacilli and how long the bacilli would survive within the arthropod.

A variety of arthropods, bred and raised in the laboratory, were made to feed on untreated patients who had disseminated Hansen's disease. Invariably these untreated patients were found to have Hansen's bacilli in their blood. Hansen's bacilli have not yet been grown on bacteriological culture media. To prove the presence of these bacilli, we ground up the arthropods and inoculated part of the suspension into mouse foot pads. If there are living leprosy bacilli in the injected specimens, even in very small numbers, they will eventually grow in the mouse footpads to easily detectable numbers. We were able to show that the bacilli were readily taken up by mosquitoes, bedbugs, ticks, and fleas and that they survived in these arthropods until the next blood meal.

As a result of the study, it is now known that insects in and around dwellings in areas where Hansen's disease is prevalent can harbor living bacilli of the disease. It is also known that a variety of arthropods harbor living bacilli after a blood meal from patients with the disseminated form of Hansen's disease. Thus, it is reasonable to assume that arthropods can transmit the disease to highly susceptible human beings.

—"Living Hansen's Bacilli Found in Mosquitoes," *Public Health Reports* 90, March–April 1975

19.   A large rock balanced on a small protuberance is an object of a certain wonder. Such rocks are not rare; for example, in Goblin Valley in southern Utah there are more than 1,000 of them. But how do the rocks stay balanced?

Balanced rocks originate when a bed of sediments is dissected by erosion until a column is formed. If the strata at the top of the column are harder than the strata farther down, erosion will whittle the softer rock down to a pillar narrower than the capstone.

Nothing about the erosion process, however, guarantees that the end product will be symmetrical, and so what keeps the capstone in place? Two investigators at Kansas State University, Wilson Tripp, an engineer, and Fredric C. Appl, whose specialty is rock mechanics, suggest that a dynamic process is responsible, that it starts when the capstone first begins to tilt in any direction and that the point of contact between the capstone and its supporting pillar continuously shifts, thereby remaining exactly under the capstone's center of gravity. The principle that underlies the process is simply that rock under the stress of compression is more resistant to erosion than unstressed rock.

When the capstone first begins to tilt, Tripp and Appl note, the movement will shift the stress of compression from one section of the supporting pillar to another. Thereafter the unstressed section will erode more rapidly than before and the stressed section will erode more slowly. Successive tilts in other directions will stress successive sections of the pillar, and the differential erosion that results will make the process self-leveling. As a consequence the capstone will remain poised on the pillar until the inevitable day when the area of contact becomes too small for the self-leveling to continue, and the balancing rock, ceasing its apparent defiance of the laws of statistical mechanics, crashes satisfyingly to the ground.

—"Science and the Citizen," *Scientific American* 230, March 1974

■ ***20.***   Nearly everyone has seen sleeping pets whimper, twitch their whiskers, and seemingly pump their legs in pursuit of dream rabbits. But are they really dreaming? Since animals can't wake up the next morning and describe their dreams, the question seemed unanswerable. But recently, Dr. Charles Vaughan of the University of Pittsburgh devised an ingenious experiment so animals could tell us, at last, that they were indeed dreaming. Rhesus monkeys were placed in booths in front of a screen and taught to press on a bar every time they saw an image on the screen. Then the monkeys were wired to an electroencephalograph machine and placed back in the special booths. Eventually they fell asleep. Soon the EEG was recording the special tracings produced by the dreaming brains of the monkeys. But most important—the sleeping monkeys were eagerly pressing the bars. Clearly they were seeing images on the screens of their minds—they were dreaming. Or so Dr. Vaughan believes.

—BOB GAINES, "You and Your Sleep"

21. Perutz first read Pauling and Corey's seven papers on a Saturday morning at the laboratory. He saw that the alpha helix was obviously right. He saw, further, that if the alpha helix was right, the diffraction pattern of natural, unstretched keratin ought to show a spot at a position where nobody had ever reported one, which would confirm the model's uniform but very small rise—about 1.5 angstroms—along the axis of the helix between one amino-acid residue and the next. Perutz wondered why Astbury, who had taken hundreds of X-ray-diffraction pictures of fibres containing keratin, had never noticed this spot. But he remembered, from visits to Leeds, that Astbury's customary laboratory setup for taking diffraction pictures employed too small a photographic plate, and the wrong angle between the fibre and the X-ray beam, to reveal the 1.5 angstrom spot. So after lunch Perutz got a single horsehair, set it up at the angle he had calculated, and took a single picture. There was the predicted spot.

—HORACE FREELAND JUDSON, "Annals of Science (DNA)," *The New Yorker,* 4 December 1978

22. Early in the 18th century Edmund Halley asked: "Why is the sky dark at night?" This apparently naive question is not easy to answer, because if the universe had the simplest imaginable structure on the largest possible scale, the background radiation of the sky would be intense. Imagine a static infinite universe, that is, a universe of infinite size in which the stars and galaxies are stationary with respect to one another. A line of sight in any direction will ultimately cross the surface of a star, and the sky should appear to be made up of overlapping stellar disks. The apparent brightness of a star's surface is independent of its distance, so that everywhere the sky should be as bright as the surface of an average star. Since the sun is an average star, the entire sky, day and night, should be about as bright as the surface of the sun. The fact that it is not was later characterized as Olbers' paradox (after the 18th-century German astronomer Heinrich Olbers). The paradox applies not only to starlight but also to all other regions of the electromagnetic spectrum. It indicates that there is something fundamentally wrong with the model of a static infinite universe, but it does not specify what.

—ADRIAN WEBSTER, "The Cosmic Radiation Background," *Scientific American,* August 1974

23. Find a sociological puzzle, and one gets, usually, a slew of esoteric explanations, couched, of course, in opaque sociological jargon. Take the question which has befuddled a number of commentators recently: Why is it that women today seem to be marrying later than before? We shall not try to list all the ingenious explanations that have been advanced, from the rise of women's liberation to the increasing proportion of open homosexuality, male and female. Suffice to say that simple statistics, once understood, provide the most likely explanations. Here is Paul C. Glick, of the U.S. Bureau of the Census, writing in *Current Population Reports:*

> One of the tangible factors that probably helps to explain the increasing postpone-ment of marriage is the 5- to 10-percent excess of women as compared with men dur-ing recent years in those ages when most first marriages occur (18 to 24 years for women and 20 to 26 years for men). This imbalance is a consequence of past fluctua-tions in the birth rate. For example, women born in 1947 after the baby boom had begun were ready to marry in 20 years, but the men they were most likely to marry were born in 1944 or 1945 (about one-half in each year) when the birth rate was still low; these men were about 8 percent less numerous than the 20-year-old women. (By contrast, girls who were born during the last 15 years, while the birth rate has been declining, will be scarce as compared with eligible men when they reach the main age for marriage.)
> —VICTOR R. FUCHS, "The Economics of Health in a Post-Industrial Society," *The Public Interest,*
> Summer 1979

24. That nuclear fission can occur has been repeatedly demonstrated. How it occurs is still a subject of investigation after 30 years.

One of the first pictures of nuclear fission put forth was the liquid-drop model suggested by the late Niels Bohr. He proposed that the matter of a nucleus was a kind of uniform fluid and that a fissioning nucleus was like a drop of liquid that had become too large for its surface tension to hold in a spherical shape. Gradually it deformed itself until it split into two.

Liquid drops split symmetrically into two equal parts. But nuclei that fissioned did so asymmetrically, into unequal parts. So the original liquid-drop model appeared less than adequate.

Nevertheless, at the annual meeting of the American Physical Society in New York last week—a meeting that nowadays seems noteworthy more for politics than sci-ence—the discovery of symmetric fission in the early liquid-drop model was reported by Dr. Walter John of the Lawrence Radiation Laboratory at Livermore, Calif., on behalf of himself and colleagues Drs. E. Kenneth Hulet, R. W. Lougheed, and J. J. Wesolowski.

The symmetric fission was found to happen to the element fermium. It comes, however, in company with asymmetric fission—some nuclei divide unevenly and some divide evenly—and it is taken as evidence in favor of an emendation of the liquid-drop model, the so-called double-hump theory.

—"Symmetric Fission," *Science News* 99, 13 February 1971

25. Because plausible scientific evidence of causation in the social sciences has been difficult to establish, the causal flow of relationships between phenomena can often be interpreted as going either way, depending on the world view the interpreter fancies. For over a generation, many of the dominant explanations for the state of things in our important institutions were generated within a liberal framework and its assumptions about causation. Is the crime rate among those who have been to tough prisons higher than among those who have not? Then prisons obviously teach people to be criminals. (But, perhaps, the reverse is true, and the worst criminals are more likely to end up in the tough prisons.) Do satisfied workers have bosses who supervise loosely? Then if we teach bosses not to supervise closely we can increase the number of happy workers, the liberal explanation runs. (Or, is supervisory style a reaction to happy or unhappy work groups?) Do children who don't get proper breakfasts have difficulty in learning, as advocates of federal food programs insist? (Or, are children with learning difficulties likely to be members of families who do not provide either pressures to learn in school, or good breakfasts?) Do children's positive views of themselves derive from positive evaluations by adults around them? (Or, do adults feel positively about children with strong egos, hence high self-esteem?)

— S. M. MILLER, "Hard Realities and Soft Social Science," *Public Interest,* Spring 1980

26. Toxin-antitoxin reactions were the first immunological processes to which experimental precision could be applied, and the discovery of principles of great importance resulted from such studies. . . . The simplest assumption to account for the manner in which an antitoxin renders a toxin innocuous would be that the antitoxin destroys the toxin. Roux and Buchner, however, advanced the opinion that the antitoxins did not act directly upon toxin, but affected it indirectly through the mediation of tissue cells. Ehrlich, on the other hand, conceived the reaction of toxin and antitoxin as a direct union, analogous to the chemical neutralization of an acid by a base.

The conception of toxin destruction was conclusively refuted by the experiments of Calmette. This observer, working with snake poison, found that the poison itself (unlike most other toxins) possessed the property of resisting heat to 100° C., while its specific antitoxin, like other antitoxins, was destroyed at or about 70° C. Nontoxic mixtures of the two substances, when subjected to heat, regained their toxic properties. The natural inference from these observations was that the toxin in the original mixture had not been destroyed, but had been merely inactivated by the presence of the antitoxin, and again set free after destruction of the antitoxin by heat.

— HANS ZINSSER and STANHOPE BAYNE-JONES, *A Textbook of Bacteriology*

27. One morning, Bruno Pontecorvo and Edoardo Amaldi were testing some metals for radioactivity. The metals had been given the shape of hollow cylinders of equal size, inside which the source of neutrons could fit. To irradiate a cylinder, they placed the source inside it, and then set it in a lead box. On that particular morning Amaldi and Pontecorvo were experimenting with silver. Pontecorvo was the first to observe that the silver cylinder behaved strangely, that its activity was not always the same, but was different if it had been placed in the middle or in a corner of the lead box.

Baffled, Amaldi and Pontecorvo went to report to Fermi and Rasetti. Franco was inclined to blame the anomalies on statistical error and inaccuracy of measurements. Enrico, who takes an agnostic view of all phenomena, suggested that they try irradiating the silver cylinder outside the lead box and see what happened. More wonders were in store for the next few days. The objects around the cylinder seemed to influence its activity. If the cylinder had been on a wooden table while being irradiated, its activity was greater than if it had been on a piece of metal. By now the whole group's interest had been aroused, and everybody was participating in the work. They placed the neutron source outside the cylinder and interposed objects between them. A plate of lead made the activity increase slightly. Lead is a heavy substance. "Let's try a light one next," Fermi said, "for instance, paraffin." The experiment with paraffin was performed on the morning of October 22 [1934].

They took a big block of paraffin, dug a cavity in it, put the neutron source inside the cavity, irradiated the silver cylinder, and brought it to a Geiger counter to measure its activity. The counter clicked madly. The halls of the physics building resounded with loud exclamations: "Fantastic! Incredible! Black magic!" Paraffin increased the artificially induced radioactivity of silver up to one hundred times.

At noon the group parted reluctantly for the usual lunch recess . . . and by the time he [Fermi] went back to the laboratory he had a theory worked out to explain the strange action of paraffin.

Paraffin contains a great deal of hydrogen. Hydrogen nuclei are protons, particles having the same mass as neutrons. When the source is inclosed in a paraffin block, the neutrons hit the protons in the paraffin before reaching the silver nuclei. In collision with a proton, a neutron loses part of its energy, in the same manner as a billiard ball is slowed down when it hits a ball of its same size. Before emerging from the paraffin, a neutron will have collided with many protons in succession, and its velocity will be greatly reduced. This slow neutron will have a much better chance of being captured by a silver nucleus than a fast one, much as a slow golf ball has a better chance of making a hole than one which zooms fast and may bypass it.

If Enrico's explanations were correct, any other substance containing a large proportion of hydrogen should have the same effect as paraffin. "Let's try and see what a considerable quantity of water does to the silver activity," Enrico said on that same afternoon.

There was no better place to find a "considerable quantity of water" than the goldfish fountain in Corbino's private garden behind the laboratory. . . . On that afternoon of October 22, they rushed their source of neutrons and their silver cylinder to that fountain, and they placed both under water. The goldfish, I am sure, retained their calm and dignity, despite the neutron shower, more than did the crowd outside. The men's excitement was fed on the results of this experiment. It confirmed Fermi's theory. Water also increased the artificial radioactivity of silver by many times.

—LAURA FERMI, *Atoms in the Family*[44]

---

[44] By kind permission of Laura Fermi and The University of Chicago Press, from *Atoms in the Family* by Laura Fermi. Copyright 1954 by The University of Chicago. Copyright 1954 under the International Copyright Union. Published 1954. Eleventh Impression 1965.

Solutions to Selected Exercises

Exercises on pages 12–16

1. PREMISS: During the next century the average values of temperature and precipitation are likely to change over large areas of the globe.
   CONCLUSION: During the next century widespread adjustments are likely to occur in the distribution of terrestrial vegetation.

5. PREMISSES: (1) Women whose partners are aggressively uncommunicative have little chance of experiencing sexual pleasure.
   (2) It is not reasonable for women to consent to what they have little chance of enjoying.
   CONCLUSION: It is not reasonable for women to consent to aggressive noncommunicative sex.

10. PREMISS: The pastoral letter is a thoughtful and comprehensive effort to bring religious and moral principles to bear on nuclear weapons.
    CONCLUSION: The pastoral letter fully deserves the wide audience it seeks.

15. PREMISSES: (1) A free society is a pluralistic society.
    (2) A pluralistic society is one with countless propaganda from many sources.
    (3) Coping with propaganda requires a wide-spread critical intelligence which is largely the product of education.
    CONCLUSION: (unstated) A free society requires education.

20. PREMISS: Citizens who so value their "independence" that they will not enroll in a political party . . . abandon a share in decision-making at the primary level: the choice of the candidate.
    CONCLUSION: Citizens who so value their "independence" that they will not enroll in a political party are really forfeiting independence.

25. PREMISS: Monopoly destroys incentive to control corporate expenses and maintain maximum production.
    CONCLUSION: Monopoly is the enemy of good management.

30. PREMISES: (1) Thinking is a function of man's immortal soul.
         (2) God has given an immortal soul to every man and woman, but not to any other animal or to machines.
  CONCLUSION: No animal or machine can think.

35. PREMISES: (1) U.S. trade with Central America is minuscule.
         (2) Our investment in Central America is insignificant.
         (3) Overblown Pan-American rhetoric aside, we share few values with the countries of Central America.
         (4) Except for Costa Rica, the region has not known democracy and the governments have traditionally allowed a few corrupt families to run whole countries like giant plantations for private profit.
  CONCLUSION: The United States has no vital interests in Central America.

Exercises on pages 21–26

1. Incidentally I never miss [Roseanne Barr's TV] show. ①[I never see it.] ⑤⓪ ②[I never miss it.]

5. ①[If we have known freedom, then we love it;] ②[if we love freedom, then we fear, at some level (individually or collectively), its loss.] ③[If we have known freedom, then we fear its loss.]

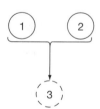

10. ①[Modern technology can tell us very well, down to the millimeter; what the brain matter of a baby's cortex is,] and ⓣⓗⓤⓢ ②[we know very accurately through brain scans and other tests what sort of life is in store for deplorably handicapped infants.]

15. ① [A just society cannot possibly pay everyone the same income,] ⟨since⟩ ② [the aptitudes and efforts of individuals diverge dramatically,] and ⟨since⟩③ [the common good is far better served, accordingly, by systematic inequalities of reward.]

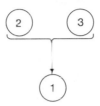

20. ① [the government need[s] to intervene in the treatment of handicapped infants.] ②[The Rehabilitation Act of 1973 states that it is illegal in any institution that receives federal aid to discriminate against anyone on the basis of race, creed, color, religion, ethnic origin or handicap.] ③[We have good evidence that many children are deprived of their civil rights by being treated in a different way than they would be treated if they were not handicapped.]

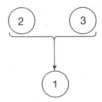

25. ①[Over the last quarter-century, as this is written, the average work week in industry has increased moderately.] ②[The standard work week has declined but this has been more than offset by increased demand for overtime work and the companion willingness to supply it.] ③[During this period average weekly earnings, adjusted for price increases, have nearly doubled.] ⟨On the evidence, one must conclude that⟩④[as their incomes rise, people will work longer hours and seek less leisure.]

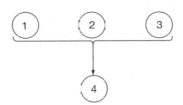

30. ①[There is no such thing as free will.] ②[The mind is induced to wish this or that by some cause,] and ③[that cause is determined by another cause,] ④[and so on back to infinity.]

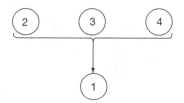

35. ①[The United States economy is still the most powerful in the world;] and ②[if the country's position as a manufacturer is now less secure, its position as supplier of food to the world was never more important.] ③[Unlike France, Italy, or England, it has no opposition party whose policies would force large-scale adaptations of the system or an attempt at conversion to socialism.] ④[The American recession, costly though it has been, has not produced serious political or social unrest.] ⑤[We have been mercifully spared Europe's terrorism.]

⑥[America's inflation is still below that of most of the rest of the industrial world,] and ⑦[the prices of shares on its stock exchanges are, by comparative standards, cheap.] (Thus,)⑧[by all the criteria of history or common sense, the dollar would seem to be one of the soundest, not one of the frailest, currencies.]

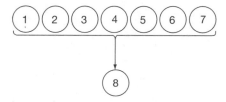

Exercises on pages 31–36

1. In my opinion ①[the preamble to the Missouri statute is unconstitutional] (for two reasons.) ②[To the extent that the preamble has substantive impact on the freedom to use contraceptive procedures, it is inconsistent with the central holding in *Griswold.*] ③[To the extent that the preamble merely makes "legislative findings without operative effect," as the State argues, . . . it violates the Establishment Clause of the First Amendment.]

5. An explanation. The fact to be explained is the presence of so many fossils in the region south and west of Ulan Bator. The propositions that do the explaining are as follows: (1) In the time of the dinosaurs and the rise of mammals, the area south and west of Ulan Bator was marked by large basins where bones deposited in sand were more certain to become fossilized. (2) In the 40 million years since the time of the dinosaurs, the area has been little disturbed by geological turmoil or people. ③ Erosion by wind and weather has exposed the relics of many dinosaurs and early mammals.

10. An explanation. The fact to be explained is the aggressive wooing of merchants by American Express. The proposition that does the explaining is that American Express has come under increasing attack from Visa (a competitor).

15. A (partial) explanation. What is (partially) explained is why Honolulu businessman Robert W. Hall shot three men at the Waikiki Yacht Club in May 1980. The proffered (partial) explanation is that he was suffering an allergic reaction to a specific ingredient in wine he drank earlier in the evening.

    This is said to be a partial explanation because it mentions only "one of the reasons . . ." rather than "the reason. . . ."

20. But ①[the peculiar evil of silencing the expression of an opinion is, that it is robbing the human race; posterity as well as the existing generation; those who dissent from the opinion, still more than those who hold it.] ②[If the opinion is right, they are deprived of the opportunity of exchanging error for truth:] ③[if wrong, they lose, what is almost as great a benefit, the clearer perception and livelier impression of truth, produced by its collision with error.]

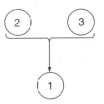

25. An explanation. What is explained is that businessmen praise competition and love monopoly. The explanation proposed is not, as some economists have contended, that monopoly ensures a "quiet life"—it rarely does—but that it promises bigger profits.

30. An explanation. What is explained is the Russians' having become more cautious in the third world. The proposed explanation is in terms of a combination of their own economic weakness, the unpredictability of many of their assumed new friends, the Reagan administration's reassertiveness, and South Africa's recent pugnacity.

35. Important voices, both internal and external to the university community, are suggesting that ①[academic tenure is inconsistent with the vitality of higher education in the coming decades.] ②[Tenure, (some would argue), not only works to shield incompetency], ③[create a kind of "academic aristocracy,"] and ④[block the access of women and minorities to university positions,] but also ⑤[deprives a university community of the necessary flexibility and adaptability to meet the particular demands of the 1980s and 1990s.]

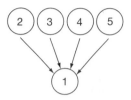

40. ①[The Russian warriors are now armed with nuclear weapons on a vast scale.] ②[The strategic rocket forces of the Soviet Union are comparable in size and quality with those of the United States.] ③[The Soviet rocket commanders could, if they were ordered to do so, obliterate the cities of the United States within thirty minutes.] ④[It has (therefore) become a matter of some importance for us in the United States to understand what may be in the Soviet commanders' minds.]

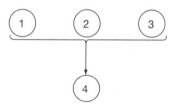

Exercises on pages 44–50

1. Opponents of the death penalty sometimes argue for its abolition on the ground that it is cruel and unusual and therefore impermissible punishment. According to them, ①[nothing that deprives a person of his life can be a usual punishment,] and ②[it is cruel for anyone to have his days ended by a period of waiting to be hanged, electrocuted or gassed.] (So)③[however effective it is as a means of preventing crime, execution is wrong] and ④[execution must be avoided.]

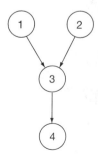

5. ①[[I]f we can cause animals to suffer, then what we do to them not only can hurt them, it can harm them;] and ②[if we can harm animals, then we can detract from the experiential quality of their lives, considered over time;] and ③[Implicit conclusion: If we can cause animals to suffer, then we can detract from the experiential quality of their lives.] ④[If we can detract from the experiential quality of animal lives, then we must view animals as retaining their identity over time and as having a good or ill of their own.] ⑤[Implicit conclusion: If we can cause animals to suffer, then we must view them as retaining their identity over time and as having a good or ill of their own.]

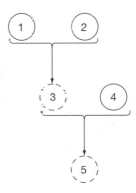

10. ①[If you want your computer to be able to handle a bit of data within a nanosecond [a nanosecond is a billionth of a second], no signal path can be much longer than 15 centimetres], (because) ②[that is roughly the distance an electrical signal can travel in a billionth of a second.] So ③[your computer will have to be tiny.]

15. ①[Bodies become heavier with increasing speed,] (thus) ②[requiring more force to accelerate them further;] ③[in the end an infinity strong force would be required to make them reach the speed of light.] (Therefore) ④[no object can be accelerated to that speed, let alone beyond.]

20. ①[The death penalty does not deter criminals] (because) ②[at the time the crime is done they do not expect to be arrested.] Also, (since) ③[many offenders are mentally unbalanced,] ④[they do not consider the rational consequences of their irrational activities.]

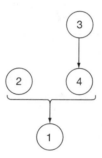

25. ① [While the dollar will eventually return to more reasonable levels, the damage to industrial America is permanent.] ②[Once a major international competitor such as Caterpillar loses foreign and domestic sales because of an overvalued dollar it won't easily get them back.] ③[Foreign competitors will have established the contacts and service networks they do not now have] and ④[customers will have little reason to change suppliers unless there is a substantial period when the dollar is grossly undervalued.] ⑤ [A return to parity won't repair the damage done.]

(Consequently) ⑥[the Reagan administration is making a major mistake when it refuses to intervene in foreign-exchange markets to force the dollar back to levels where American companies can compete on world markets.]

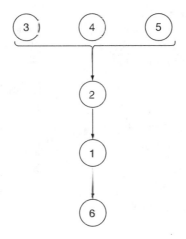

30. ①[In inflationary times it is obviously advantageous to borrow money at normal interest rates] (because) ②[dollars will be cheaper and more plentiful when it comes time to repay the loan.] (Therefore) ③[businesses seek to borrow funds]— but ④[banks are loath to lend,] (for exactly the same reasons.)

    (Two results follow.) ⑤[First, interest rates go ever higher to compensate banks for the falling value of the dollars they will receive. . . .]

    ⑥[Second, banks refuse to lend for more than short periods of time.] (The result is that) ⑦[business has to take on short term loans at high interest rates.]

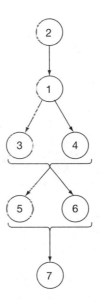

35. ". . . You appeared to be surprised when I told you, on our first meeting, that you had come from Afghanistan."

"You were told, no doubt."

"Nothing of the sort. I *knew* you came from Afghanistan. From long habit the train of thoughts ran so swiftly through my mind that I arrived at the conclusion without being conscious of intermediate steps. There were such steps, however. The train of reasoning ran, ① [Here is a gentleman of a medical type,] but ② [with the air of a military man.] Ⓒlearly ③ [an army doctor,] then. ④[He has just come from the tropics,] [his face is dark,] and ⑥[that is not the natural tint of his skin,] Ⓕor ⑦ [his wrists are fair.] ⑧[He has undergone hardship and sickness,] Ⓐs ⑨[his haggard face says clearly.] ⑩[His left arm has been injured.] ⑪[He holds it in a stiff and unnatural manner.] ⑫[Where in the tropics could an English army doctor have seen much hardship and got his arm wounded? Clearly in Afghanistan.] The whole train of thought did not occupy a second. I then remarked that you came from Afghanistan, and you were astonished."

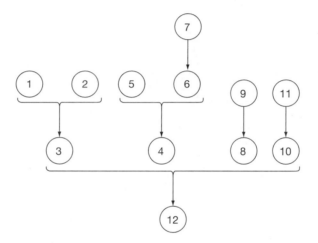

Exercises on pages 62–67

1. If the first native is a politician, then he lies and denies being a politician. If the first native is not a politician, then he tells the truth and denies being a politician. In either case, then, the first native denies being a politician.

   Since the second native reports that the first native denies being a politician, he tells the truth, and is, therefore, a nonpolitician.

   The third native asserts that the first native is a politician. If the first native is a politician, then the third native speaks the truth and is, therefore, a nonpolitician. If the first native is a nonpolitician, then the third native lies and is, therefore, a politician. Hence only one of the first and third natives is a politician, and since the second is a nonpolitician, there is only one politician among the three natives.

5. Since Lefty said that Spike did it, Spike's first and third statements are equivalent in meaning and therefore either both true or both false. Since only one statement is false, they are both true.

Dopey's third statement is, therefore, false, and so his first two are true. Therefore Butch's third statement is false and so his first two are true, of which the second reveals that Red is the guilty man.

(An alternative method of solving this problem was communicated to me by Professor Peter M. Longley of the University of Alaska. All but Red both assert their innocence *and* accuse someone else. If their professions of innocence are false, so are their accusations of other persons. But no one makes two false statements, so their statements that they are innocent must be true. Hence Red is the guilty one. This solution, however, presupposes that only one of the men is guilty.)

(Still another method of solving this problem is due to James I. Campbell of Eisenhower College and Walter Charen of Rutgers College. Dopey's second statement and Butch's third statement are contradictory, so at least one must be false. But if Dopey's second statement were false, his third statement would be true and Spike would be guilty. However, if Spike were guilty, his first and third statements would both be false, so he cannot be guilty and hence Dopey's second statement cannot be false. Therefore, Butch's third statement must be false, whence his second statement is true and Red is the guilty man.)

10. Green is an outfielder (i) and is married (o), but the right fielder and the center fielder are bachelors (e); so *Green is the left fielder* (p).

    Knight or Adams played outfield (f), but Adams played infield or battery (i), so Knight is an outfielder (q).

    White, Miller, and Brown are not outfielders (p and e), nor are Jones, Smith, and Adams (i); so Hunter is an outfielder (r).

    Hunter and Knight play right field and center field (p, q, and r); the right fielder is shorter than the center fielder (g); Knight is shorter than Hunter (b); so *Knight is the right fielder* (s) and *Hunter is the center fielder* (t).

    Brown is not the pitcher (a), nor the catcher (e and o), nor the shortstop (n), nor the second baseman (l), nor the third baseman (e and o); so *Brown is the first baseman* (u).

    The second baseman is a bachelor (k), so he is either White, Miller, or Brown (e). But he is neither Brown (u) nor Miller (k), so *White is the second baseman* (v).

    The catcher is neither Jones, Brown, nor Hunter (l), neither Miller nor White (e and o), not Adams (m), neither Green (p) nor Knight (s); so *Smith is the catcher* (w).

    The third baseman is neither Green (p), nor Knight (s), nor Hunter (t), nor Brown (u), nor White (v), nor Smith (w), nor Miller (e and o), nor Jones (c); so *Adams is the third baseman* (x).

    Miller is a bachelor (e) and therefore not the pitcher (h); nor is Miller the catcher (w), nor an outfielder (p, s, and t), nor a baseman (u, v, and x), so *Miller is the shortstop* (y).

    And by elimination, *Jones is the pitcher* (z).

15. 1. Mr. Robinson lives in Detroit (given: a).
        Therefore,
    2. If the brakeman's next-door neighbor is Mr. Robinson, then the brakeman lives in Detroit (from 1 and common knowledge).

3.   The brakeman lives halfway between Detroit and Chicago (given: b).
     Therefore,

4.   The brakeman does not live in Detroit (from 3 and common knowledge).
     Therefore,

5.   The brakeman's next-door neighbor is not Mr. Robinson (from 2 and 4).

6.   The brakeman's next-door neighbor is one of the three passengers (given: e).
     Therefore,

7.   The brakeman's next-door neighbor is either Mr. Jones or Mr. Smith (from 5, 6, and the initial statement of facts).

8.   The brakeman's next-door neighbor earns exactly three times as much as the brakeman (given: e).

9.   Mr. Jones earns exactly $20,000 a year (given: c).

10. If the brakeman's next-door neighbor is Mr. Jones, then the brakeman earns exactly one-third of $20,000 (from 8 and 9).

11. Nobody earns exactly one-third of $20,000 (common knowledge).
     Therefore,

12. The brakeman does not earn exactly one-third of $20,000 (from 11).
     Therefore,

13. The brakeman's next-door neighbor is not Mr. Jones (from 10 and 12).
     Therefore,

14. The brakeman's next-door neighbor is Mr. Smith (from 7 and 13).
     Therefore,

15. Mr. Smith lives halfway between Detroit and Chicago (from 3 and 14).
     Therefore,

16. Mr. Smith does not live in Chicago (from 15 and common knowledge).
     Therefore,

17. Mr. Robinson does not live in Chicago (from 1 and common knowledge).

18. At least one passenger lives in Chicago (presuppostion of f).
     Therefore,

19. The passenger living in Chicago is Mr. Jones (from 16, 17, 18, and facts).

20. The passenger living in Chicago has the same name as the brakeman (given: f).
     Therefore,

21. Mr. Jones has the same name as the brakeman (from 19 and 20).
     Therefore,

22. Jones is the brakeman (from 21).
     Therefore,

23. Smith is not the brakeman (from 22 and facts).

24. Smith once beat the fireman at billiards (given: d).
     Therefore,

25. Smith is not the fireman (from 24).
     Therefore,

26. Smith is the engineer (from 23, 25, and facts).

Exercises on pages 79–82

I. 1.   Directive—the minister is trying to get the groom to answer.

Commissive—the groom commits himself to the bride and to the relationship.

Expressive—the groom expresses his love and devotion to the bride.

5. Expressive—Lincoln expresses his love of country and tries to evoke a similar sentiment in his audience.

Directive—Lincoln tries to get his audience to defend the Union.

10. Directive—let us stand fast together.

Expressive—to evoke strong feelings of solidarity.

Informative—if we do not stand together, we shall all lose our lives.

15. Directive—the speaker is trying to get the jury to reach a verdict against Pickwick.

Expressive—the speaker expresses scorn for and tries to evoke feelings of hostility toward Pickwick.

Informative—the speaker informs the jury that Pickwick is a revoltingly heartless, systematic villain.

II. 1. Asserts that the government's classification of ice as a "food product" implies that Antarctica is one of the world's foremost food producers.

Intended to cause rejection of government bureaus' rulings and classifications.

Provides evidence that the speaker (writer) has a sharp wit and that he is opposed to (some) governmental intrusion into business.

5. Asserts that turbulence and all other evil tempers of this evil age belong to the middle classes rather than to the lower classes.

Intended to cause hostility toward the middle classes rather than toward the lower classes.

Provides evidence that the speaker is hostile towards the middle classes, and not (or at least does not regard himself as) middle class himself.

10. Asserts that egoism is generally the reason why a person who is reasonably well off does not enjoy life.

Intended to cause people to take an active interest in others.

Provides evidence that the speaker dislikes egoism and takes an interest in others.

Provides evidence that the speaker is eloquent.

Exercises on pages 90–92

1. Disagreement in belief: a believes that it is important (prudent) to reflect on one's actions before undertaking them, whereas b believes that it is important (prudent), in at least some cases, to be bold and impetuous.

Disagreement in attitude: a has a positive attitude toward reflection, whereas b has a neutral or negative attitude toward reflection.

5. Disagreement in belief: a believes that absence makes the heart grow fonder, whereas b believes that absence loosens the bonds of love and affection.

Disagreement in attitude: a has a positive attitude toward absence, since it strengthens the bonds of love and affection, whereas b has a negative attitude toward absence.

10. Disagreement in belief: Mussolini believes that war is noble and honorable, whereas Sumner believes that it is ignoble and dishonorable.

   Disagreement in attitude: Mussolini has a positive attitude toward war, whereas Sumner has a negative attitude toward war.

15. Disagreement in belief: Decatur believes that one's country is worthy even if it acts wrongly, whereas Schurz believes that one's country is worthy only if it acts rightly.

   Agreement in attitude: Decatur and Schurz have a positive attitude toward their country (the United States) and a negative attitude toward wrong-doing.

Exercises on pages 103–105

1. Fallacy of complex question. The question presupposes that Crest is a good toothpaste. It may not be. The advertiser shifts attention from the quality of the toothpaste to whether the prospective consumer's children are "worth" it. A parent might respond as follows: "First let's determine whether your toothpaste is any good; then we'll decide whether it's worth my kids!"

5. Fallacy of equivocation. The word "deter" is used in two senses: first, to mean "give reason not to do something"; second, to mean "prevent." While those who are executed are deterred in the second sense (they are prevented from committing further crimes), they are not deterred in the first sense. Usually, when people say that the death penalty does not deter, or is not a sufficient deterrent, they are claiming that the execution of person A does not give *other* people reason to refrain from doing what A did. Lybrand shifts from this sense to the other and is thereby able to "refute" the popular argument.

10. Fallacy of amphiboly. The colon in the first sentence makes it sound as though *York* died on the expedition, when in fact he did not. The colon should be replaced with a semicolon.

Exercises on pages 110–111

1. Straw-person fallacy. S's argument is not that the economy is improving because *nobody* lost a job; it is that more people gained than lost jobs. T misstates S's argument, dismisses the misstated version, and concludes that S's argument is defective.

5. Fallacy of composition (part to whole). The characteristic of sphericity cannot be transferred from part to whole. This is the part-to-whole version of the fallacy because the universe is a functioning or systemic collection of parts.

10. Fallacy of division (whole to part). The Senate is a functional body, therefore a whole as opposed to a mere collection of members. Unfortunately for the arguer, powerfulness cannot be transferred from whole to part. Each senator has only one vote and cannot, alone, pass laws.

Exercises on pages 120–121

1. Fallacy of appeal to authority. Physicians are rightly revered in our society, for they prevent and cure disease, but this does not mean that they are authoritative on all matters. Dolan's letter is not about medical matters, about which he, a medical doctor, might be presumed to be authoritative. It is about moral matters. By affix-

ing "M.D." to his name, he tempts readers to transfer his medical authority to the moral realm. *However,* those who accept Dolan as a moral authority, and not just a medical authority, do not commit the fallacy of appeal to authority.

5. Fallacy of appeal to emotion (fear). Instead of giving readers *reason* to believe that the newspaper is worth purchasing, the Nazis tried to frighten them into buying it.

10. Fallacy of attack on the person (poisoning the well). Instead of addressing the arguments of those who vote against extending protection of rape laws to married women (presumably they had reasons), the authors question the motives of the legislators, suggesting that they vote as they do out of self-interest (self-preservation).

Exercises on pages 127–129

1. Fallacy of hasty generalization. Unless the two female bosses happen to be representative of women, which is unlikely, the argument is fallacious.

5. Slippery slope (logical version). The claim is that the situations described are relevantly alike, so if one allows one type of lawsuit, one must, on pain of inconsistency, allow *all* of them. But that would be unacceptable (because it would cause the "collapse" of the courts), so group defamation lawsuits by women against pornographers should not be allowed. Whether the argument is fallacious depends on whether the situations are relevantly alike. The more relevant differences, the weaker the argument.

10. Weak analogy. Dyson is arguing that because science and music are relevantly alike, their practitioners should be treated alike. Since "waywardness" is tolerated in musicians, it should therefore be tolerated in scientists. Whether this argument is fallacious depends on the number of relevant similarities and dissimilarities between science and music. The greater the number of relevant similarities, the stronger the argument.

Exercises on pages 129–131

1. Fallacy of begging the question. The issue (question) is why the man with three pearls gets three. In the course of *justifying* his having three, he cites the *fact* that he has three.

5. Fallacy of appeal to the people. The mere fact that 80 percent (or even 100 percent) of the people believe something doesn't make it true. It may provide a reason to vote a certain way, but it doesn't make the belief true.

10. Fallacy of complex question. Connors's question presupposes that the official *did* miss the call. The official, of course, will deny this.

15. Fallacy of hasty generalization. Unless these two Schwinns are representative of Schwinn bicycles, which is unlikely, the generalization is hasty.

20. Fallacy of false cause (*post hoc ergo propter hoc*). The inference is that, because the deaths occurred *after* treatment by the doctor, they occurred *because* of treatment by the doctor.

Exercises on page 148

I. 1. animal, vertebrate, mammal, feline, wildcat, lynx.

5. number, real number, rational number; integer, positive integer, prime.

Exercises on page 150–151

I. 1. Louis F. Gossett, Jr., Clint Eastwood, Meryl Streep.
    5. gold, silver, platinum.
    10. Robert Penn Warren, Edgar Allan Poe, Walt Whitman.
    15. Boston University, Harvard University, Massachusetts Institute of Technology.
II. 1. movie star
    5. metal
    10. American
    15. employer

Exercises on pages 154–155

I. 1. ridiculous.
    5. vanity.
    10. danger.
    15. portent.
    20. wigwam.
    25. custom.
II. 1. unmarried man.
    5. male sibling.
    10. male parent.
    15. young sheep.
    20. small horse.
    25. male offspring.

Exercises on pages 158–162

II. 1. Violates Rules 1, 3, and 4. The main problem is the obscurity of the definition. If someone does not know the meaning of "freedom," is he or she likely to understand it better after reading Giamatti's definition?
    5. Violates Rule 2. The word "base" appears in the definiens as well as in the definiendum.
    10. Violates Rule 2. While the word "hazard" does not appear in the definiendum, its synonym, "dangerous," does.
    15. Violates Rules 1, 3, and 4. The definition is obscure.
    20. Violates Rule 2. The same word or a derivation appears in both the definiendum and the definiens.
III. 1. Expressed in figurative language, violates Rule 4. It also fails to state the essence (which is that faith is a virtue), thus violating Rule 1.
    5. Too broad, since some prose also records such moments; and too narrow, since some (great) poetry is tragic; violates Rule 3. It also may be criticized as being phrased in figurative language, violating Rule 4, although this is not altogether obvious.
    10. Too broad, because some persons with a very low opinion of themselves tend to behave this way; and too narrow, because some supremely conceited persons do not stoop to such vainglory or social climbing; violates Rule 3. It also may be criticized for violating Rule 1 in not stating the essence, which is a trait of character rather than a tendency to overt behavior of the kinds specified.

15. Too narrow: not all political power is exercised "for the public good," certainly not "*only* for the public good"; violates Rule 3.

20. Too broad, violates Rule 3. In his *A History of Western Philosophy*, Bertrand Russell criticized this definition on the grounds that "the dealings of a drill-sergeant with a crowd of recruits, or of a bricklayer with a heap of bricks . . . exactly fulfill Dewey's definition of 'inquiry.'"

25. This is a beautiful definition. If a fault is to be found, it is that people can be patriotic to only some civic groups such as a nation, which if true would make Sumner's definition too broad; violates Rule 3.

Exercises on pages 167–171

1. Analogical argument. *Hamlet* without poetry or the Prince of Denmark would lose its character; it would cease to be the sort of thing it is. Baseball is said to be analogous to *Hamlet*, so baseball without romance and heroism would lose its character. That is, romance and heroism are essential to the sport.

5. Analogical argument. The comparison is between aiding the Soviets and Al Capone's receiving aid from the government. Because the latter is unconscionable, so is the former.

10. Nonargumentative use of analogy. Specifically, the use is descriptive. Thinking is a familiar activity, so the author's aim is to leave a vivid picture in the reader's mind.

15. Analogical argument. The author points out a similarity between persons and infers that because one of them feels pain while having a tooth extracted without an anaesthetic, so does the other.

20. Analogical argument. The author points out that malaria parasites and microfilariae behave similarly. He concludes that they have the same "biological purpose": to facilitate transmission by mosquitoes.

25. Analogical argument. There is obviously water in the ocean. Saying this is like saying that Dorothy (Dodo) Cheney comes from a tennis-playing family. Hence, Dorothy (Dodo) Cheney obviously comes from a tennis-playing family.

Exercises on pages 176–183

I. 1. (a) strengthens (criterion 2); (b) strengthens (criterion 1); (c) strengthens (criterion 3); (d) strengthens (criterion 5); (e) weakens (criterion 4); (f) leaves the argument unaffected (criterion 6).

5. (a) strengthens (criterion 5); (b) weakens (criterion 4); (c) strengthens (criterion 2); (d) leaves the argument unaffected (criterion 6); (e) strengthens (criterion 3); (f) strengthens (criterion 1).

II. 1. Large diamonds, armies, and great intellects all have the attributes of greatness [of value for diamonds, of military strength for armies, of mental superiority for intellects] and of divisibility [through cutting for diamonds; dispersion for armies; interruption, disturbance, and distraction for intellects].

Large diamonds and armies all have the attribute of having their greatness diminish when they are divided.

Therefore great intellects also have the attribute of having their greatness diminish when they are divided.

(1) There are only three kinds of instances among which the analogies

are said to hold, which is not very many. On the other hand, there are many, many instances of these kinds. By our first criterion the argument is fairly cogent.

(2) There are only three respects in which the things involved are said to be analogous. This is not many and the argument is accordingly rather weak.

(3) The conclusion states only that, when "divided," a great intellect will sink to the level of an ordinary one. This is not a terribly strong conclusion relative to the premisses, and so by our third criterion the argument is fairly cogent.

(4) The instances with which the conclusion deals are enormously, fantastically different from the instances mentioned in the premisses. There are so many disanalogies between intellects, on the one hand, and large diamonds and armies, on the other, that by our fourth criterion Schopenhauer's argument is almost totally lacking in probative force.

(5) There are but two kinds of instances in the premisses with which the conclusion's instances are compared. Armies and large diamonds are, however, quite dissimilar to each other, so from the point of view of our fifth criterion, the argument is moderately cogent.

(6) Schopenhauer recognizes that the question of relevance is important, for he introduces a separate little discussion on this point. He urges that superiority (the "greatness") of a great intellect "depends upon" its concentration or undividedness. Here he invokes the illustrative or explanatory (nonargumentative) analogy of the concave mirror which focuses all its available light on one point. There is indeed some merit in this claim, and by our sixth criterion the argument has a fairly high degree of cogency.

Finally, however, it must be admitted that the whole passage might plausibly be analyzed as invoking large diamonds and armies for illustrative and explanatory rather than argumentative purposes. The plausibility of this alternative analysis, however, derives more from the weakness of the analogical argument than from what is explicitly stated in the passage in question.

5. This passage can be analyzed in two different ways. In both ways the analogical argument is presented primarily as an illustration of the biologist's reasoning

(I) Porpoises and men all have lungs, warm blood, and hair.

   Men are mammals.

   Therefore porpoises are also mammals.

   (1) There are many instances examined, which makes the conclusion probable.

   (2) There are only three respects noted in the premisses in which porpoises and men resemble each other. In terms of their sheer number, this is not many; not enough to make the argument plausible.

   (3) The conclusion is enormously strong relative to the premisses, because so many attributes are summarized in the term "mammal" (shown by the variety of other, specific attributes confidently predicted by the zoologist). This tends, of course, to weaken the argument.

(4) There are many disanalogies between men and porpoises; porpoises are aquatic, men are terrestrial, porpoises have tails, men do not, porpoises do not have the well-developed, highly differentiated limbs characteristics of men, and so on. These tend to weaken the argument.

(5) There are very few dissimilarities among men—biologically speaking—and by our fifth criterion this tends to weaken the argument too.

(6) But in terms of relevance the argument is superlatively good, because biologists have found the three attributes remarked in the premises to be such remarkably dependable indicators of other mammalian characteristics.

(II) Porpoises and men all have lungs, warm blood, and hair. Men also nurse their young with milk, have a four-chambered heart, bones of a particular type, a certain general pattern of nerves and blood vessels, and red blood cells that lack nuclei.

Therefore porpoises also nurse their young with milk, have a four-chambered heart, bones of the same particular type, the same general pattern of nerves and blood vessels, and red blood cells that lack nuclei.

This version of the analogical argument contained in the given passage is evaluated in much the same way as the first one discussed. It is somewhat stronger an argument than the first one according to the third criterion, because in spite of the apparently greater detail in the second version's conclusion, it is weaker than that of the first version because being a mammal entails all these details plus many more.

Nature has a way of reminding us that such arguments are only probable, however, and never demonstrative. For the platypus resembles all other mammals in having lungs, warm blood, hair, nursing their young with milk, and so on. Other mammals are viviparous (bearing their young alive). Therefore the platypus . . .? No, the platypus lays eggs.

10. Gram-positive bacteria in culture mediums and gram-positive bacteria in the living body all have much the same properties: ways of growing, or reproducing, etc. Gram-positive bacteria in culture mediums have the property of being destroyed by the presence of penicillium. Therefore gram-positive bacteria in the living body also will be destroyed by the presence of penicillium.

(1) There are very many kinds and instances that have been examined, which makes the conclusion very probable.

(2) There are very many respects hidden in the "etc." in which gram-positive bacteria resemble each other whether in culture mediums or in the living body. These make the conclusion highly probable.

(3) The conclusion is strong relative to the premises, though it could have been stronger. A weaker conclusion would have been that the presence of penicillium in the living body would have inhibited the growth of gram-positive bacteria there. A stronger conclusion would have stated that exactly that same amount of penicillium in the living body would destroy the gram-positive bacteria there in exactly the same time that it did in a culture medium. I think (especially in the light of subsequent knowledge!) that the conclusion could have been regarded at the time as highly probable.

(4) There are relatively few disanalogies between the living body and culture mediums *relative to the growth in them of bacteria.* (Of course, this is a consequence of bacteriologists designing culture mediums to simulate the living body in the respects in which it is an acceptable habitat for bacteria.) So from this point of view also the conclusion is probable.

(5) There were many disanalogies among the instances mentioned in the premisses: Dr. Fleming "found that quite a number of species" were destroyed by penicillium. So here too the conclusion is highly probable.

(6) The analogy is relevant because it was well known long before Dr. Fleming's discovery that a fungus subsists on organic matter. By this criterion also the conclusion is very probable.

15. Physicists study ideal (abstract) entities and draw practical conclusions from them. Since mathematical biophysics also studies ideal (abstract) entities, probably it, too, can draw practical conclusions.

(1) Only two instances are cited: physics and mathematical biophysics. This weakens the argument.

(2) The instances have a number of common characteristics: both sciences study ideal (abstract) entities; both have a methodology; both have a goal of understanding the world; and so on.

(3) The conclusion is vague. If the "practical" results of mathematical biophysics were more clearly specified, it may be that the conclusion is too strong relative to the premises, in which case the argument is weakened.

(4) There are obvious disanalogies between physics and mathematical biophysics—for example, physics has been around longer.

(5) Since only one instance besides mathematical biophysics is cited, this criterion—diversity of instances—cannot be satisfied. This weakens the argument. What the author needs to show is that *several* diverse disciplines have the characteristics of studying ideal (abstract) entities; having a methodology; having a goal of understanding the world; and so on.

(6) The analogies cited in (2) are relevant because having a methodology and a goal of understanding the world make it more likely that the disciplines in question have practical uses. The disanalogy cited in (4) is arguably irrelevant, for the age of the science appears to have nothing to do with whether it will achieve practical results.

Exercises on pages 185–189

1. The argument being refuted is alleged to be the following:
Psychoanalysis is very difficult and time-consuming. Therefore psychoanalysis is the most valuable method of psychotherapy.
The refuting analogy is:
The Model T (a Ford car last produced during the 1920s) is very difficult and time consuming (which it was: because of its stiff springs it was uncomfortable to ride in, and it was hazardous in traffic because of its low horsepower; and it was prone to breakdown because of its ancient vintage). Therefore the Model T is the most valuable method of wheeled transportation.
These two arguments have the same form, and since the refuting analogy has a

true premiss and a false conclusion, it is invalid and therefore a very effective refutation of the given argument.

5. The argument being refuted is alleged to be the following:

There are many things wrong with society—some of which are increasingly conspicuous. We have also had decades of uninterrupted growth. Therefore the growth must be the cause of the various social and economic ills that we see around us.

The refuting analogy is:

There are many ills of society. People spend more time these days in cleaning their teeth. Therefore the fact that people spend more time these days in cleaning their teeth must be the cause of all the ills of society.

The two arguments have the same form, and since the refuting analogy has true premisses and a false conclusion, it is obviously invalid and therefore a very effective refutation of the given argument.

In fact, both arguments commit the Fallacy of False Cause, of the *post hoc ergo propter hoc* variety discussed in section 3.5.

10. The argument being refuted is alleged to be the following:

The death penalty gives rise to inevitable litigation. That inevitable litigation makes the cost of the death penalty prohibitive in time and money. Therefore the death penalty is not a practical sanction (penalty).

The refuting analogy is:

I have poured glue in the works of your watch. As a consequence your watch is worthless. Therefore you ought to throw your watch away.

These two arguments have rather different forms, and as a consequence the refuting analogy is not a very effective refutation of the given argument.

More specifically, it is not obvious that the "abolitionists" are the ones who file the large numbers of petitions in each case—indeed, it is explicitly stated that it is the convicted murderer who does so. So the original arguer might object that it is not he who pours glue into the watch, but might rather insist that the watch in question is inescapably prone to collect glue in its works. And for *that* reason it is worthless as a timepiece, and ought to be thrown away.

There are so many arguments both for and against capital punishment that not much turns on the given argument and its proposed refutation.

15. The argument being refuted is the following: Price increases are the cause of inflation; therefore, budget deficits are not the cause of inflation (or they play nothing more than a minimal role in causing inflation).

The refuting analogy is: Meals cause hunger; therefore, poverty, crop failures, overpopulation, transportation breakdowns, etc., are not the cause of hunger (or they play nothing more than a minimal role in causing hunger).

These two arguments have much the same form, and since the refuting analogy has a false conclusion, it shows that there is something wrong with the original argument. What is wrong is much the same thing that is wrong with the given argument. There is a causal connection between price increases and inflation, just as there is a causal connection between meals and hunger. But it is hunger that causes meals (to be eaten), not the other way around. And that shows—it could be argued (and has often been argued)—that it is the inflating of wages, so that more money is paid for fewer goods produced, that causes the price rises in the goods produced. And it is that spiraling which constitutes inflation. Needless to say, what is the cause—or causes—of inflation is a matter that has been much debated. But it is surely a mistake to say that price increases are the cause of inflation, just as obviously as the silly claim that meals cause hunger!

20. Here we have a tangle of analogical argument, refutation by logical analogy, nonargumentative use of analogy, and explanation.

　The first analogical argument is: Although the use of force is wrong, at times force can justly be used to counter force; therefore, although lying is wrong, at times lies can rightly be used to counter lies.

　The second analogical argument (perhaps just another formulation of the first one) is: Just as someone forfeits his right to noninterference by others when he threatens them forcibly, so a liar has forfeited the ordinary right to be dealt with honestly.

　The conclusion inferred is offered as an *explanation* of why "Many find it easier to lie to those they take to be untruthful themselves. It is as though a barrier had been let down." (The second sentence here is a nonargumentative use of analogy.)

　Augustine's argument against the conclusion is that countering a lie with a lie is like countering sacrilege with sacrilege. And since sacrilege is *absolutely* wrong, so is lying.

　This is not *exactly* a refutation by logical analogy as the term is explained in the book. But it is one in an extended sense, because it is an analogical argument used to refute another analogical argument.

Exercises on pages 199–200

1. The instances are six students. The phenomenon to be explained is sickness. The one circumstance that all of the sick students have in common is having eaten canned pears, so that is probably the cause of the sickness.

5. The instances are three patients. The phenomenon to be explained is the development of cold sores. The one circumstance that all of the patients have in common is having been exposed to hypnotic suggestion, so that is probably the cause of the cold sores.

Exercises on pages 204–205

1. The instances are the twins. The phenomenon to be explained is X's alcoholism. X and Y, being identical twins, have the same genetic endowment. The only respect in which they differ is having different upbringings, so that is probably the cause of X's alcoholism.

5. The instances are two monkeys. The phenomenon to be explained is contraction of typhus. The monkeys are alike in all but one respect: One monkey is exposed to the feces of lice and the other is not. Since only the monkey exposed to the lice feces contracts typhus, that is probably its cause.

Exercises on pages 210–211

1. The instances are conditioned rats. The phenomenon to be explained is fearfulness. The two groups of rats are allowed to differ in only one respect: how long

they lack hippocampuses. None of the rats that lacked hippocampuses for one day exhibited fear, while all of those that lacked hippocampuses for longer periods of time exhibited fear. Therefore, the presence of a hippocampus is causally related to fearfulness. Specifically, the hippocampus stores memory that provides the basis of fearfulness.

5. The instances are 400 people exposed to the cold virus. The phenomenon to be explained is catching a cold. The people are divided into two groups and allowed to differ in only one respect, namely, consuming alcohol. Since the percentage of each group catching a cold differed significantly, alcohol probably inhibits catching colds.

Exercises on pages 214–215

1. The phenomenon to be explained is the increase in the earth's surface temperature since 1880. Changes in the sun's output explains much, but not all, of the increase. The only remaining circumstance is an increased concentration of greenhouse gases, so that is probably the cause of the remaining (residual) increase in temperature.

5. The phenomenon to be explained is radioactivity in a pile of pitchblende. Much, but not all, of the radioactivity could be explained by known radioactive elements. The residue was probably caused by an unknown radioactive element, which turned out to be (what is now known as) radium.

Exercises on pages 219–221

1. The instances are rats. The phenomenon to be explained is the development of cancerous tumors. Since the number of tumors varied directly with the amount of protein ingested, the protein probably causes the development of cancerous tumors.

5. The instances are rats. The phenomenon to be explained is cancer. Since the number of cancerous tumors varied directly with the amount of alcohol ingested, the alcohol probably causes the development of cancer.

Exercises on pages 227–235

Set One

1. Joint method of agreement and difference (quantitative, percentage version). The instances are 61 male sex offenders. The phenomenon to be explained is criminal recidivism (repeating a crime). The men were divided into two groups and allowed to differ in only one respect, namely, the presence or absence of the drug Depo Provera. A greater percentage of those who did not use the drug than those who used the drug repeated their crimes, so probably Depo Provera reduces recidivism.

5. Method of difference. The instances are two rabbits—or rather, one rabbit at different times, t and t+1. The only difference is that the rabbit at t+1 was injected with solution 606, while the rabbit at t was not. The rabbit at time t had spirochetes; the rabbit at time t+1 did not. Therefore, solution 606 probably cures (causes the disappearance of) spirochetes.

10. Method of concomitant variation. The phenomenon to be explained is global temperature change. This is found to vary directly with the length of the solar cycle, so probably the sun's activity causally affects global temperature.

Set Two

1. Method of agreement. The instances are people. The phenomenon to be explained

is retinitis pigmentosa. The one circumstance all of the people had in common is belonging to a particular family, so probably a single gene, common to that family (and others), causes retinitis pigmentosa.

5. Method of residues. The phenomenon to be explained is the amount of time it takes a magnetic needle to come to rest. Much, but not all, of the elapsed time can be explained by air resistance and lack of perfect mobility in the thread holding the needle. The residual amount of time is probably caused by the remaining circumstance, namely the fact that the needle was suspended over a plate of copper.

10. Joint method of agreement and difference (qualitative). The instances are airline passengers. Two groups of passengers are allowed to differ in only one respect, namely traveling between time zones. All of those who traveled between time zones experienced physiological changes and a drop in mental acuity, while none of those who flew in the same time zone experienced these changes. Therefore, probably, crossing time zones causes the physiological and mental changes.

Exercises on pages 272–283

1. The data to be explained are the striking differences in appearance between objects that are very far away and objects that are (relatively) nearby. The hypothesis astronomers adopt to explain these differences is that the distant objects are much younger than nearby objects.

 The hypothesis surely is relevant, because it is well known that the passage of time, or aging, makes a difference to things both in their character and in their appearance.

 Because of the immense distances involved (and the limiting character of the velocity of light), there is little chance of any *direct* testing of the hypothesis. But if astronomers could manage to acquire good data on the appearances of galaxies at various intermediate distances between our own and the most distant ones, and found that their appearances differed in ways that could be correlated with the differences in their distances from us, that would constitute a test (and a verification) of the hypothesis, since aging produces relatively continuous or gradual change.

 The hypothesis is compatible with previously well-established hypotheses and physical laws, which assign no influence to spatial location *as such,* and which therefore require some explanation of *why* things at different distances present different appearances. That light travels at finite velocity, and thus *takes time* to move from one place to another, entails that what we see at any time is the way things looked at an earlier time. The further the light has to travel to reach us, the longer ago it must have left the surface of the object seen. Where the distances are vast, that would entail that the time elapsed was sufficient for the distant galaxies to age perceptibly, and thus not only to be different but to look different from galaxies closer by.

 The hypothesis has some predictive power, as suggested in what was said about testing it. And it has explanatory power not only in accounting for the data to be explained but also, by implication, in explaining what *our* galaxy was like in its earlier, formative period.

 Finally, the hypothesis is reasonably simple, being based on well-established views such as that light travels at a finite velocity and that aging changes the appearances of things.

5. The data to be explained are that a plant's roots grow *down* and its stem grows *up* regardless of the orientation in which a young seedling is fixed. Knight's hypothesis to explain this data was that "this behavior was due to gravity," meaning by this that the plant's roots are positively gravity-sensitive, and its stem negatively gravity-sensitive.

   The hypothesis is relevant because the gravitational attraction of the earth is well established and would exercise a constant "pull" on the gravity-sensitive roots regardless of how the seedling is placed.

   The hypothesis is testable in a variety of ways, some only recently available. If the astronauts who reached the moon had been able to stay there longer, they could have arranged seedlings in various positions and then observed the direction in which their roots and stems grew. If the roots grew in the direction of the moon and their stems in the opposite direction, that would show that its gravity rather than anything else about the earth (e.g., its magnetic field or its iron core) was the cause of the phenomenon observed on earth. Or if in an artificial satellite far removed from all external massive bodies, the roots and stems of seedlings arranged in different positions continued to grow in quite different directions, that too would provide an affirmative test of Knight's hypothesis. Knight's own test using centrifugal force stronger than gravity was extremely ingenious.

   The hypothesis seems to be perfectly compatible with previously well-established hypotheses. Its predictive power is also considerable, because it enables us to predict how plants would grow on the moon or in artificial satellites.

   The hypothesis is simple in the sense that it explains the data in terms of an already well-established theory concerning the earth's gravity. It is incomplete, of course, in that it leaves unanswered the question of what makes the roots positively gravity-sensitive, and what there is in the stem to make it negatively gravity-sensitive.

10. The first datum to be explained is the apparent slowness of rotation of the planet Venus. The first hypothesis considered is that Venus, like Mercury, rotates at the same rate that it revolves about the sun, thus keeping the same side always toward the sun and the other side always dark.

    This hypothesis is surely relevant: if Venus does rotate slowly, that would explain why it appears to rotate slowly. It is testable by various means, not all of which are as yet technically feasible. It is especially compatible with the previously established hypothesis that Mercury behaves the same way. It has predictive power not only to explain the original datum, but also other phenomena that can be used in testing it. It is an admirably simple hypothesis.

    The first hypothesis leads to the prediction that the dark side of Venus must be exceedingly cold. But Pettit and Nicholson measured the temperature of the dark side of Venus and found it to be comparatively mild: -9°F. This disconfirms the first hypothesis, unless it can be salvaged by some other hypothesis that could explain the apparent discrepancy.

    The second hypothesis considered as a possible way to save the first one is that atmospheric currents from the warm and bright side of Venus could perpetually heat the cold and dark side. This second hypothesis could save the first one.

    The second hypothesis is clearly relevant. It is testable by various means, not all technically feasible at present. It has predictive power and is fairly simple. But it is not compatible with previously well-established hypotheses about the size of Venus and—especially—the behavior of atmospheric currents. So the second hypothesis is rejected, and with it the first.

The third hypothesis intended to replace the first two is that Venus rotates "fairly often."

This third hypothesis is relevant, for if Venus rotates only *fairly* often that would explain the original datum that Venus appears to rotate slowly, and if it rotates fairly *often* that would explain why the dark side does not cool excessively. This is of course very loose: the actual hypothesis in this case must ultimately be made quantitative to take account of the actual measurements that are made. The third hypothesis also satisfies the several other criteria discussed in the text.

15. The data to be explained here are the steep rates at which the surface of the moon cools down and heats up during and after lunar eclipses.

The hypothesis that the surface of the moon is solid rock, or composed of rocks of macroscopic size, is rejected because it is incompatible with the previously well-established hypothesis that "no solid piece of rock can cool down and heat up so quickly."

The alternative hypothesis is that the upper surface of the moon is "a thick layer of heat-insulating dust as fine as face powder." This hypothesis is relevant, for it would certainly explain the extremely rapid changes of surface temperature: only the few inches of dust change temperature; the insulated substratum remains relatively constant in temperature. It is testable, though at the time it was proposed the techniques were not technically feasible. It is compatible with the previously established hypothesis. It has predictive power: it could be used to predict what would happen if a meteorite should land on the surface of the moon. And it is fairly simple.

But there is the question: How did the surface of the moon become so minutely pulverized? Here Dr. Buettner proposed his hypothesis that the moon's rocks have been ground to dust not merely by "the sandblasting of meteoric dust" but by "the everlasting influx of cosmic rays."

This hypothesis is relevant, testable, compatible with previously well-established hypotheses, has predictive and explanatory power, and is simple.

And yet moon rocks our Apollo flights brought back to earth show that the moon is not covered by "dust as fine as face powder." This should help emphasize the fact that scientific theories and hypotheses are continually subject to revision as new data are accumulated.

20. The data to be explained are the sleep movements of animals: whimpering, whisker twitching, and leg pumping. The hypothesis is that they are dreaming.

The hypothesis is certainly relevant even though it rests only on an analogy with human behavior, which has been tested through human subjects' reporting (on awakening) dreams that were earlier manifested by their sleep movements.

But the hypothesis applied to animal behavior is not testable in the same way, because animals cannot give postdreaming reports.

The experimenter devised two tests of the hypothesis based on deductions from it. The first test (not quite adequately reported in the brief excerpt) pertains to the electroencephalograph (EEG). Characteristic EEG tracings were associated with visual perceptions of rhesus monkeys while awake. It was further hypothesized that the same EEG tracings would accompany the hypothesized dream "visual perceptions" of the sleeping monkeys. Then it was predicted that during the sleep movements of the monkeys that suggest that they are dreaming, EEG tracings would occur. This test verified the prediction and thus tended to confirm the original hypothesis.

The second test of the original hypothesis involved conditioning monkeys to make a specific motor response to visual perceptions in their waking state. It was further hypothesized that the conditioning would be carried over from the waking to the sleeping state. Then it was predicted that during the sleep movements of the monkeys that suggest they are dreaming, the conditioned specific motor response would occur to the hypothesized dream "visual perceptions." This test verified the prediction and thus tended to confirm the original hypothesis also.

The hypothesis that animals dream is relevant, testable, compatible with previously well-established hypotheses, has predictive and explanatory power, and is simple.

Index